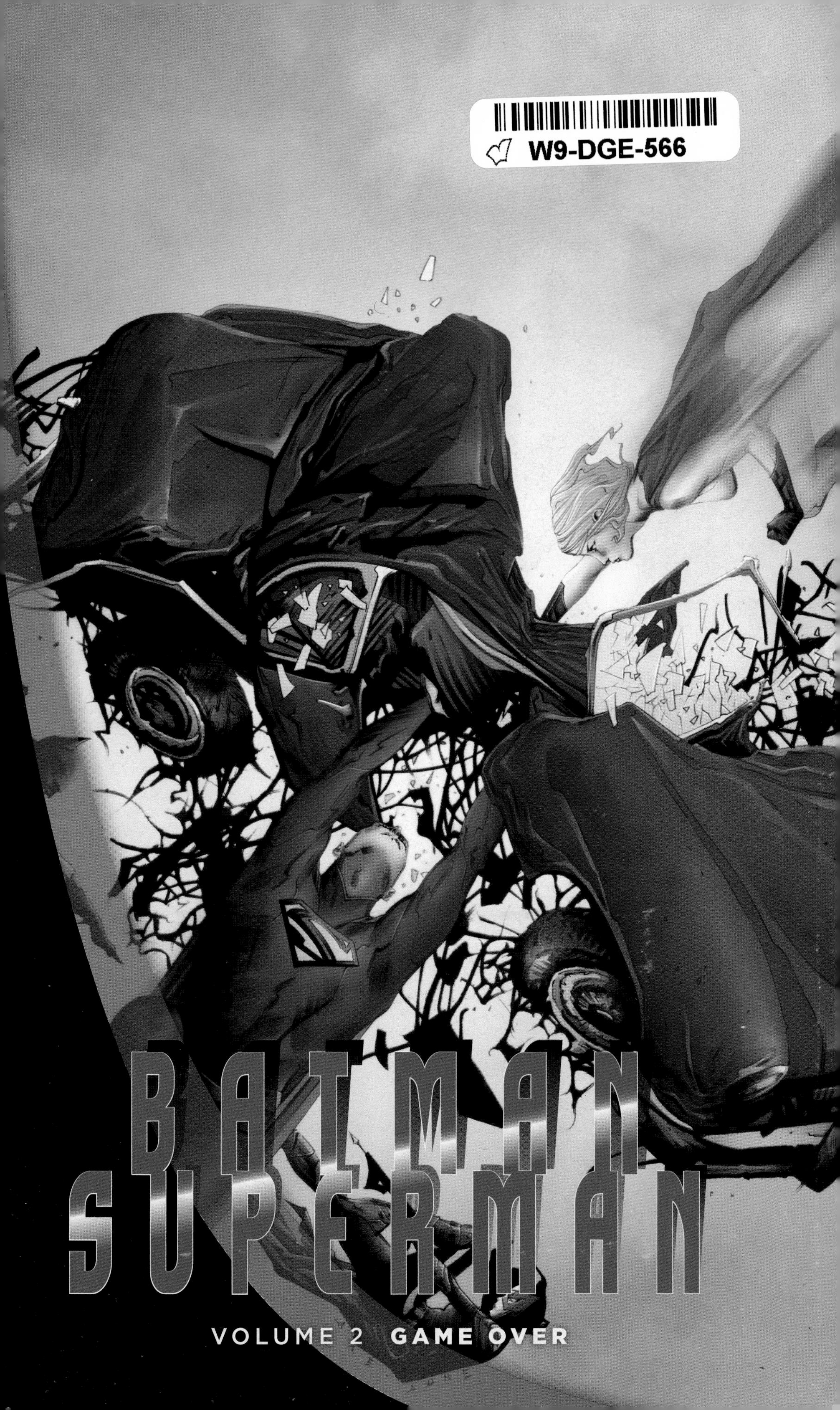

BATMAN SUPERMAN

VOLUME 2 **GAME OVER**

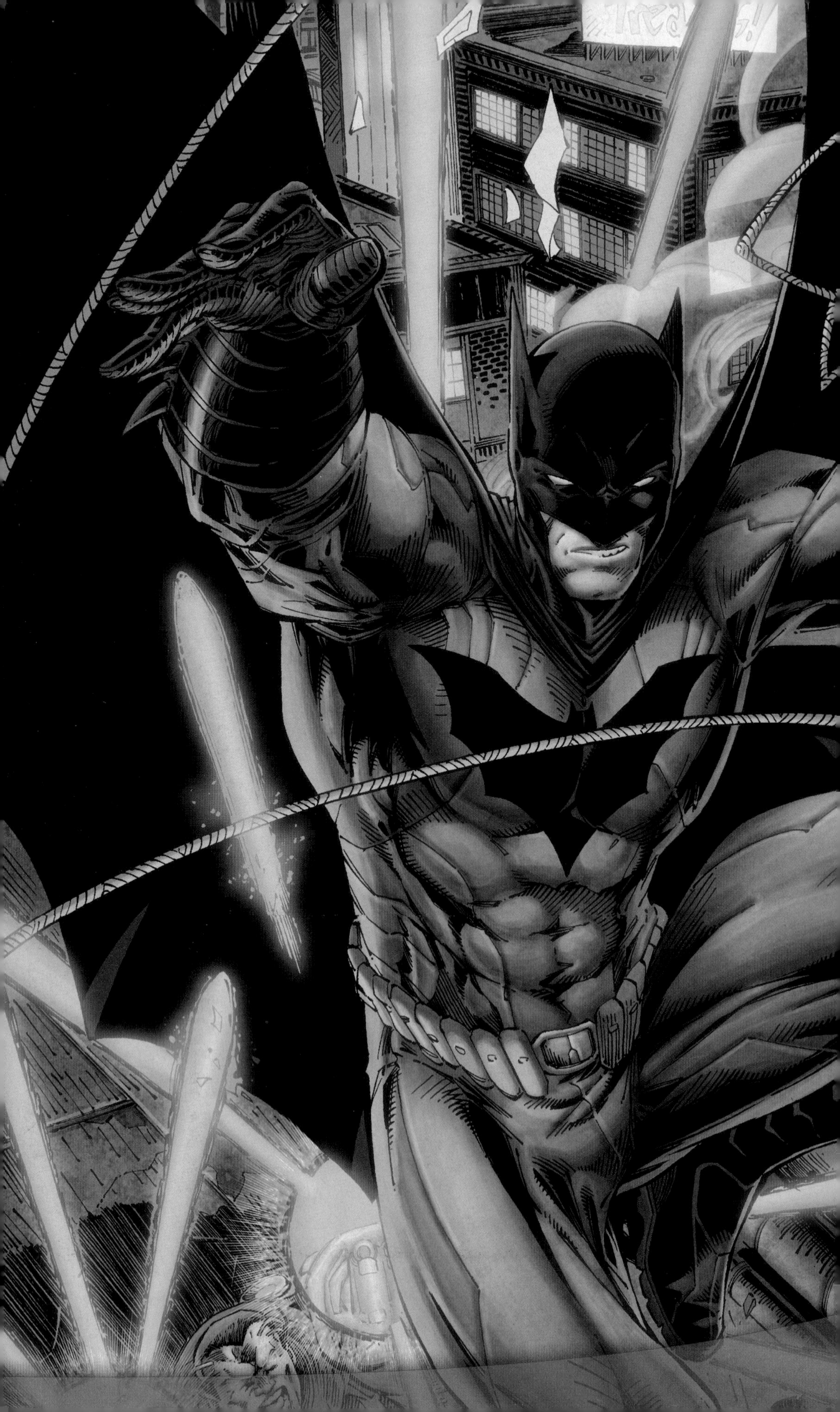

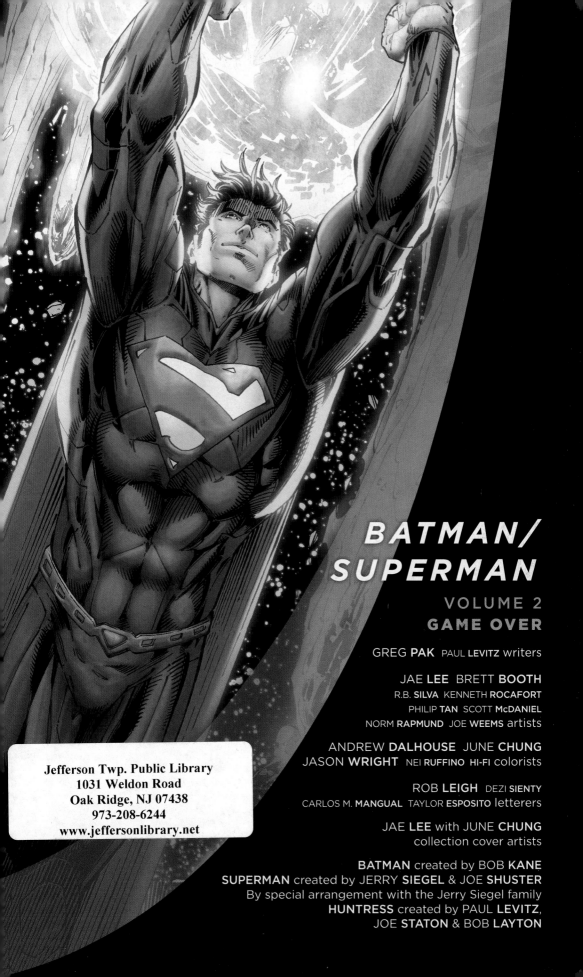

BATMAN/ SUPERMAN

VOLUME 2
GAME OVER

GREG **PAK**   PAUL **LEVITZ** writers

JAE **LEE**   BRETT **BOOTH**
R.B. **SILVA**   KENNETH **ROCAFORT**
PHILIP **TAN**   SCOTT **McDANIEL**
NORM **RAPMUND**   JOE **WEEMS** artists

ANDREW **DALHOUSE**   JUNE **CHUNG**
JASON **WRIGHT**   NEI **RUFFINO**   HI-FI colorists

ROB **LEIGH**   DEZI **SIENTY**
CARLOS M. **MANGUAL**   TAYLOR **ESPOSITO** letterers

JAE **LEE** with JUNE **CHUNG**
collection cover artists

BATMAN created by BOB **KANE**
SUPERMAN created by JERRY **SIEGEL** & JOE **SHUSTER**
By special arrangement with the Jerry Siegel family
HUNTRESS created by PAUL **LEVITZ**,
JOE **STATON** & BOB **LAYTON**

EDDIE BERGANZA MIKE COTTON Editors – Original Series RICKEY PURDIN Associate Editor – Original Series
ANTHONY MARQUES Assistant Editor – Original Series ROBIN WILDMAN Editor ROBBIN BROSTERMAN Design Director – Books
ROBBIE BIEDERMAN Publication Design

BOB HARRAS Senior VP – Editor-in-Chief, DC Comics

DIANE NELSON President DAN DIDIO and JIM LEE Co-Publishers GEOFF JOHNS Chief Creative Officer
AMIT DESAI Senior VP – Marketing and Franchise Management
AMY GENKINS Senior VP – Business and Legal Affairs NAIRI GARDINER Senior VP – Finance
JEFF BOISON VP – Publishing Planning MARK CHIARELLO VP – Art Direction and Design
JOHN CUNNINGHAM VP – Marketing TERRI CUNNINGHAM VP – Editorial Administration
LARRY GANEM VP – Talent Relations and Services ALISON GILL Senior VP – Manufacturing and Operations
HANK KANALZ Senior VP – Vertigo and Integrated Publishing JAY KOGAN VP – Business and Legal Affairs, Publishing
JACK MAHAN VP – Business Affairs, Talent NICK NAPOLITANO VP – Manufacturing Administration SUE POHJA VP – Book Sales
FRED RUIZ VP – Manufacturing Operations COURTNEY SIMMONS Senior VP – Publicity BOB WAYNE Senior VP – Sales

BATMAN/SUPERMAN VOLUME 2: GAME OVER

DC Comics, 1700 Broadway, New York, NY 10019
A Warner Bros. Entertainment Company.
Printed by RR Donnelley, Salem, VA, USA. 4/3/15. First Printing.

ISBN: 978-1-4012-5423-0

Library of Congress Cataloging-in-Publication Data

Pak, Greg, author.
Batman/Superman. Volume 2, Game Over / Greg Pak ; illustrated by Jae Lee.
pages cm. — (The New 52!)
Batman created by Bob Kane.
Superman created by Jerry Siegel and Joe Shuster.
ISBN 978-1-4012-5423-0
1. Graphic novels. I. Lee, Jae, 1972- illustrator. II. Title. III. Title: Game Over.
PN6728.B36P34 2014
741.5'973—dc23
2014000327

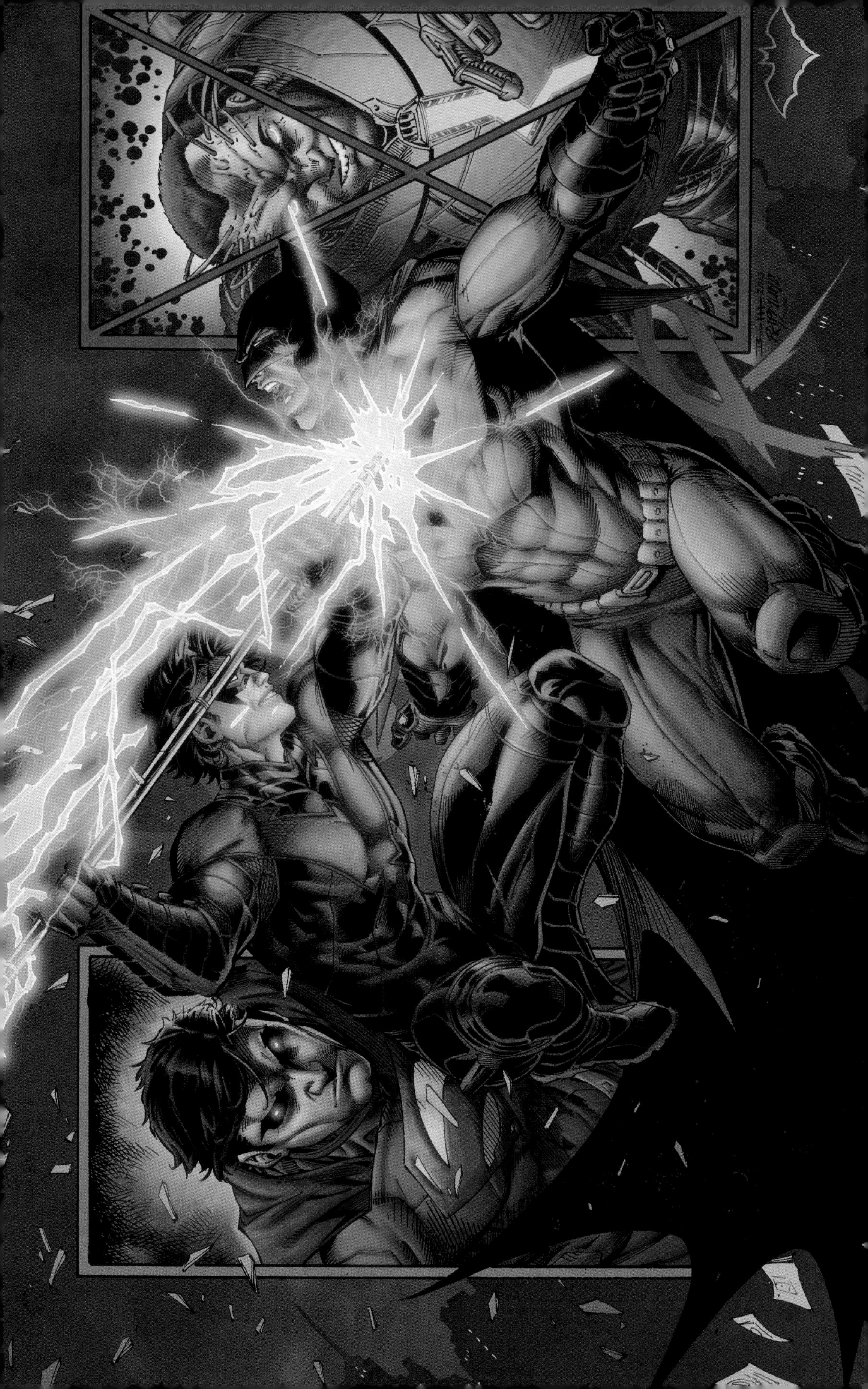

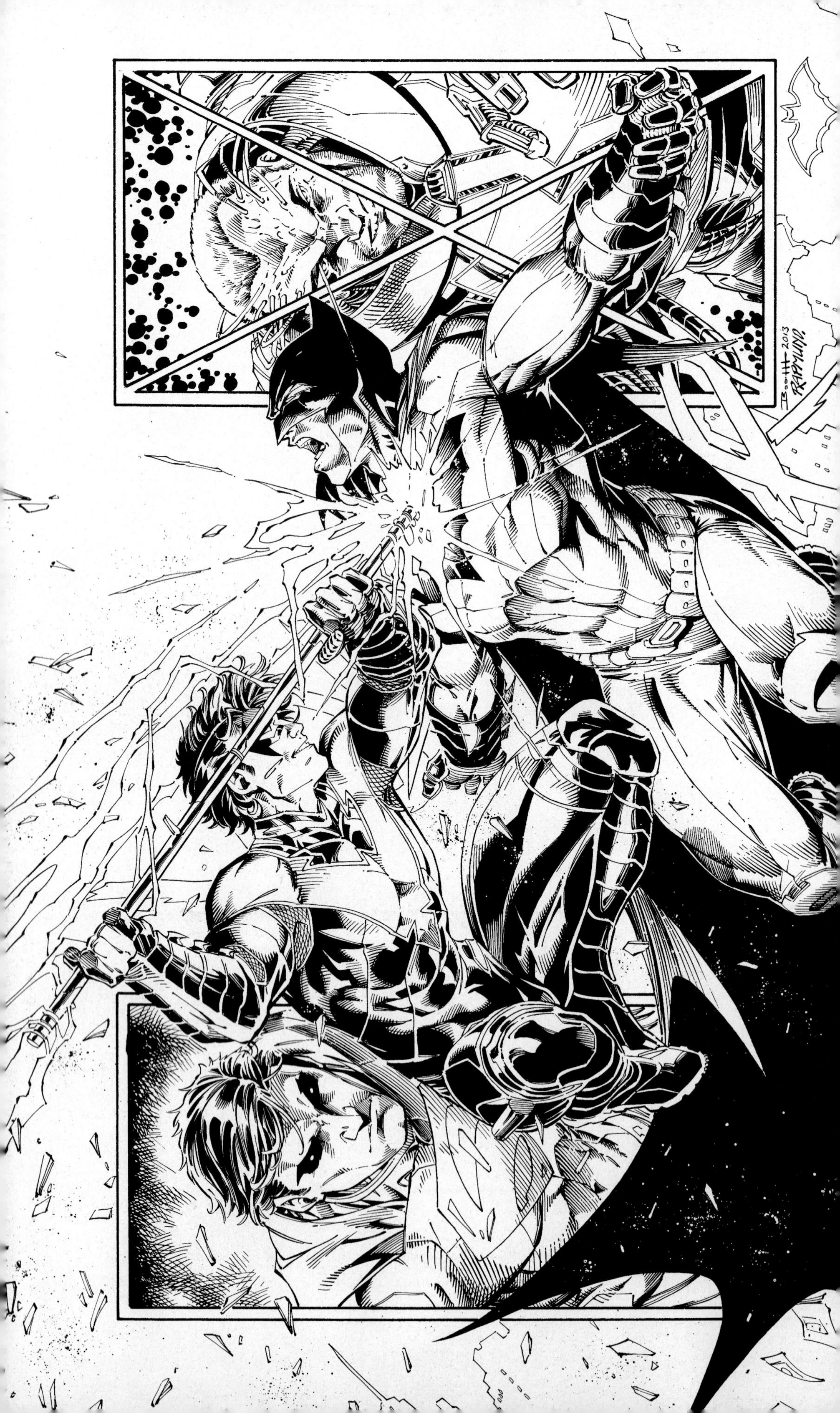

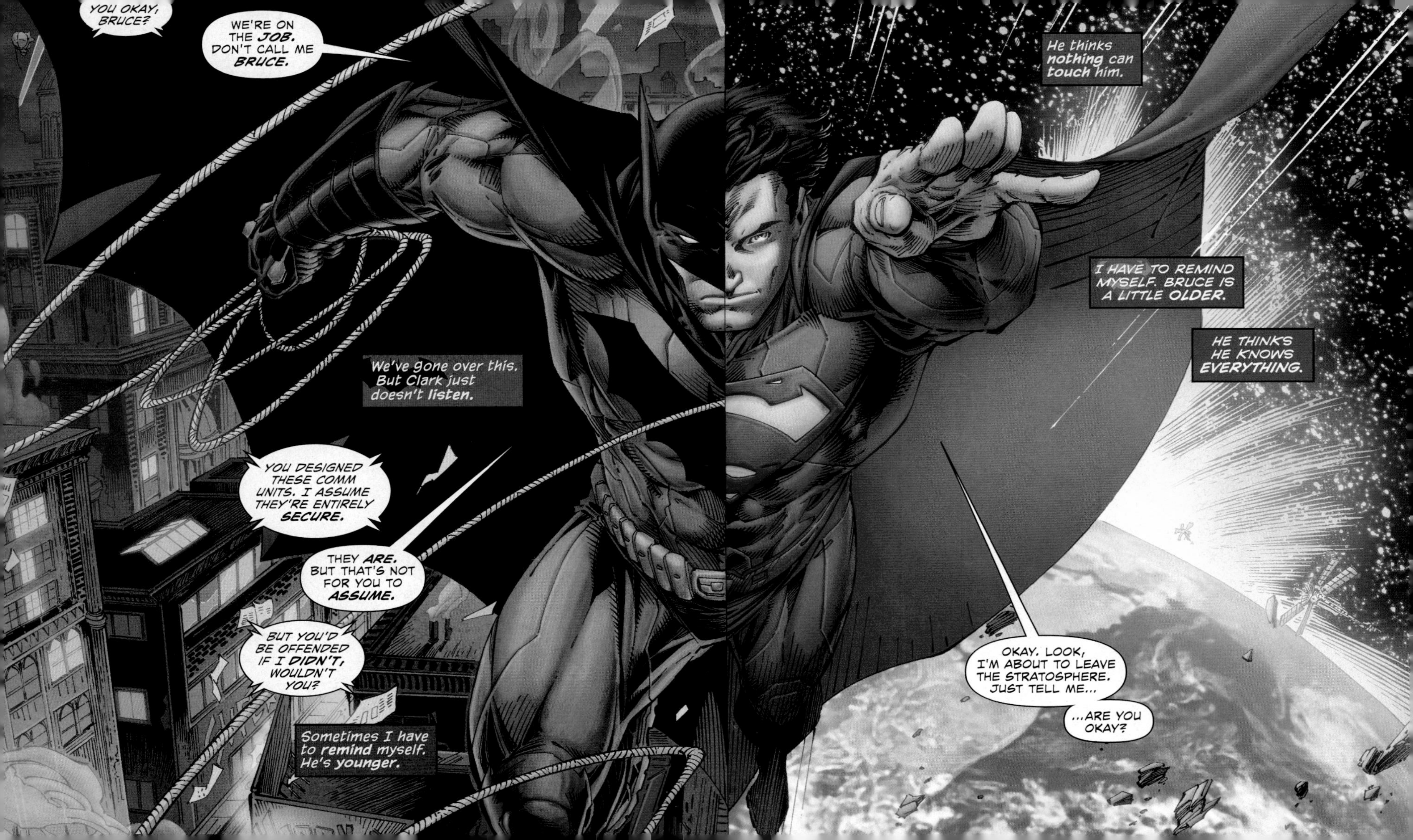

YOU OKAY, BRUCE?
WE'RE ON THE **JOB.** DON'T CALL ME **BRUCE.**
We've gone over this. But Clark just doesn't **listen.**
YOU DESIGNED THESE COMM UNITS. I ASSUME THEY'RE ENTIRELY **SECURE.**
THEY **ARE.** BUT THAT'S NOT FOR YOU TO **ASSUME.**
BUT YOU'D BE OFFENDED IF I **DIDN'T,** WOULDN'T YOU?
Sometimes I have to **remind** myself. He's **younger.**
He thinks **nothing** can **touch** him.
I HAVE TO REMIND MYSELF. BRUCE IS A LITTLE **OLDER.**
HE THINKS HE KNOWS **EVERYTHING.**
OKAY. LOOK, I'M ABOUT TO LEAVE THE STRATOSPHERE. JUST TELL ME...
...ARE YOU OKAY?

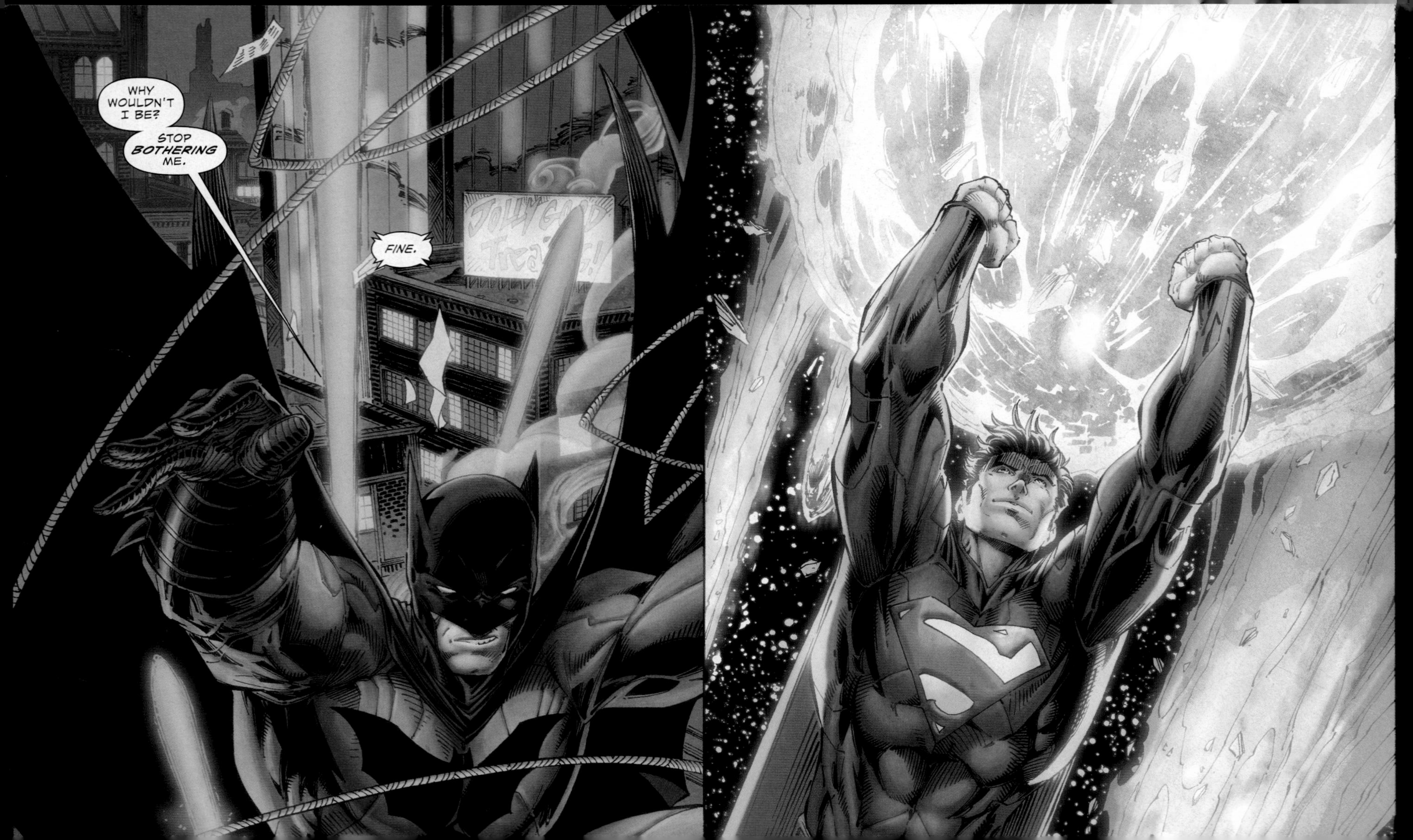
WHY WOULDN'T I BE?
STOP ***BOTHERING*** ME.
FINE.

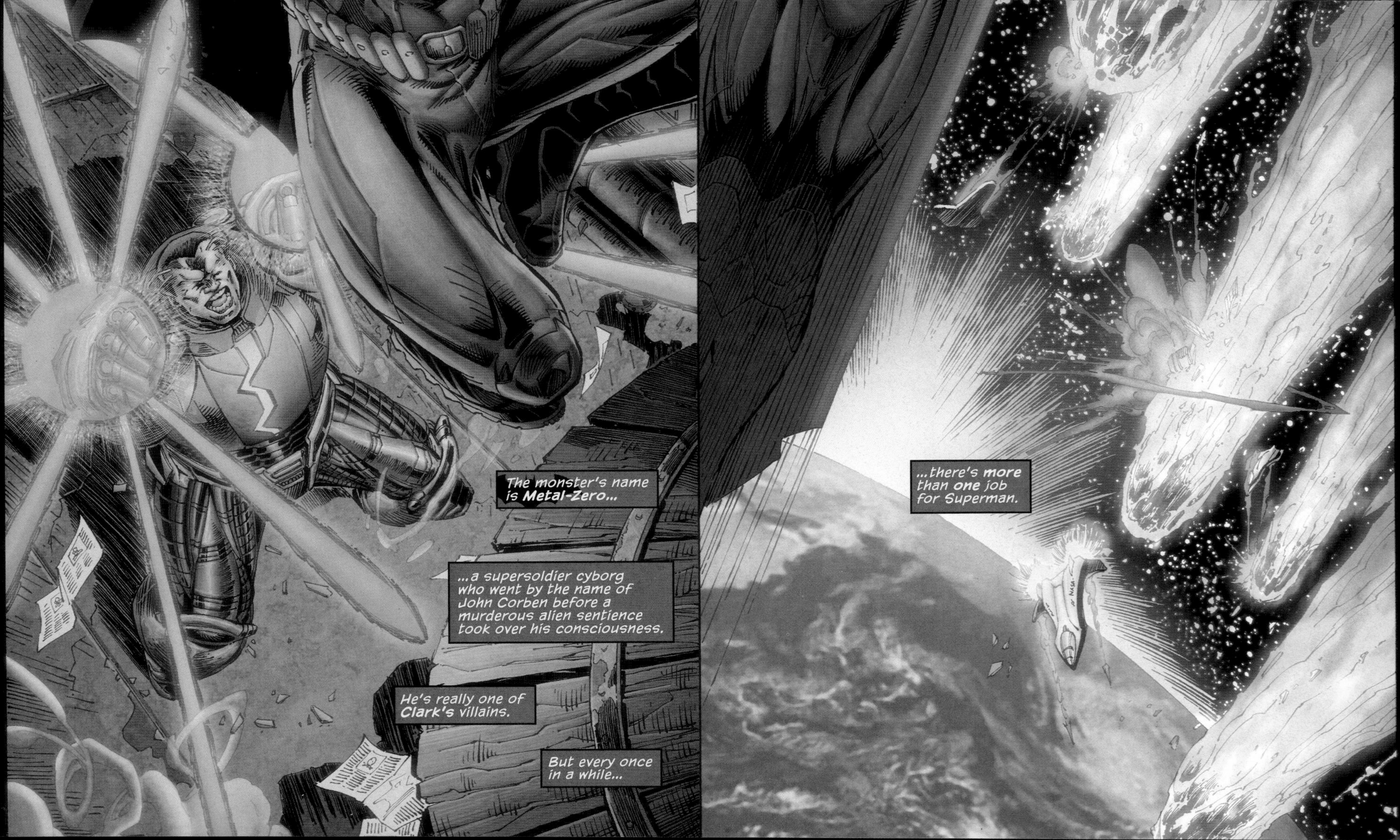
The monster's name is **Metal-Zero**...
...a supersoldier cyborg who went by the name of John Corben before a murderous alien sentience took over his consciousness.
He's really one of **Clark's** villains.
But every once in a while...
...there's **more** than **one** job for Superman.
NASA

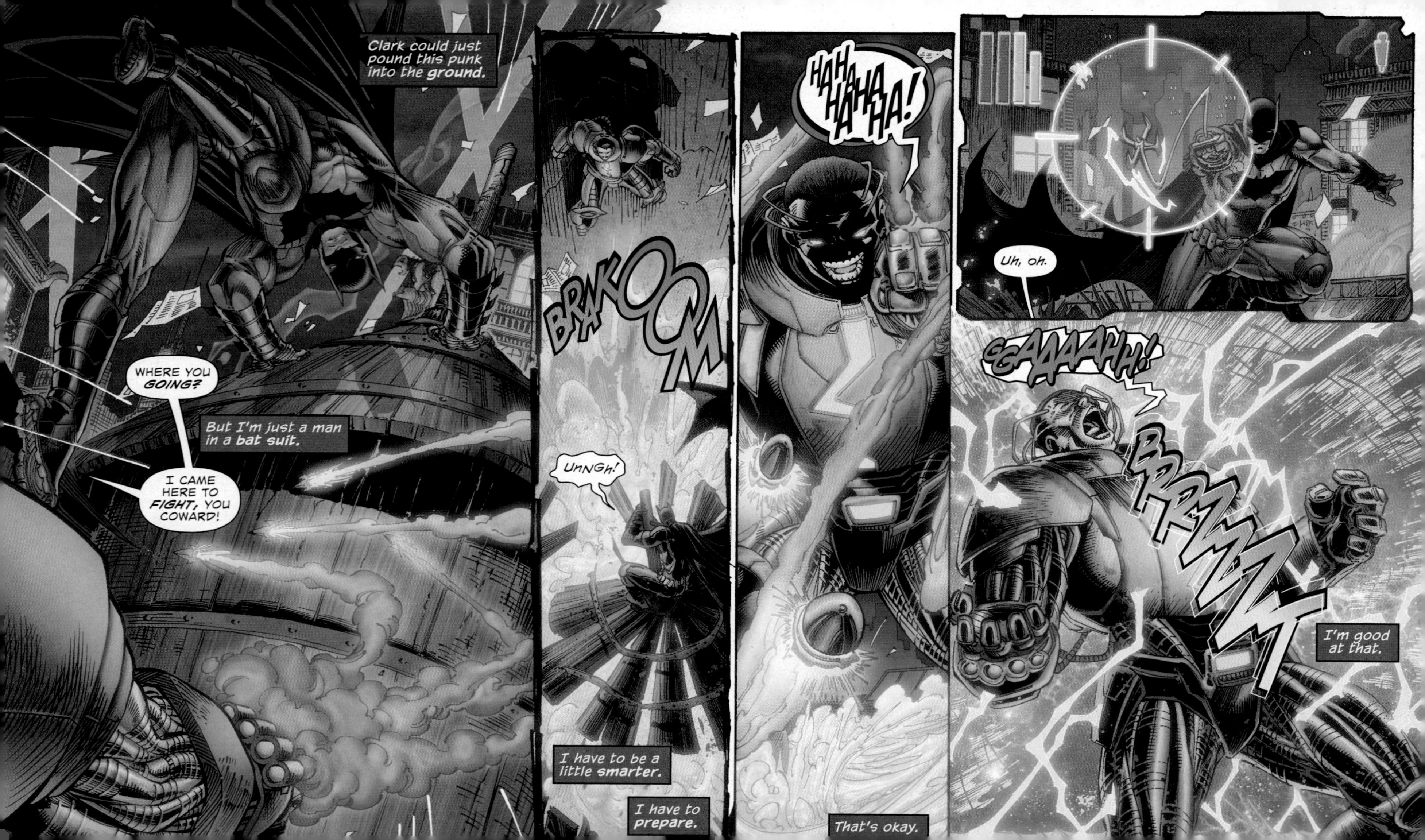

Clark could just pound this punk into the ground.
WHERE YOU GOING?
But I'm just a man in a bat suit.
I CAME HERE TO FIGHT, YOU COWARD!
BRAKOOOM
UNNGH!
I have to be a little smarter.
I have to prepare.
HAHAHAHAHAHA!
That's okay.
Uh, oh.
GGAAAAAHH!
BRRZZZZT
I'm good at that.

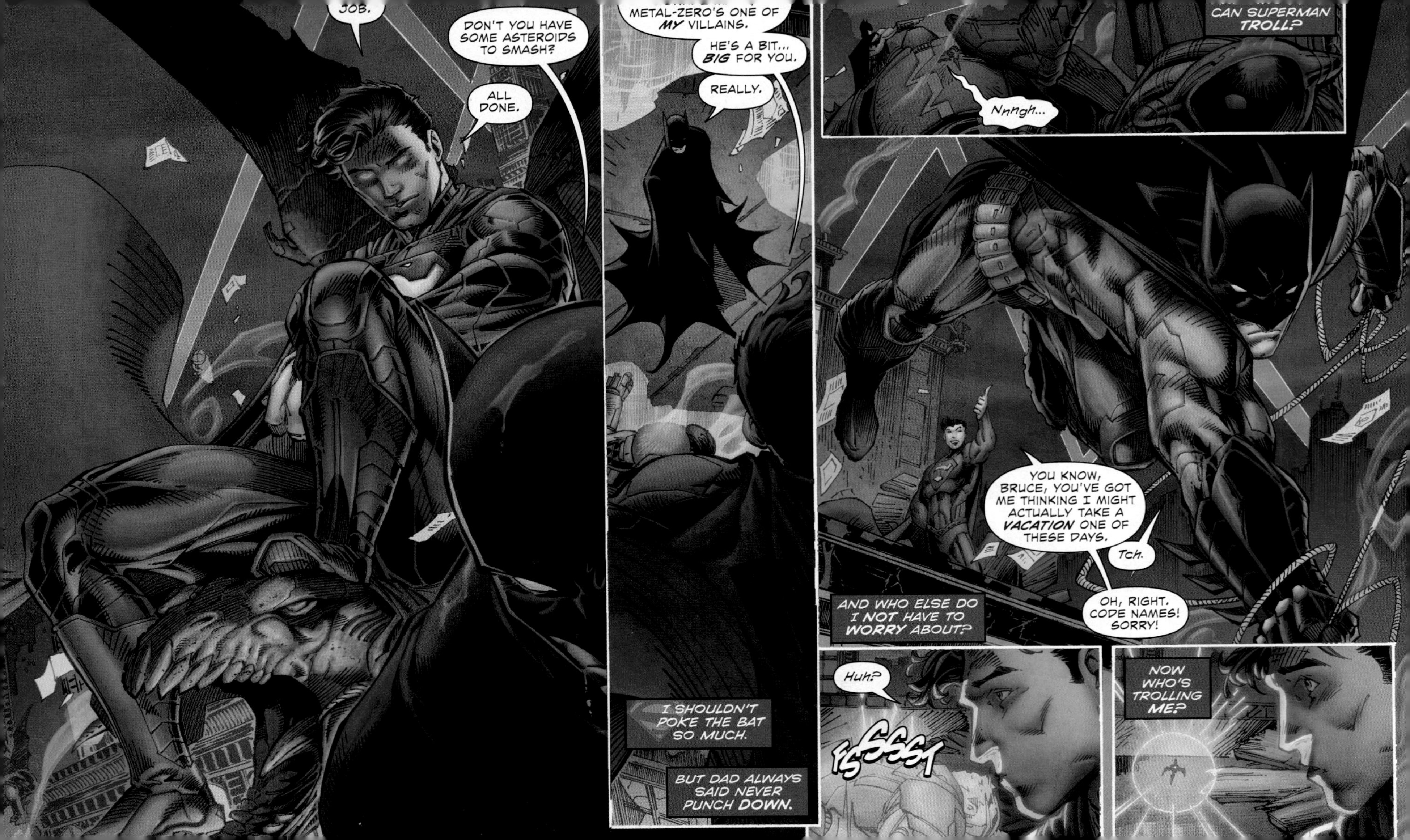
JOB.
DON'T YOU HAVE SOME ASTEROIDS TO SMASH?
ALL DONE.
METAL-ZERO'S ONE OF MY VILLAINS.
HE'S A BIT... BIG FOR YOU.
REALLY.
I SHOULDN'T POKE THE BAT SO MUCH.
BUT DAD ALWAYS SAID NEVER PUNCH DOWN.
CAN SUPERMAN TROLL?
Nnngh...
YOU KNOW, BRUCE, YOU'VE GOT ME THINKING I MIGHT ACTUALLY TAKE A VACATION ONE OF THESE DAYS.
Tch.
OH, RIGHT. CODE NAMES! SORRY!
AND WHO ELSE DO I NOT HAVE TO WORRY ABOUT?
Huh?
FSSSST
NOW WHO'S TROLLING ME?

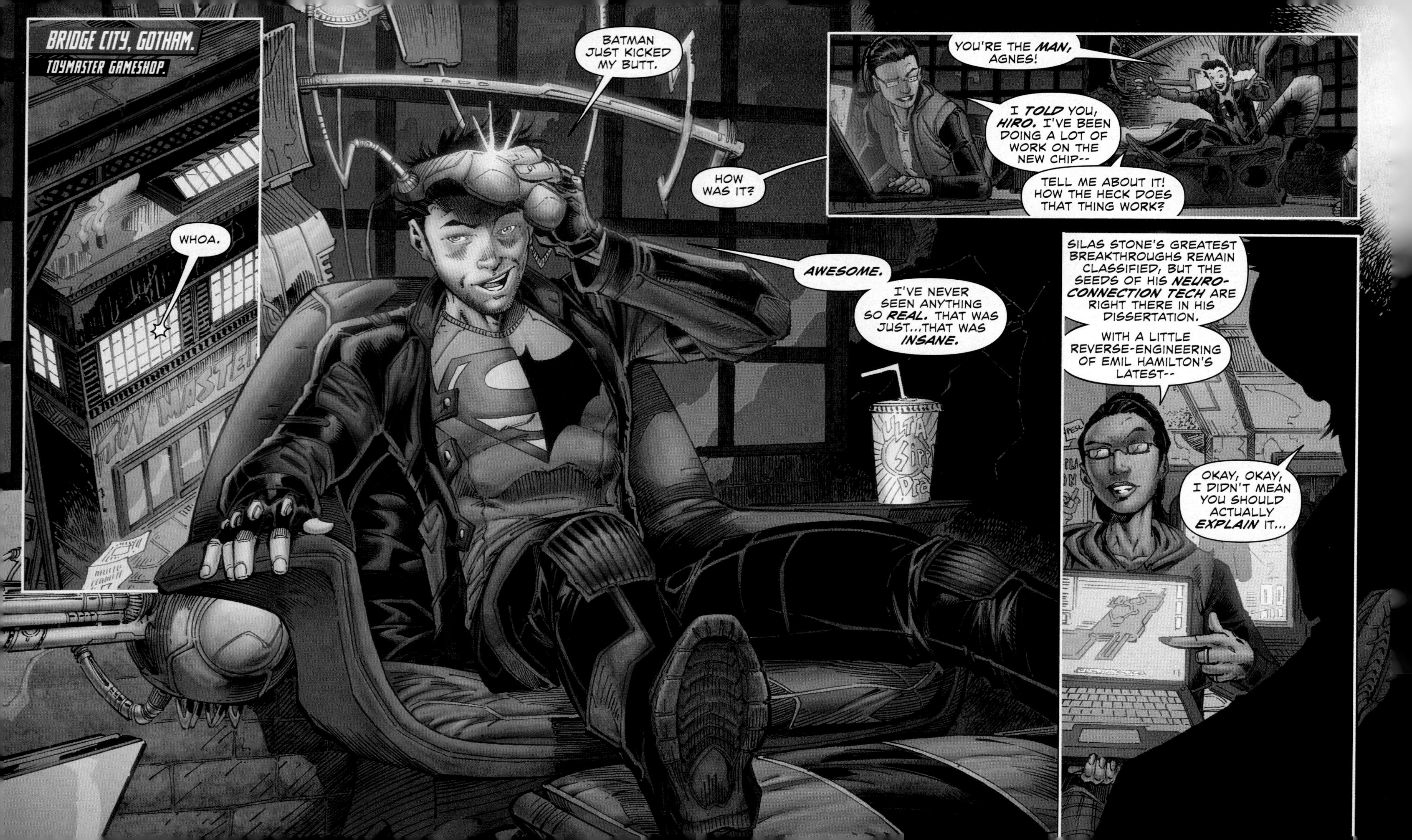
BRIDGE CITY, GOTHAM.
TOYMASTER GAMESHOP.
WHOA.
BATMAN JUST KICKED MY BUTT.
HOW WAS IT?
AWESOME.
I'VE NEVER SEEN ANYTHING SO REAL. THAT WAS JUST...THAT WAS INSANE.
YOU'RE THE MAN, AGNES!
I TOLD YOU, HIRO. I'VE BEEN DOING A LOT OF WORK ON THE NEW CHIP--
TELL ME ABOUT IT! HOW THE HECK DOES THAT THING WORK?
SILAS STONE'S GREATEST BREAKTHROUGHS REMAIN CLASSIFIED, BUT THE SEEDS OF HIS NEURO-CONNECTION TECH ARE RIGHT THERE IN HIS DISSERTATION.
WITH A LITTLE REVERSE-ENGINEERING OF EMIL HAMILTON'S LATEST--
OKAY, OKAY, I DIDN'T MEAN YOU SHOULD ACTUALLY EXPLAIN IT...

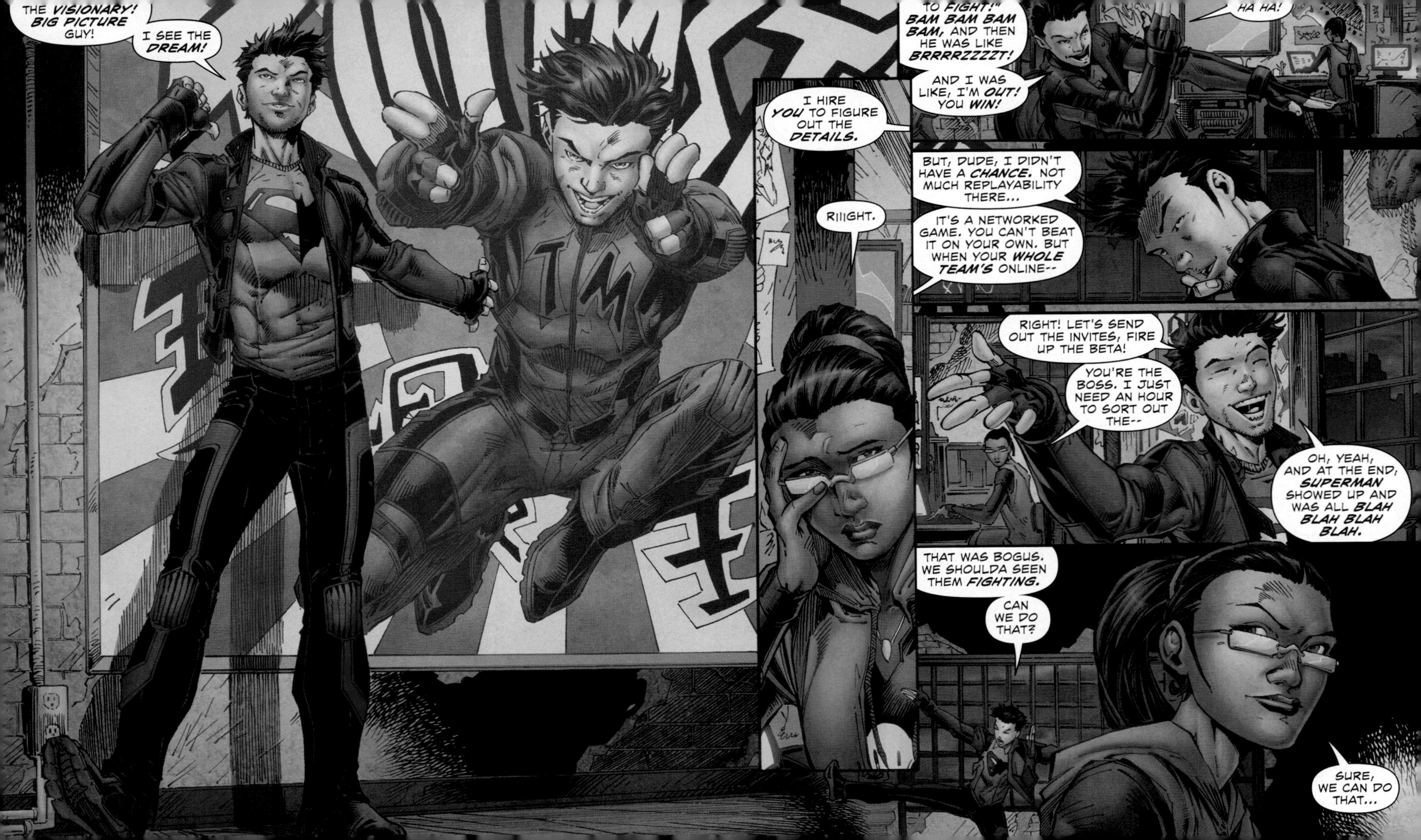
THE VISIONARY! BIG PICTURE GUY!
I SEE THE DREAM!
I HIRE YOU TO FIGURE OUT THE DETAILS.
RIIIGHT.
TO FIGHT!" BAM BAM BAM BAM, AND THEN HE WAS LIKE BRRRRZZZZZT!
AND I WAS LIKE, I'M OUT! YOU WIN!
HA HA!
BUT, DUDE, I DIDN'T HAVE A CHANCE. NOT MUCH REPLAYABILITY THERE...
IT'S A NETWORKED GAME. YOU CAN'T BEAT IT ON YOUR OWN. BUT WHEN YOUR WHOLE TEAM'S ONLINE--
RIGHT! LET'S SEND OUT THE INVITES, FIRE UP THE BETA!
YOU'RE THE BOSS. I JUST NEED AN HOUR TO SORT OUT THE--
OH, YEAH, AND AT THE END, SUPERMAN SHOWED UP AND WAS ALL BLAH BLAH BLAH BLAH.
THAT WAS BOGUS. WE SHOULDA SEEN THEM FIGHTING.
CAN WE DO THAT?
SURE, WE CAN DO THAT...

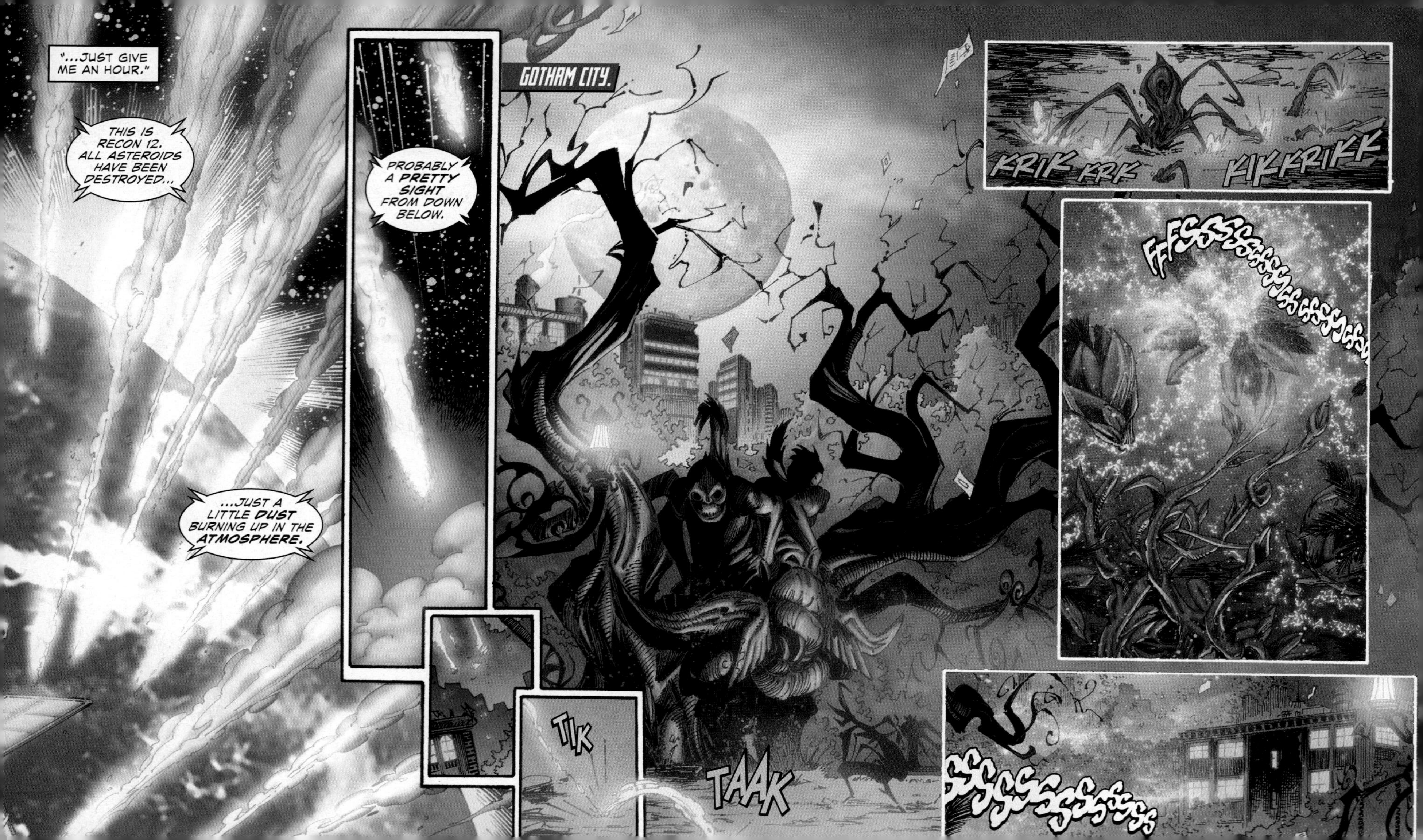
"...JUST GIVE ME AN HOUR."
THIS IS RECON 12. ALL ASTEROIDS HAVE BEEN DESTROYED...
...JUST A LITTLE DUST BURNING UP IN THE ATMOSPHERE.
PROBABLY A PRETTY SIGHT FROM DOWN BELOW.
GOTHAM CITY.
TIK
TAAK
KRIK KRIK
KIKKRIKK
FFFSSSSSSSSSSSSSSSSSS
SSSSSSSSSSSSSSSS

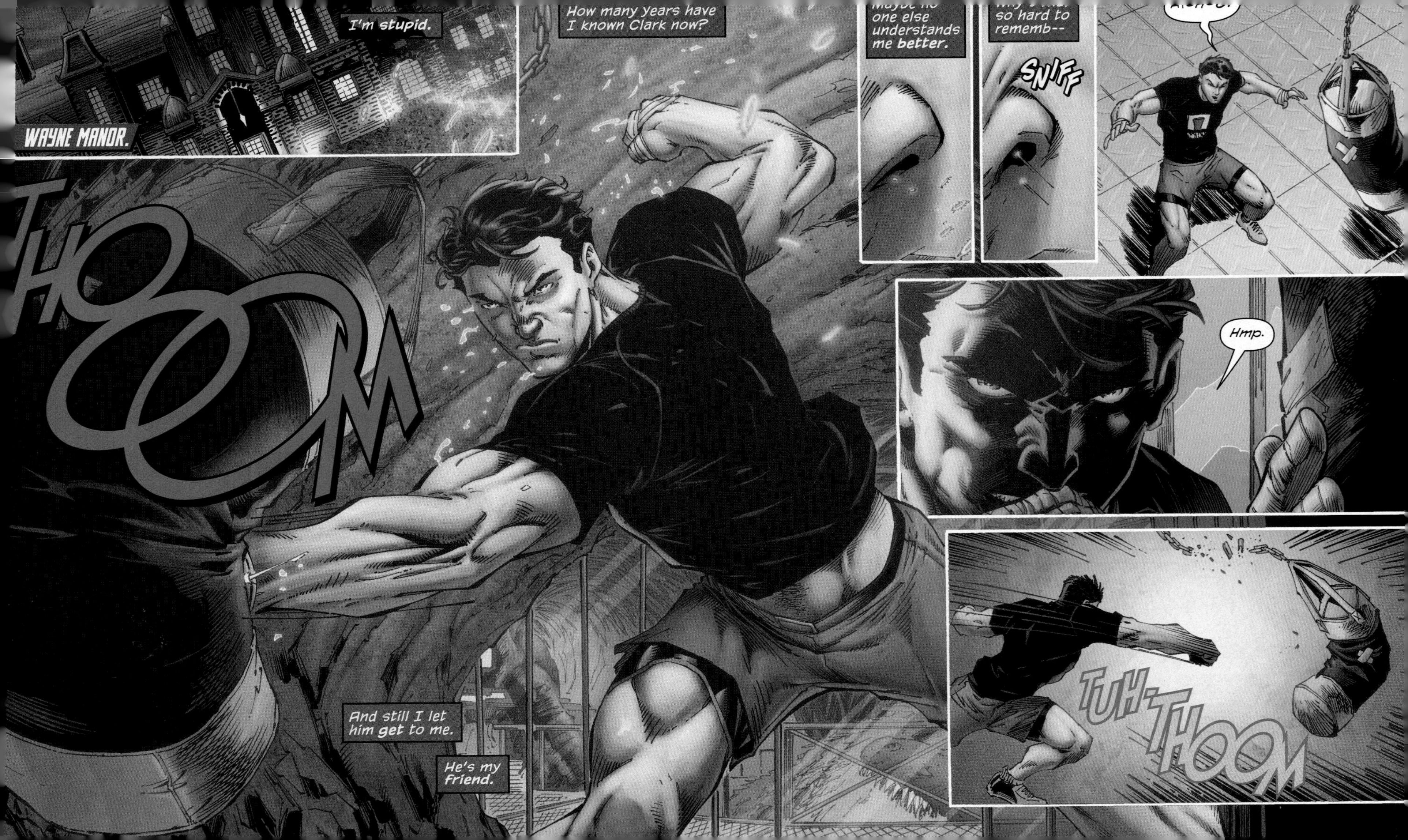
WAYNE MANOR.
I'm stupid.
THOOM
How many years have I known Clark now?
And still I let him get to me.
He's my friend.
one else understands me better.
so hard to rememb--
SNIFF
Hmp.
TUH-THOOM

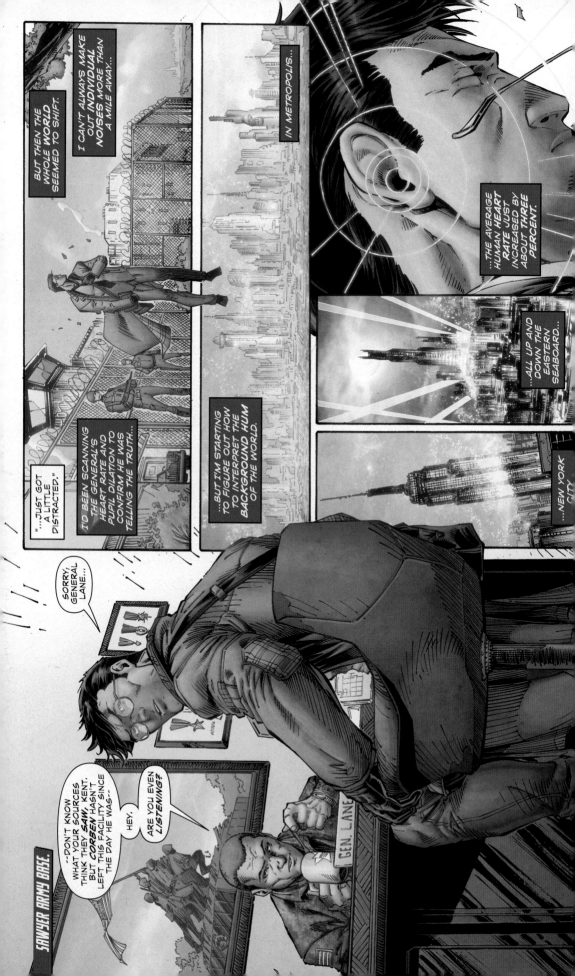

BUT THEN THE WHOLE WORLD SEEMED TO SHIFT.

I CAN'T ALWAYS MAKE OUT INDIVIDUAL NOISES MORE THAN A MILE AWAY...

IN METROPOLIS...

...THE AVERAGE HUMAN HEART RATE JUST INCREASED BY ABOUT THREE PERCENT.

...ALL UP AND DOWN THE EASTERN SEABOARD...

NEW YORK CITY.

"...JUST GOT A LITTLE DISTRACTED."

I'D BEEN SCANNING THE GENERAL'S HEART RATE AND PUPIL DILATION TO CONFIRM HE WAS TELLING THE TRUTH...

...BUT I'M STARTING TO FIGURE OUT HOW TO INTERPRET THE BACKGROUND HUM OF THE WORLD.

SORRY, GENERAL LANE...

SAWYER ARMY BASE.

--DON'T KNOW WHAT YOUR SOURCES THINK THEY SAW, KENT, BUT CORBEN HASN'T LEFT THIS FACILITY SINCE THE DAY HE WAS--

HEY, ARE YOU EVEN LISTENING?

GEN. LANE

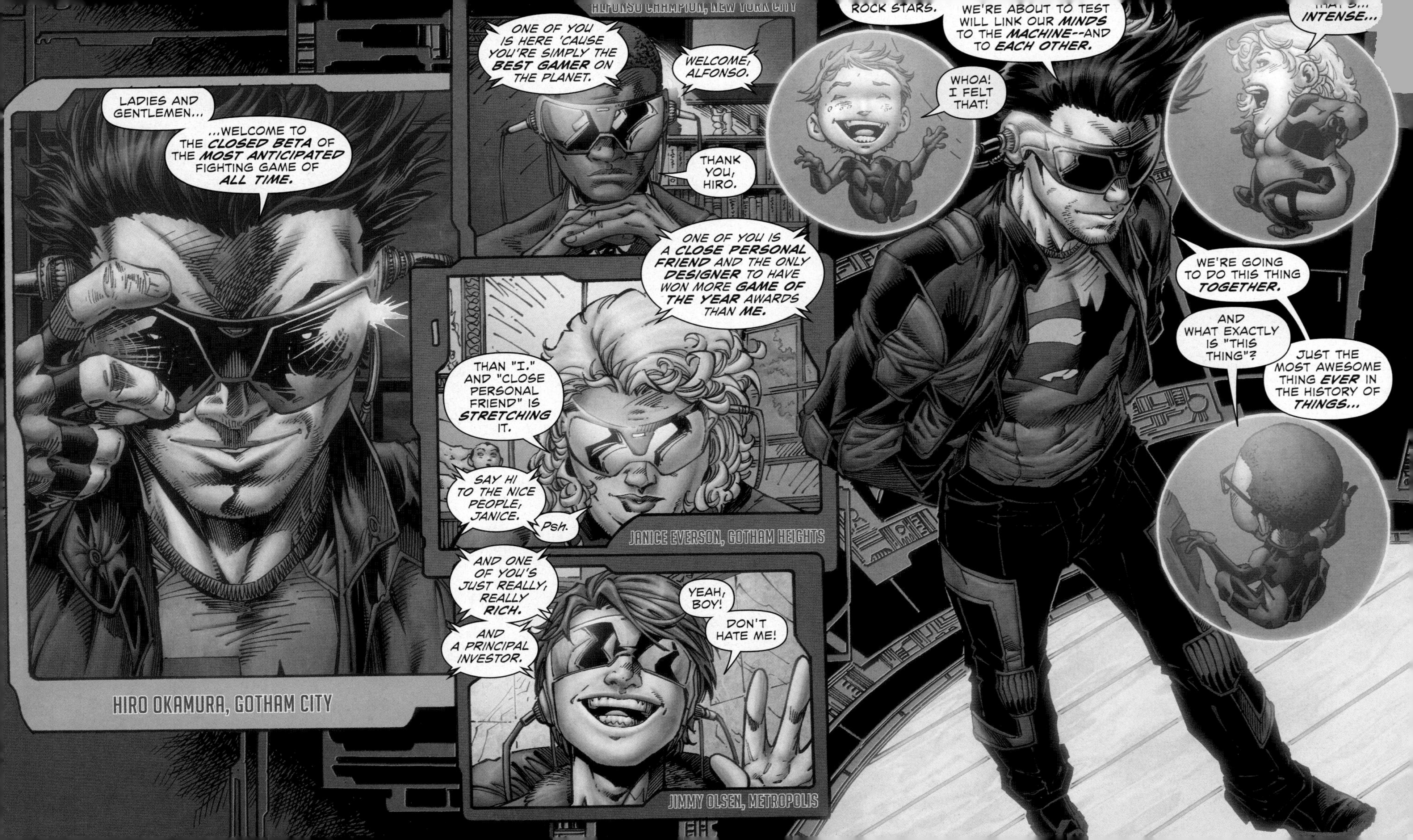

LADIES AND GENTLEMEN...
...WELCOME TO THE CLOSED BETA OF THE MOST ANTICIPATED FIGHTING GAME OF ALL TIME.
HIRO OKAMURA, GOTHAM CITY
ALFONSO CHAMPION, NEW YORK CITY
ONE OF YOU IS HERE 'CAUSE YOU'RE SIMPLY THE BEST GAMER ON THE PLANET.
WELCOME, ALFONSO.
THANK YOU, HIRO.
ONE OF YOU IS A CLOSE PERSONAL FRIEND AND THE ONLY DESIGNER TO HAVE WON MORE GAME OF THE YEAR AWARDS THAN ME.
THAN "I." AND "CLOSE PERSONAL FRIEND" IS STRETCHING IT.
SAY HI TO THE NICE PEOPLE, JANICE.
Psh.
JANICE EVERSON, GOTHAM HEIGHTS
AND ONE OF YOU'S JUST REALLY, REALLY RICH.
AND A PRINCIPAL INVESTOR.
YEAH, BOY!
DON'T HATE ME!
JIMMY OLSEN, METROPOLIS
ROCK STARS.
WE'RE ABOUT TO TEST WILL LINK OUR MINDS TO THE MACHINE--AND TO EACH OTHER.
WHOA! I FELT THAT!
INTENSE...
WE'RE GOING TO DO THIS THING TOGETHER.
AND WHAT EXACTLY IS "THIS THING"?
JUST THE MOST AWESOME THING EVER IN THE HISTORY OF THINGS...

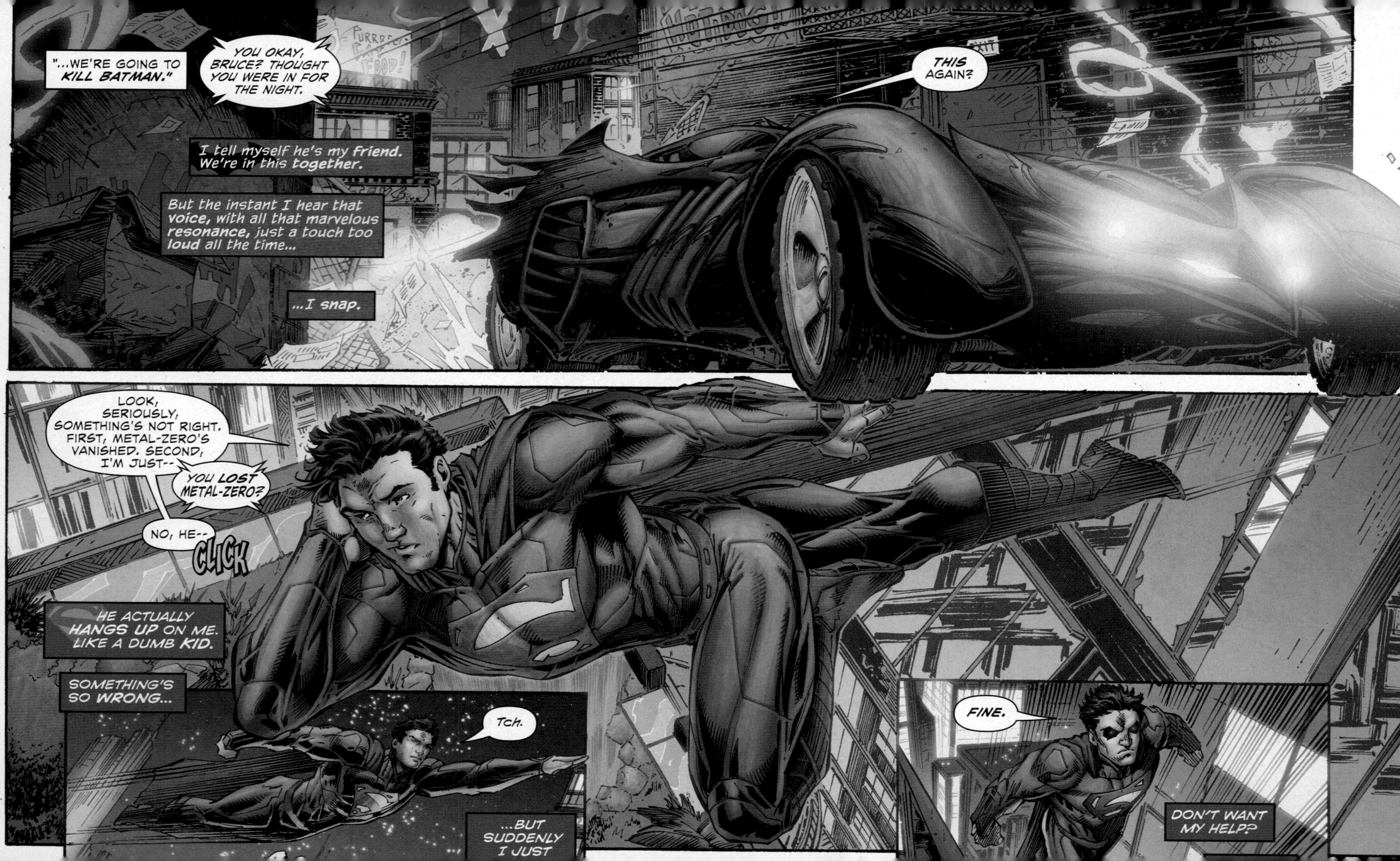
"...WE'RE GOING TO KILL BATMAN."
YOU OKAY, BRUCE? THOUGHT YOU WERE IN FOR THE NIGHT.
I tell myself he's my friend. We're in this together.
But the instant I hear that voice, with all that marvelous resonance, just a touch too loud all the time...
...I snap.
THIS AGAIN?
LOOK, SERIOUSLY, SOMETHING'S NOT RIGHT. FIRST, METAL-ZERO'S VANISHED. SECOND, I'M JUST--
YOU LOST METAL-ZERO?
NO, HE--
CLICK
HE ACTUALLY HANGS UP ON ME. LIKE A DUMB KID.
SOMETHING'S SO WRONG...
Tch.
...BUT SUDDENLY I JUST
FINE.
DON'T WANT MY HELP?

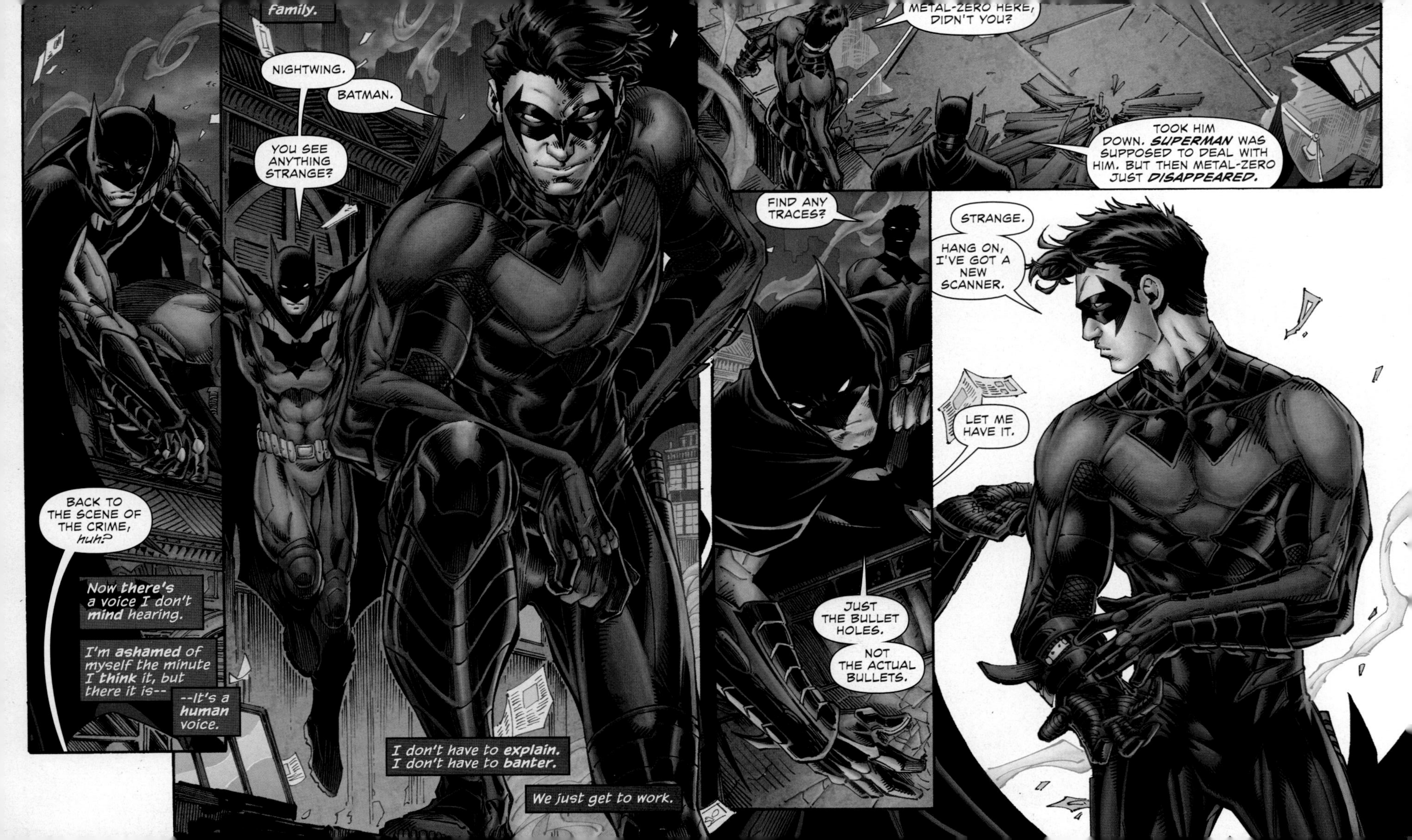
BACK TO THE SCENE OF THE CRIME, huh?
Now there's a voice I don't mind hearing.
I'm ashamed of myself the minute I think it, but there it is--
--It's a human voice.
family.
NIGHTWING.
BATMAN.
YOU SEE ANYTHING STRANGE?
I don't have to explain. I don't have to banter.
We just get to work.
METAL-ZERO HERE, DIDN'T YOU?
TOOK HIM DOWN. SUPERMAN WAS SUPPOSED TO DEAL WITH HIM. BUT THEN METAL-ZERO JUST DISAPPEARED.
FIND ANY TRACES?
JUST THE BULLET HOLES.
NOT THE ACTUAL BULLETS.
STRANGE.
HANG ON, I'VE GOT A NEW SCANNER.
LET ME HAVE IT.

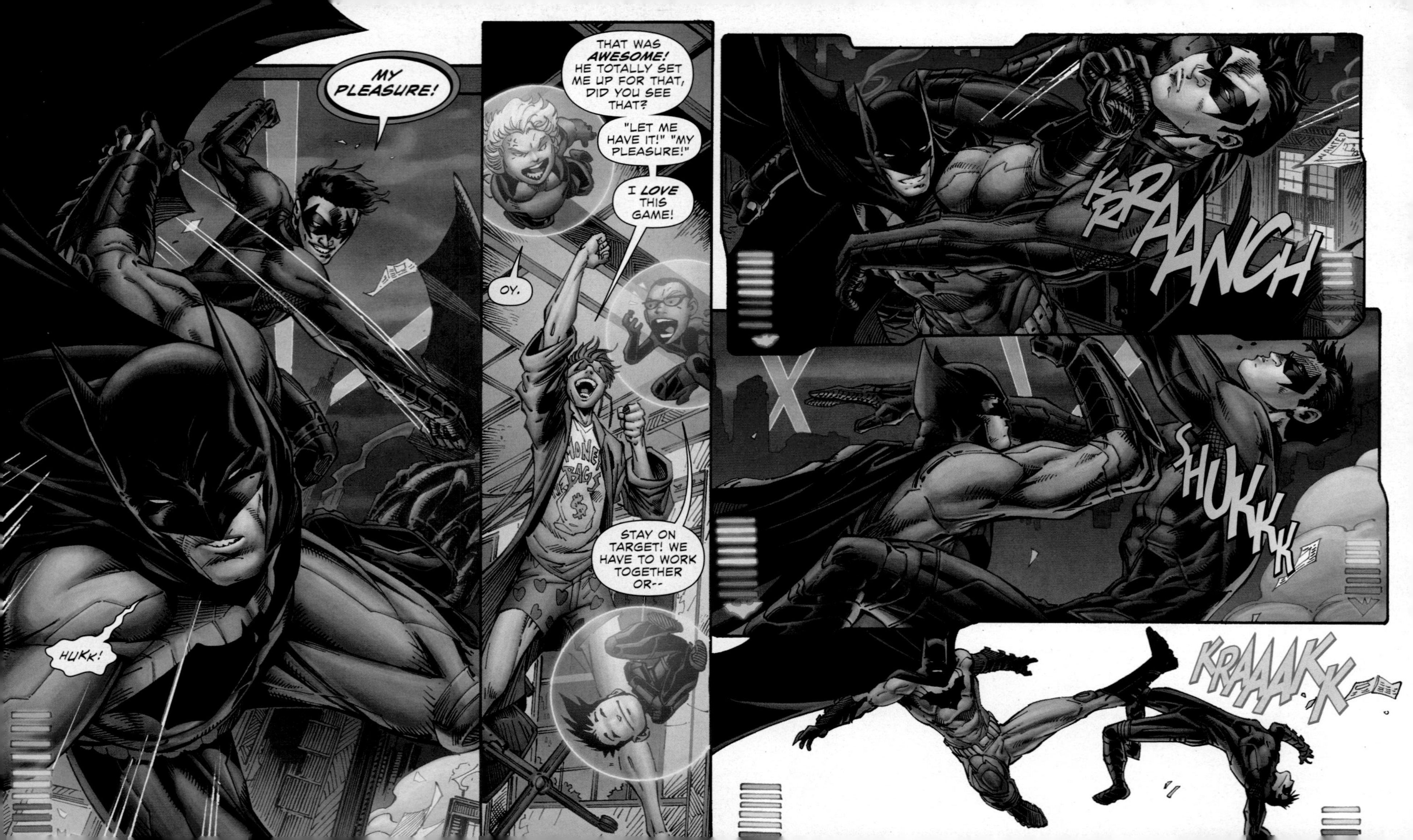
MY PLEASURE!
HUKK!
THAT WAS *AWESOME!* HE TOTALLY SET ME UP FOR THAT, DID YOU SEE THAT?
"LET ME HAVE IT!" "MY PLEASURE!"
I *LOVE* THIS GAME!
OY.
STAY ON TARGET! WE HAVE TO WORK TOGETHER OR--
KRRAANCH
SHUKKK
KRAAAKK

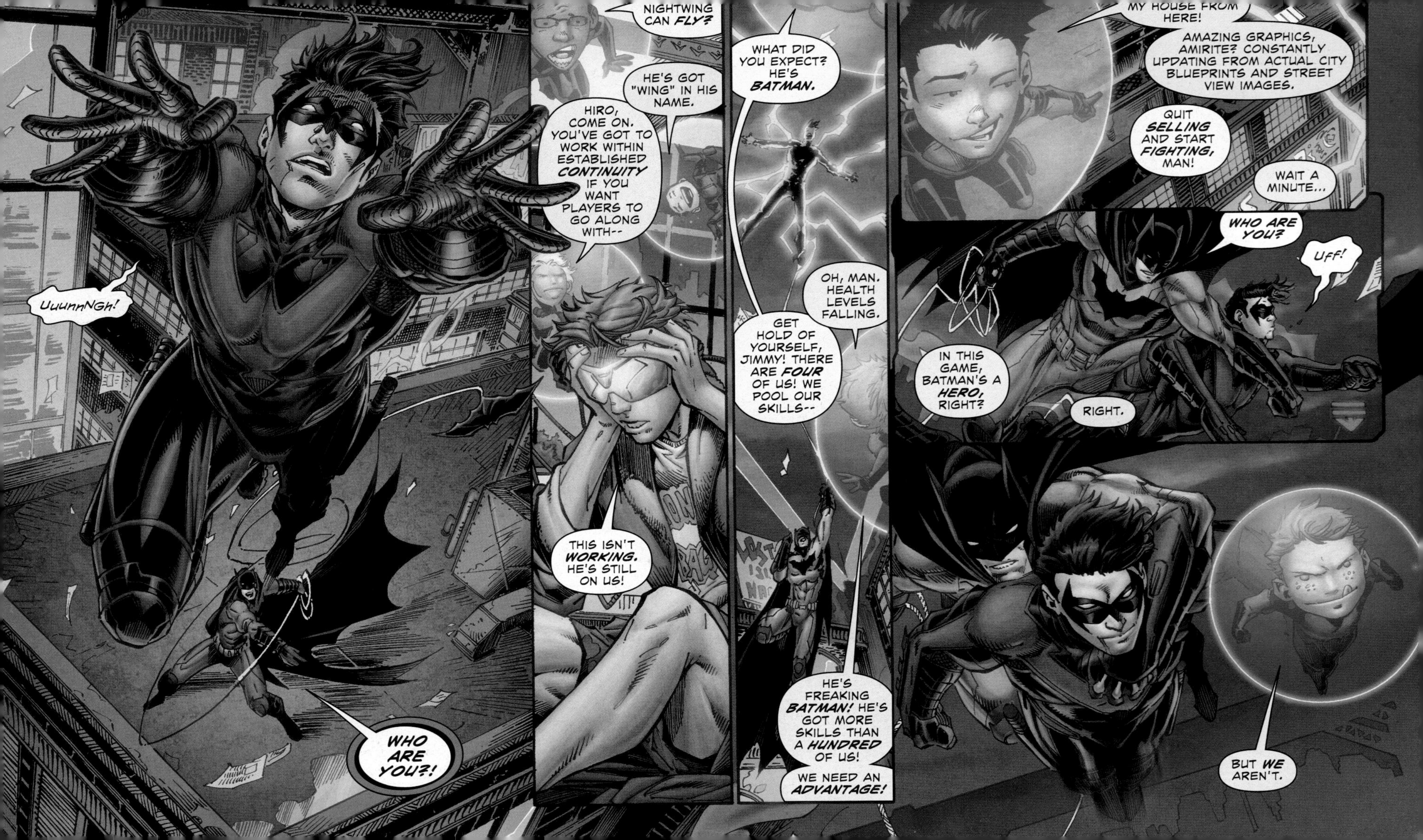
UuunnNGh!
WHO ARE YOU?!
NIGHTWING CAN *FLY?*
HE'S GOT "WING" IN HIS NAME.
HIRO, COME ON. YOU'VE GOT TO WORK WITHIN ESTABLISHED *CONTINUITY* IF YOU WANT PLAYERS TO GO ALONG WITH--
THIS ISN'T *WORKING.* HE'S STILL ON US!
WHAT DID YOU EXPECT? HE'S *BATMAN.*
OH, MAN. HEALTH LEVELS FALLING.
GET HOLD OF YOURSELF, JIMMY! THERE ARE *FOUR* OF US! WE POOL OUR SKILLS--
HE'S FREAKING *BATMAN!* HE'S GOT MORE SKILLS THAN A *HUNDRED* OF US!
WE NEED AN *ADVANTAGE!*
MY HOUSE FROM HERE!
AMAZING GRAPHICS, AMIRITE? CONSTANTLY UPDATING FROM ACTUAL CITY BLUEPRINTS AND STREET VIEW IMAGES.
QUIT *SELLING* AND START *FIGHTING,* MAN!
WAIT A MINUTE...
WHO ARE YOU?
Uff!
IN THIS GAME, BATMAN'S A *HERO,* RIGHT?
RIGHT.
BUT *WE* AREN'T.

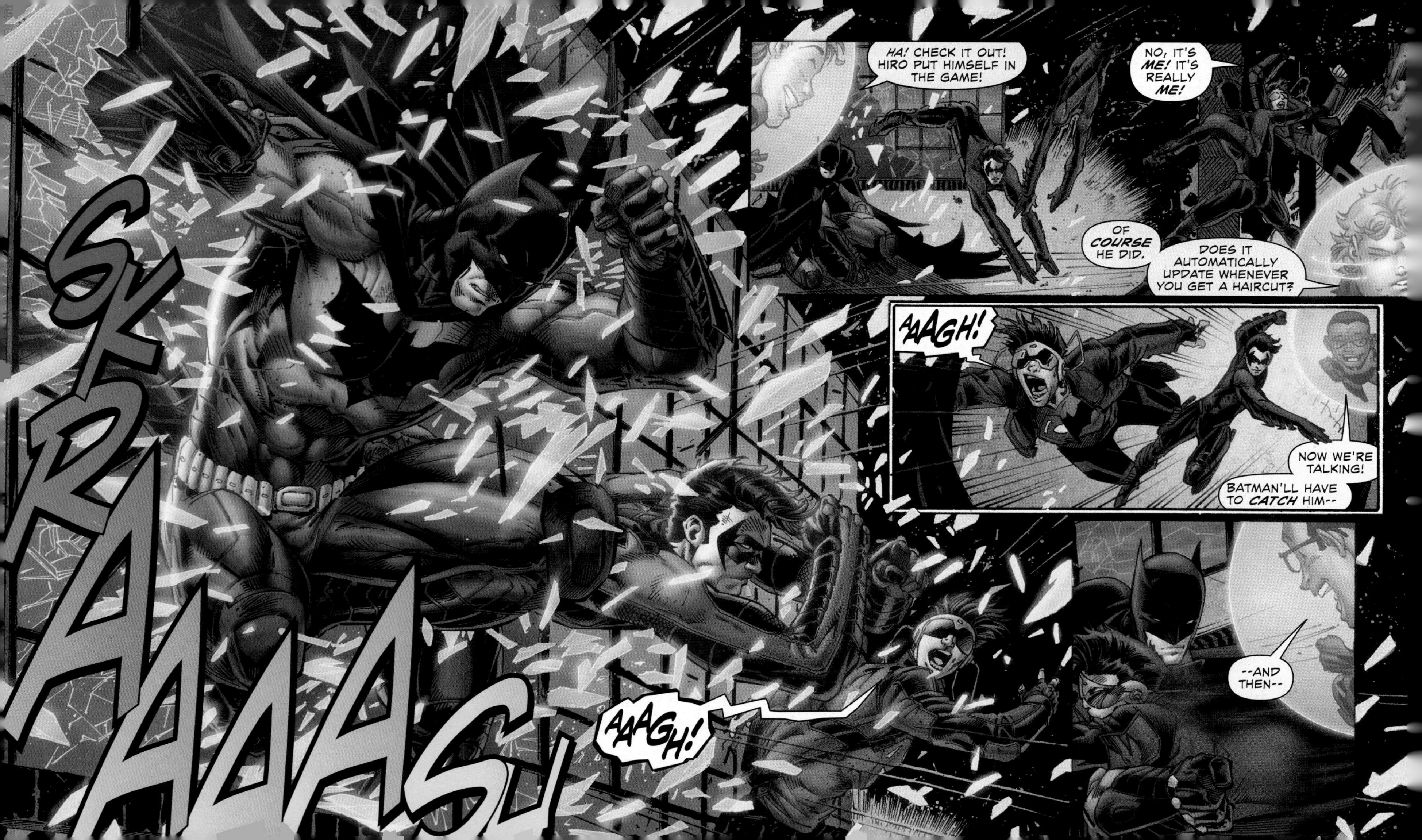
HA! CHECK IT OUT! HIRO PUT HIMSELF IN THE GAME!
NO, IT'S ME! IT'S REALLY ME!
OF COURSE HE DID.
DOES IT AUTOMATICALLY UPDATE WHENEVER YOU GET A HAIRCUT?
AAAGH!
NOW WE'RE TALKING!
BATMAN'LL HAVE TO CATCH HIM--
--AND THEN--
AAAGH!
SKRAAAASH!

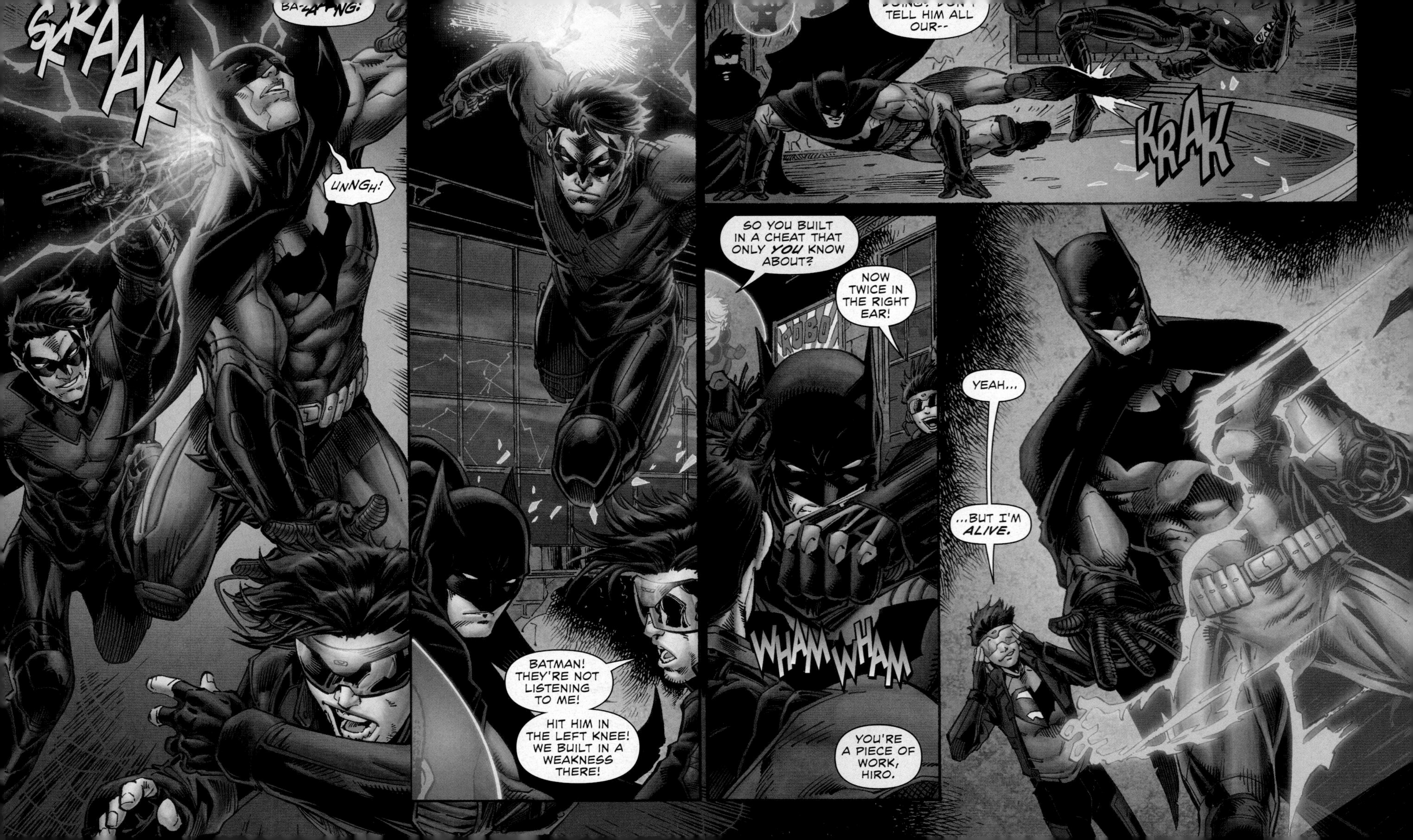
SKKAAK
UNNGH!
TELL HIM ALL
OUR--
KRAK
SO YOU BUILT IN A CHEAT THAT ONLY YOU KNOW ABOUT?
NOW TWICE IN THE RIGHT EAR!
WHAM WHAM
YOU'RE A PIECE OF WORK, HIRO.
BATMAN! THEY'RE NOT LISTENING TO ME!
HIT HIM IN THE LEFT KNEE! WE BUILT IN A WEAKNESS THERE!
YEAH...
...BUT I'M ALIVE.

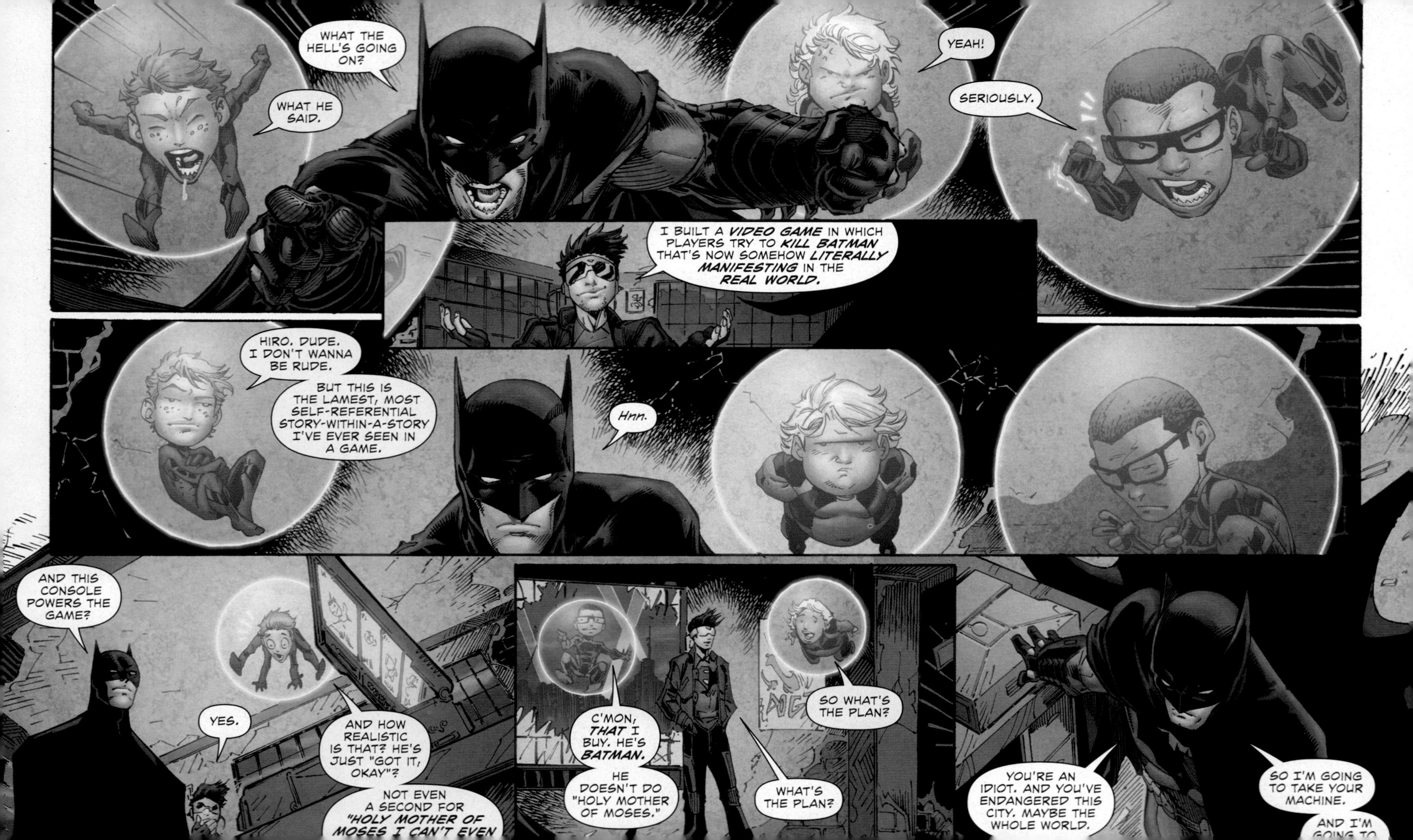

WHAT THE HELL'S GOING ON?
WHAT HE SAID.
YEAH!
SERIOUSLY.
I BUILT A ***VIDEO GAME*** IN WHICH PLAYERS TRY TO ***KILL BATMAN*** THAT'S NOW SOMEHOW ***LITERALLY MANIFESTING*** IN THE ***REAL WORLD.***
HIRO. DUDE. I DON'T WANNA BE RUDE.
BUT THIS IS THE LAMEST, MOST SELF-REFERENTIAL STORY-WITHIN-A-STORY I'VE EVER SEEN IN A GAME.
Hnn.
AND THIS CONSOLE POWERS THE GAME?
YES.
AND HOW REALISTIC IS THAT? HE'S JUST "GOT IT, OKAY"?
NOT EVEN A SECOND FOR ***"HOLY MOTHER OF MOSES I CAN'T EVEN***
C'MON, ***THAT*** I BUY. HE'S ***BATMAN.***
HE DOESN'T DO "HOLY MOTHER OF MOSES."
WHAT'S THE PLAN?
SO WHAT'S THE PLAN?
YOU'RE AN IDIOT. AND YOU'VE ENDANGERED THIS CITY. MAYBE THE WHOLE WORLD.
SO I'M GOING TO TAKE YOUR MACHINE.
AND I'M

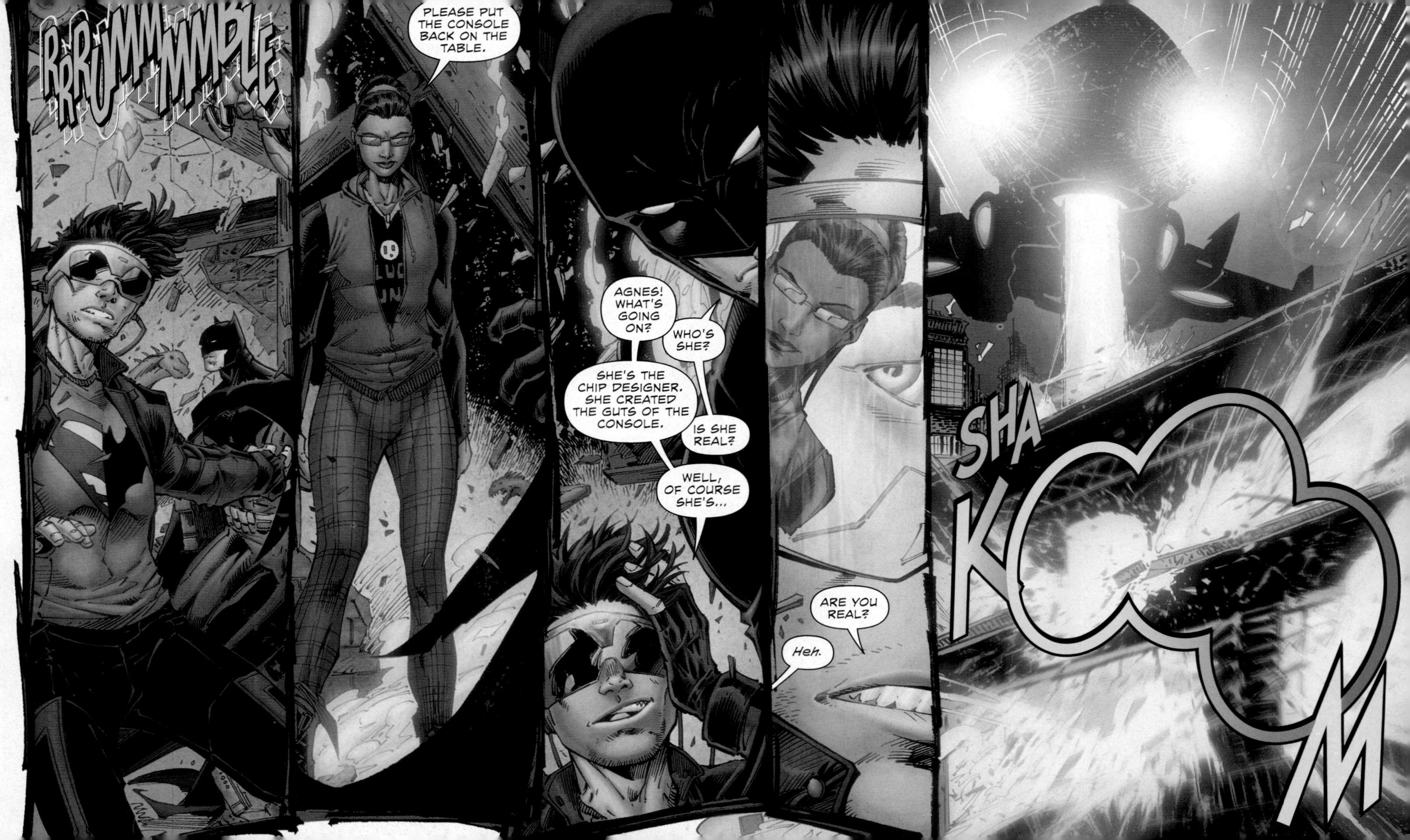
RRRUMMMMBLE
PLEASE PUT THE CONSOLE BACK ON THE TABLE.
AGNES! WHAT'S GOING ON?
WHO'S SHE?
SHE'S THE CHIP DESIGNER. SHE CREATED THE GUTS OF THE CONSOLE.
IS SHE REAL?
WELL, OF COURSE SHE'S...
ARE YOU REAL?
Heh.
SHAKOOM

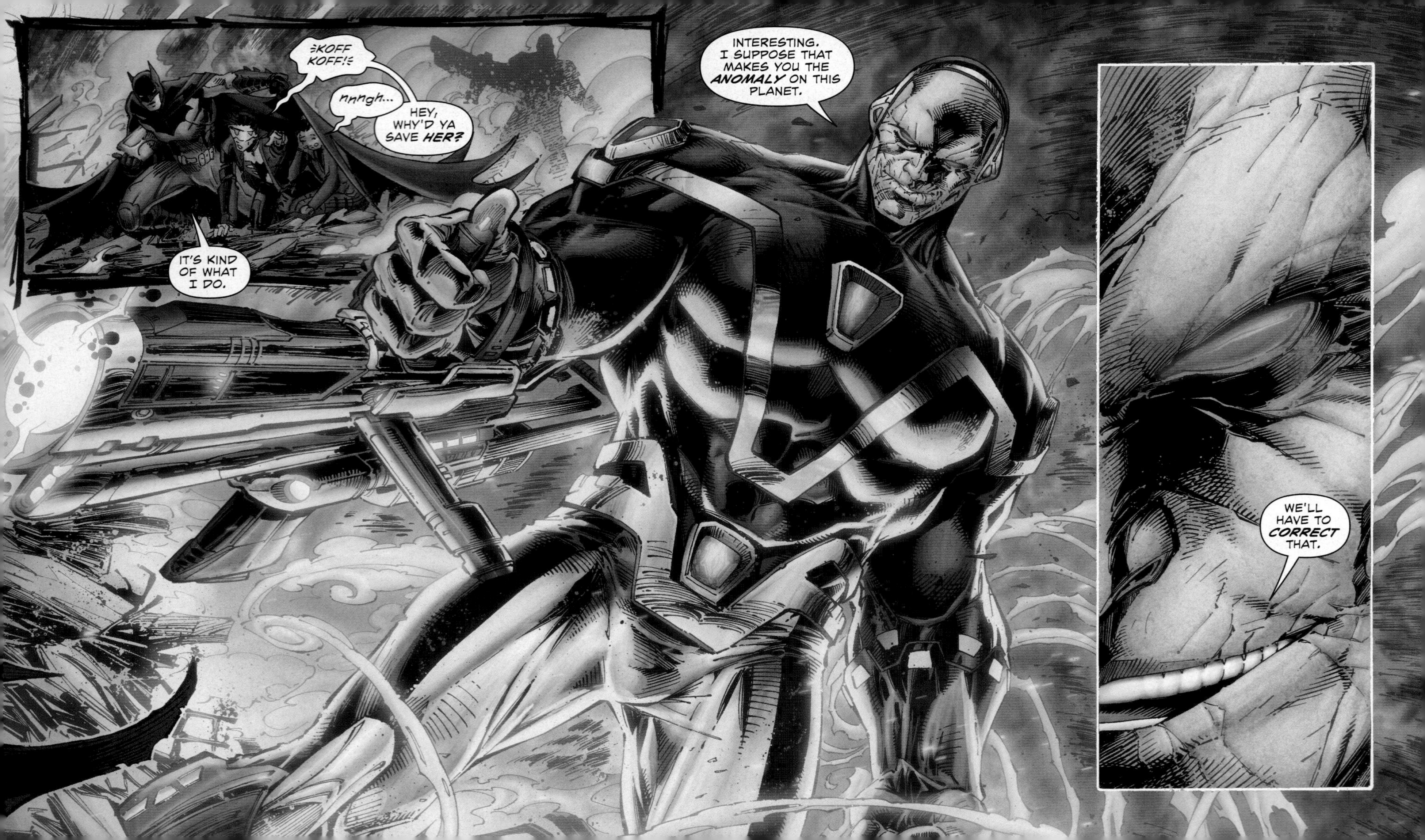

¡KOFF KOFF!¡
nnngh...
HEY, WHY'D YA SAVE HER?
IT'S KIND OF WHAT I DO.
INTERESTING. I SUPPOSE THAT MAKES YOU THE ANOMALY ON THIS PLANET.
WE'LL HAVE TO CORRECT THAT.

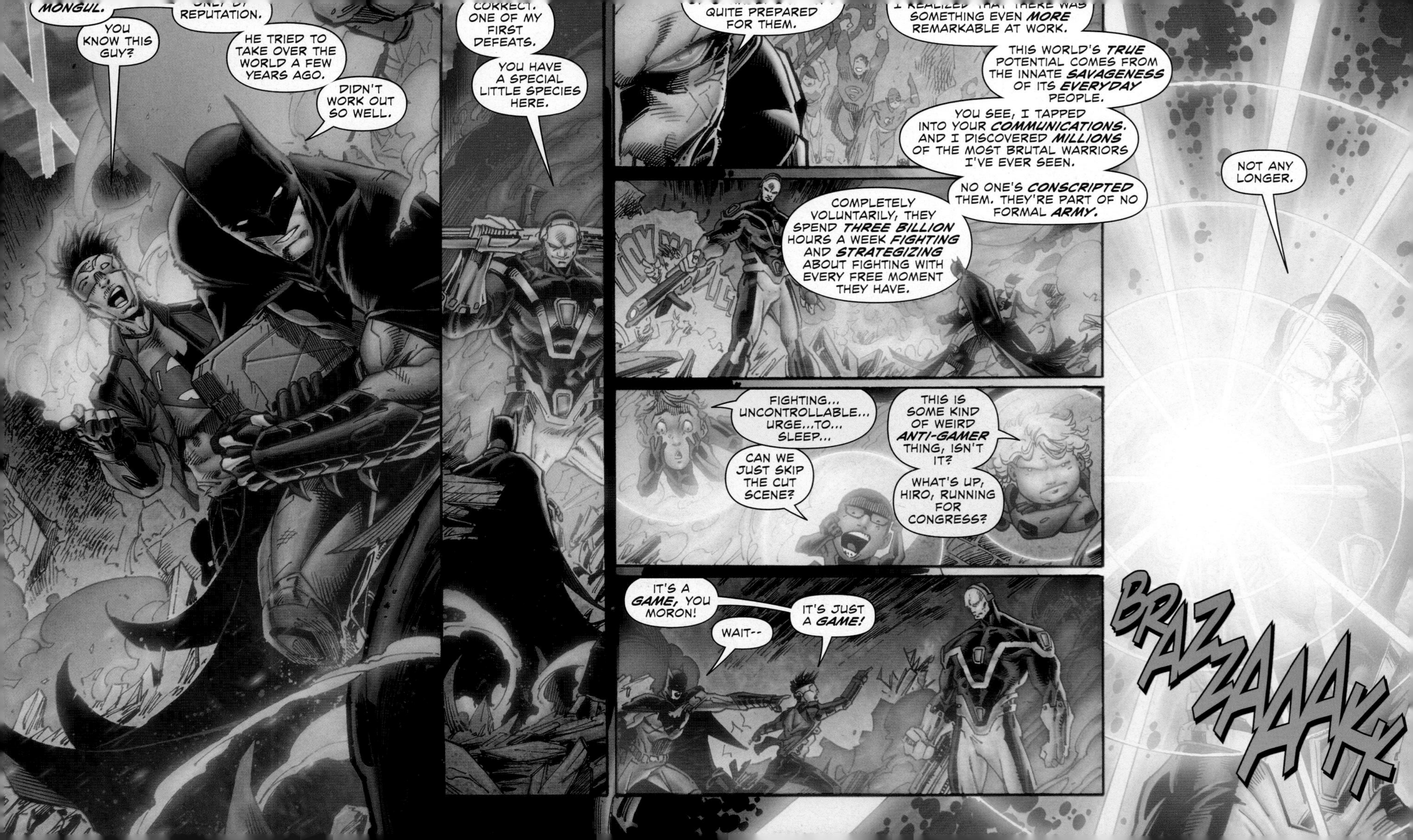
MONGUL.
YOU KNOW THIS GUY?
REPUTATION.
HE TRIED TO TAKE OVER THE WORLD A FEW YEARS AGO.
DIDN'T WORK OUT SO WELL.
CORRECT. ONE OF MY FIRST DEFEATS.
YOU HAVE A SPECIAL LITTLE SPECIES HERE.
QUITE PREPARED FOR THEM.
SOMETHING EVEN MORE REMARKABLE AT WORK.
THIS WORLD'S TRUE POTENTIAL COMES FROM THE INNATE SAVAGENESS OF ITS EVERYDAY PEOPLE.
YOU SEE, I TAPPED INTO YOUR COMMUNICATIONS. AND I DISCOVERED MILLIONS OF THE MOST BRUTAL WARRIORS I'VE EVER SEEN.
NO ONE'S CONSCRIPTED THEM. THEY'RE PART OF NO FORMAL ARMY.
COMPLETELY VOLUNTARILY, THEY SPEND THREE BILLION HOURS A WEEK FIGHTING AND STRATEGIZING ABOUT FIGHTING WITH EVERY FREE MOMENT THEY HAVE.
FIGHTING... UNCONTROLLABLE... URGE...TO... SLEEP...
CAN WE JUST SKIP THE CUT SCENE?
THIS IS SOME KIND OF WEIRD ANTI-GAMER THING, ISN'T IT?
WHAT'S UP, HIRO, RUNNING FOR CONGRESS?
IT'S A GAME, YOU MORON!
WAIT--
IT'S JUST A GAME!
NOT ANY LONGER.
BRAZZAAAKK

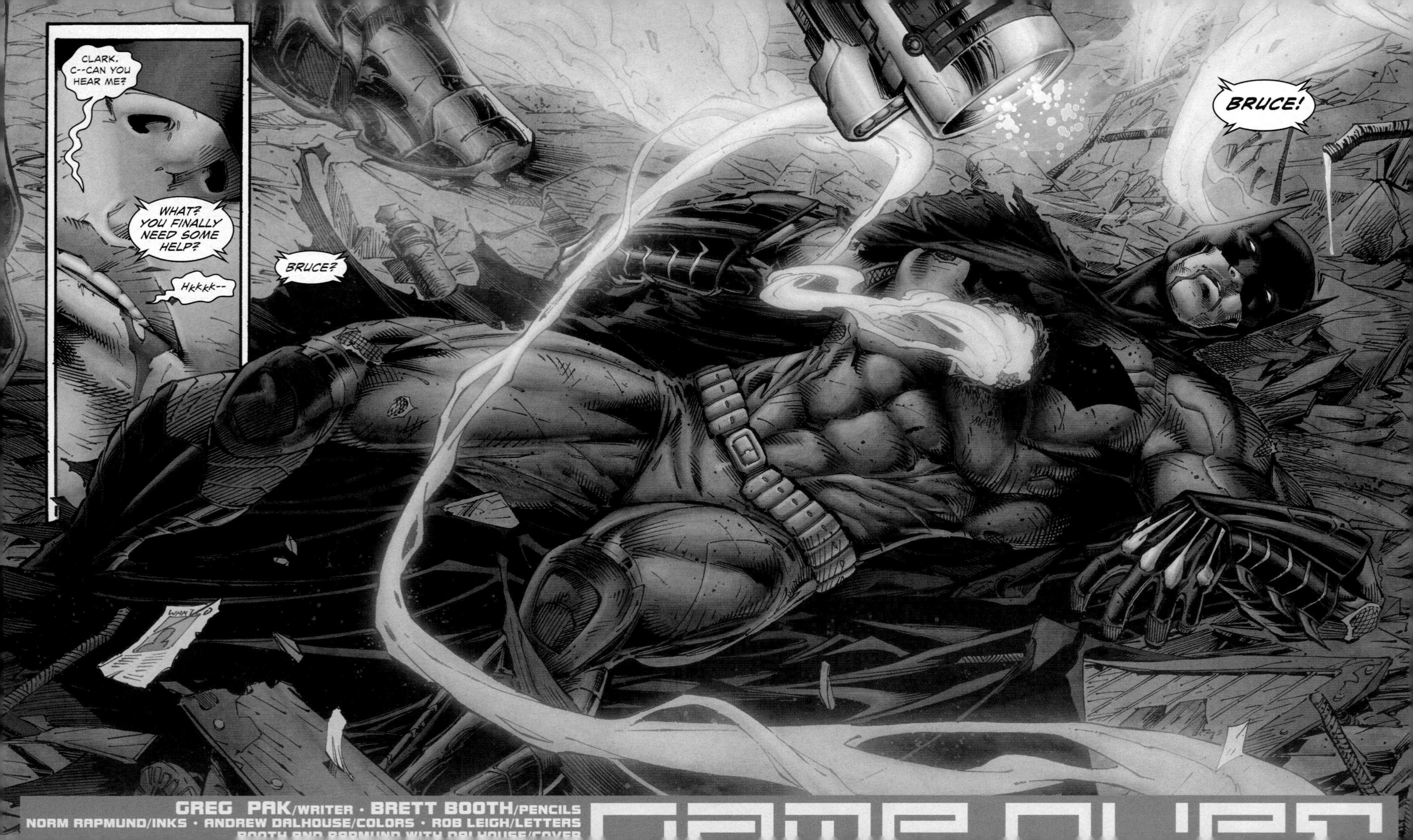
CLARK. C--CAN YOU HEAR ME?
WHAT? YOU FINALLY NEED SOME HELP?
HKKKK--
BRUCE?
BRUCE!
GREG PAK/WRITER · BRETT BOOTH/PENCILS
NORM RAPMUND/INKS · ANDREW DALHOUSE/COLORS · ROB LEIGH/LETTERS

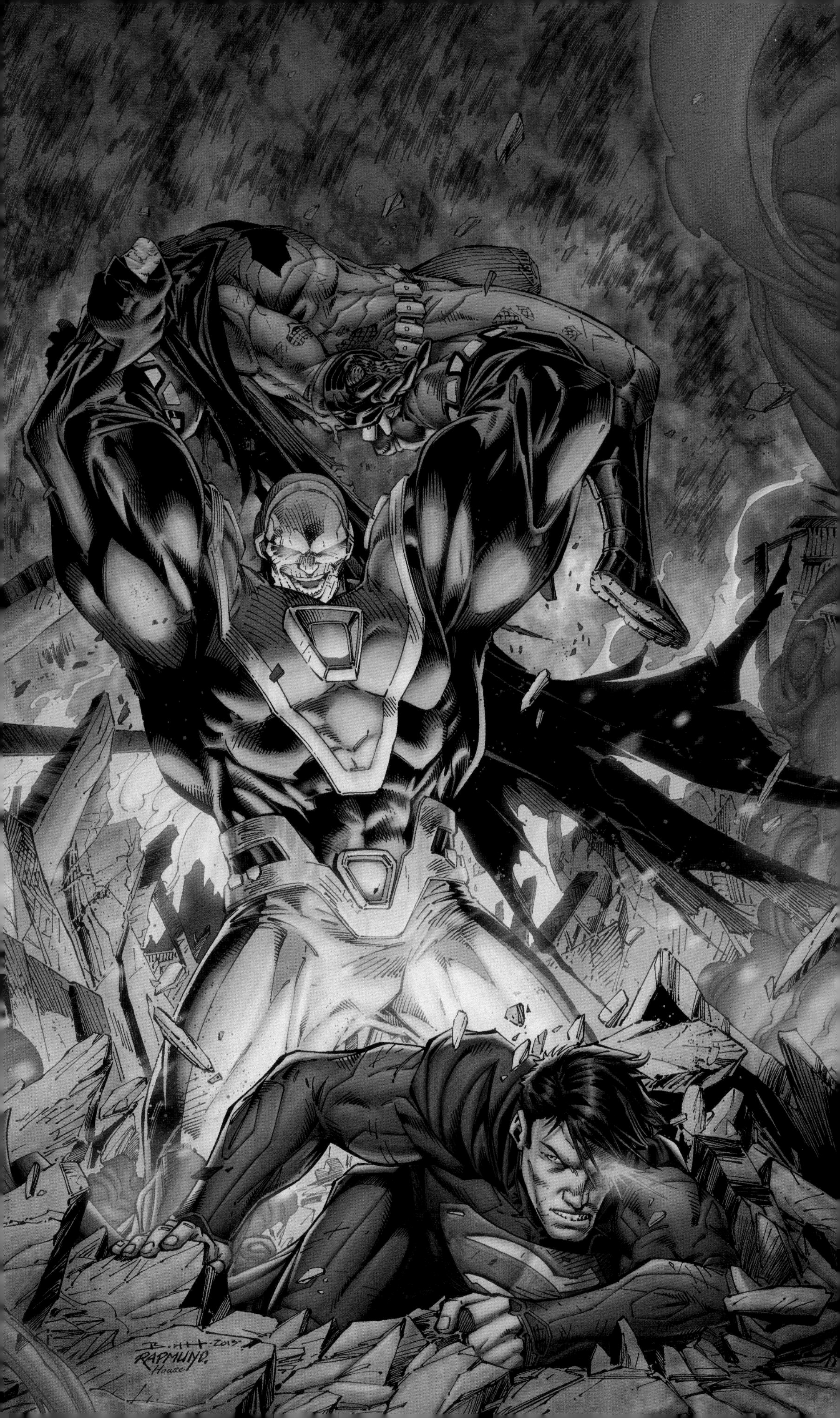
RAPMUND.
House

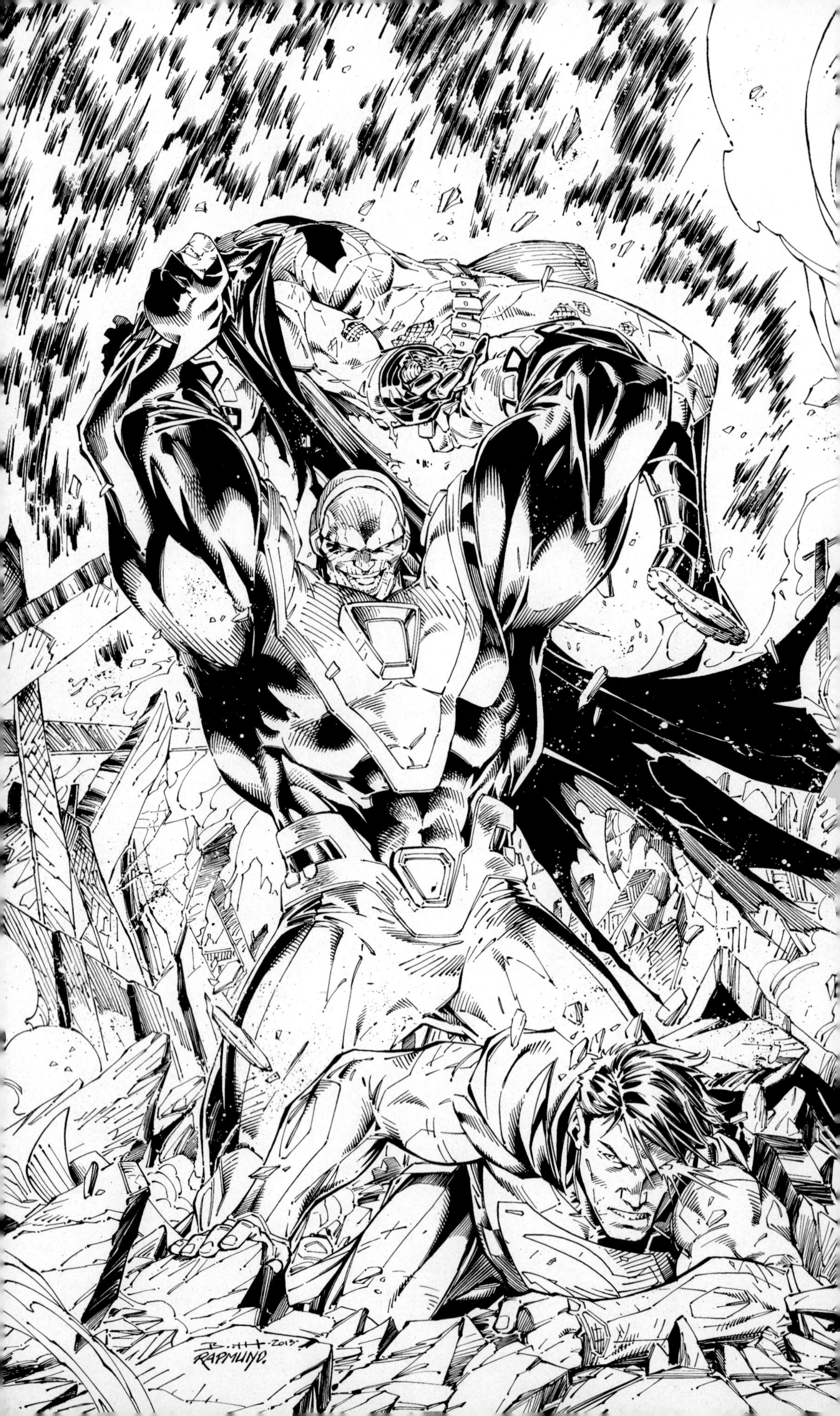
RAPMUND.

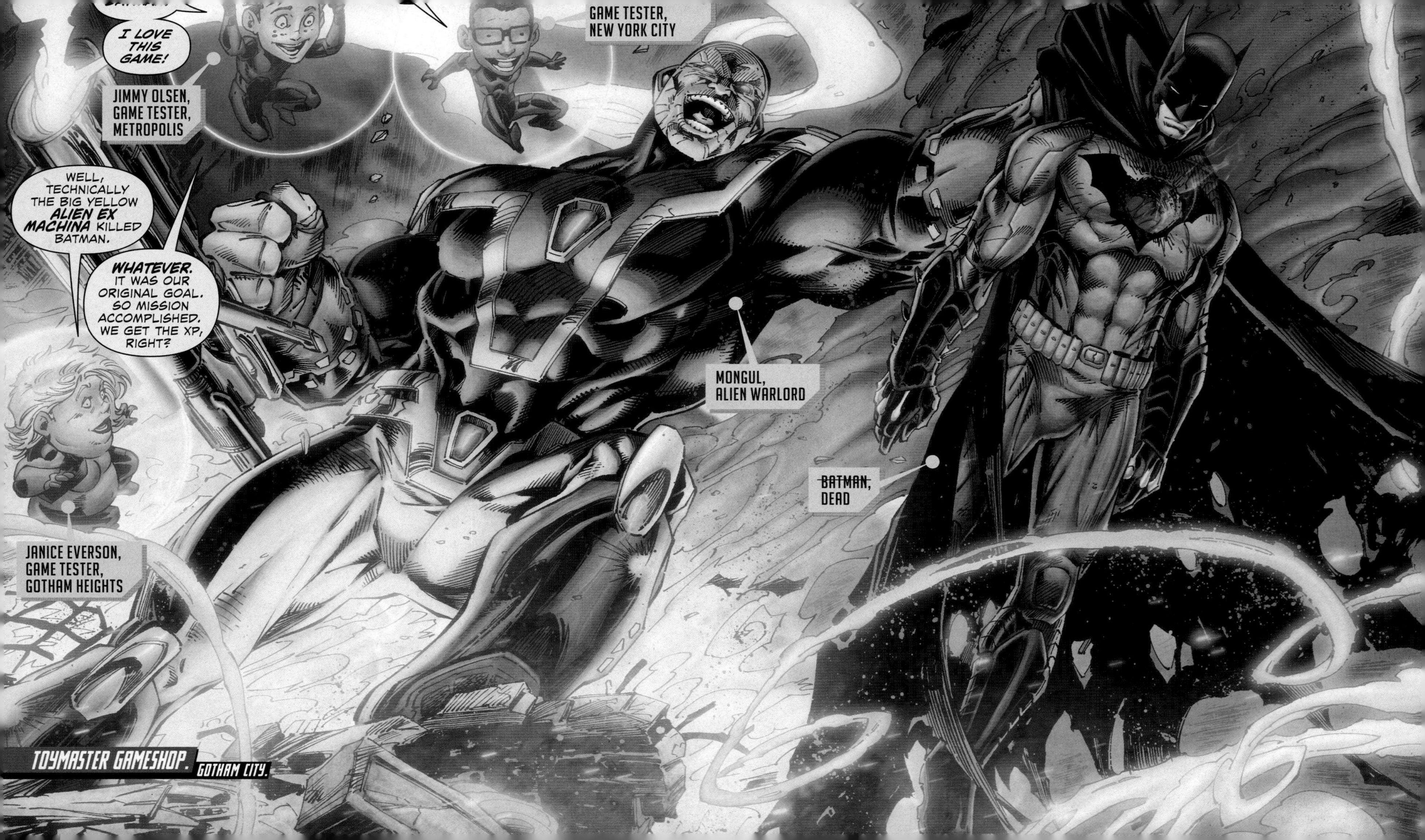
I LOVE THIS GAME!
JIMMY OLSEN, GAME TESTER, METROPOLIS
GAME TESTER, NEW YORK CITY
WELL, TECHNICALLY THE BIG YELLOW ALIEN EX MACHINA KILLED BATMAN.
WHATEVER. IT WAS OUR ORIGINAL GOAL. SO MISSION ACCOMPLISHED. WE GET THE XP, RIGHT?
MONGUL, ALIEN WARLORD
~~BATMAN~~, DEAD
JANICE EVERSON, GAME TESTER, GOTHAM HEIGHTS
TOYMASTER GAMESHOP. GOTHAM CITY.

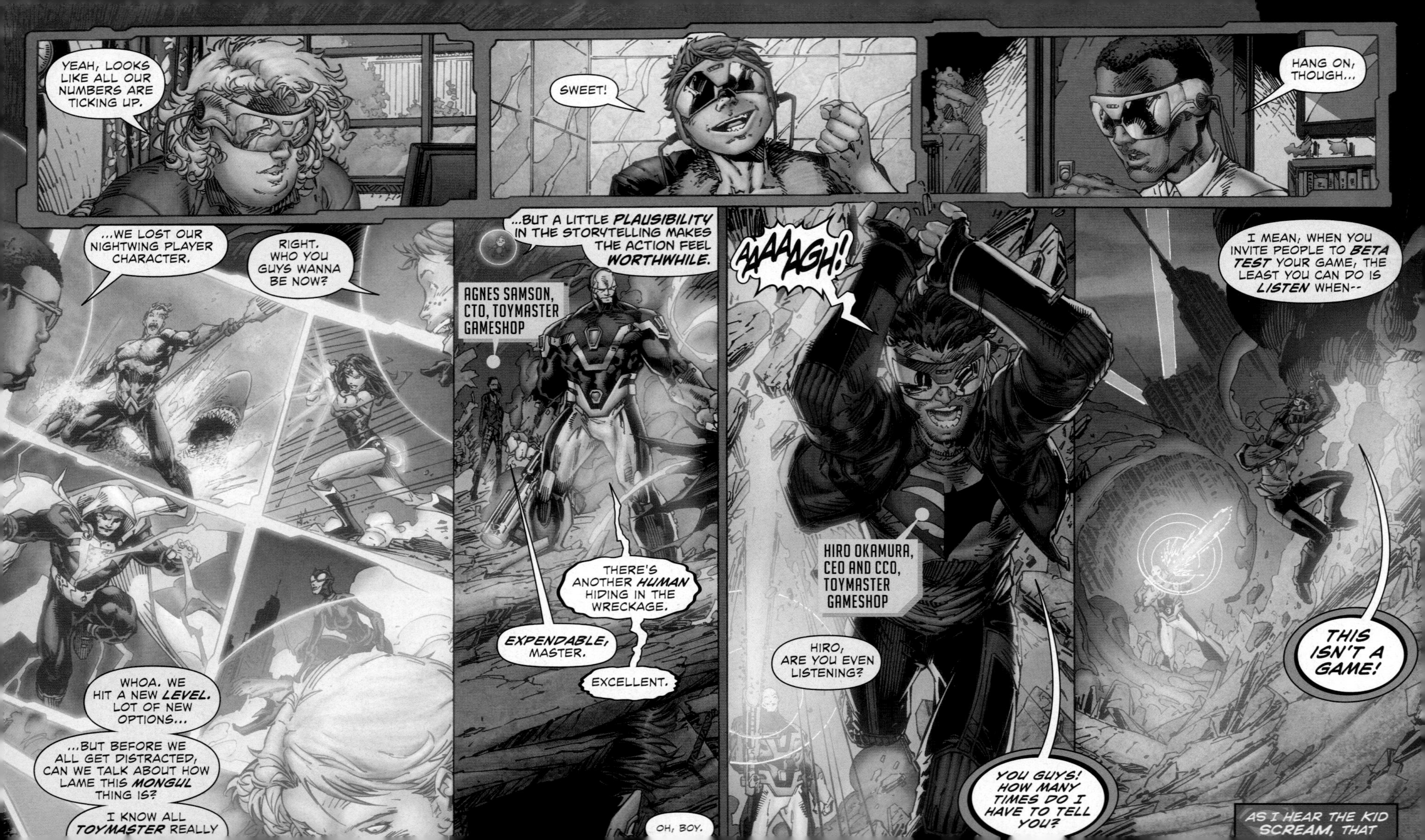
YEAH, LOOKS LIKE ALL OUR NUMBERS ARE TICKING UP.
SWEET!
HANG ON, THOUGH...
...WE LOST OUR NIGHTWING PLAYER CHARACTER.
RIGHT. WHO YOU GUYS WANNA BE NOW?
WHOA. WE HIT A NEW *LEVEL.* LOT OF NEW OPTIONS...
...BUT BEFORE WE ALL GET DISTRACTED, CAN WE TALK ABOUT HOW LAME THIS *MONGUL* THING IS?
I KNOW ALL *TOYMASTER* REALLY
...BUT A LITTLE *PLAUSIBILITY* IN THE STORYTELLING MAKES THE ACTION FEEL *WORTHWHILE.*
AGNES SAMSON, CTO, TOYMASTER GAMESHOP
THERE'S ANOTHER *HUMAN* HIDING IN THE WRECKAGE.
EXPENDABLE, MASTER.
EXCELLENT.
OH, BOY.
AAAAAGH!
HIRO OKAMURA, CEO AND CCO, TOYMASTER GAMESHOP
HIRO, ARE YOU EVEN LISTENING?
YOU GUYS! HOW MANY TIMES DO I HAVE TO TELL YOU?
I MEAN, WHEN YOU INVITE PEOPLE TO *BETA TEST* YOUR GAME, THE LEAST YOU CAN DO IS *LISTEN* WHEN--
THIS ISN'T A GAME!
AS I HEAR THE KID SCREAM, THAT

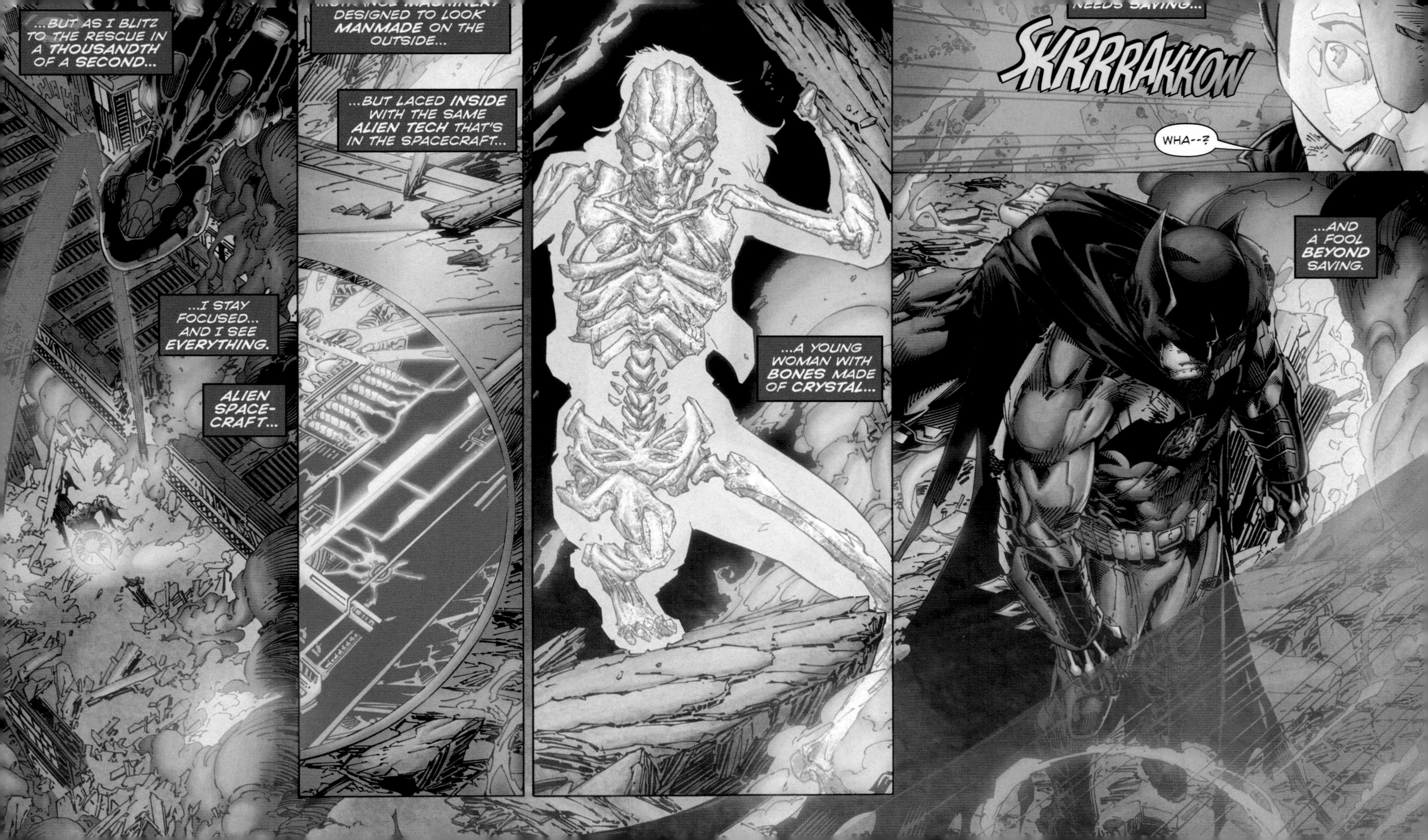
...BUT AS I BLITZ TO THE RESCUE IN A THOUSANDTH OF A SECOND...
...I STAY FOCUSED... AND I SEE EVERYTHING.
ALIEN SPACE-CRAFT...
DESIGNED TO LOOK MANMADE ON THE OUTSIDE...
...BUT LACED INSIDE WITH THE SAME ALIEN TECH THAT'S IN THE SPACECRAFT...
...A YOUNG WOMAN WITH BONES MADE OF CRYSTAL...
SKRRRAKKOW
WHA--?
...AND A FOOL BEYOND SAVING.

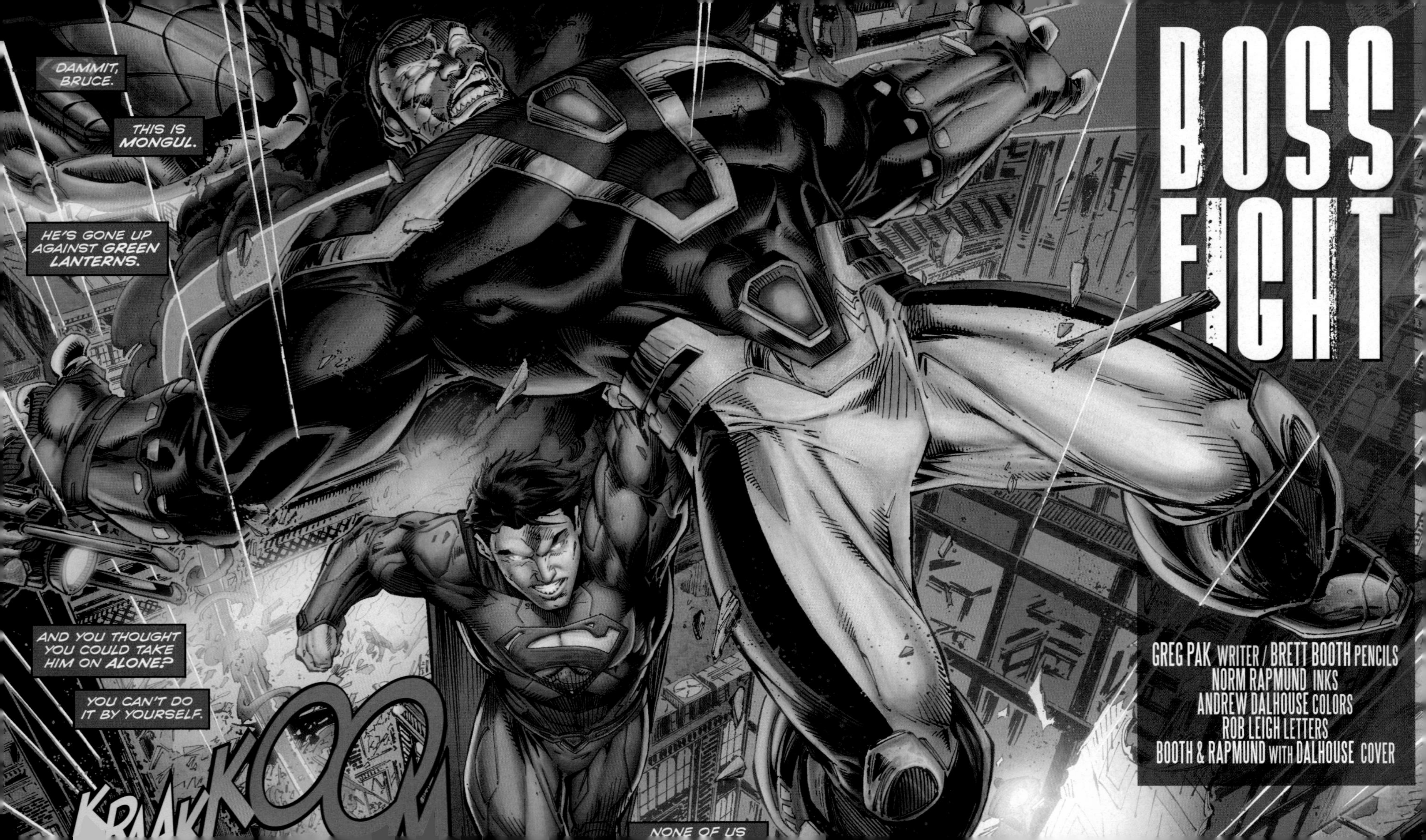
DAMMIT, BRUCE.
THIS IS MONGUL.
HE'S GONE UP AGAINST GREEN LANTERNS.
AND YOU THOUGHT YOU COULD TAKE HIM ON ALONE?
YOU CAN'T DO IT BY YOURSELF.
NONE OF US
BOSS FIGHT
GREG PAK WRITER / BRETT BOOTH PENCILS
NORM RAPMUND INKS
ANDREW DALHOUSE COLORS
ROB LEIGH LETTERS
BOOTH & RAPMUND WITH DALHOUSE COVER

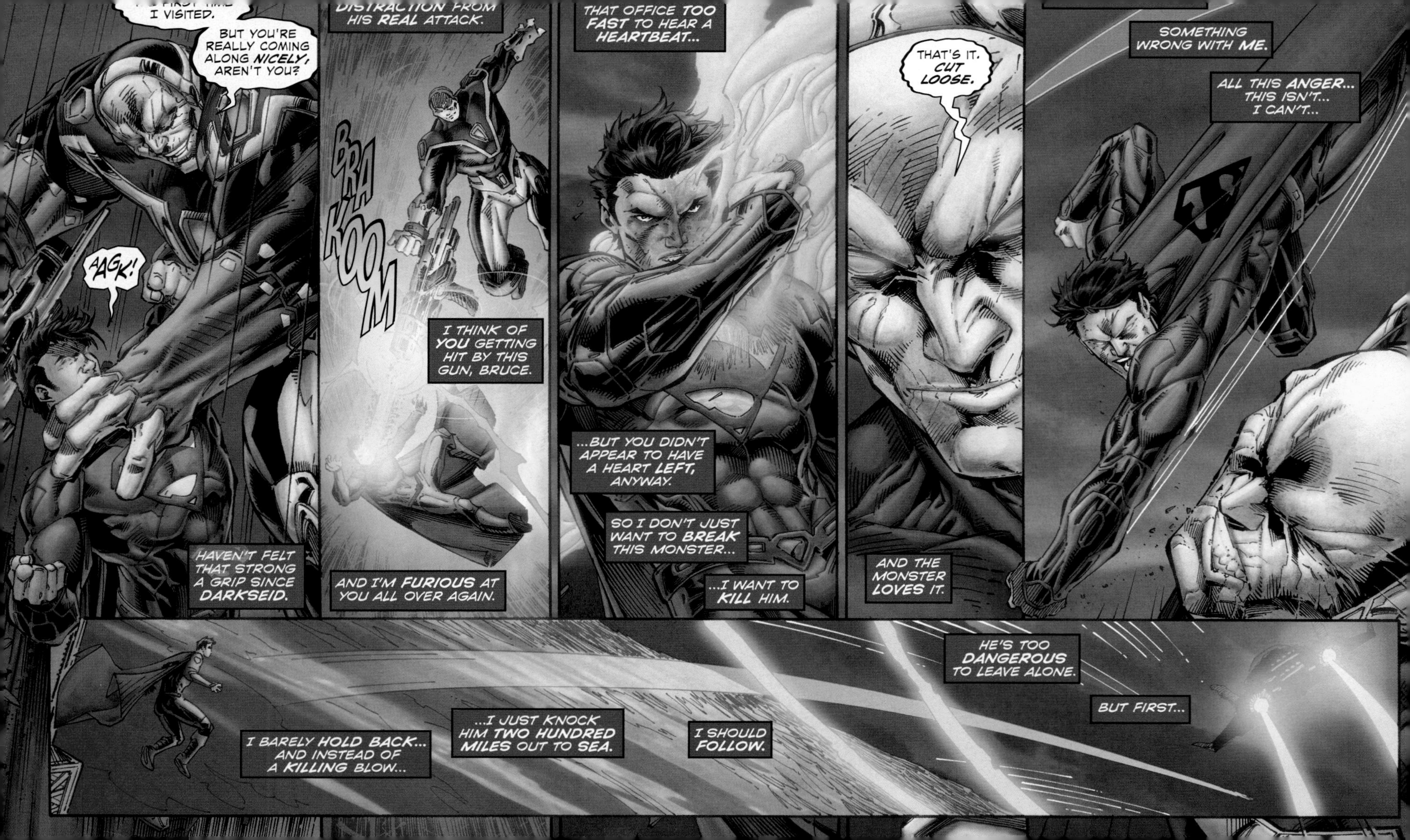
I VISITED.
BUT YOU'RE REALLY COMING ALONG NICELY, AREN'T YOU?
AAGK!
HAVEN'T FELT THAT STRONG A GRIP SINCE DARKSEID.
DISTRACTION FROM HIS REAL ATTACK.
BRAKOOM
I THINK OF YOU GETTING HIT BY THIS GUN, BRUCE.
AND I'M FURIOUS AT YOU ALL OVER AGAIN.
THAT OFFICE TOO FAST TO HEAR A HEARTBEAT...
...BUT YOU DIDN'T APPEAR TO HAVE A HEART LEFT, ANYWAY.
SO I DON'T JUST WANT TO BREAK THIS MONSTER...
...I WANT TO KILL HIM.
THAT'S IT. CUT LOOSE.
AND THE MONSTER LOVES IT.
SOMETHING WRONG WITH ME.
ALL THIS ANGER... THIS ISN'T... I CAN'T...
I BARELY HOLD BACK... AND INSTEAD OF A KILLING BLOW...
...I JUST KNOCK HIM TWO HUNDRED MILES OUT TO SEA.
I SHOULD FOLLOW.
HE'S TOO DANGEROUS TO LEAVE ALONE.
BUT FIRST...

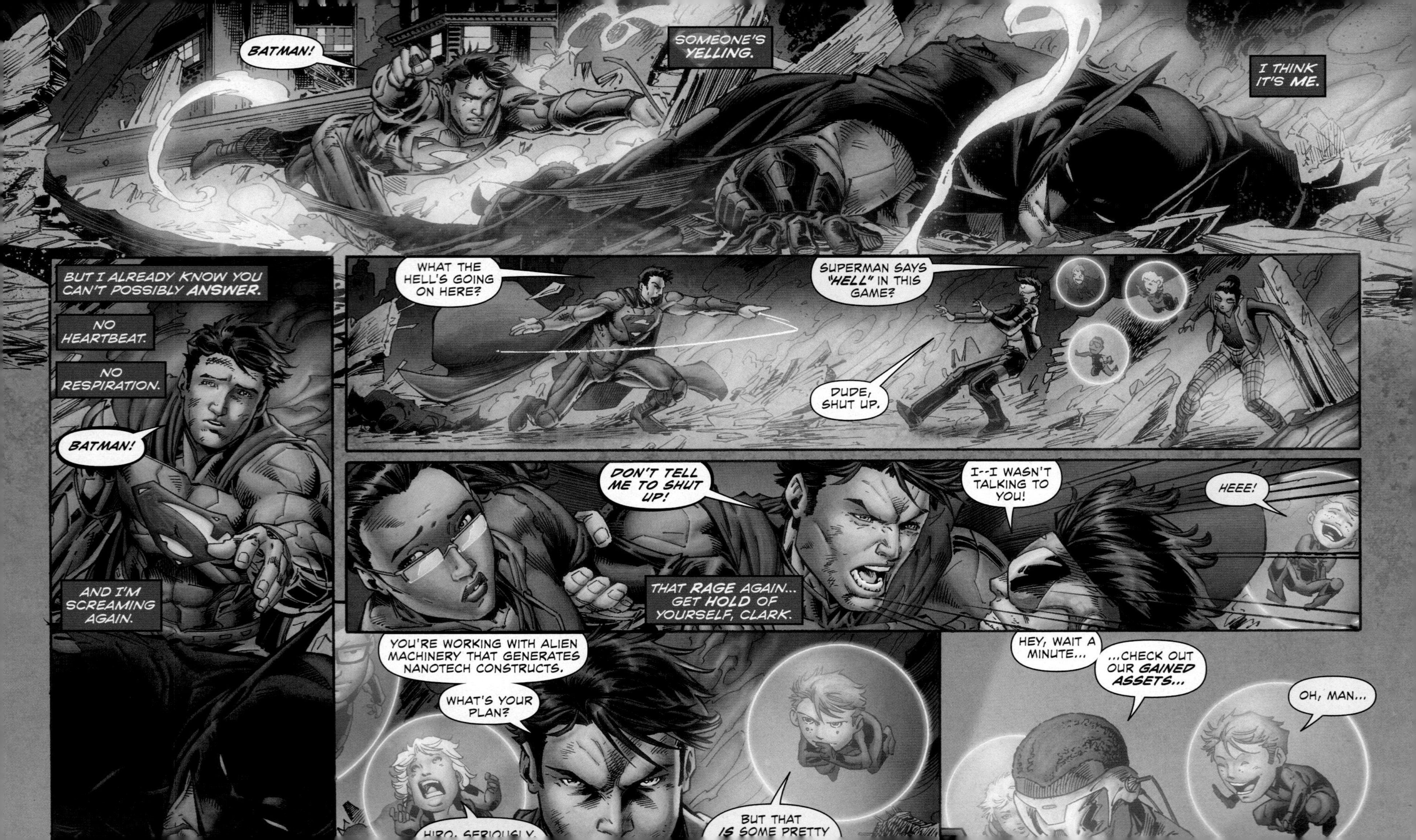
BATMAN!
SOMEONE'S YELLING.
I THINK IT'S ME.
BUT I ALREADY KNOW YOU CAN'T POSSIBLY ANSWER.
NO HEARTBEAT.
NO RESPIRATION.
BATMAN!
AND I'M SCREAMING AGAIN.
WHAT THE HELL'S GOING ON HERE?
SUPERMAN SAYS "HELL" IN THIS GAME?
DUDE, SHUT UP.
DON'T TELL ME TO SHUT UP!
I--I WASN'T TALKING TO YOU!
HEEE!
THAT RAGE AGAIN... GET HOLD OF YOURSELF, CLARK.
YOU'RE WORKING WITH ALIEN MACHINERY THAT GENERATES NANOTECH CONSTRUCTS.
WHAT'S YOUR PLAN?
BUT THAT IS SOME PRETTY
HEY, WAIT A MINUTE...
...CHECK OUT OUR GAINED ASSETS...
OH, MAN...

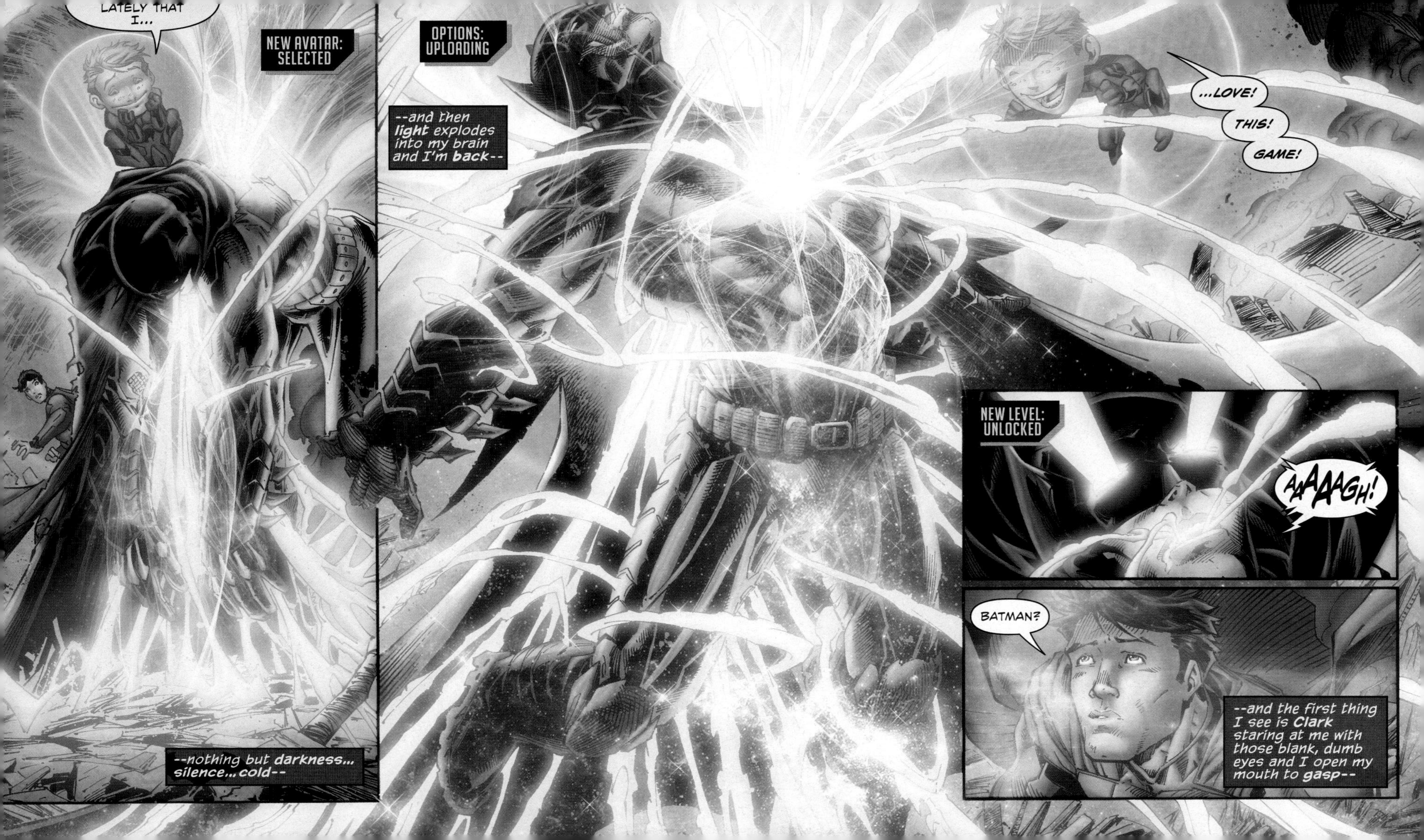

LATELY THAT I...
NEW AVATAR: SELECTED
--nothing but *darkness*... *silence*... *cold*--
OPTIONS: UPLOADING
--and then *light* explodes into my brain and I'm *back*--
...LOVE!
THIS!
GAME!
NEW LEVEL: UNLOCKED
AAAAAGH!
BATMAN?
--and the first thing I see is *Clark* staring at me with those blank, dumb eyes and I open my mouth to *gasp*--

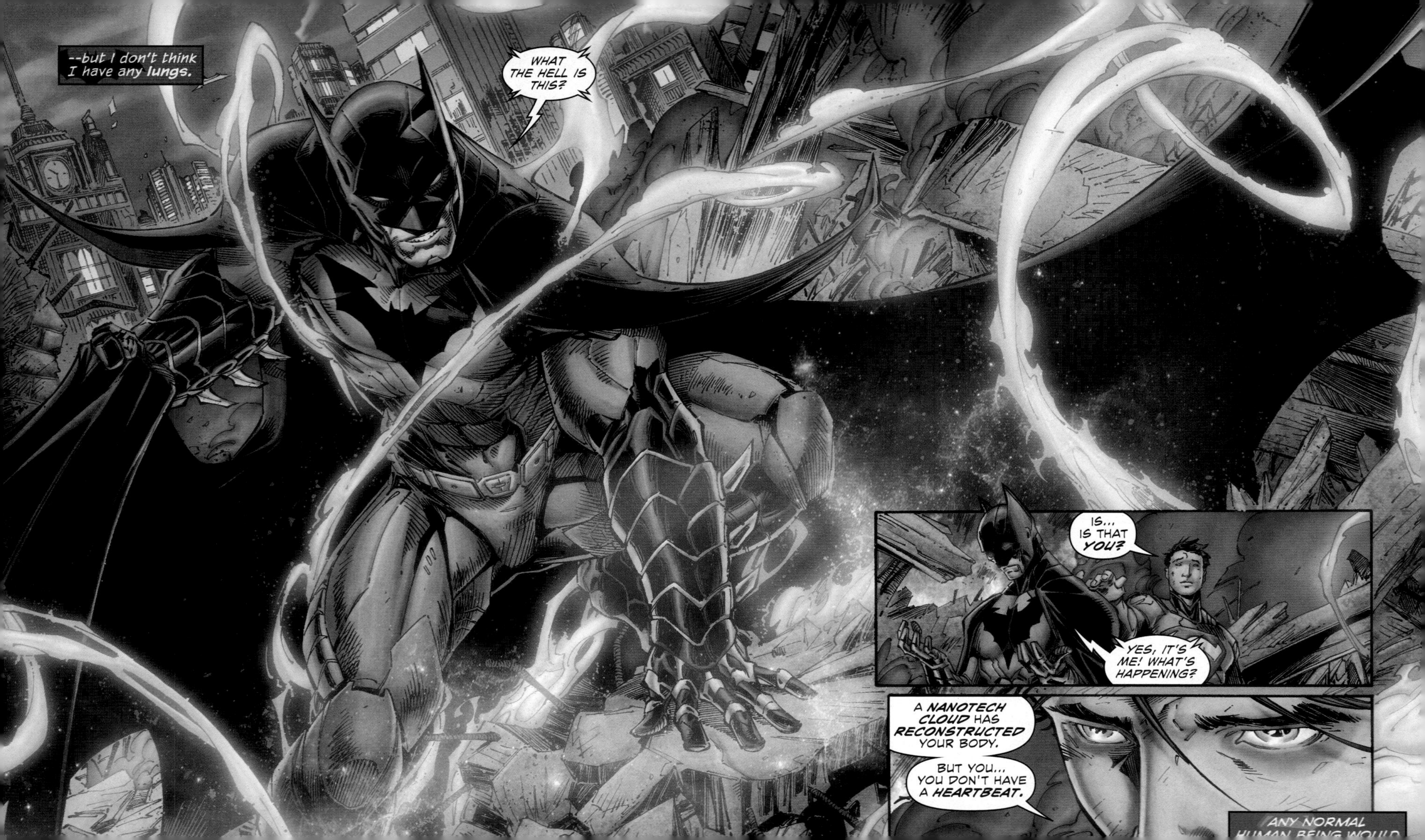
--but I don't think I have any lungs.
WHAT THE HELL IS THIS?
IS... IS THAT YOU?
YES, IT'S ME! WHAT'S HAPPENING?
A NANOTECH CLOUD HAS RECONSTRUCTED YOUR BODY.
BUT YOU... YOU DON'T HAVE A HEARTBEAT.
ANY NORMAL

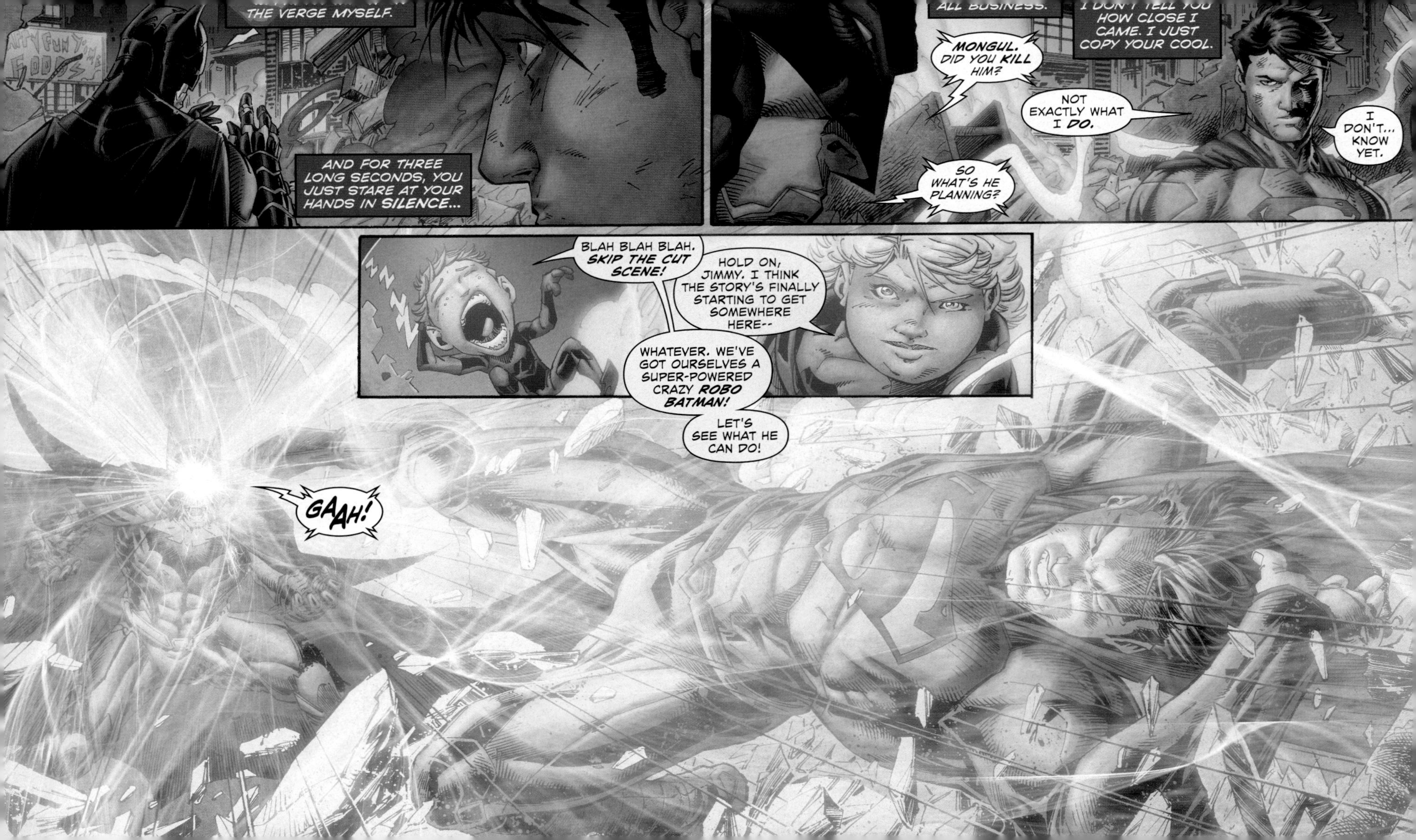
THE VERGE MYSELF.
AND FOR THREE LONG SECONDS, YOU JUST STARE AT YOUR HANDS IN SILENCE...
ALL BUSINESS.
MONGUL. DID YOU KILL HIM?
I DON'T TELL YOU HOW CLOSE I CAME. I JUST COPY YOUR COOL.
NOT EXACTLY WHAT I DO.
SO WHAT'S HE PLANNING?
I DON'T... KNOW YET.
BLAH BLAH BLAH. SKIP THE CUT SCENE!
HOLD ON, JIMMY. I THINK THE STORY'S FINALLY STARTING TO GET SOMEWHERE HERE--
WHATEVER. WE'VE GOT OURSELVES A SUPER-POWERED CRAZY ROBO BATMAN!
LET'S SEE WHAT HE CAN DO!
GAAH!

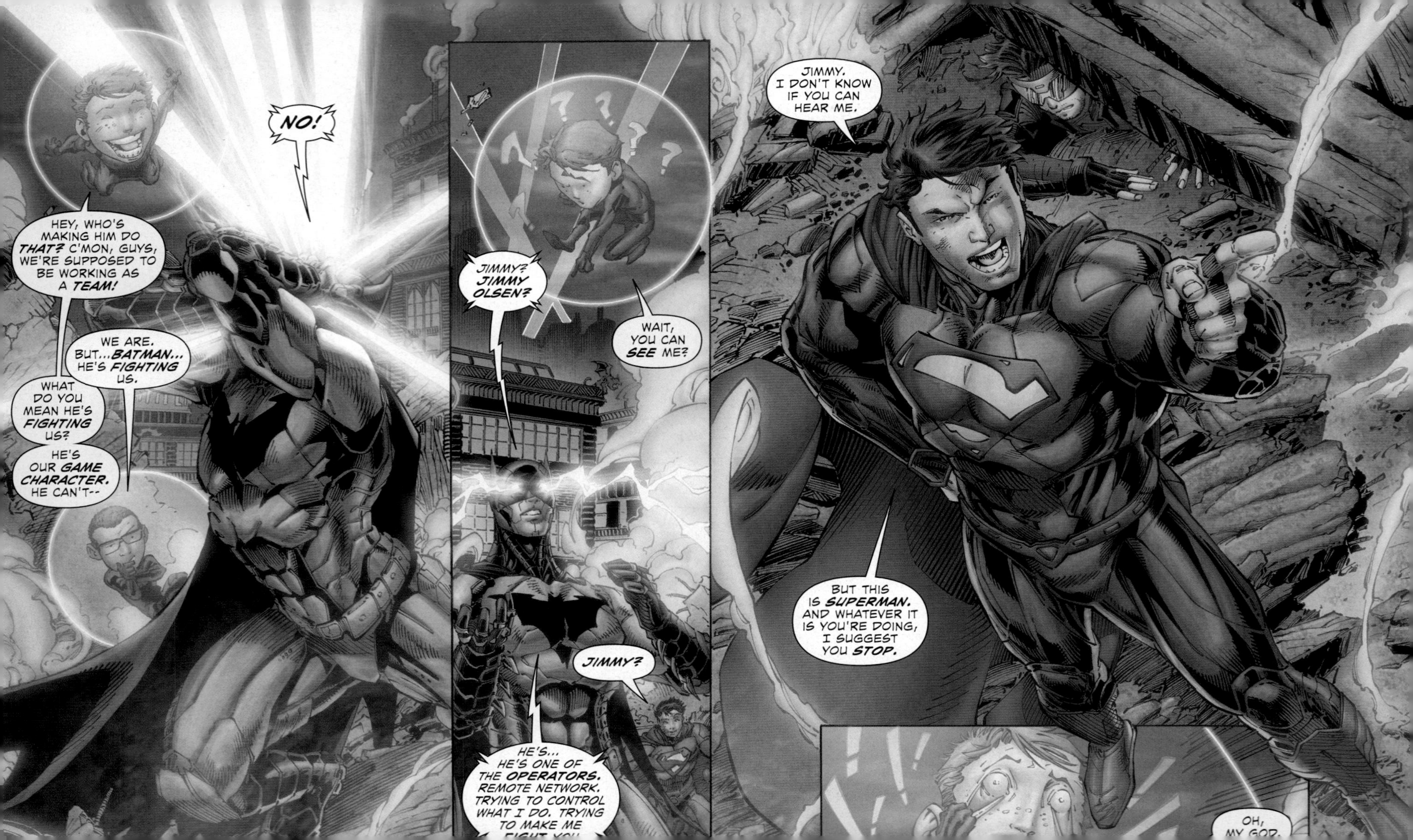

NO!
HEY, WHO'S MAKING HIM DO THAT? C'MON, GUYS, WE'RE SUPPOSED TO BE WORKING AS A TEAM!
WE ARE. BUT...BATMAN... HE'S FIGHTING US.
WHAT DO YOU MEAN HE'S FIGHTING US?
HE'S OUR GAME CHARACTER. HE CAN'T--
JIMMY? JIMMY OLSEN?
WAIT, YOU CAN SEE ME?
JIMMY?
HE'S... HE'S ONE OF THE OPERATORS. REMOTE NETWORK. TRYING TO CONTROL WHAT I DO. TRYING TO MAKE ME
JIMMY. I DON'T KNOW IF YOU CAN HEAR ME.
BUT THIS IS SUPERMAN. AND WHATEVER IT IS YOU'RE DOING, I SUGGEST YOU STOP.
OH,

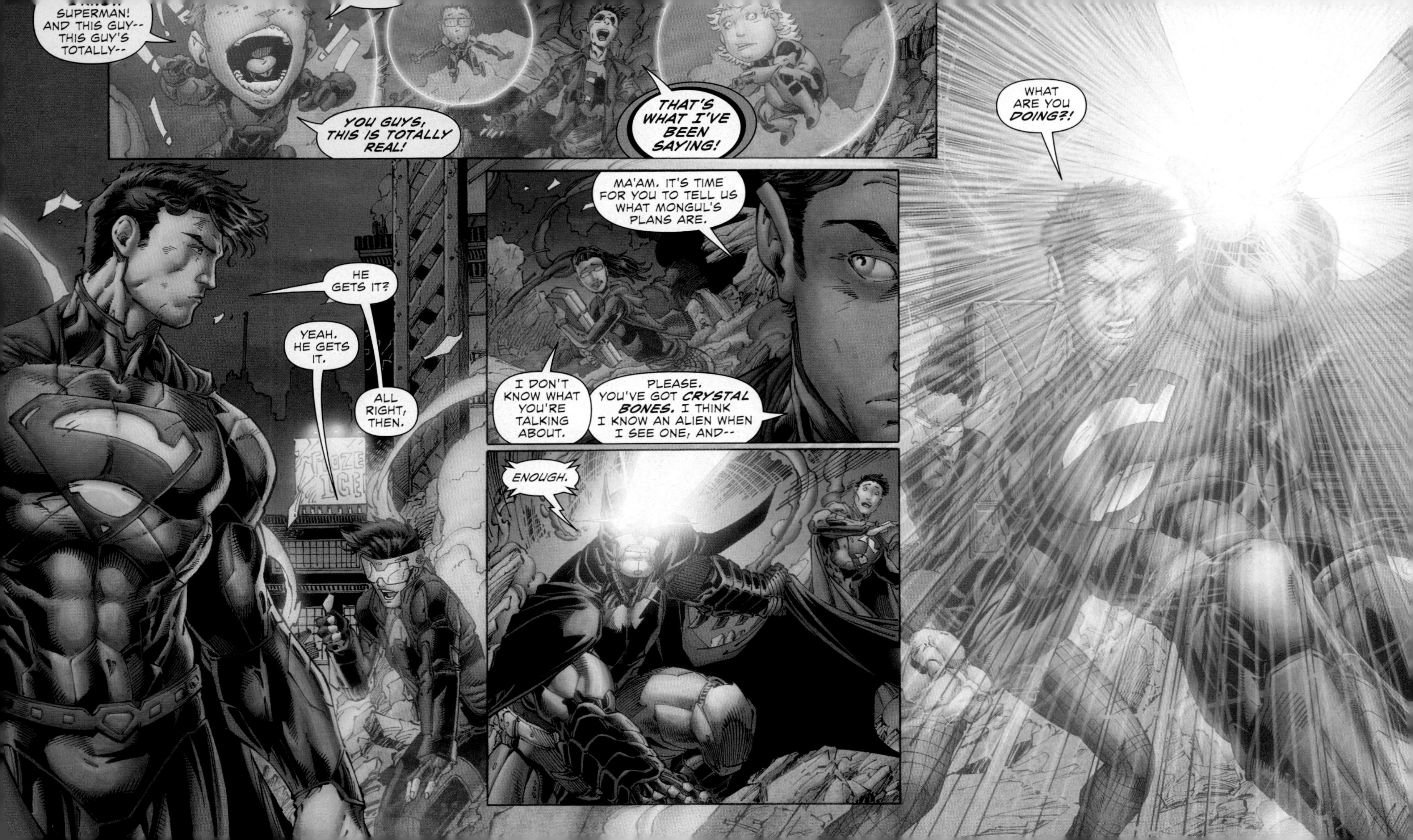
SUPERMAN! AND THIS GUY-- THIS GUY'S TOTALLY--
YOU GUYS, THIS IS TOTALLY REAL!
THAT'S WHAT I'VE BEEN SAYING!
HE GETS IT?
YEAH. HE GETS IT.
ALL RIGHT, THEN.
MA'AM. IT'S TIME FOR YOU TO TELL US WHAT MONGUL'S PLANS ARE.
I DON'T KNOW WHAT YOU'RE TALKING ABOUT.
PLEASE. YOU'VE GOT CRYSTAL BONES. I THINK I KNOW AN ALIEN WHEN I SEE ONE, AND--
ENOUGH.
WHAT ARE YOU DOING?!

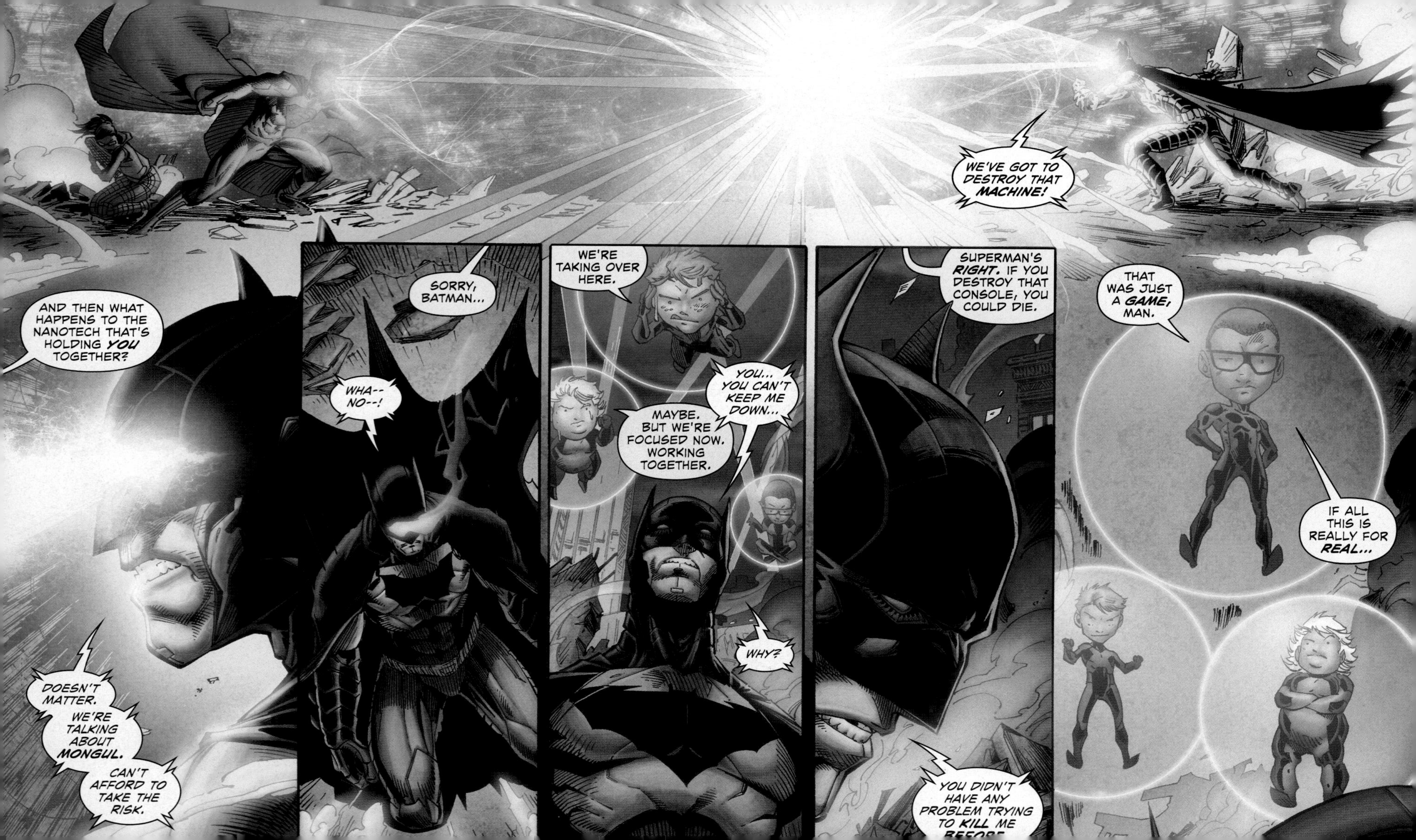
WE'VE GOT TO DESTROY THAT **MACHINE!**
AND THEN WHAT HAPPENS TO THE NANOTECH THAT'S HOLDING **YOU** TOGETHER?
DOESN'T MATTER.
WE'RE TALKING ABOUT **MONGUL.**
CAN'T AFFORD TO TAKE THE RISK.
SORRY, BATMAN...
WHA-- NO--!
WE'RE TAKING OVER HERE.
YOU... YOU CAN'T KEEP ME DOWN...
MAYBE. BUT WE'RE FOCUSED NOW. WORKING TOGETHER.
WHY?
SUPERMAN'S **RIGHT.** IF YOU DESTROY THAT CONSOLE, YOU COULD DIE.
YOU DIDN'T HAVE ANY PROBLEM TRYING TO **KILL** ME
THAT WAS JUST A **GAME,** MAN.
IF ALL THIS IS REALLY FOR **REAL...**

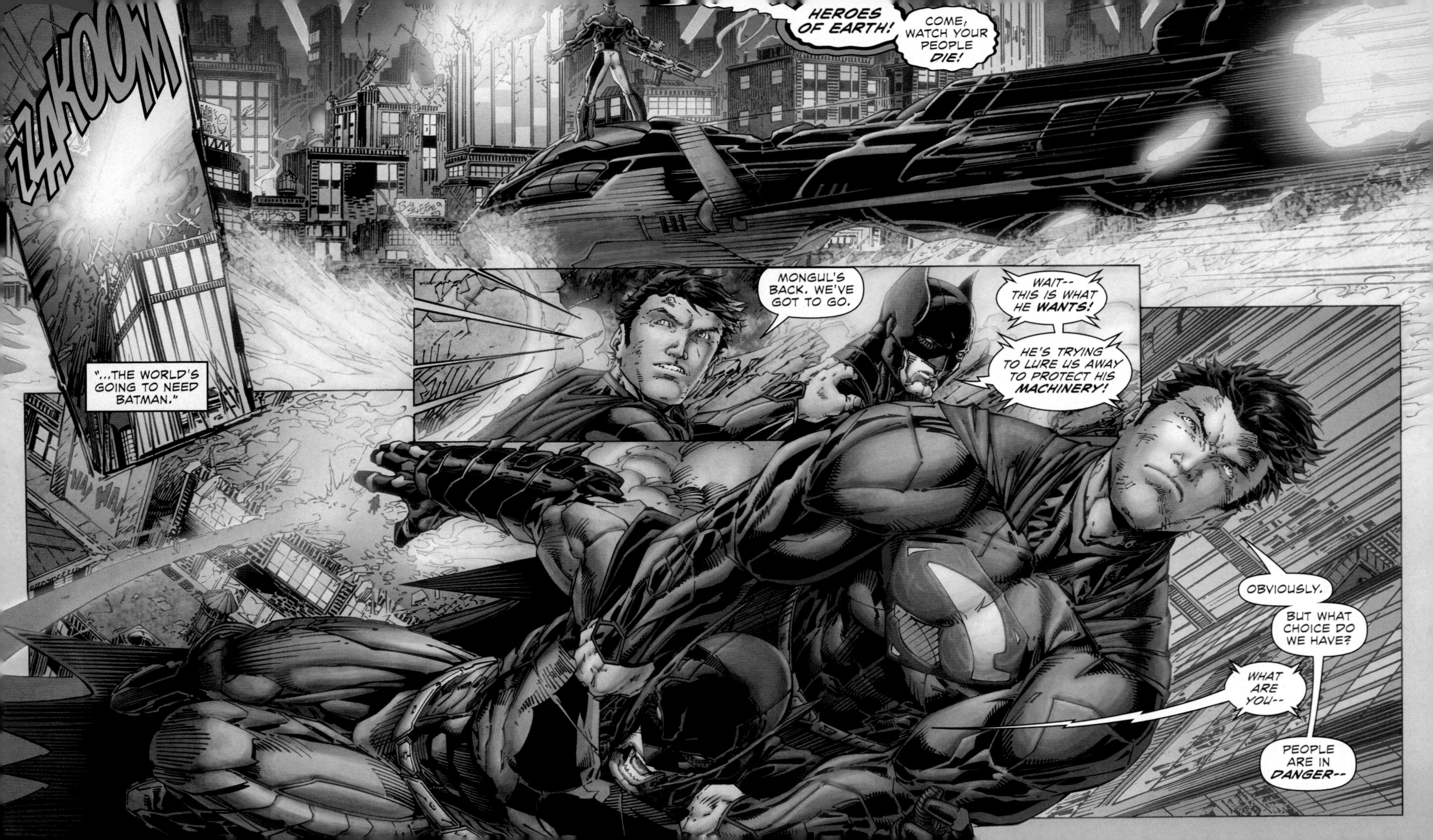
ZZAKOOM
"...THE WORLD'S GOING TO NEED BATMAN."
HEROES OF EARTH!
COME, WATCH YOUR PEOPLE DIE!
MONGUL'S BACK. WE'VE GOT TO GO.
WAIT-- THIS IS WHAT HE WANTS!
HE'S TRYING TO LURE US AWAY TO PROTECT HIS MACHINERY!
OBVIOUSLY.
BUT WHAT CHOICE DO WE HAVE?
WHAT ARE YOU--
PEOPLE ARE IN DANGER--

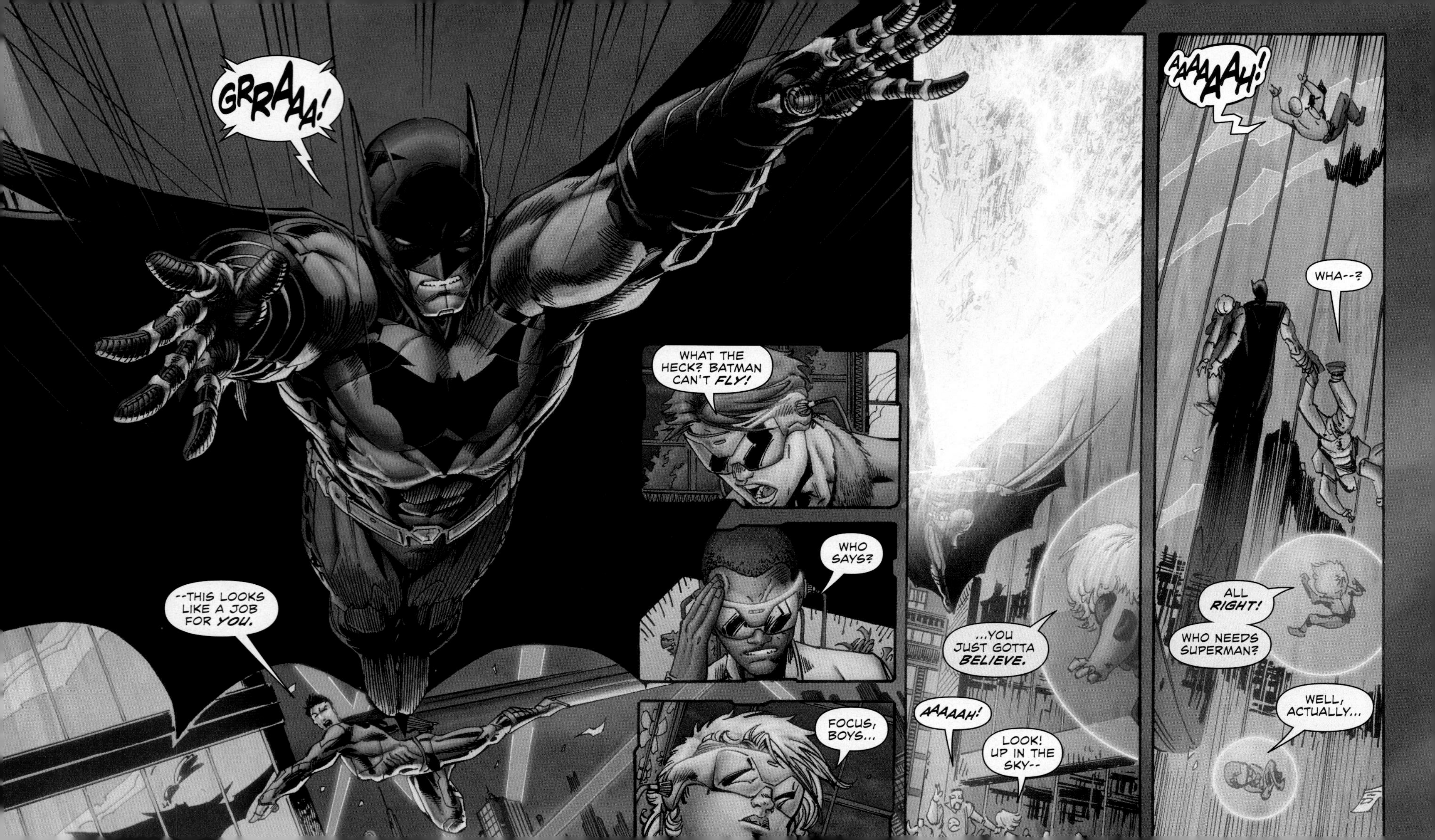

GRRAAAA!
--THIS LOOKS LIKE A JOB FOR YOU.
WHAT THE HECK? BATMAN CAN'T FLY!
WHO SAYS?
FOCUS, BOYS...
...YOU JUST GOTTA BELIEVE.
AAAAAH!
LOOK! UP IN THE SKY--
AAAAAAH!
WHA--?
ALL RIGHT!
WHO NEEDS SUPERMAN?
WELL, ACTUALLY...

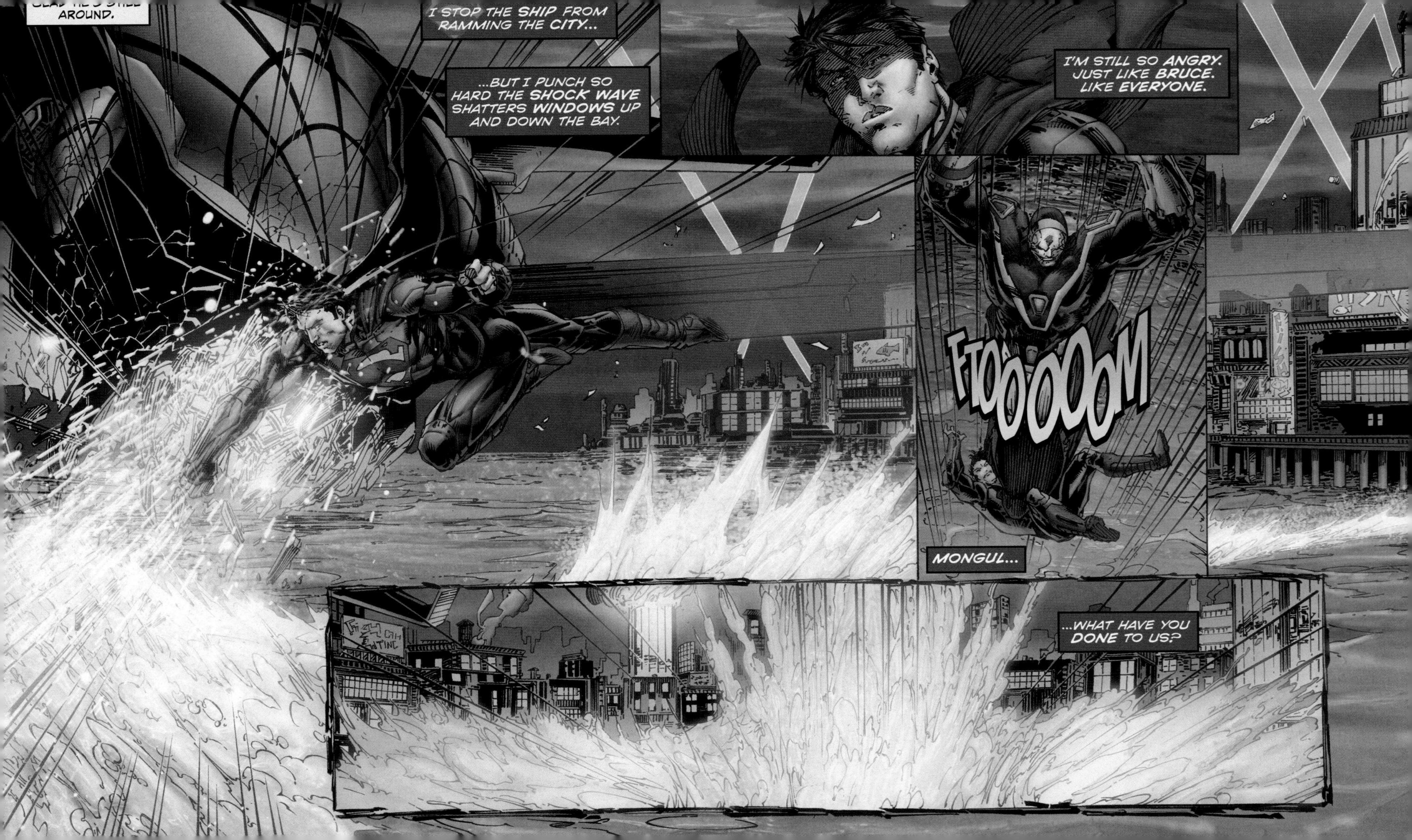
AROUND.
I STOP THE SHIP FROM RAMMING THE CITY...
...BUT I PUNCH SO HARD THE SHOCK WAVE SHATTERS WINDOWS UP AND DOWN THE BAY.
I'M STILL SO ANGRY. JUST LIKE BRUCE. LIKE EVERYONE.
FTOOOOOOM
MONGUL...
...WHAT HAVE YOU DONE TO US?

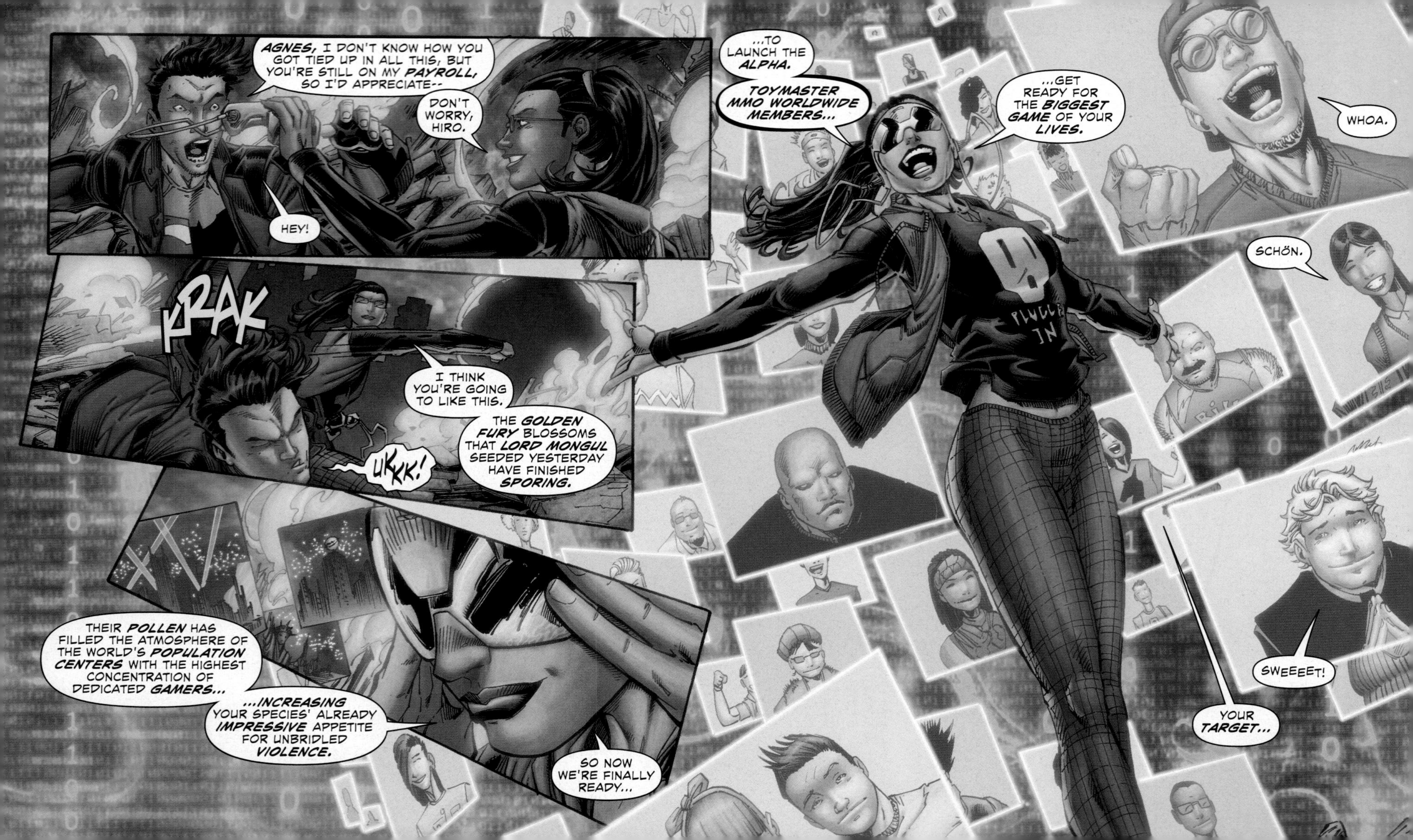
AGNES, I DON'T KNOW HOW YOU GOT TIED UP IN ALL THIS, BUT YOU'RE STILL ON MY PAYROLL, SO I'D APPRECIATE--
DON'T WORRY, HIRO.
HEY!
KRAK
I THINK YOU'RE GOING TO LIKE THIS.
THE GOLDEN FURY BLOSSOMS THAT LORD MONGUL SEEDED YESTERDAY HAVE FINISHED SPORING.
UKKK!
THEIR POLLEN HAS FILLED THE ATMOSPHERE OF THE WORLD'S POPULATION CENTERS WITH THE HIGHEST CONCENTRATION OF DEDICATED GAMERS...
...INCREASING YOUR SPECIES' ALREADY IMPRESSIVE APPETITE FOR UNBRIDLED VIOLENCE.
SO NOW WE'RE FINALLY READY...
...TO LAUNCH THE ALPHA.
TOYMASTER MMO WORLDWIDE MEMBERS...
...GET READY FOR THE BIGGEST GAME OF YOUR LIVES.
WHOA.
SCHÖN.
SWEEEET!
YOUR TARGET...

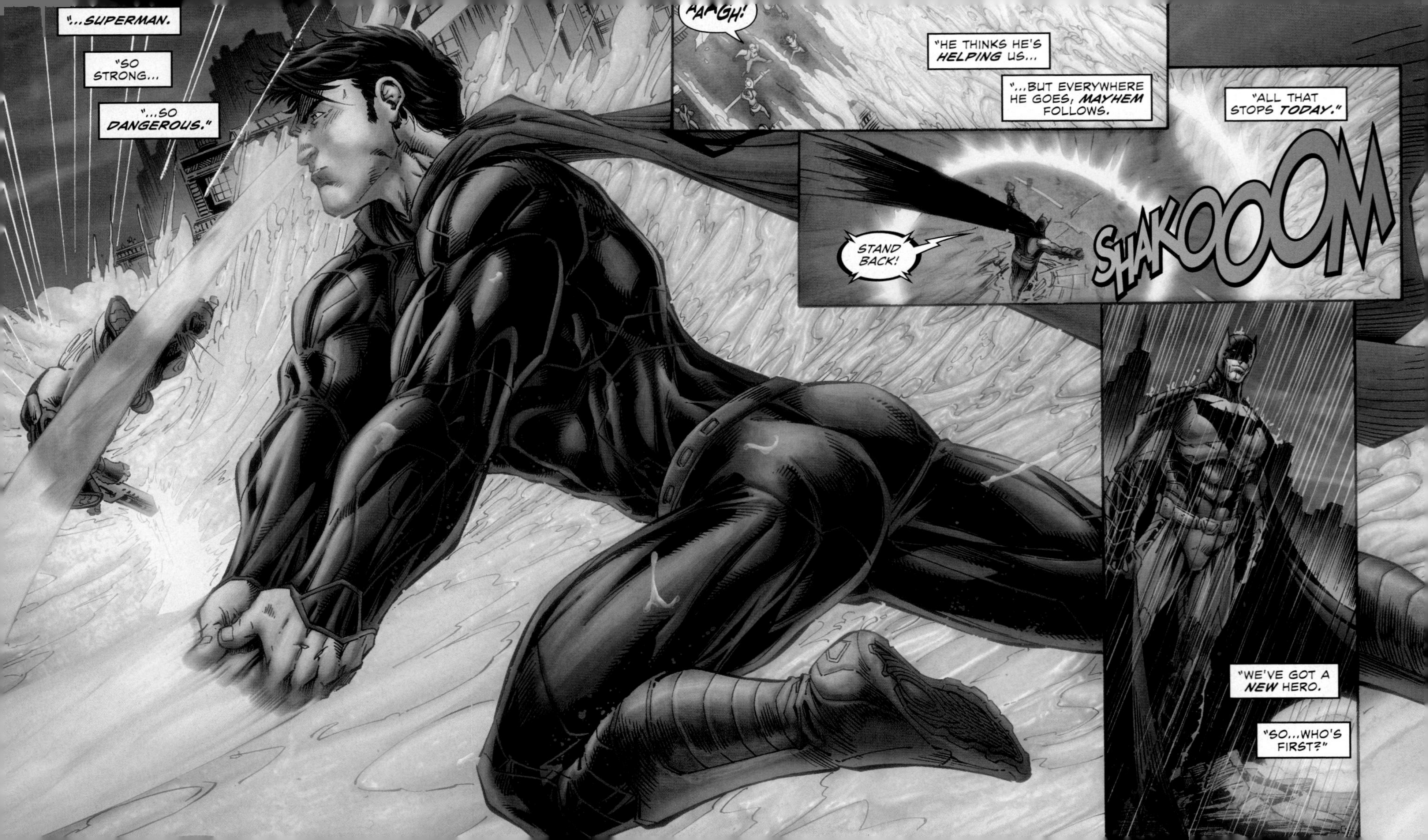
"...SUPERMAN.
"SO STRONG...
"...SO DANGEROUS."
AAAGH!
"HE THINKS HE'S HELPING US...
"...BUT EVERYWHERE HE GOES, MAYHEM FOLLOWS.
"ALL THAT STOPS TODAY."
STAND BACK!
SHAKOOOM
"WE'VE GOT A NEW HERO.
"SO...WHO'S FIRST?"

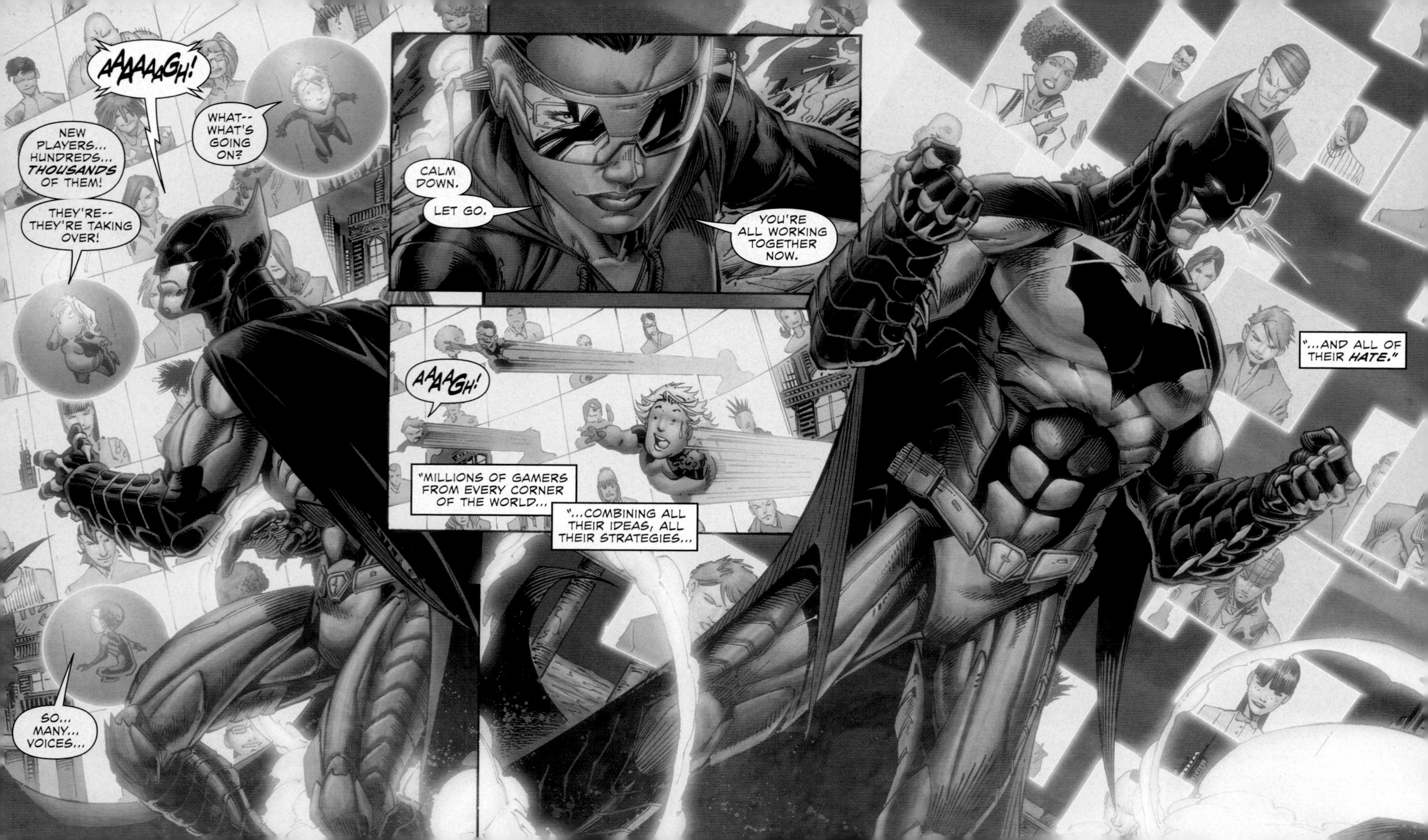
AAAAAAGH!
NEW PLAYERS... HUNDREDS... ***THOUSANDS*** OF THEM!
WHAT-- WHAT'S GOING ON?
THEY'RE-- THEY'RE TAKING OVER!
SO... MANY... VOICES...
CALM DOWN.
LET GO.
YOU'RE ALL WORKING TOGETHER NOW.
AAAAGH!
"MILLIONS OF GAMERS FROM EVERY CORNER OF THE WORLD...
"...COMBINING ALL THEIR IDEAS, ALL THEIR STRATEGIES...
"...AND ALL OF THEIR ***HATE.***"

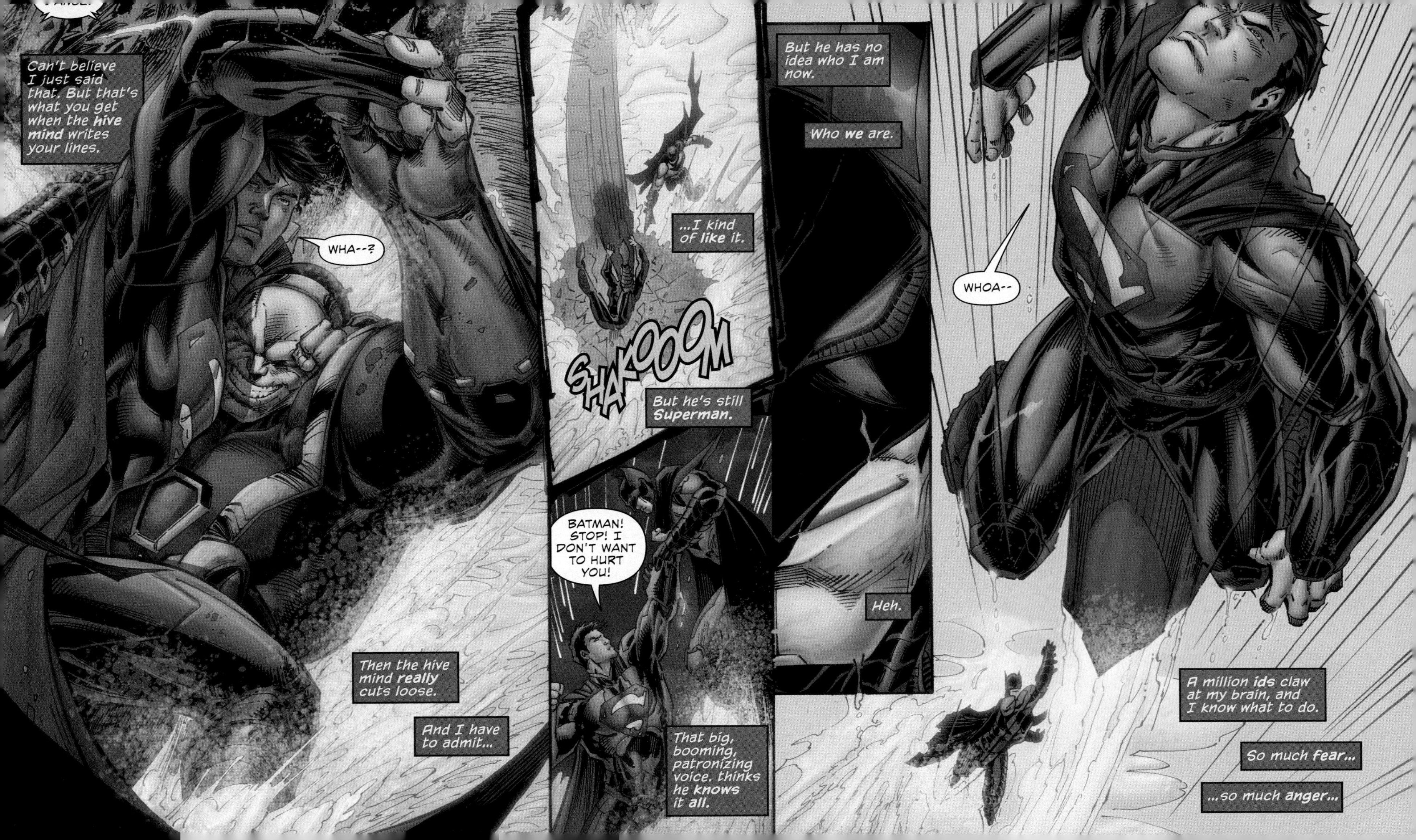
Can't believe I just said that. But that's what you get when the **hive mind** writes your lines.
WHA--?
Then the hive mind **really** cuts loose.
And I have to admit...
...I kind of **like** it.
SHAKOOOM
But he's still **Superman.**
BATMAN! STOP! I DON'T WANT TO HURT YOU!
That big, booming, patronizing voice. thinks he **knows** it **all.**
But he has no idea who I am now.
Who **we** are.
Heh.
WHOA--
A million **ids** claw at my brain, and I know what to do.
So much **fear**...
...so much **anger**...

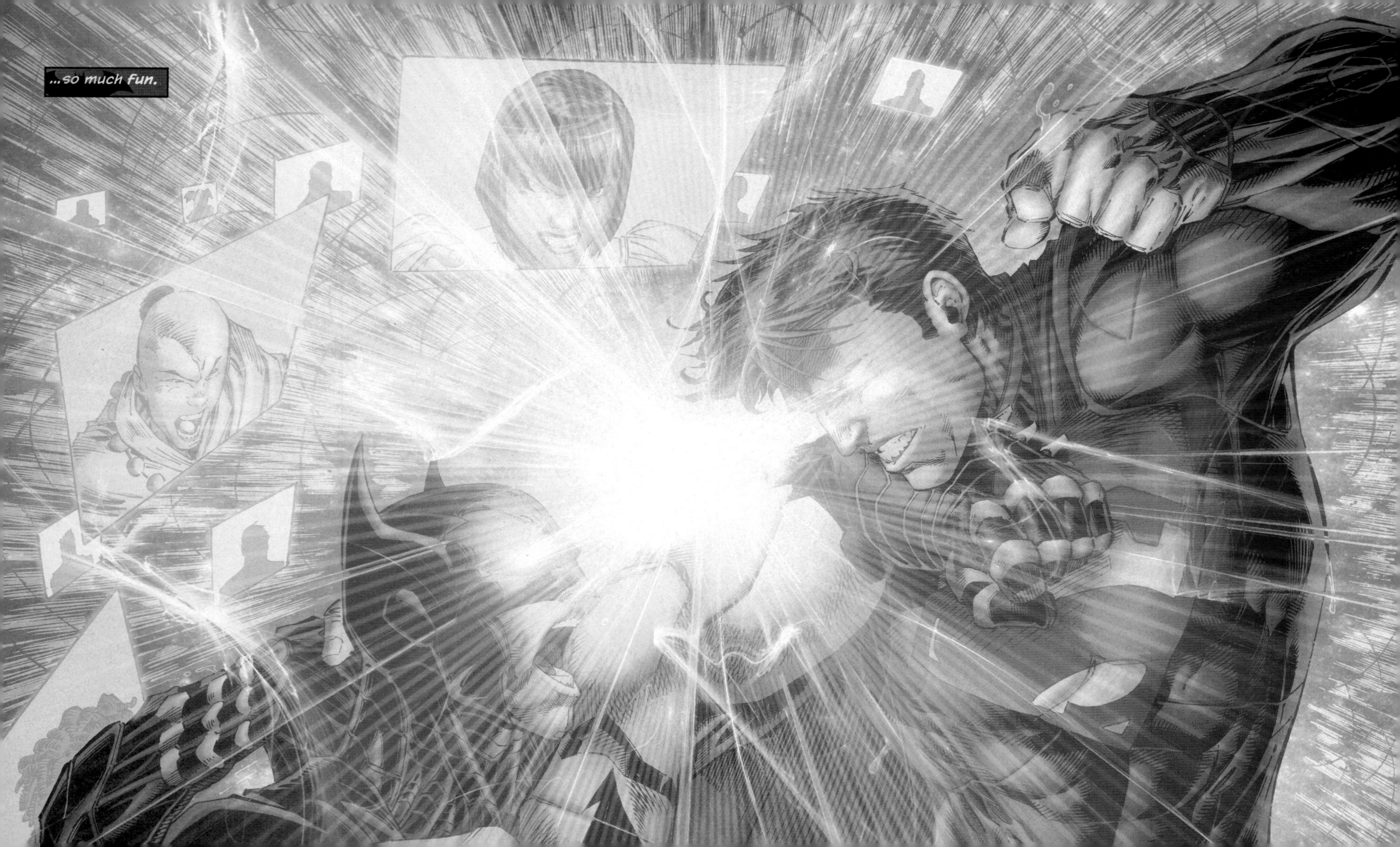
...so much fun.

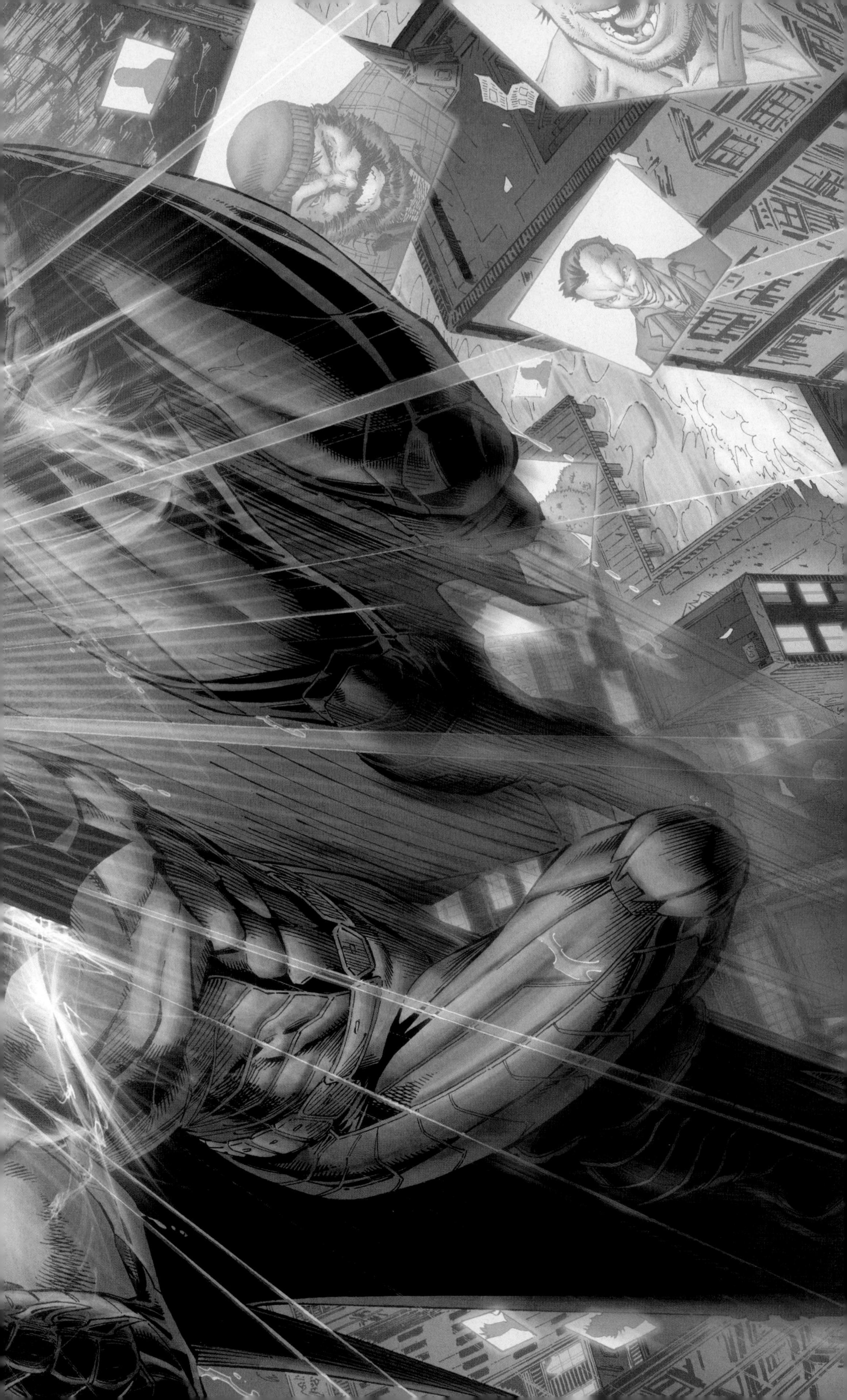

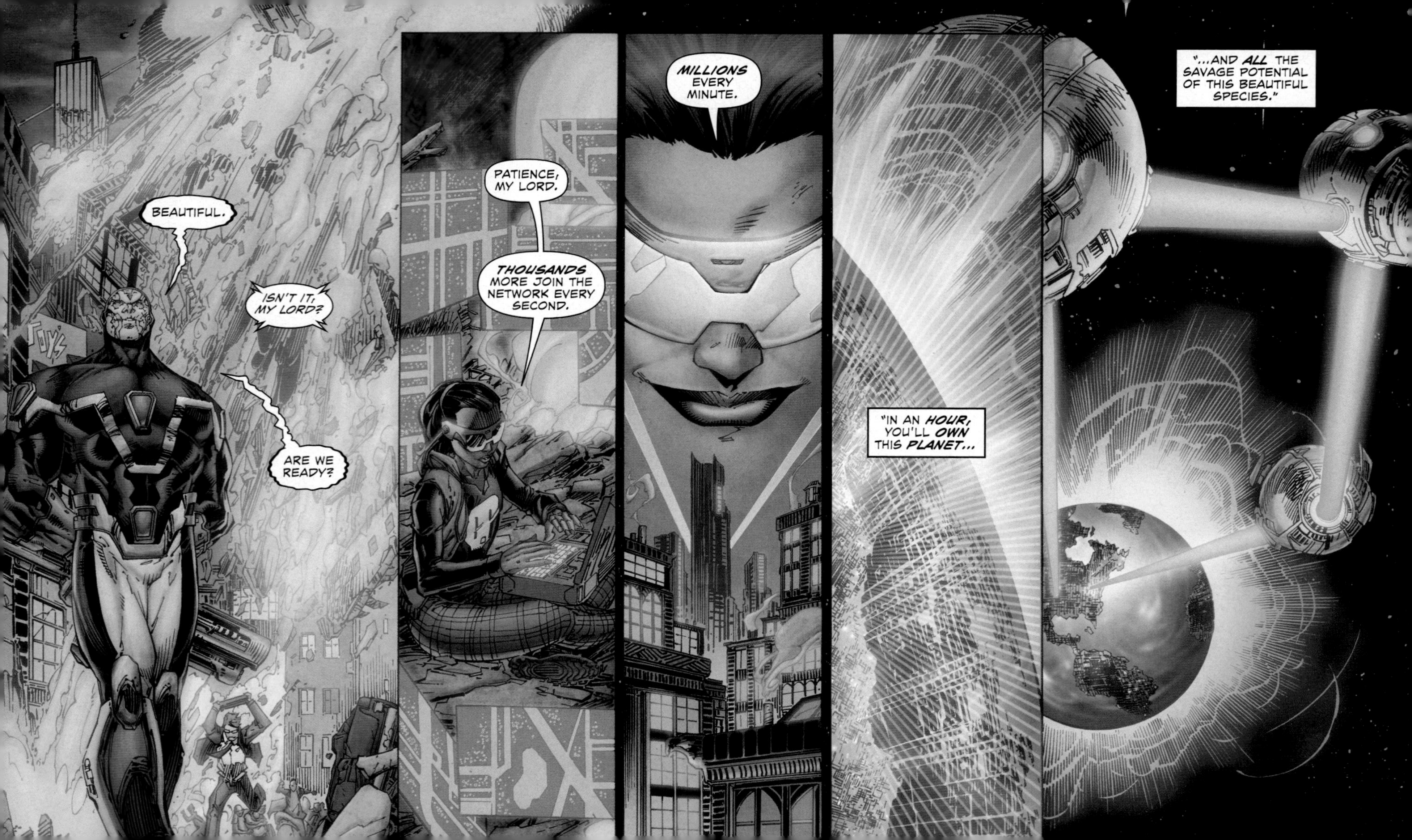
BEAUTIFUL.
ISN'T IT, MY LORD?
ARE WE READY?
PATIENCE, MY LORD.
THOUSANDS MORE JOIN THE NETWORK EVERY SECOND.
MILLIONS EVERY MINUTE.
"IN AN HOUR, YOU'LL OWN THIS PLANET...
"...AND ALL THE SAVAGE POTENTIAL OF THIS BEAUTIFUL SPECIES."

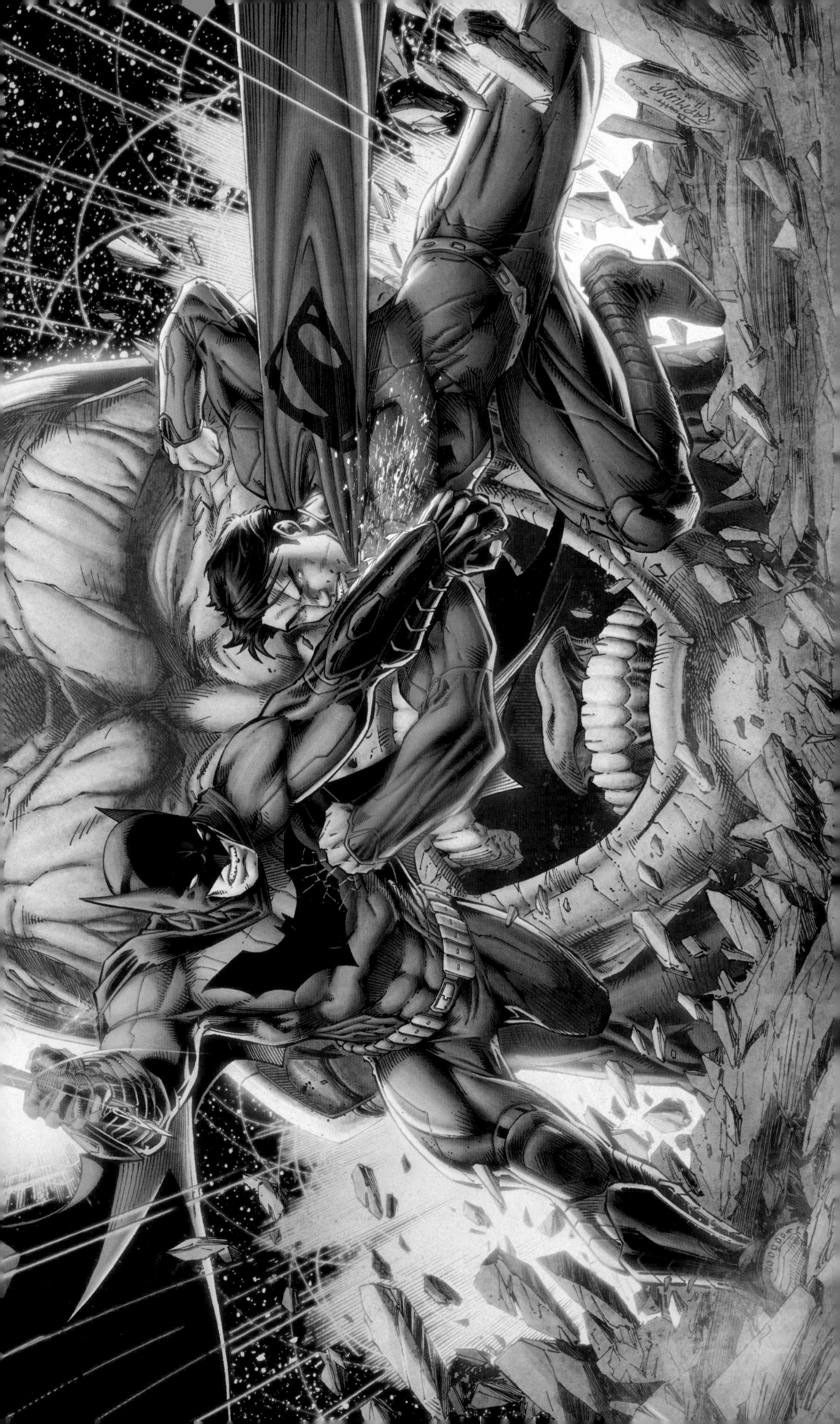

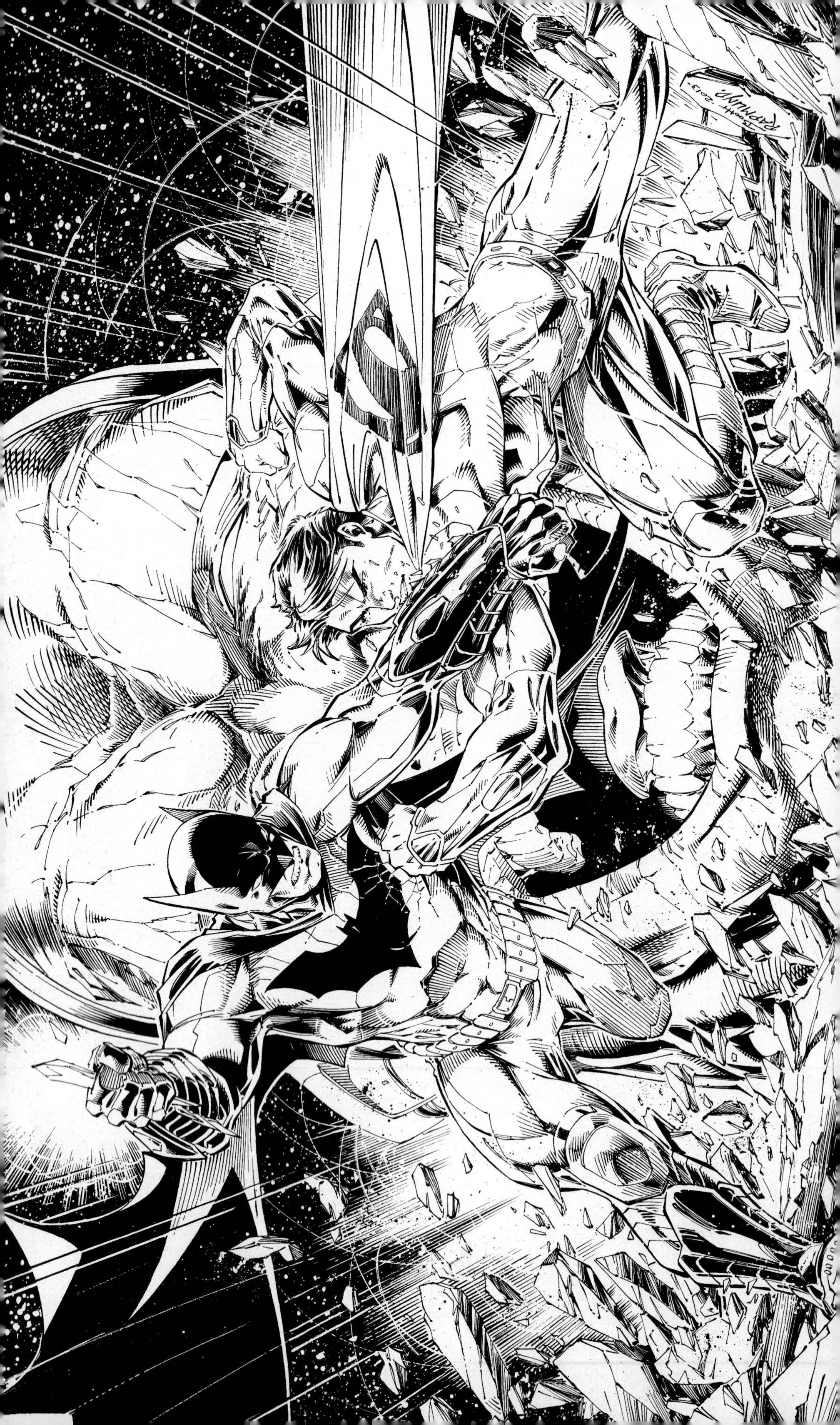

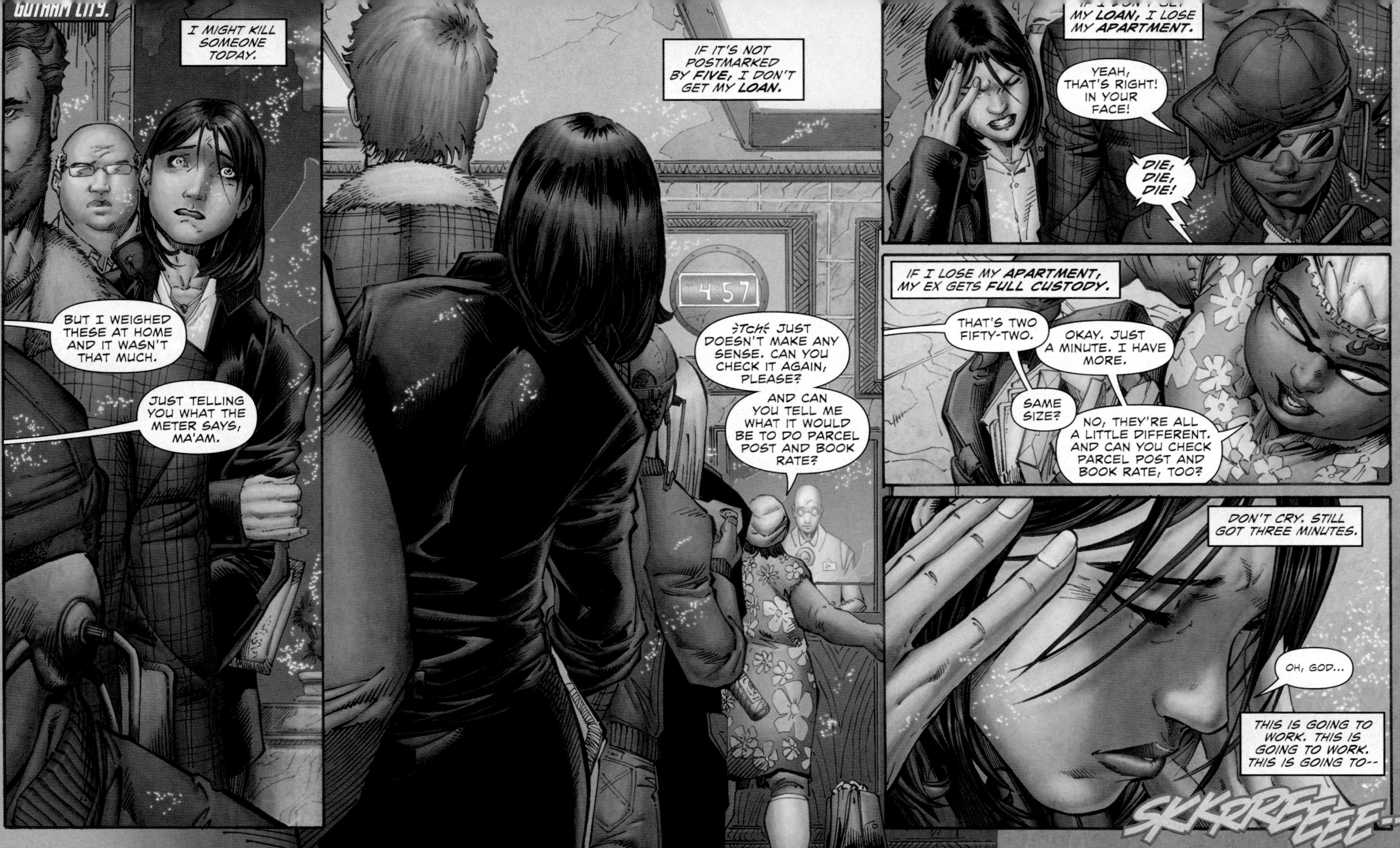
GOTHAM CITY.
I MIGHT KILL SOMEONE TODAY.
BUT I WEIGHED THESE AT HOME AND IT WASN'T THAT MUCH.
JUST TELLING YOU WHAT THE METER SAYS, MA'AM.
IF IT'S NOT POSTMARKED BY FIVE, I DON'T GET MY LOAN.
4:57
TCH JUST DOESN'T MAKE ANY SENSE. CAN YOU CHECK IT AGAIN, PLEASE?
AND CAN YOU TELL ME WHAT IT WOULD BE TO DO PARCEL POST AND BOOK RATE?
MY LOAN, I LOSE MY APARTMENT.
YEAH, THAT'S RIGHT! IN YOUR FACE!
DIE, DIE, DIE!
IF I LOSE MY APARTMENT, MY EX GETS FULL CUSTODY.
THAT'S TWO FIFTY-TWO.
OKAY. JUST A MINUTE. I HAVE MORE.
SAME SIZE?
NO, THEY'RE ALL A LITTLE DIFFERENT. AND CAN YOU CHECK PARCEL POST AND BOOK RATE, TOO?
DON'T CRY. STILL GOT THREE MINUTES.
OH, GOD...
THIS IS GOING TO WORK. THIS IS GOING TO WORK. THIS IS GOING TO--
SKKRREEEEE--

SMASHER

GREG PAK WRITER / BRETT BOOTH PENCILS
NORM RAPMUND INKS / ANDREW DALHOUSE COLORS / ROB LEIGH LETTERS
BOOTH & RAPMUND WITH DALHOUSE COVER

THIS... THIS IS INSANE.

BUT IT'S FOUR FIFTY-NINE.

AND SUDDENLY I'M FIRST IN LINE.

KKKRRAKKOOOOM

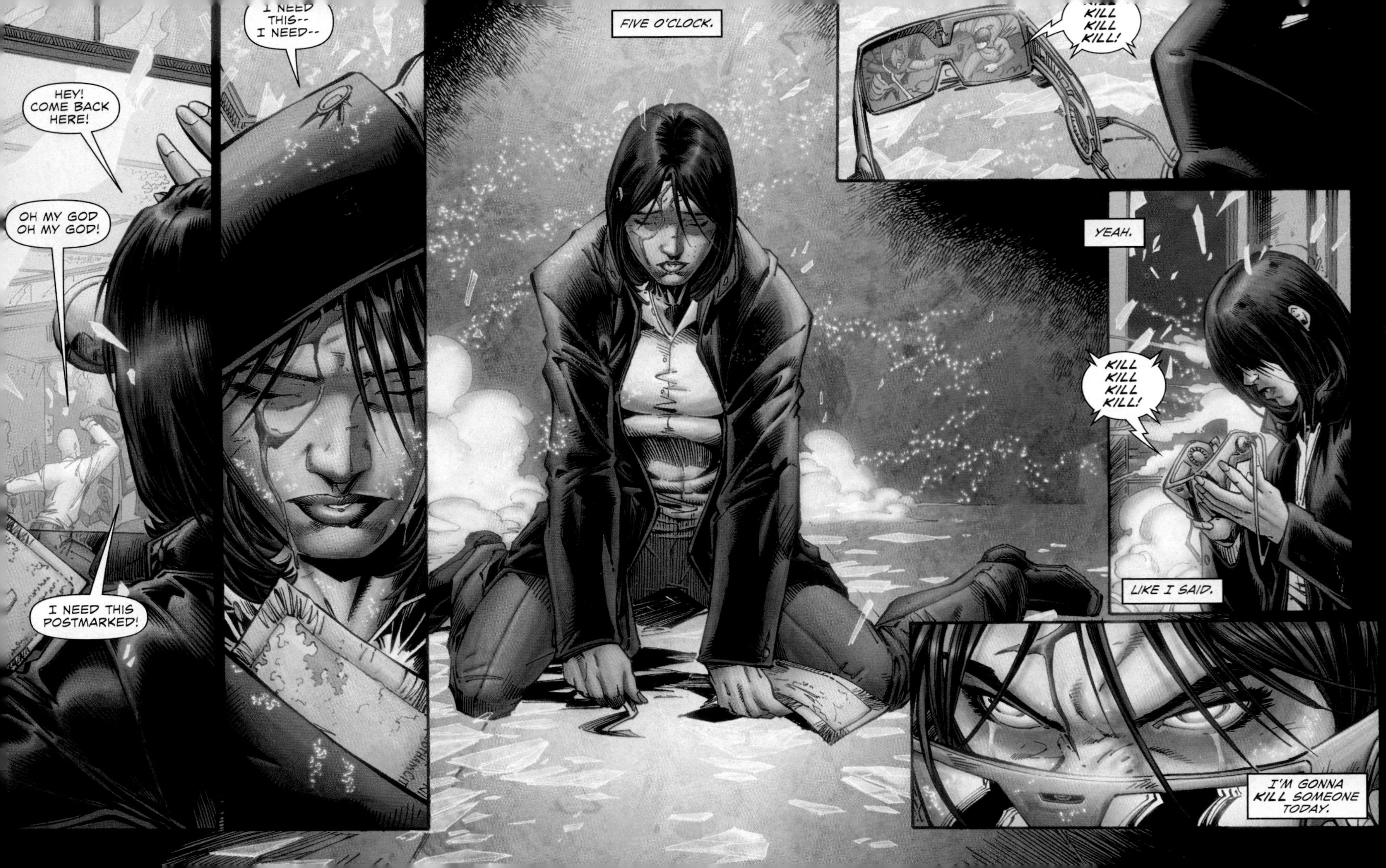

HEY! COME BACK HERE!
OH MY GOD OH MY GOD!
I NEED THIS POSTMARKED!
I NEED THIS-- I NEED--
FIVE O'CLOCK.
KILL KILL KILL!
YEAH.
KILL KILL KILL KILL!
LIKE I SAID.
I'M GONNA KILL SOMEONE TODAY.

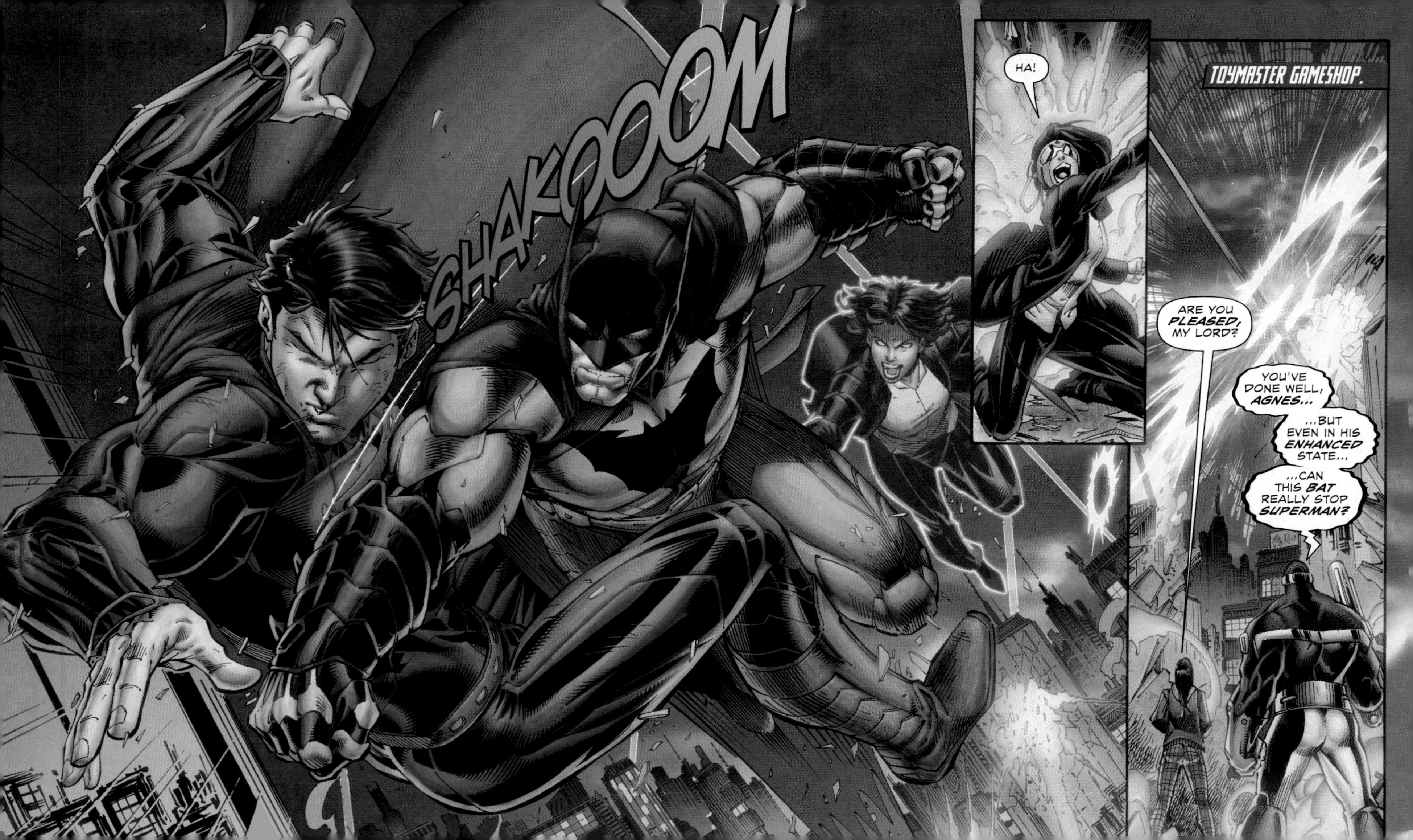
SHAKOOOM
HA!
TOYMASTER GAMESHOP.
ARE YOU PLEASED, MY LORD?
YOU'VE DONE WELL, AGNES...
...BUT EVEN IN HIS ENHANCED STATE...
...CAN THIS BAT REALLY STOP SUPERMAN?

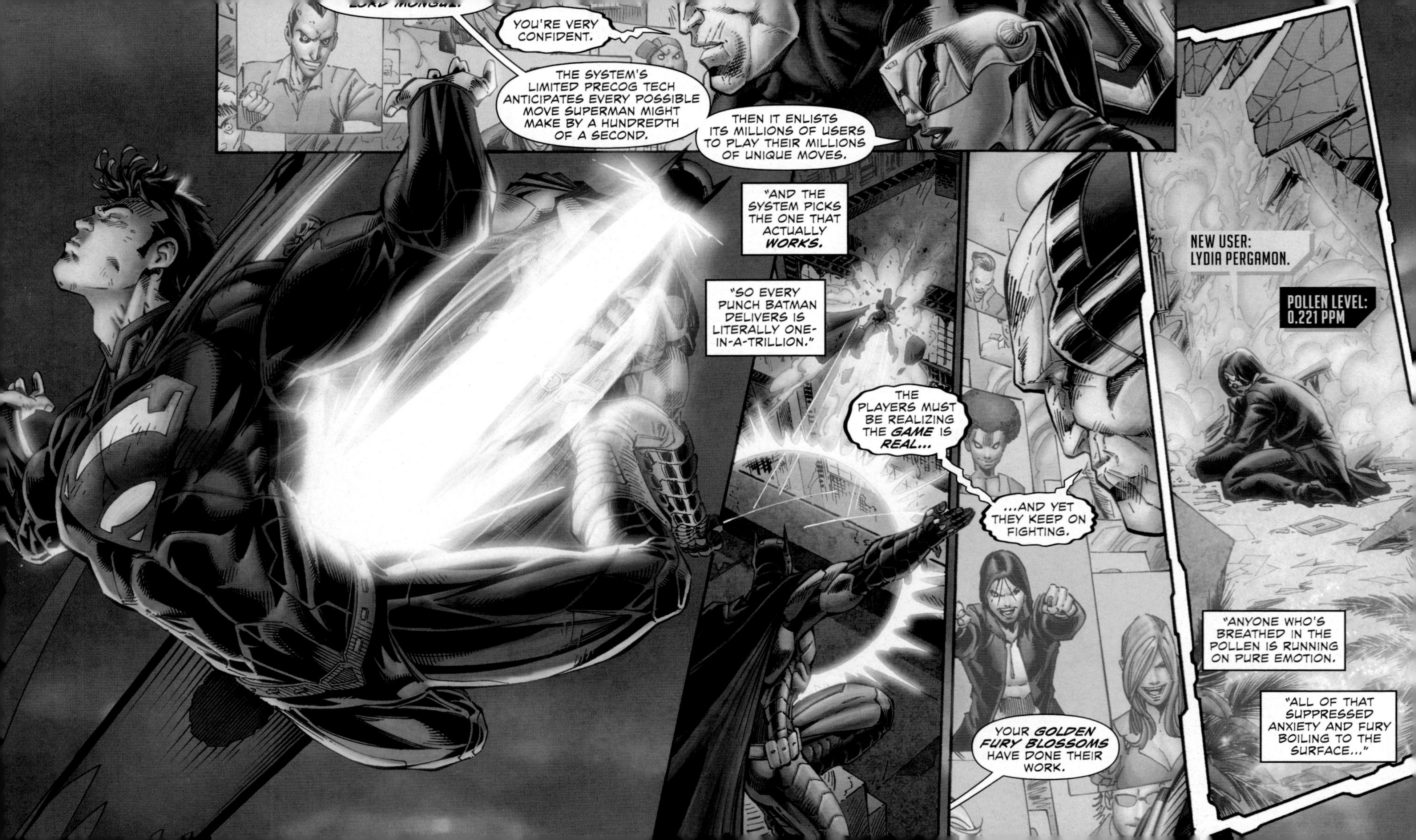
YOU'RE VERY CONFIDENT.
THE SYSTEM'S LIMITED PRECOG TECH ANTICIPATES EVERY POSSIBLE MOVE SUPERMAN MIGHT MAKE BY A HUNDREDTH OF A SECOND.
THEN IT ENLISTS ITS MILLIONS OF USERS TO PLAY THEIR MILLIONS OF UNIQUE MOVES.
"AND THE SYSTEM PICKS THE ONE THAT ACTUALLY *WORKS.*
"SO EVERY PUNCH BATMAN DELIVERS IS LITERALLY ONE-IN-A-TRILLION."
THE PLAYERS MUST BE REALIZING THE *GAME* IS *REAL*...
...AND YET THEY KEEP ON FIGHTING.
YOUR *GOLDEN FURY BLOSSOMS* HAVE DONE THEIR WORK.
NEW USER: LYDIA PERGAMON.
POLLEN LEVEL: 0.221 PPM
"ANYONE WHO'S BREATHED IN THE POLLEN IS RUNNING ON PURE EMOTION.
"ALL OF THAT SUPPRESSED ANXIETY AND FURY BOILING TO THE SURFACE..."

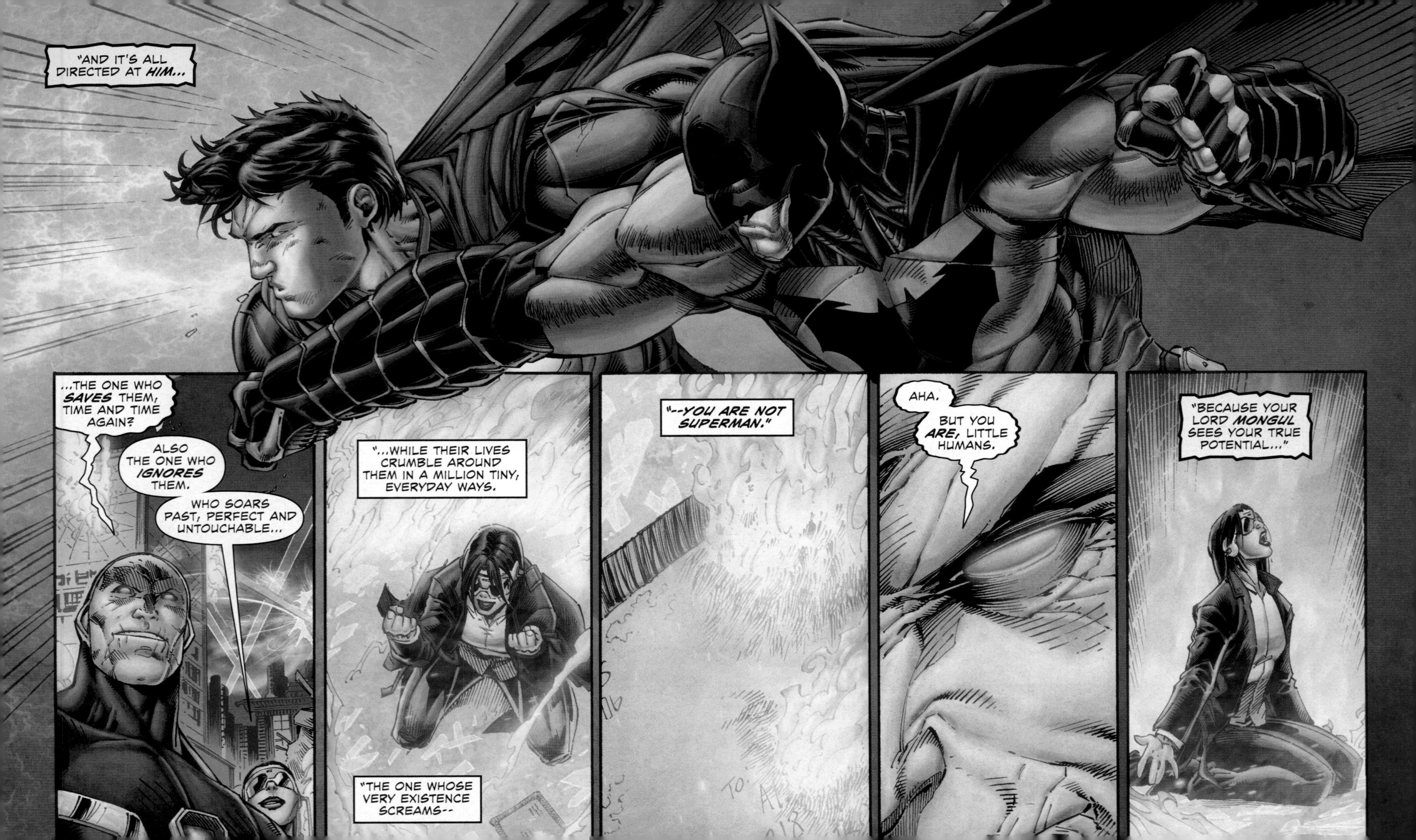
"AND IT'S ALL DIRECTED AT *HIM*...
...THE ONE WHO *SAVES* THEM, TIME AND TIME AGAIN?
ALSO THE ONE WHO *IGNORES* THEM.
WHO SOARS PAST, PERFECT AND UNTOUCHABLE...
"...WHILE THEIR LIVES CRUMBLE AROUND THEM IN A MILLION TINY, EVERYDAY WAYS.
"THE ONE WHOSE VERY EXISTENCE SCREAMS--
"--*YOU ARE NOT SUPERMAN.*"
AHA.
BUT YOU *ARE,* LITTLE HUMANS.
"BECAUSE YOUR LORD *MONGUL* SEES YOUR TRUE POTENTIAL..."

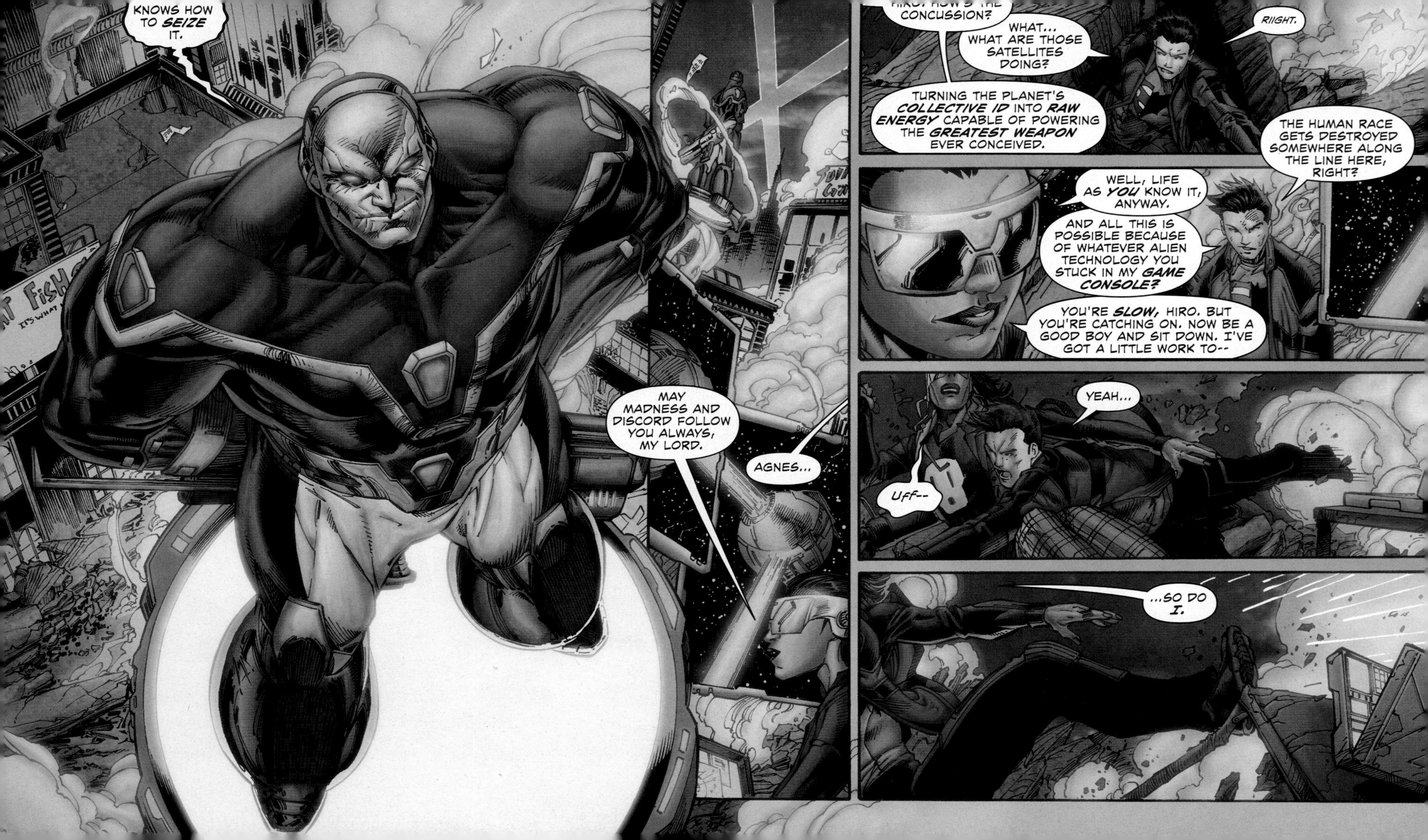
KNOWS HOW TO SEIZE IT.
MAY MADNESS AND DISCORD FOLLOW YOU ALWAYS, MY LORD.
AGNES...
CONCUSSION?
WHAT... WHAT ARE THOSE SATELLITES DOING?
TURNING THE PLANET'S COLLECTIVE ID INTO RAW ENERGY CAPABLE OF POWERING THE GREATEST WEAPON EVER CONCEIVED.
RIIGHT.
THE HUMAN RACE GETS DESTROYED SOMEWHERE ALONG THE LINE HERE, RIGHT?
WELL, LIFE AS YOU KNOW IT, ANYWAY.
AND ALL THIS IS POSSIBLE BECAUSE OF WHATEVER ALIEN TECHNOLOGY YOU STUCK IN MY GAME CONSOLE?
YOU'RE SLOW, HIRO. BUT YOU'RE CATCHING ON. NOW BE A GOOD BOY AND SIT DOWN. I'VE GOT A LITTLE WORK TO--
YEAH...
UFF--
...SO DO I.

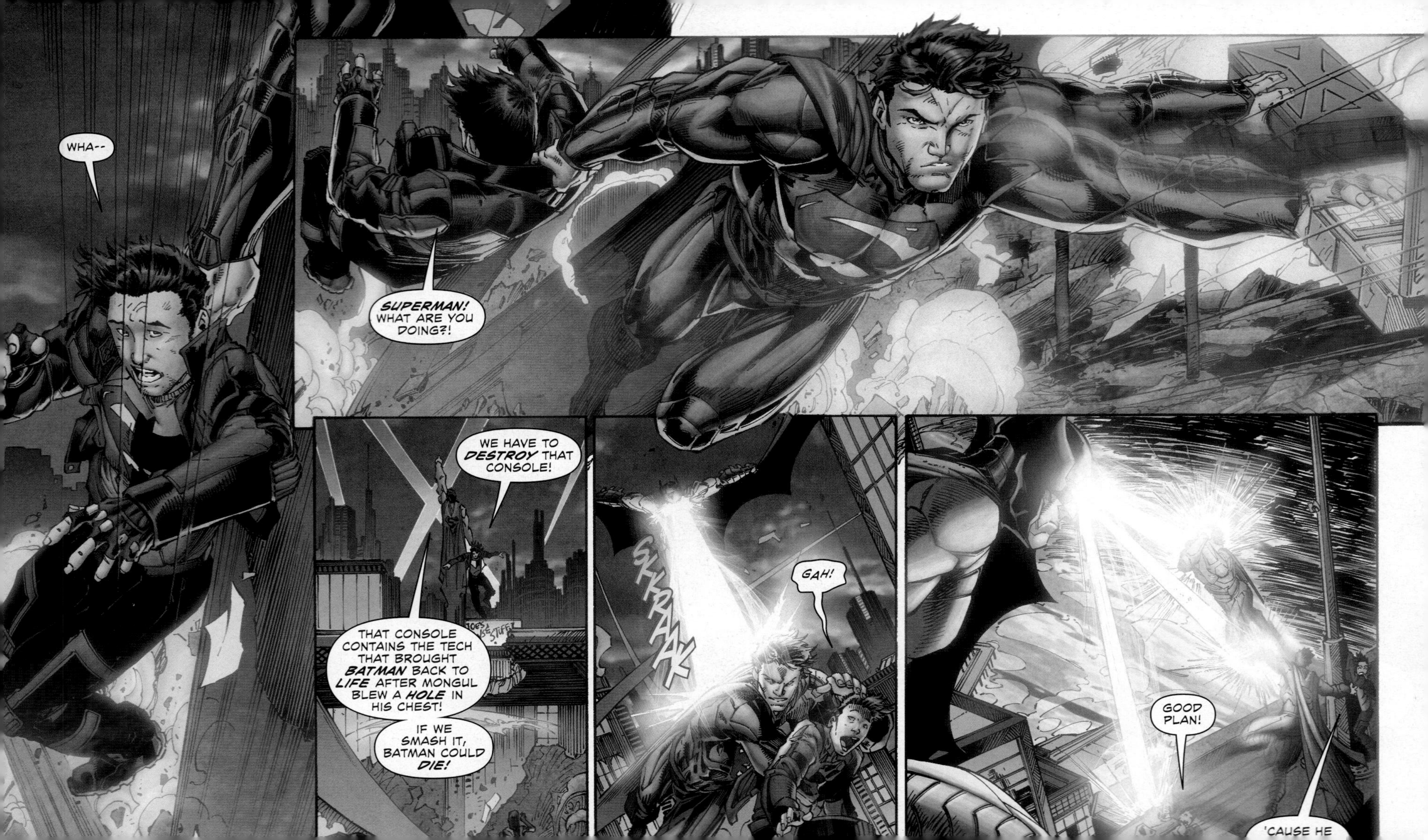
WHA--
SUPERMAN! WHAT ARE YOU DOING?!
WE HAVE TO DESTROY THAT CONSOLE!
THAT CONSOLE CONTAINS THE TECH THAT BROUGHT BATMAN BACK TO LIFE AFTER MONGUL BLEW A HOLE IN HIS CHEST!
IF WE SMASH IT, BATMAN COULD DIE!
SKKRAAAK
GAH!
GOOD PLAN!
'CAUSE HE

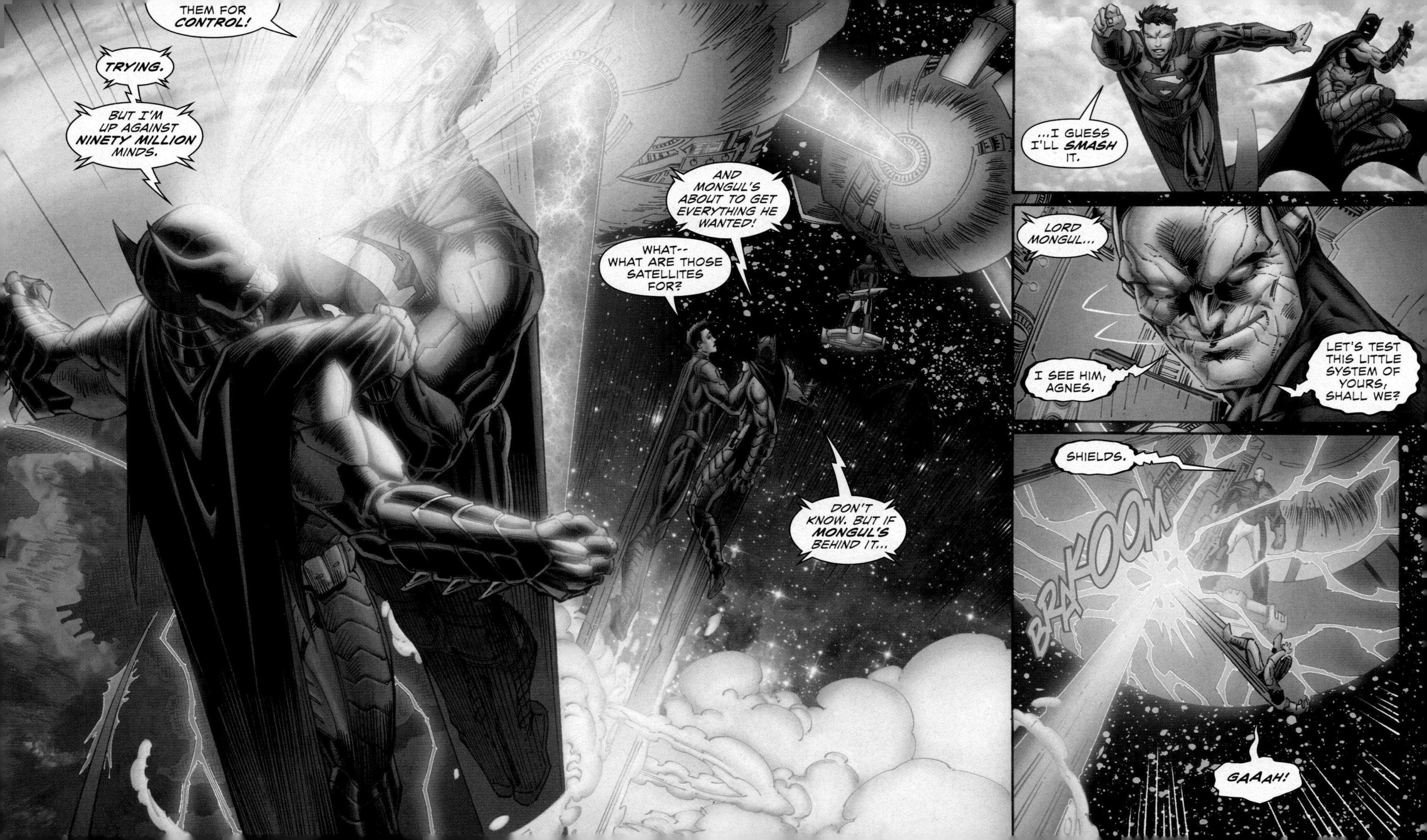
THEM FOR CONTROL!
TRYING.
BUT I'M UP AGAINST NINETY MILLION MINDS.
WHAT-- WHAT ARE THOSE SATELLITES FOR?
AND MONGUL'S ABOUT TO GET EVERYTHING HE WANTED!
DON'T KNOW. BUT IF MONGUL'S BEHIND IT...
...I GUESS I'LL SMASH IT.
LORD MONGUL...
I SEE HIM, AGNES.
LET'S TEST THIS LITTLE SYSTEM OF YOURS, SHALL WE?
SHIELDS.
BRAKOOM
GAAAH!

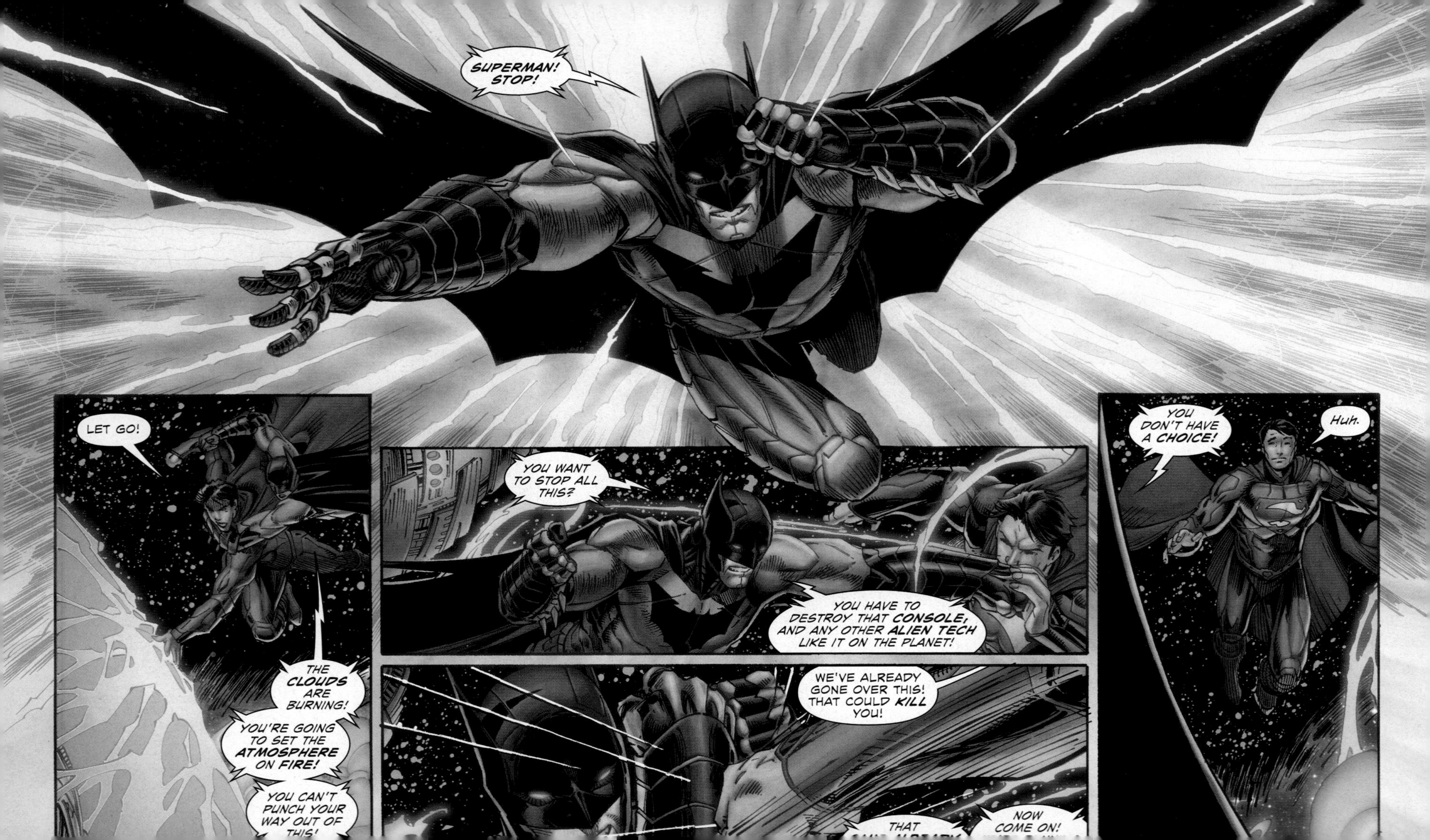
SUPERMAN! STOP!
LET GO!
THE CLOUDS ARE BURNING!
YOU'RE GOING TO SET THE ATMOSPHERE ON FIRE!
YOU CAN'T PUNCH YOUR WAY OUT OF THIS!
YOU WANT TO STOP ALL THIS?
YOU HAVE TO DESTROY THAT CONSOLE, AND ANY OTHER ALIEN TECH LIKE IT ON THE PLANET!
WE'VE ALREADY GONE OVER THIS! THAT COULD KILL YOU!
NOW COME ON!
YOU DON'T HAVE A CHOICE!
Huh.

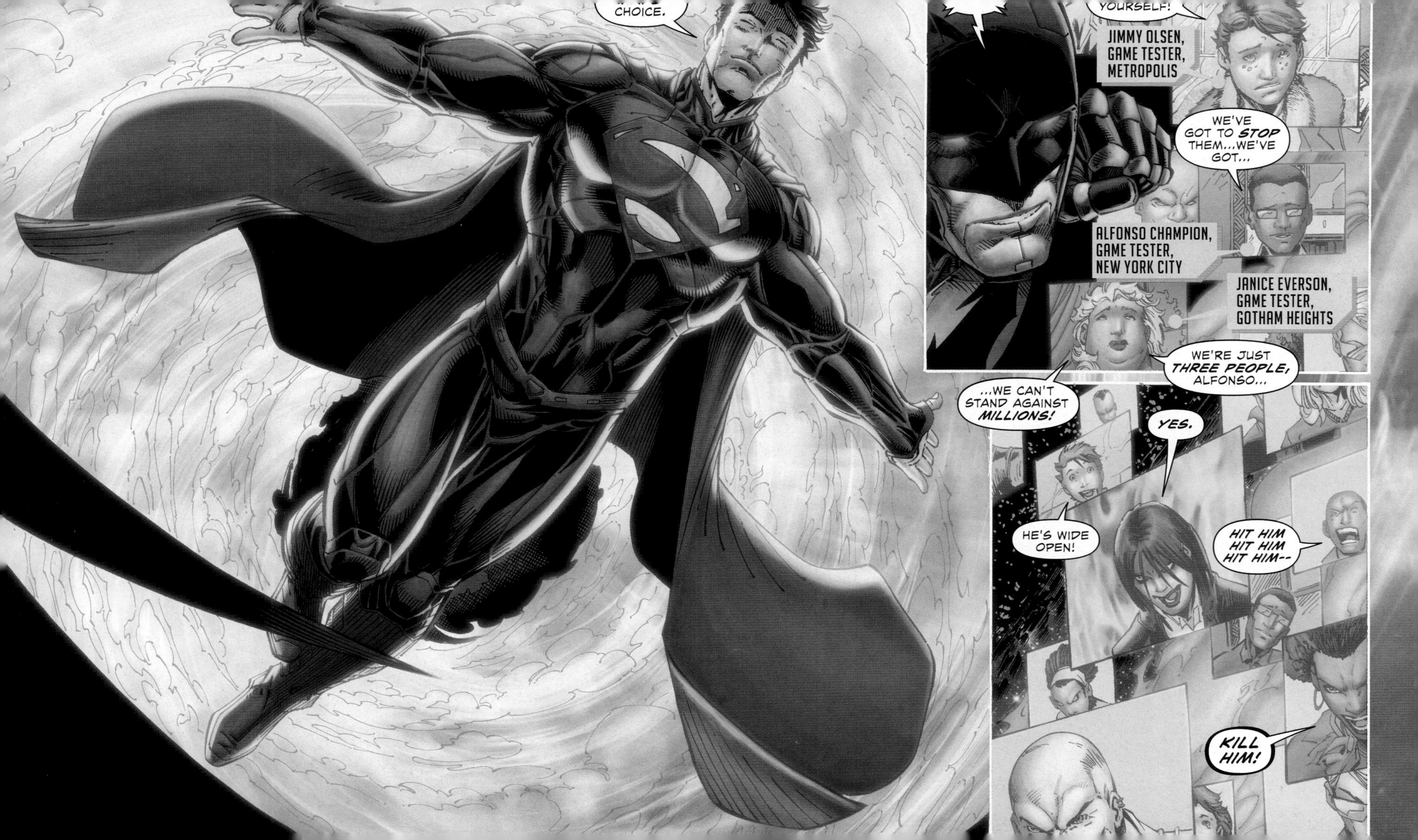
CHOICE.
YOURSELF!
JIMMY OLSEN, GAME TESTER, METROPOLIS
WE'VE GOT TO STOP THEM...WE'VE GOT...
ALFONSO CHAMPION, GAME TESTER, NEW YORK CITY
JANICE EVERSON, GAME TESTER, GOTHAM HEIGHTS
WE'RE JUST THREE PEOPLE, ALFONSO...
...WE CAN'T STAND AGAINST MILLIONS!
YES.
HE'S WIDE OPEN!
HIT HIM HIT HIM HIT HIM--
KILL HIM!

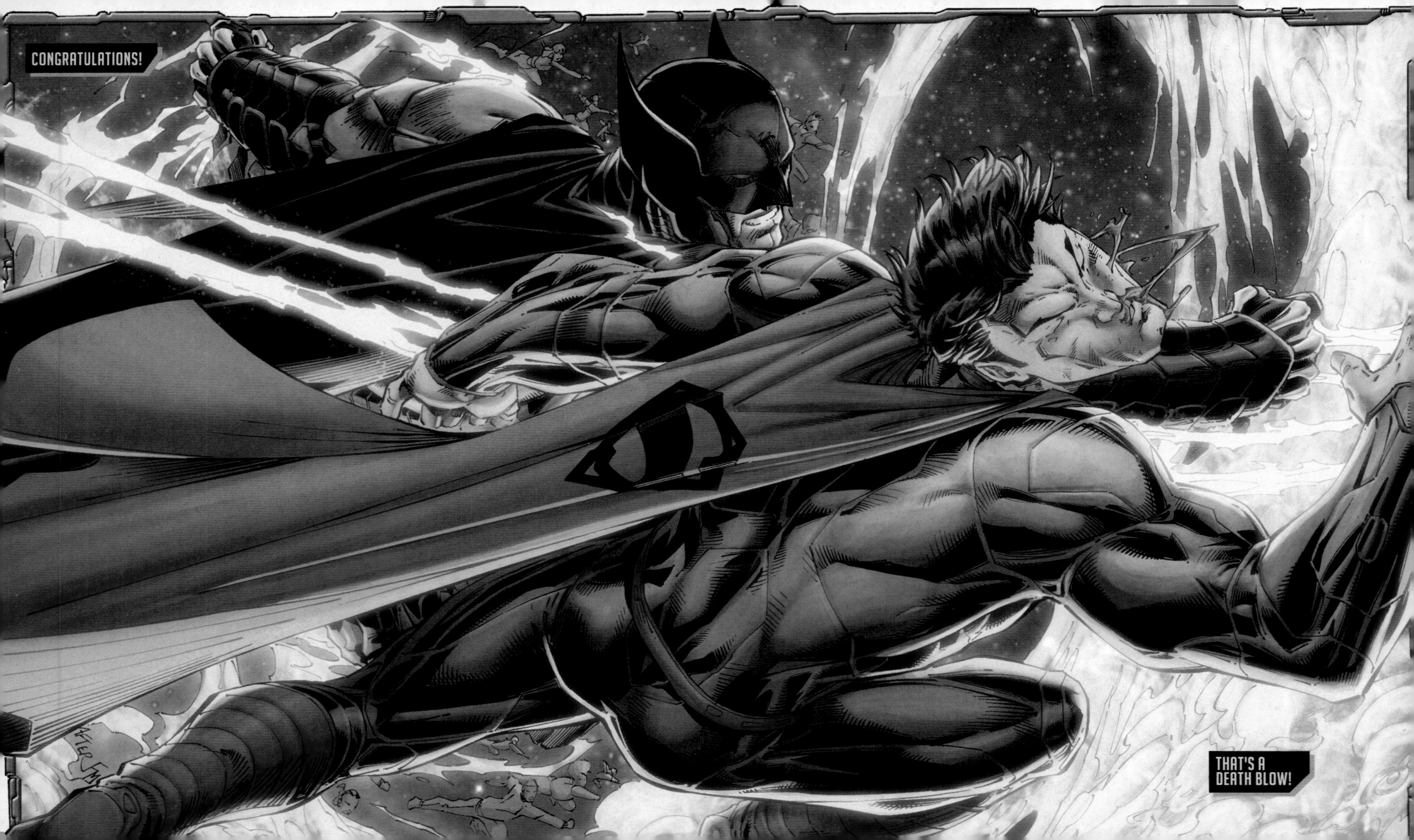
CONGRATULATIONS!
THAT'S A DEATH BLOW!

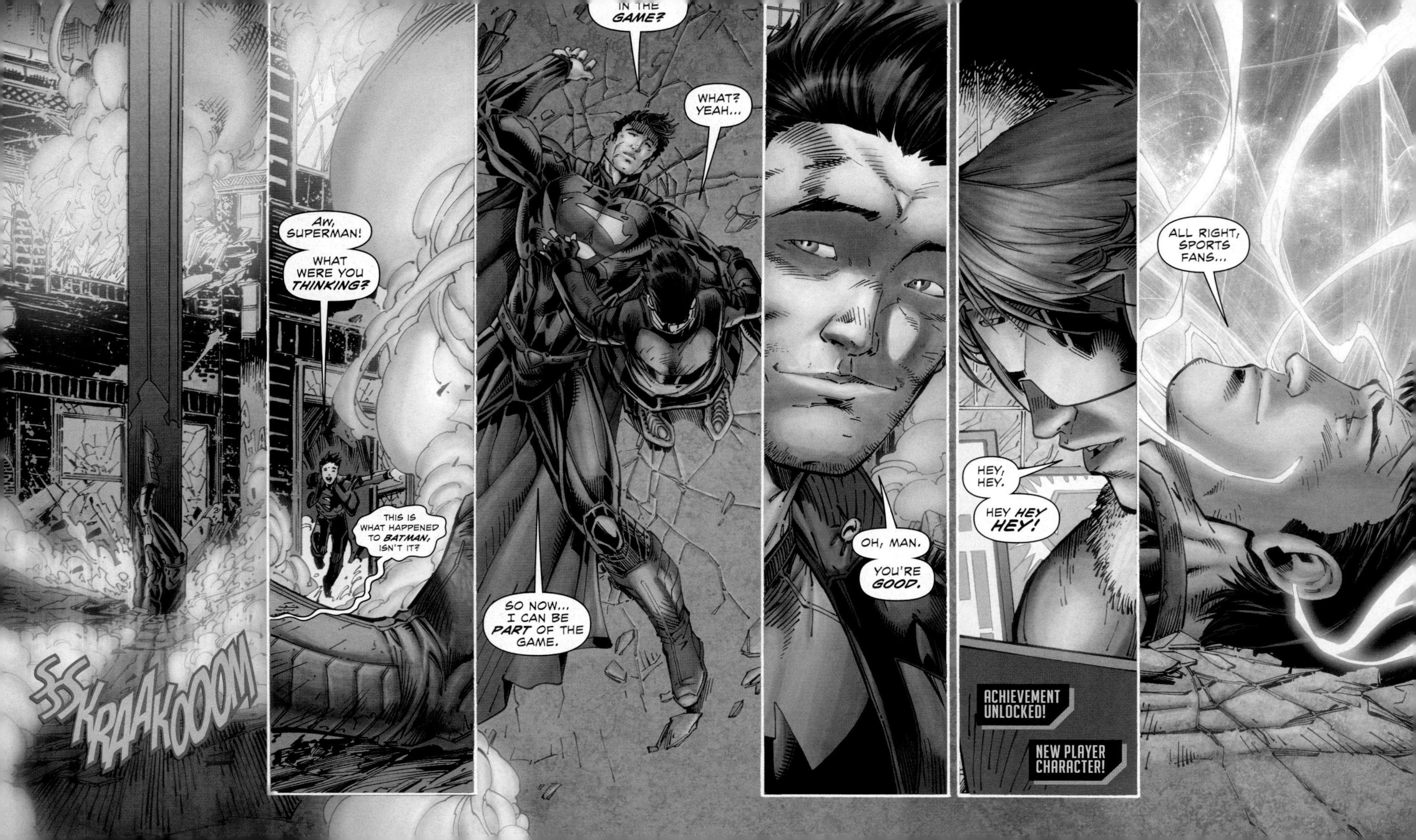
SSKRAAKOOOM
AW, SUPERMAN!
WHAT WERE YOU THINKING?
THIS IS WHAT HAPPENED TO BATMAN, ISN'T IT?
IN THE GAME?
WHAT? YEAH...
SO NOW... I CAN BE PART OF THE GAME.
OH, MAN.
YOU'RE GOOD.
HEY, HEY.
HEY HEY HEY!
ACHIEVEMENT UNLOCKED!
NEW PLAYER CHARACTER!
ALL RIGHT, SPORTS FANS...

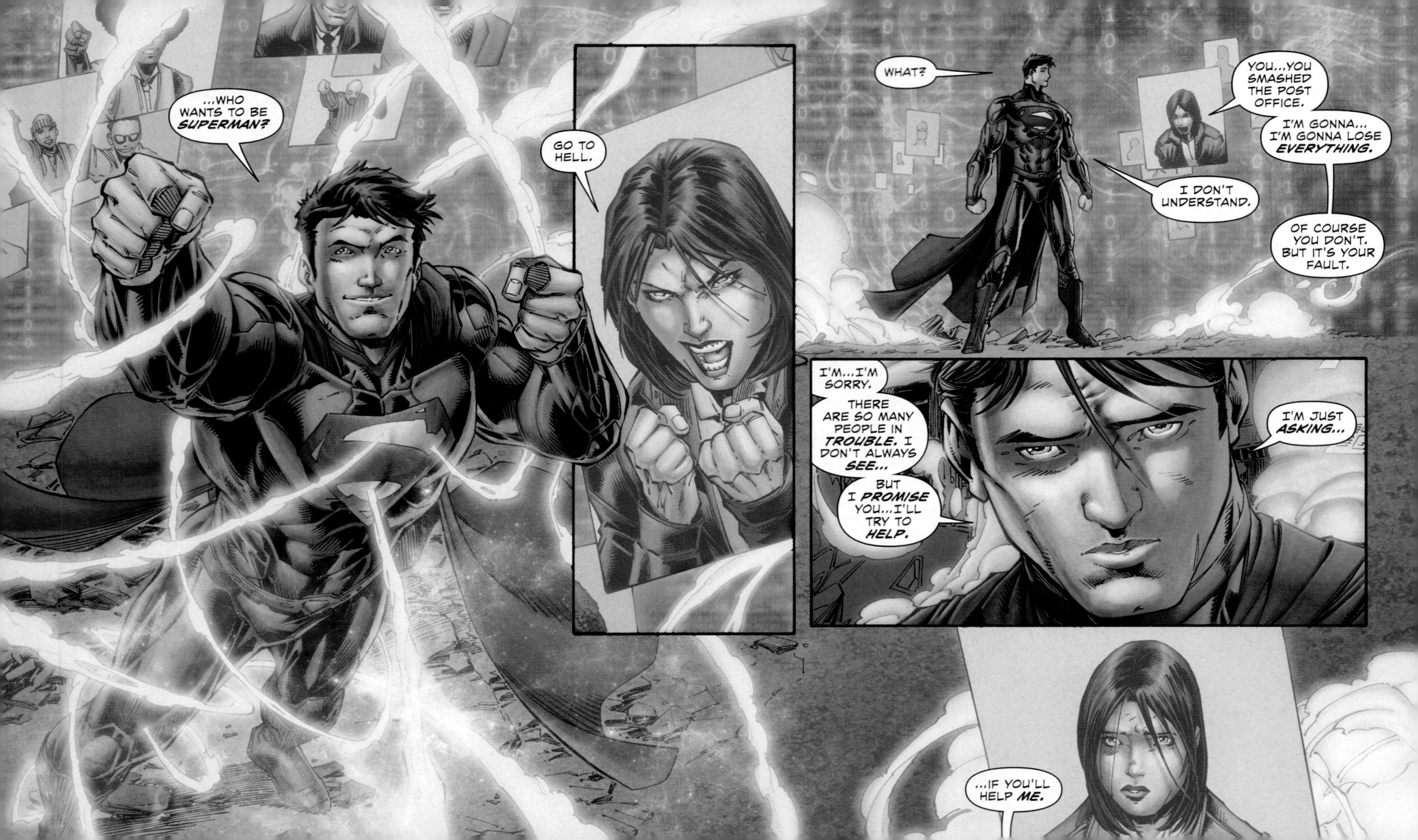
...WHO WANTS TO BE *SUPERMAN?*
GO TO HELL.
WHAT?
YOU...YOU SMASHED THE POST OFFICE.
I'M GONNA... I'M GONNA LOSE *EVERYTHING.*
I DON'T UNDERSTAND.
OF COURSE YOU DON'T. BUT IT'S YOUR FAULT.
I'M...I'M SORRY.
THERE ARE SO MANY PEOPLE IN *TROUBLE.* I DON'T ALWAYS *SEE...*
BUT I *PROMISE* YOU...I'LL TRY TO *HELP.*
I'M JUST *ASKING...*
...IF YOU'LL HELP *ME.*

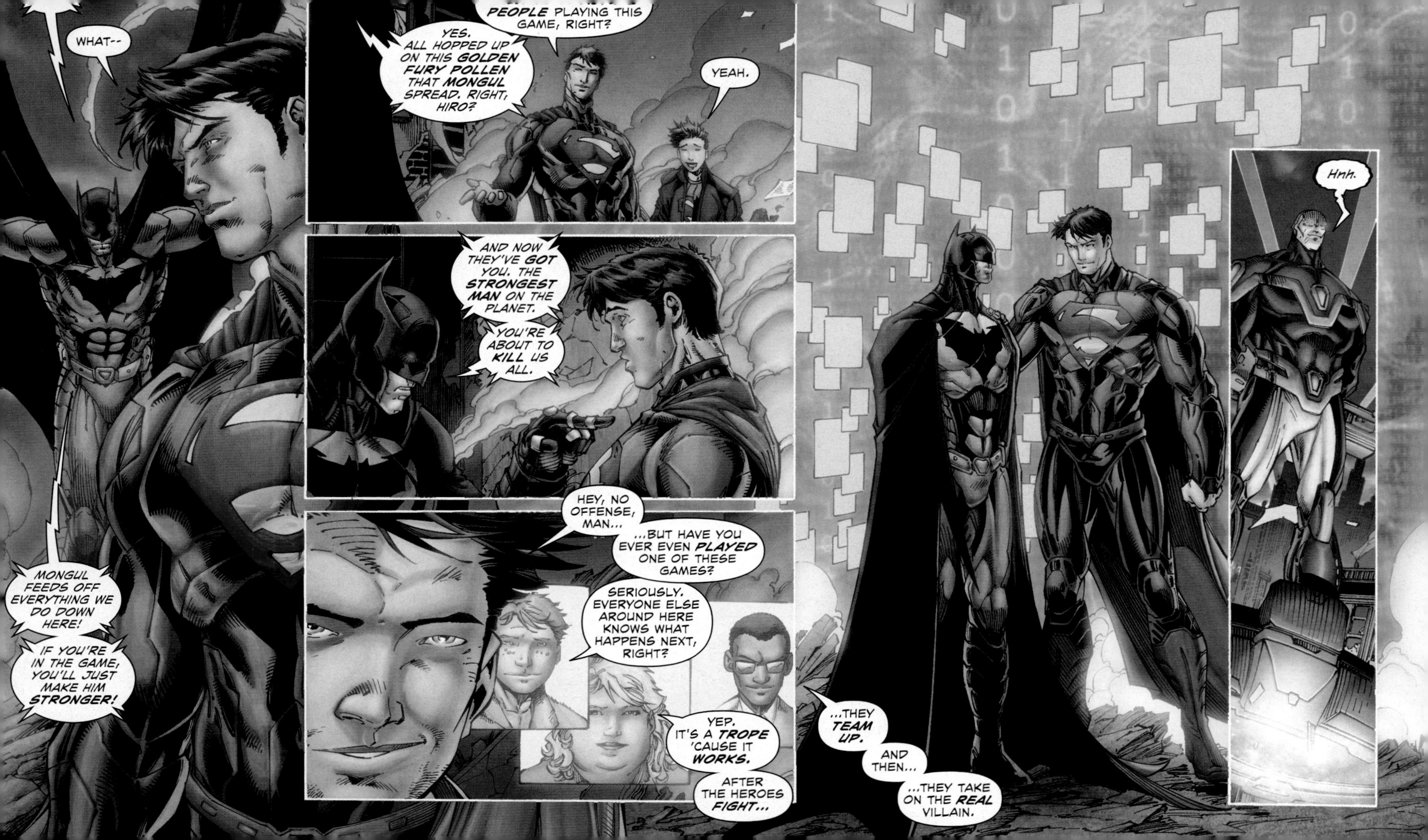
WHAT--
MONGUL FEEDS OFF EVERYTHING WE DO DOWN HERE!
IF YOU'RE IN THE GAME, YOU'LL JUST MAKE HIM STRONGER!
PEOPLE PLAYING THIS GAME, RIGHT?
YES. ALL HOPPED UP ON THIS GOLDEN FURY POLLEN THAT MONGUL SPREAD. RIGHT, HIRO?
YEAH.
AND NOW THEY'VE GOT YOU. THE STRONGEST MAN ON THE PLANET.
YOU'RE ABOUT TO KILL US ALL.
HEY, NO OFFENSE, MAN...
...BUT HAVE YOU EVER EVEN PLAYED ONE OF THESE GAMES?
SERIOUSLY. EVERYONE ELSE AROUND HERE KNOWS WHAT HAPPENS NEXT, RIGHT?
YEP. IT'S A TROPE 'CAUSE IT WORKS.
AFTER THE HEROES FIGHT...
...THEY TEAM UP.
AND THEN...
...THEY TAKE ON THE REAL VILLAIN.
Hnh.

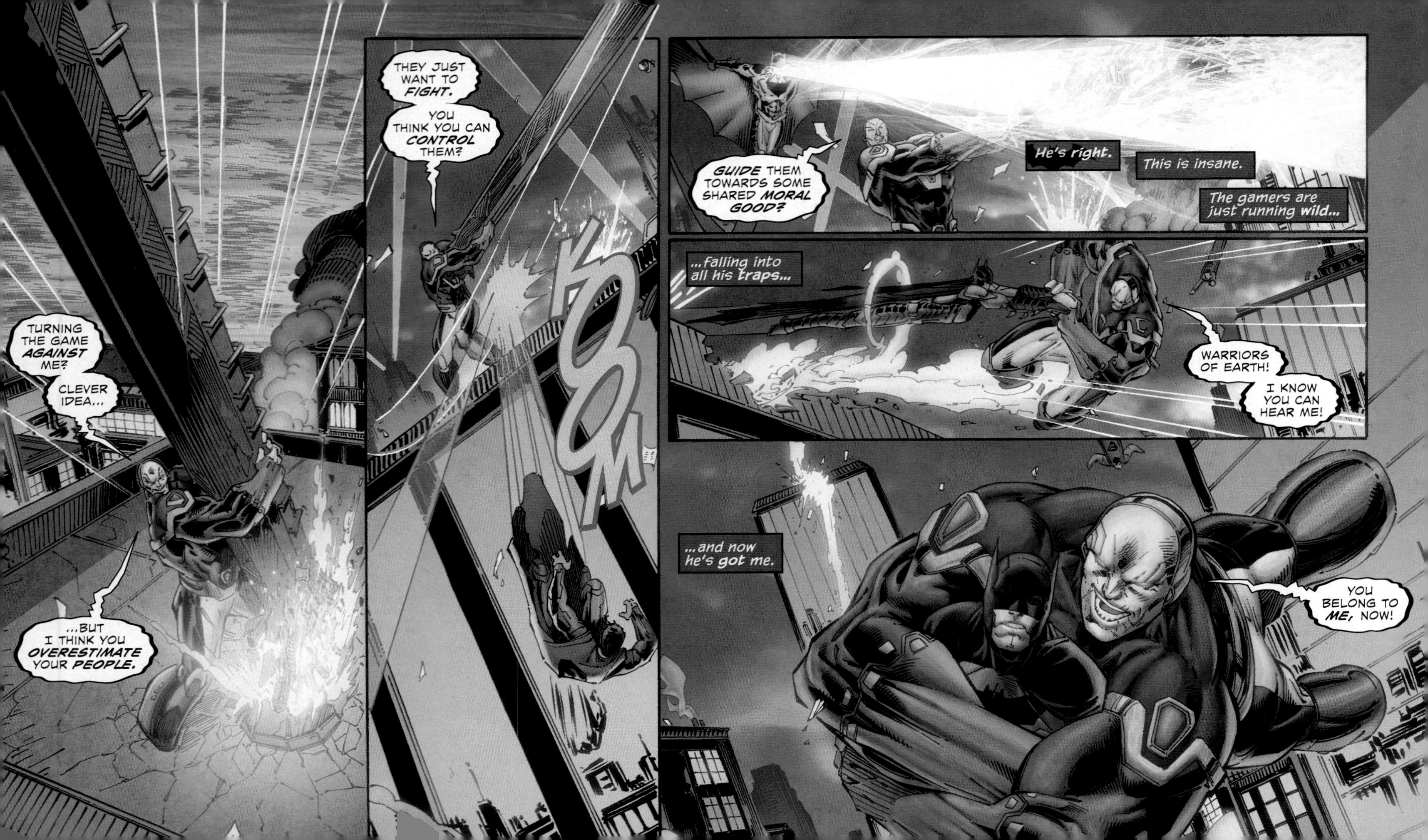
TURNING THE GAME AGAINST ME?
CLEVER IDEA...
...BUT I THINK YOU OVERESTIMATE YOUR PEOPLE.
THEY JUST WANT TO FIGHT.
YOU THINK YOU CAN CONTROL THEM?
KOOM
GUIDE THEM TOWARDS SOME SHARED MORAL GOOD?
He's right.
This is insane.
The gamers are just running wild...
...falling into all his traps...
WARRIORS OF EARTH!
I KNOW YOU CAN HEAR ME!
...and now he's got me.
YOU BELONG TO ME, NOW!

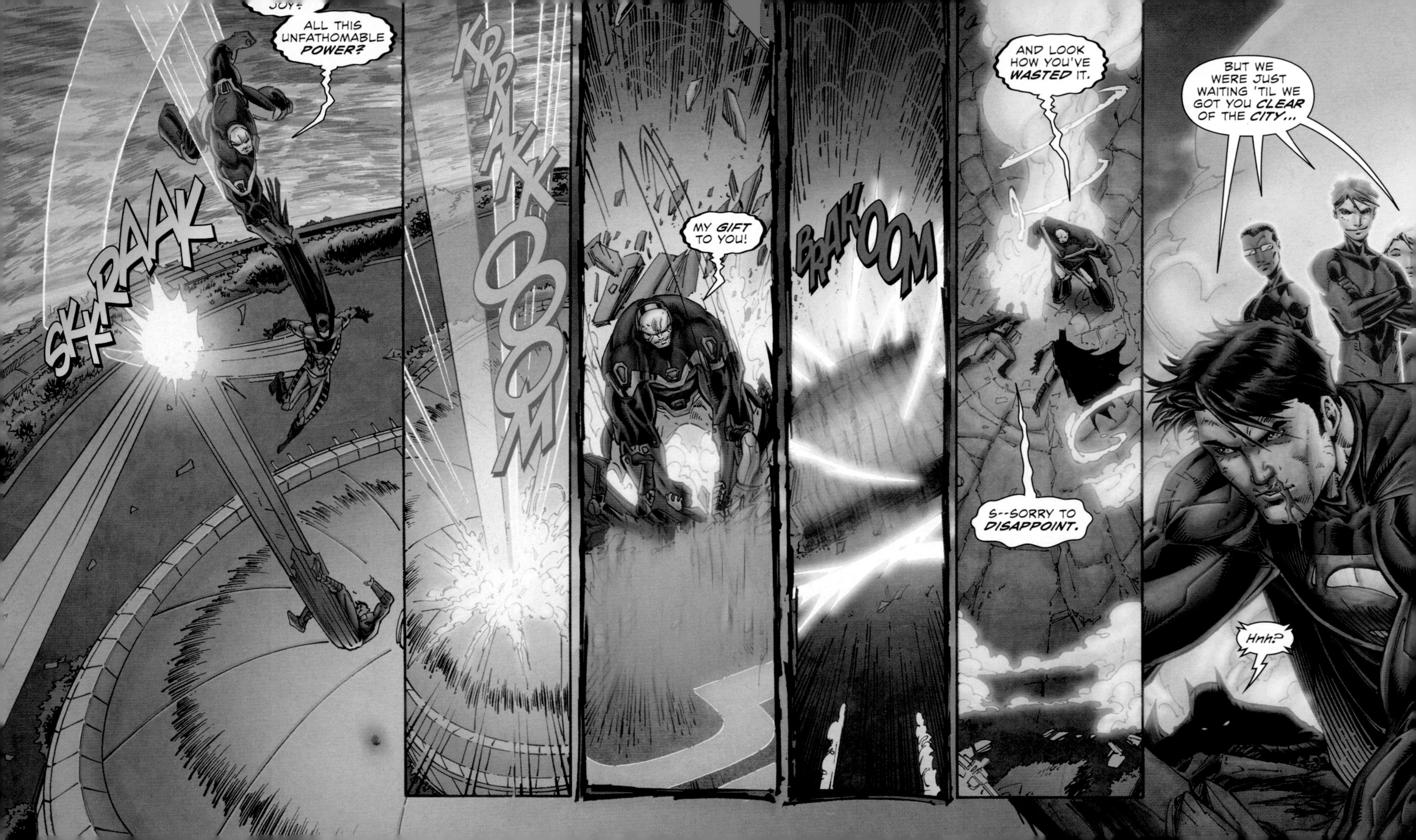
ALL THIS UNFATHOMABLE POWER?
SKRAAK
KRRAKKOOOM
MY GIFT TO YOU!
BRAKOOM
AND LOOK HOW YOU'VE WASTED IT.
S--SORRY TO DISAPPOINT.
BUT WE WERE JUST WAITING 'TIL WE GOT YOU CLEAR OF THE CITY...
Hnh?

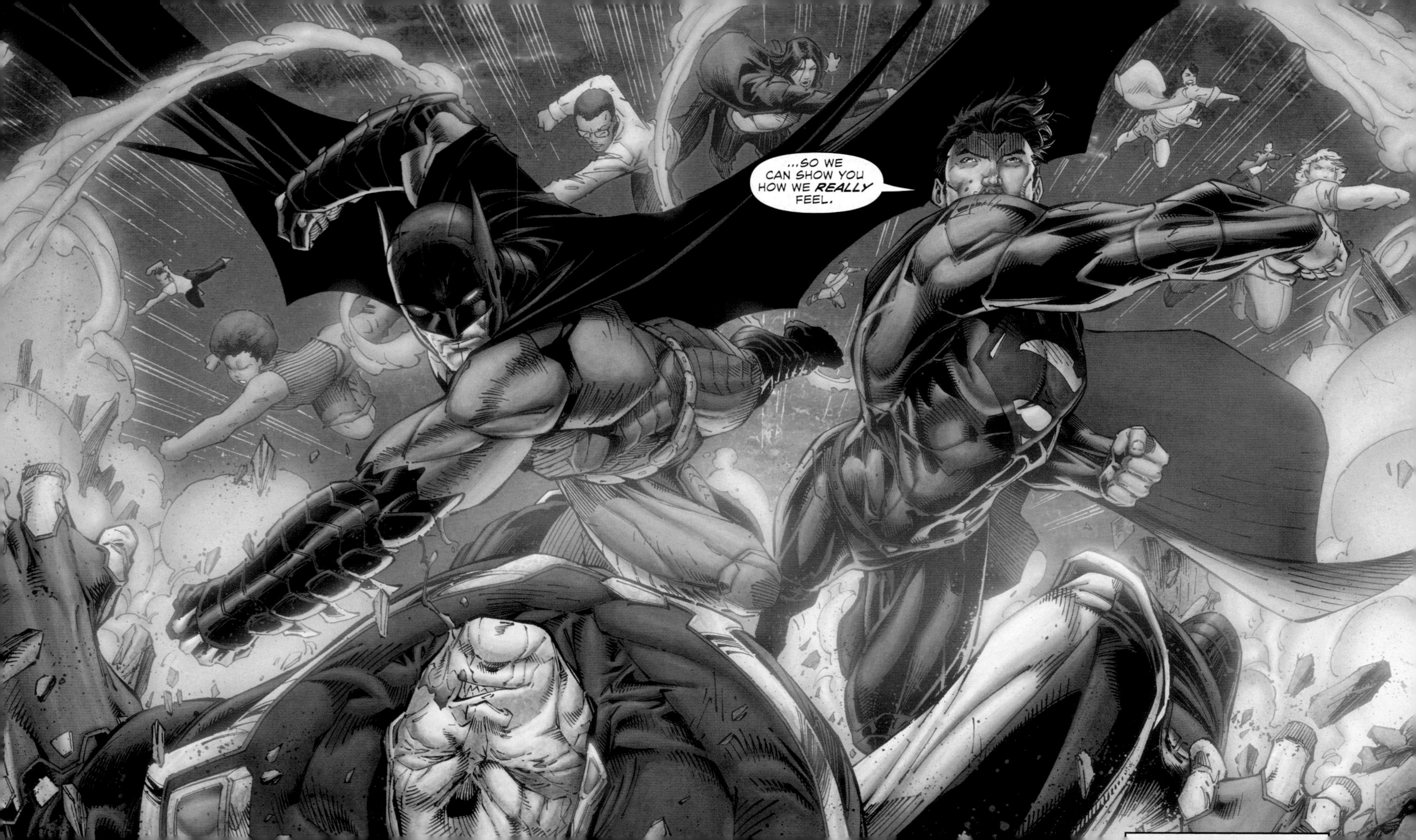
...SO WE CAN SHOW YOU HOW WE *REALLY* FEEL.

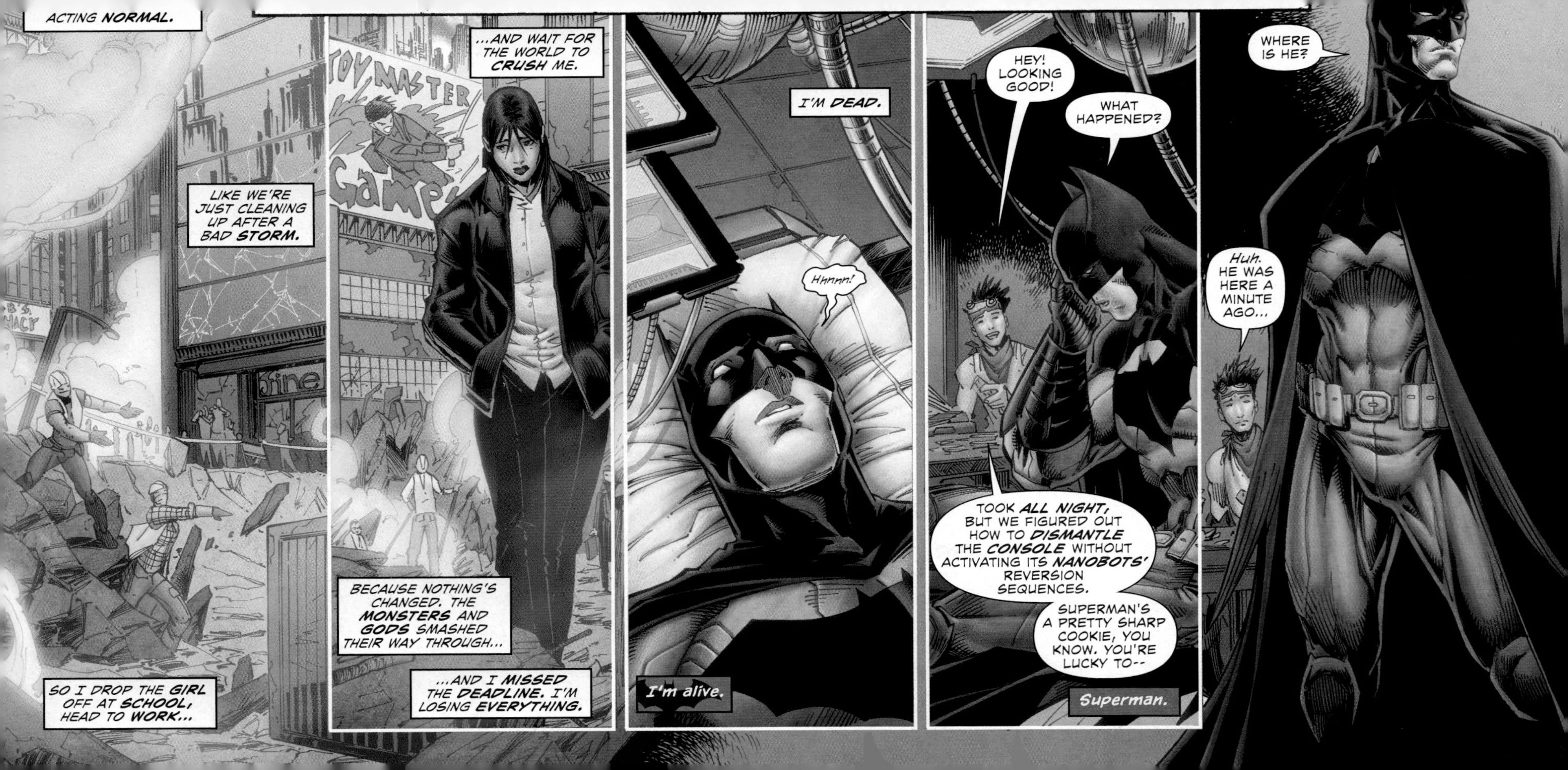
ACTING NORMAL.
LIKE WE'RE JUST CLEANING UP AFTER A BAD STORM.
SO I DROP THE GIRL OFF AT SCHOOL, HEAD TO WORK...
...AND WAIT FOR THE WORLD TO CRUSH ME.
TOYMASTER GAMES
BECAUSE NOTHING'S CHANGED. THE MONSTERS AND GODS SMASHED THEIR WAY THROUGH...
...AND I MISSED THE DEADLINE. I'M LOSING EVERYTHING.
I'M DEAD.
Hhnnn!
I'm alive.
HEY! LOOKING GOOD!
WHAT HAPPENED?
TOOK ALL NIGHT, BUT WE FIGURED OUT HOW TO DISMANTLE THE CONSOLE WITHOUT ACTIVATING ITS NANOBOTS' REVERSION SEQUENCES.
SUPERMAN'S A PRETTY SHARP COOKIE, YOU KNOW. YOU'RE LUCKY TO--
Superman.
WHERE IS HE?
Huh. HE WAS HERE A MINUTE AGO...

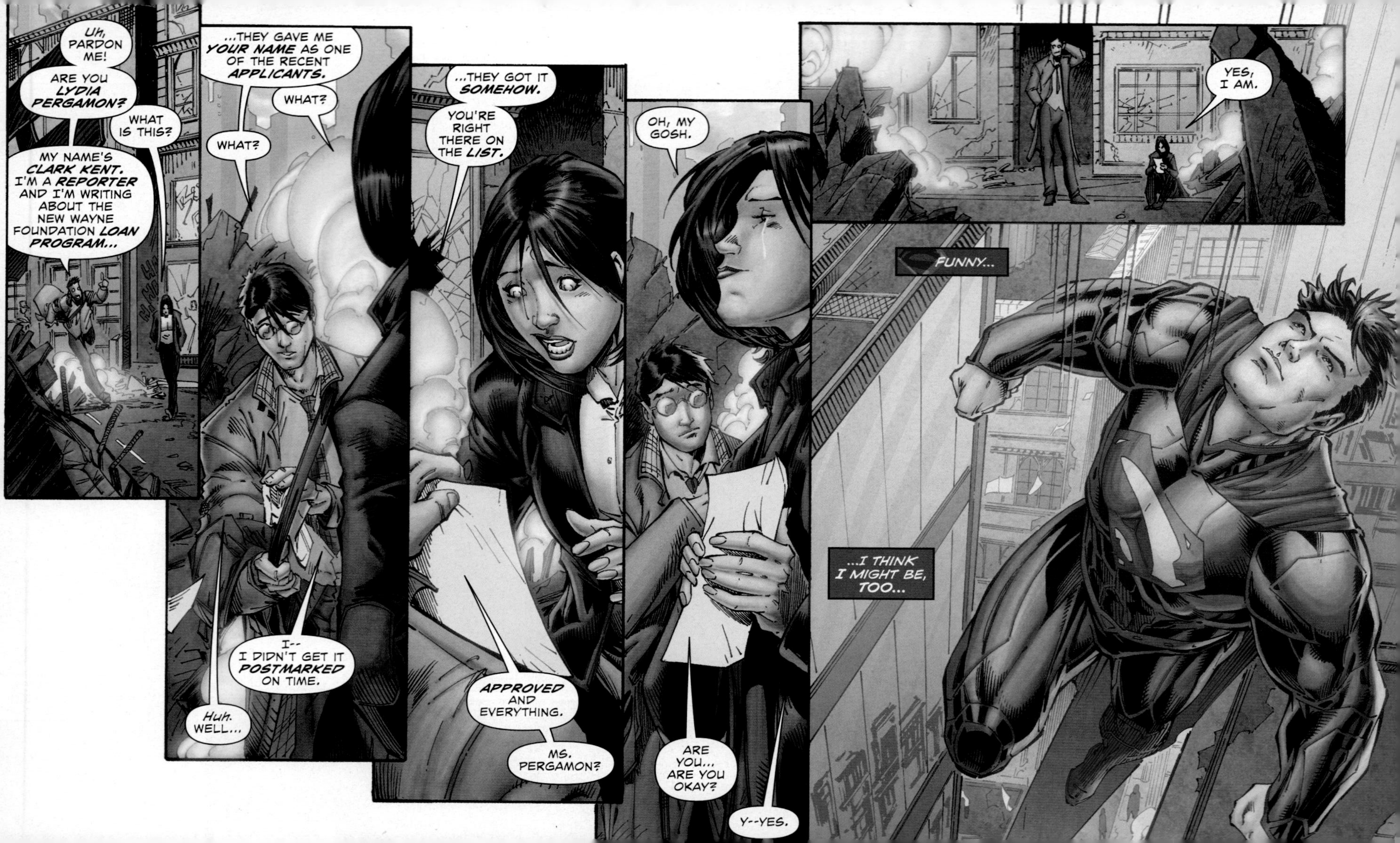
Uh, PARDON ME!
ARE YOU LYDIA PERGAMON?
WHAT IS THIS?
MY NAME'S CLARK KENT. I'M A REPORTER AND I'M WRITING ABOUT THE NEW WAYNE FOUNDATION LOAN PROGRAM...
...THEY GAVE ME YOUR NAME AS ONE OF THE RECENT APPLICANTS.
WHAT?
WHAT?
I-- I DIDN'T GET IT POSTMARKED ON TIME.
Huh. WELL...
...THEY GOT IT SOMEHOW.
YOU'RE RIGHT THERE ON THE LIST.
APPROVED AND EVERYTHING.
MS. PERGAMON?
OH, MY GOSH.
ARE YOU... ARE YOU OKAY?
Y--YES.
YES, I AM.
FUNNY...
...I THINK I MIGHT BE, TOO...

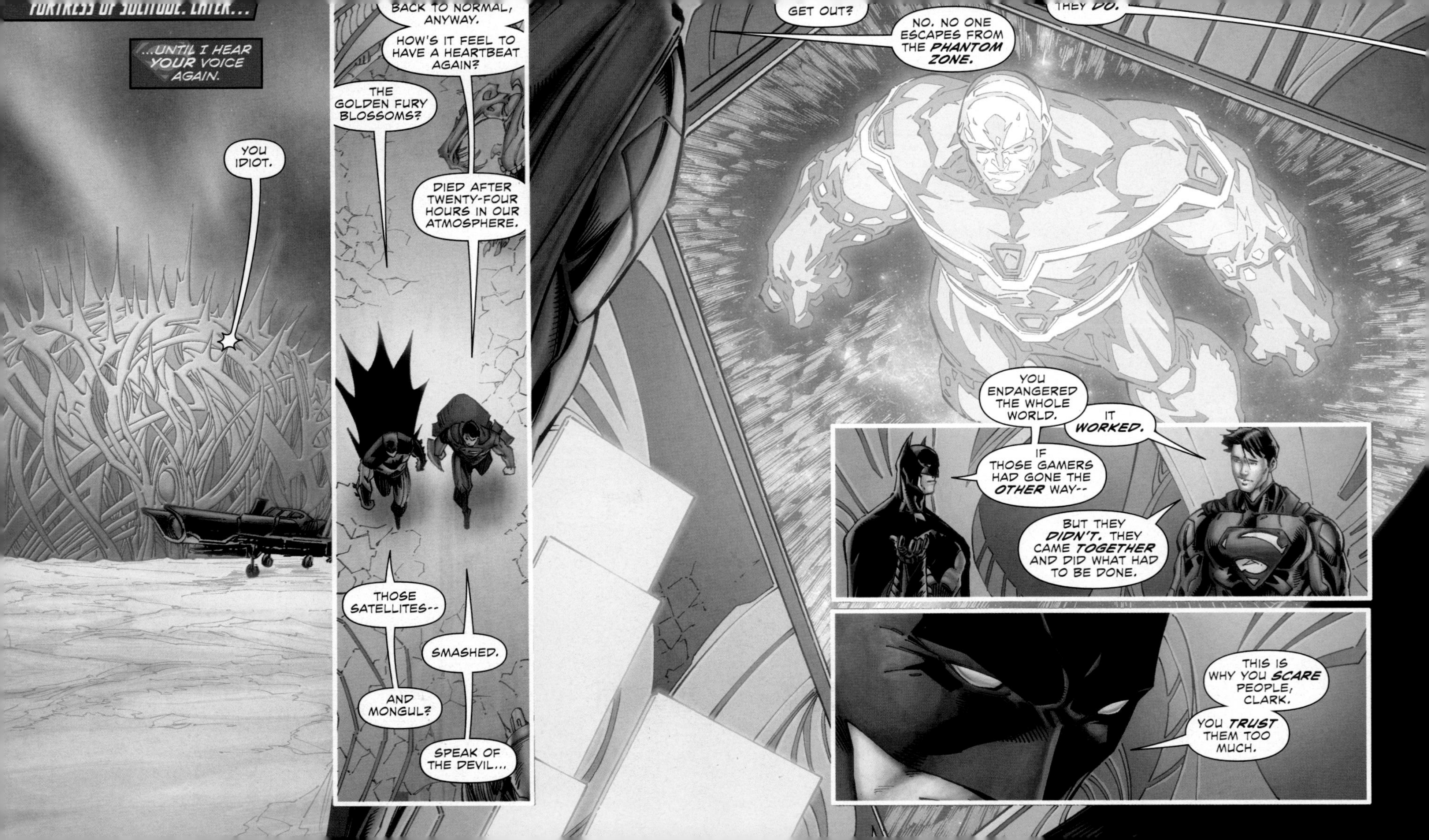
FORTRESS OF SOLITUDE. LATER...
...UNTIL I HEAR YOUR VOICE AGAIN.
YOU IDIOT.
BACK TO NORMAL, ANYWAY.
HOW'S IT FEEL TO HAVE A HEARTBEAT AGAIN?
THE GOLDEN FURY BLOSSOMS?
DIED AFTER TWENTY-FOUR HOURS IN OUR ATMOSPHERE.
THOSE SATELLITES--
SMASHED.
AND MONGUL?
SPEAK OF THE DEVIL...
GET OUT?
NO. NO ONE ESCAPES FROM THE *PHANTOM ZONE.*
THEY *DO.*
YOU ENDANGERED THE WHOLE WORLD.
IT *WORKED.*
IF THOSE GAMERS HAD GONE THE *OTHER* WAY--
BUT THEY *DIDN'T.* THEY CAME *TOGETHER* AND DID WHAT HAD TO BE DONE.
THIS IS WHY YOU *SCARE* PEOPLE, CLARK.
YOU *TRUST* THEM TOO MUCH.

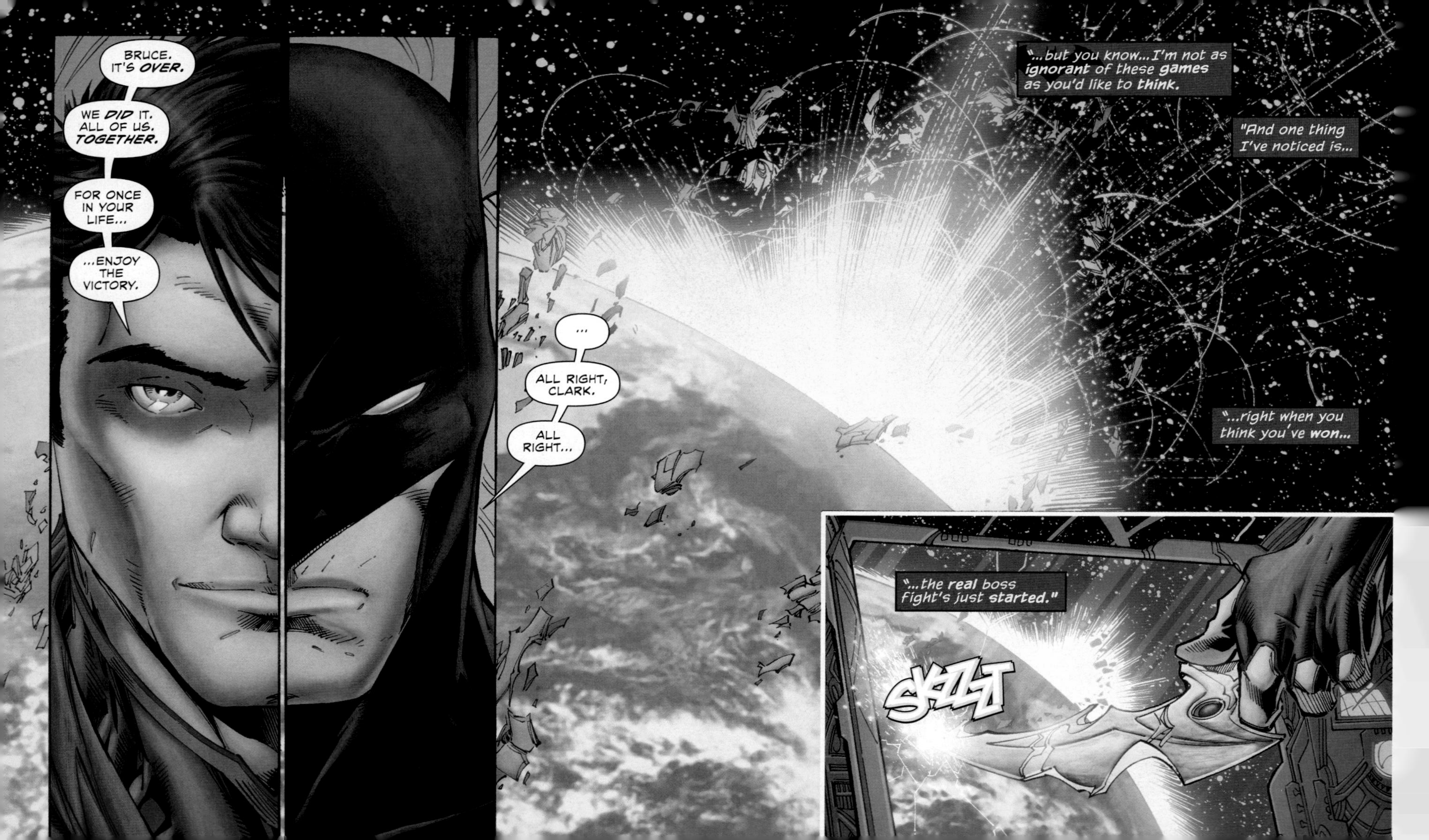
BRUCE. IT'S OVER.
WE DID IT. ALL OF US. TOGETHER.
FOR ONCE IN YOUR LIFE...
...ENJOY THE VICTORY.
...
ALL RIGHT, CLARK.
ALL RIGHT...
"...but you know...I'm not as ignorant of these games as you'd like to think.
"And one thing I've noticed is...
"...right when you think you've won...
"...the real boss fight's just started."
SKZZZT

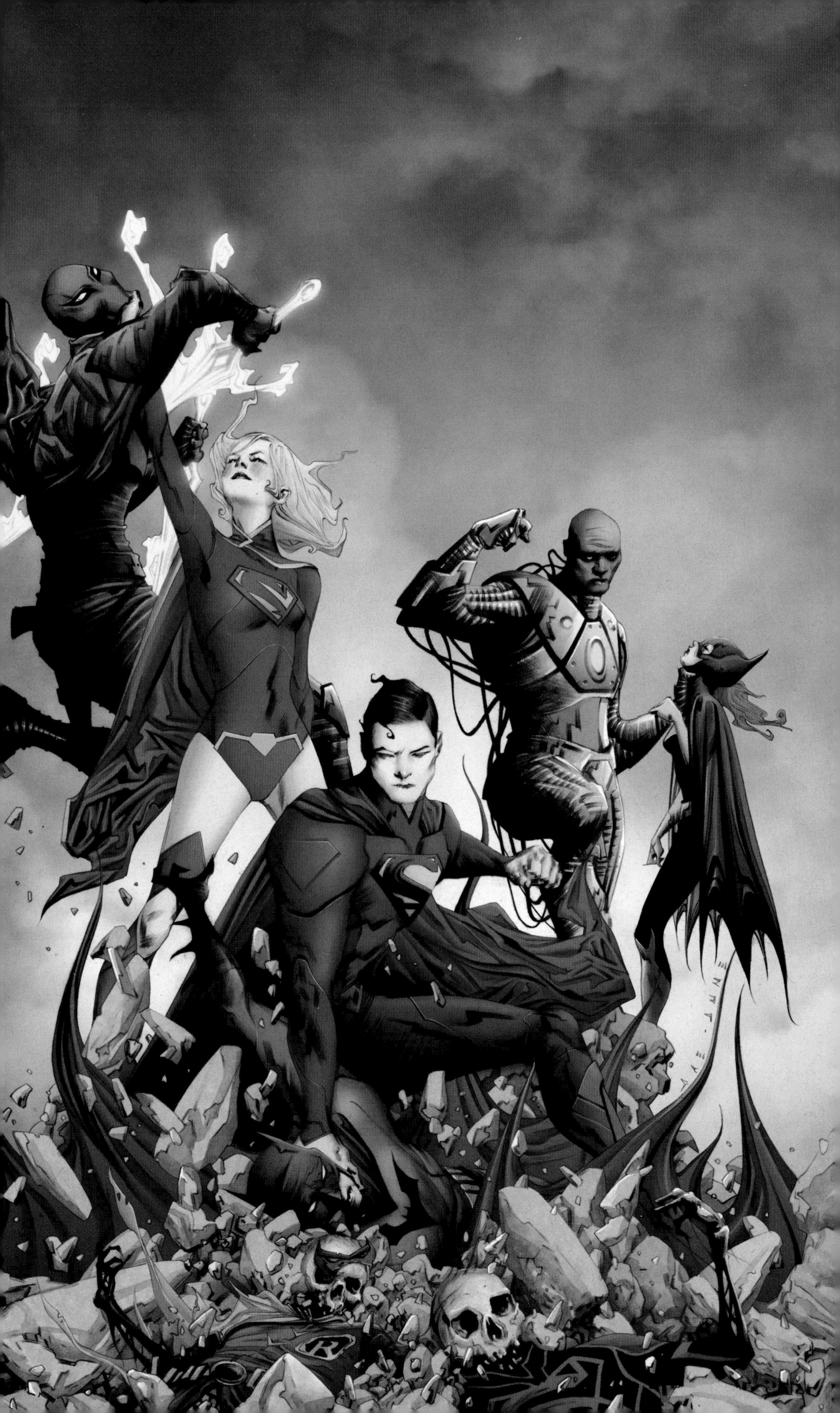

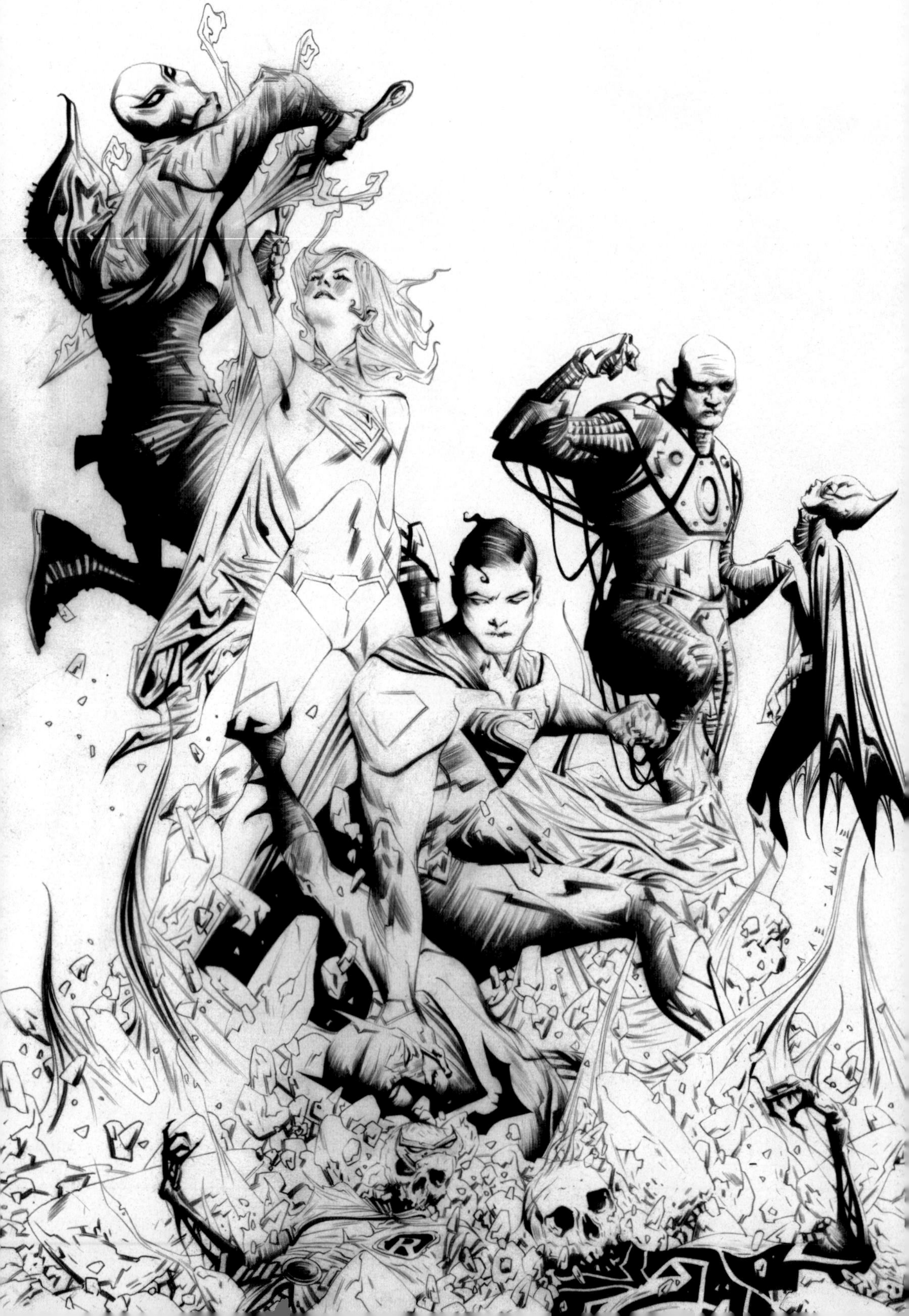

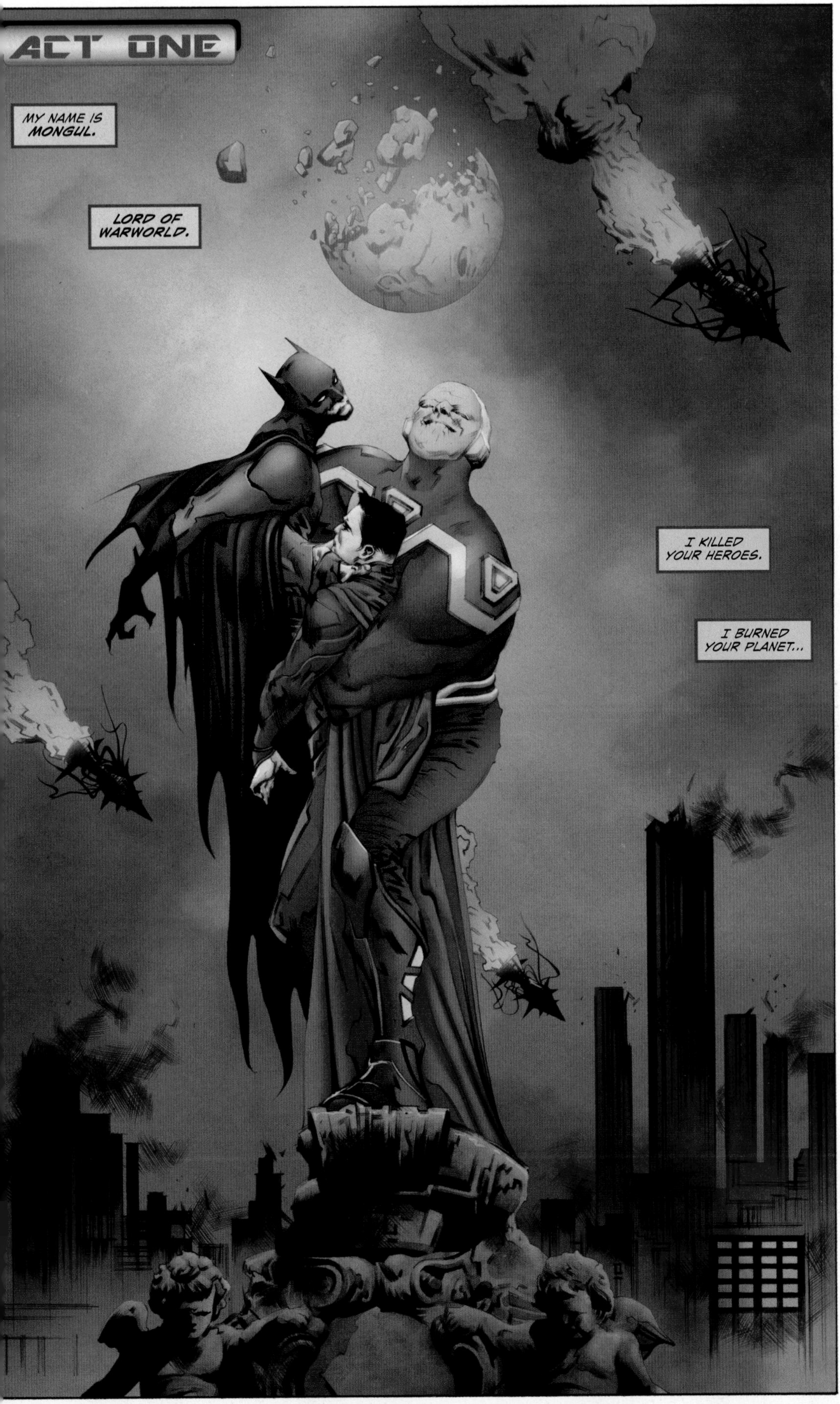
ACT ONE
MY NAME IS MONGUL.
LORD OF WARWORLD.
I KILLED YOUR HEROES.
I BURNED YOUR PLANET...

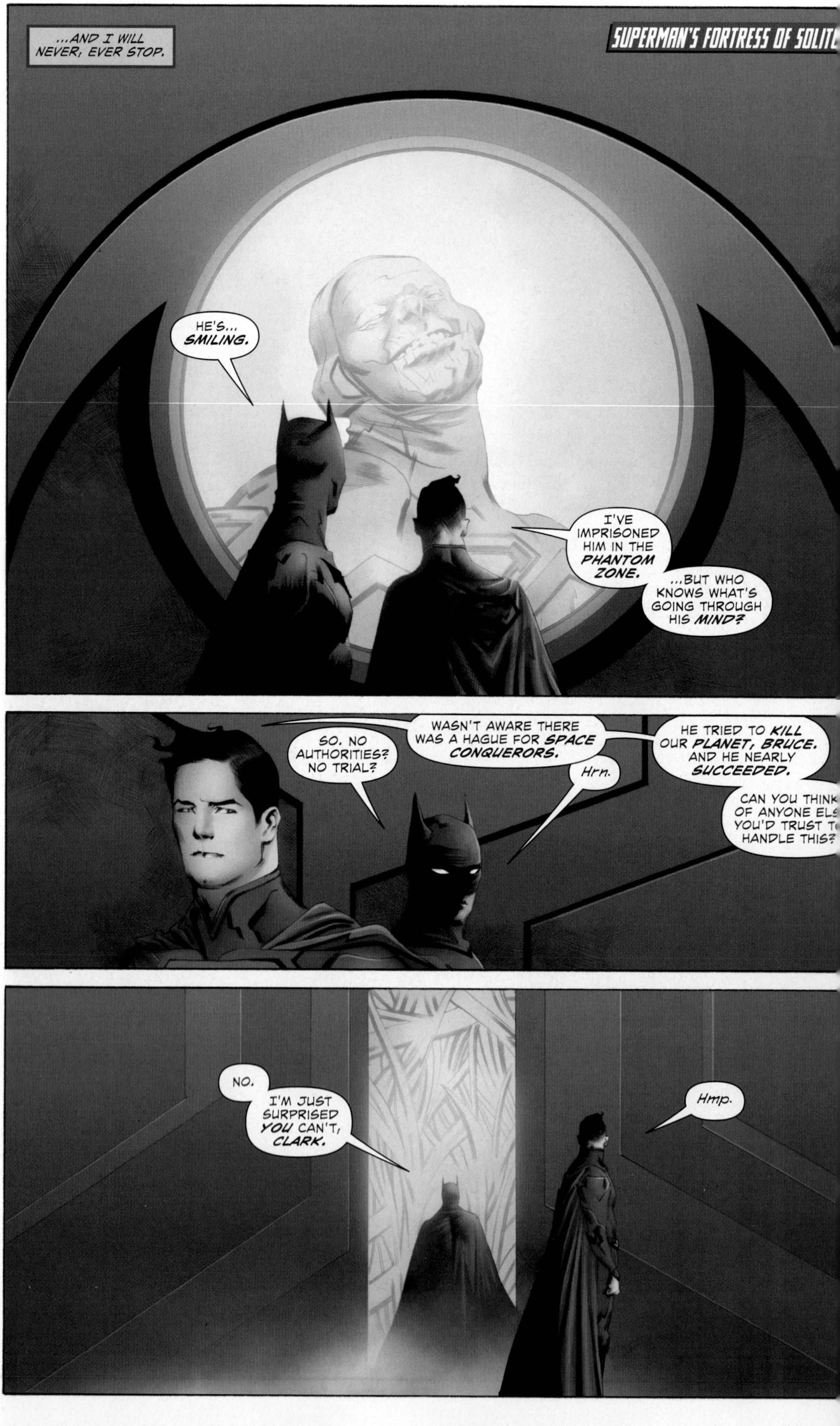
...AND I WILL NEVER, EVER STOP.
SUPERMAN'S FORTRESS OF SOLIT
HE'S... SMILING.
I'VE IMPRISONED HIM IN THE PHANTOM ZONE.
...BUT WHO KNOWS WHAT'S GOING THROUGH HIS MIND?
SO. NO AUTHORITIES? NO TRIAL?
WASN'T AWARE THERE WAS A HAGUE FOR SPACE CONQUERORS.
Hrn.
HE TRIED TO KILL OUR PLANET, BRUCE. AND HE NEARLY SUCCEEDED.
CAN YOU THINK OF ANYONE ELS YOU'D TRUST T HANDLE THIS?
NO.
I'M JUST SURPRISED YOU CAN'T, CLARK.
Hmp.

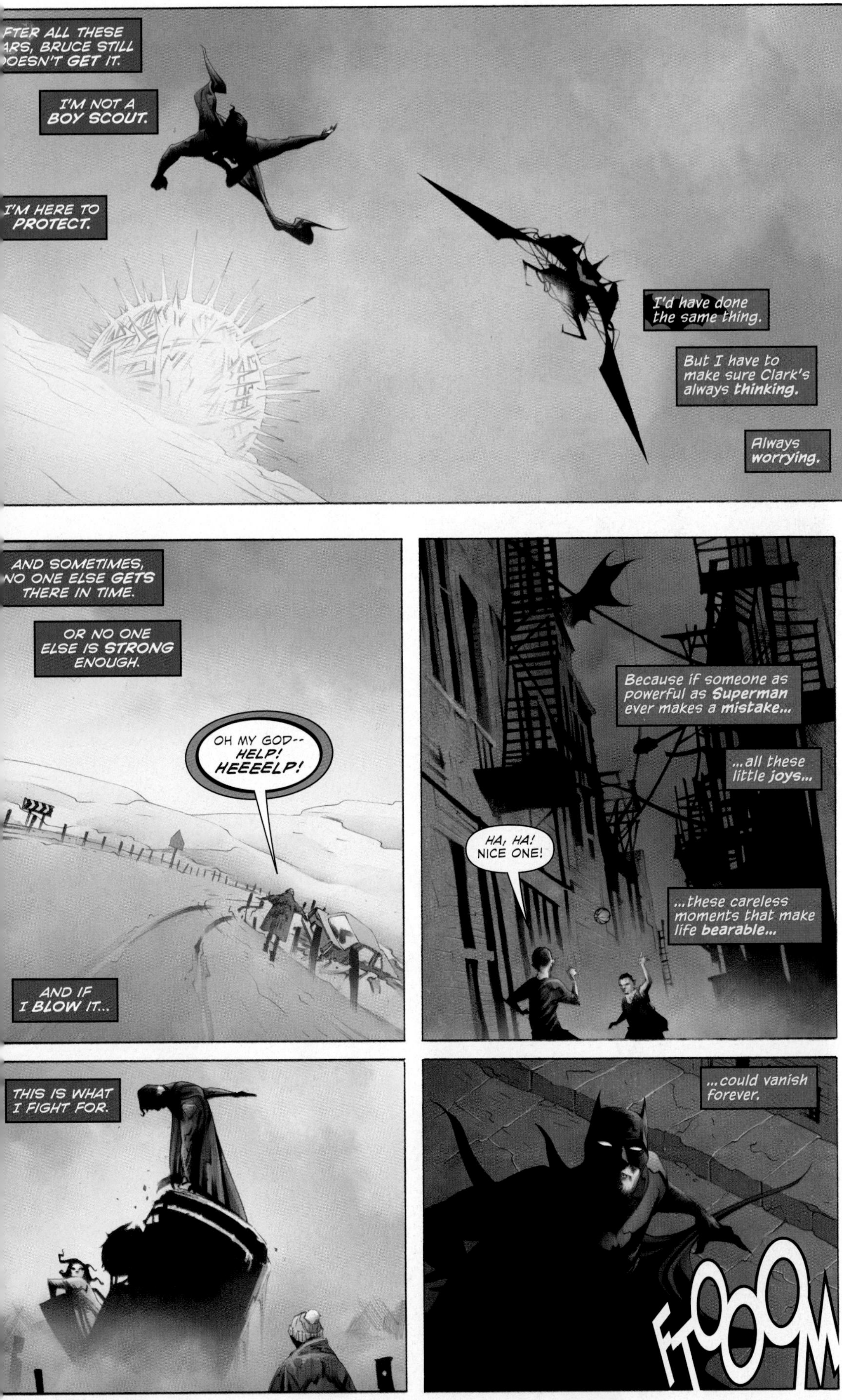
FTER ALL THESE
ARS, BRUCE STILL
OESN'T GET IT.
I'M NOT A BOY SCOUT.
I'M HERE TO PROTECT.
I'd have done the same thing.
But I have to make sure Clark's always thinking.
Always worrying.
AND SOMETIMES, NO ONE ELSE GETS THERE IN TIME.
OR NO ONE ELSE IS STRONG ENOUGH.
OH MY GOD-- HELP! HEEEELP!
AND IF I BLOW IT...
Because if someone as powerful as Superman ever makes a mistake...
...all these little joys...
HA, HA! NICE ONE!
...these careless moments that make life bearable...
THIS IS WHAT I FIGHT FOR.
...could vanish forever.
FTOOOM

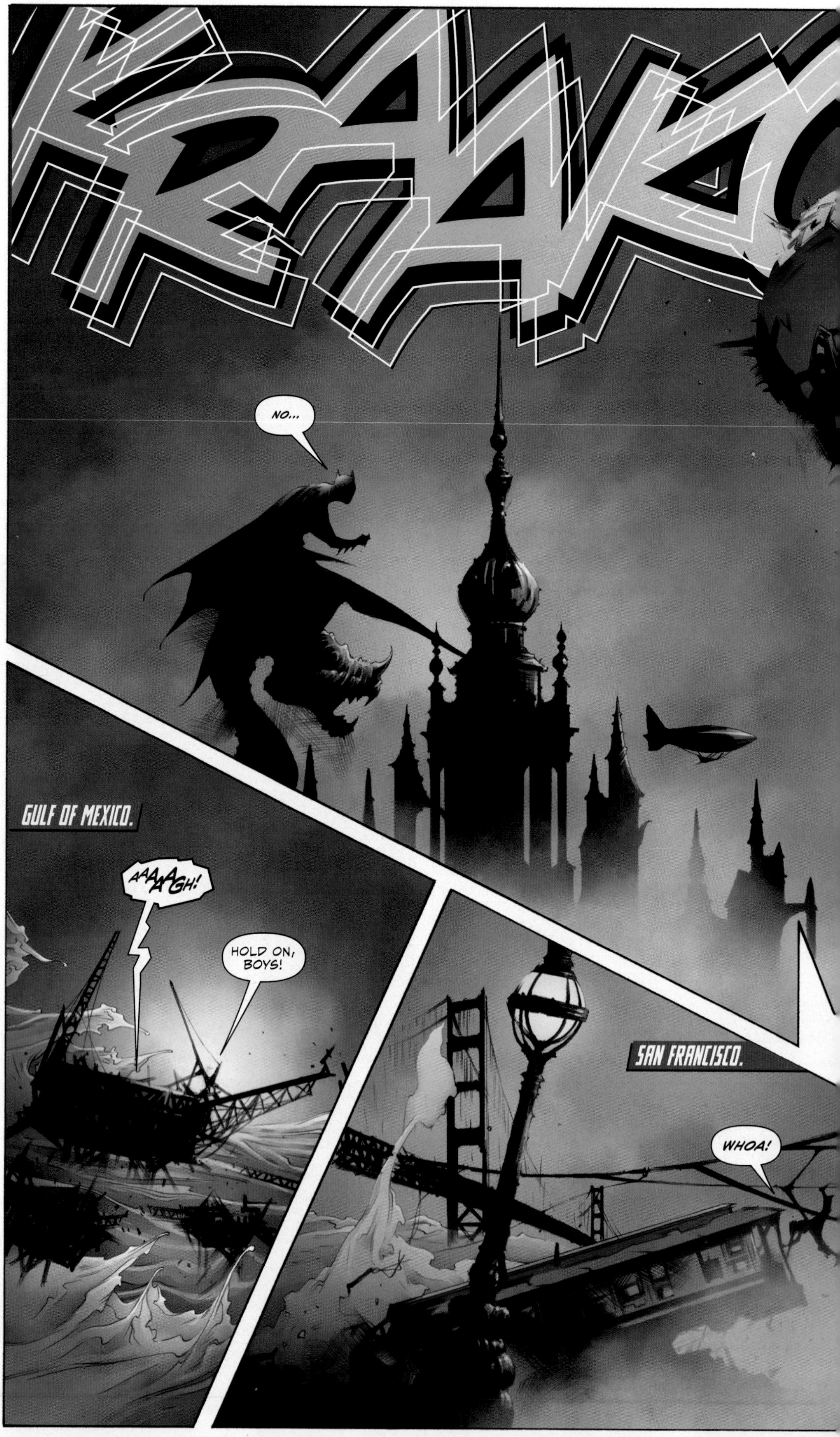

KRAKA
NO...
GULF OF MEXICO.
AAAAAGH!
HOLD ON, BOYS!
SAN FRANCISCO.
WHOA!

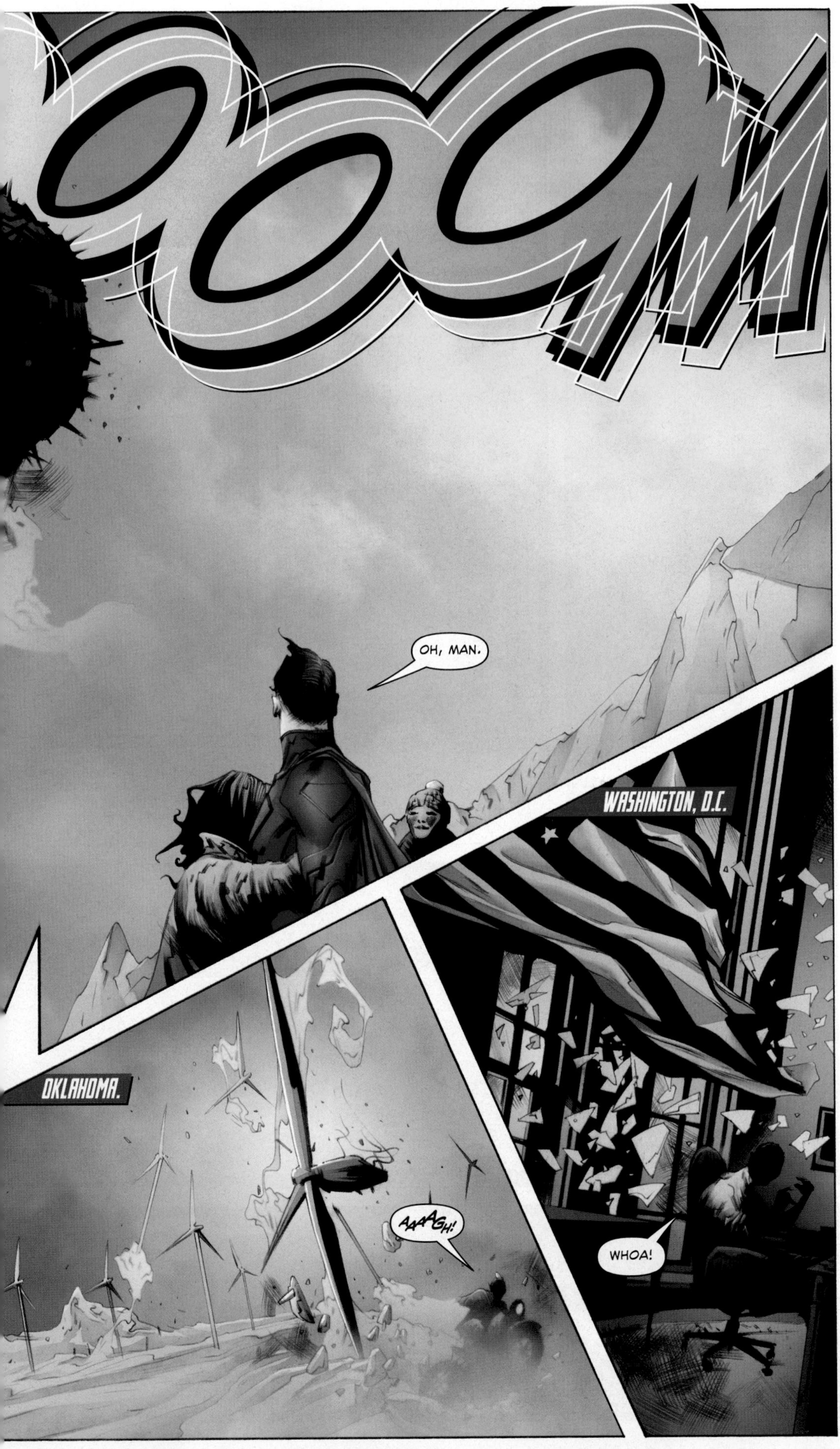
OOOM
OH, MAN.
WASHINGTON, D.C.
WHOA!
OKLAHOMA.
AAAAGH!

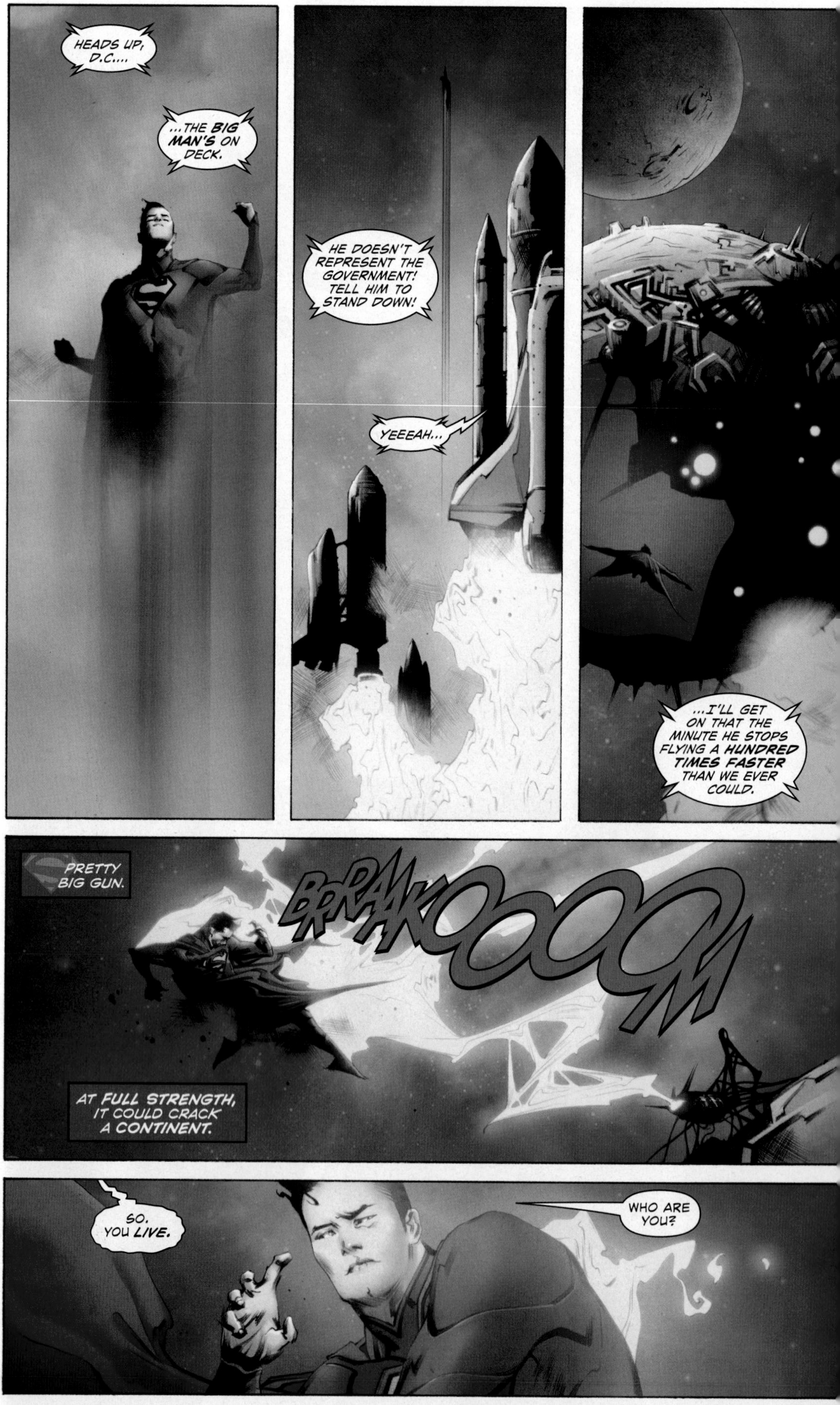
HEADS UP, D.C....
...THE BIG MAN'S ON DECK.
HE DOESN'T REPRESENT THE GOVERNMENT! TELL HIM TO STAND DOWN!
YEEEAH...
...I'LL GET ON THAT THE MINUTE HE STOPS FLYING A HUNDRED TIMES FASTER THAN WE EVER COULD.
PRETTY BIG GUN.
BRRAKOOOOM
AT FULL STRENGTH, IT COULD CRACK A CONTINENT.
SO. YOU LIVE.
WHO ARE YOU?

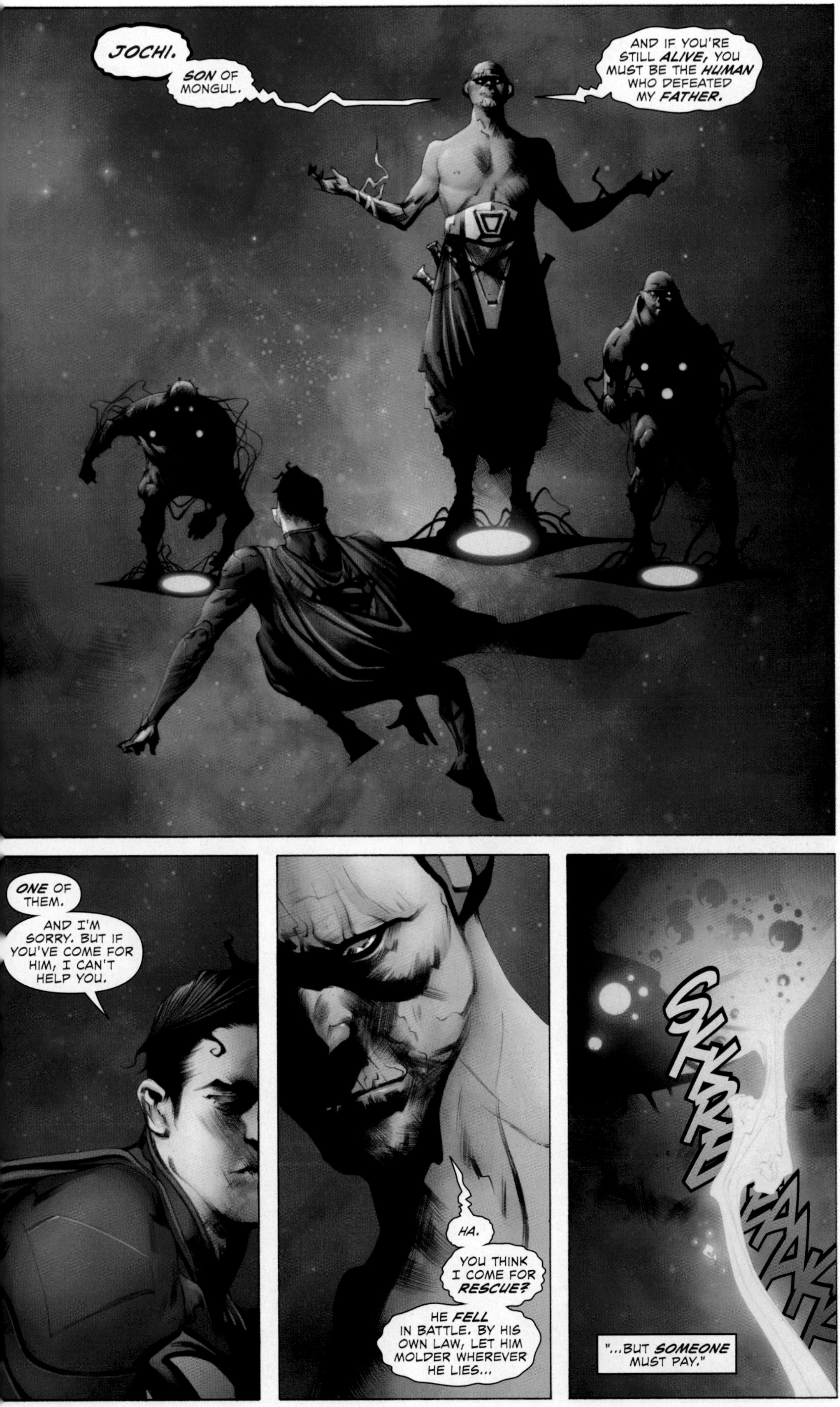
JOCHI.
SON OF MONGUL.
AND IF YOU'RE STILL ALIVE, YOU MUST BE THE HUMAN WHO DEFEATED MY FATHER.
ONE OF THEM.
AND I'M SORRY. BUT IF YOU'VE COME FOR HIM, I CAN'T HELP YOU.
HA.
YOU THINK I COME FOR RESCUE?
HE FELL IN BATTLE. BY HIS OWN LAW, LET HIM MOLDER WHEREVER HE LIES...
"...BUT SOMEONE MUST PAY."

WARRIOR CULTURE.

EYE FOR AN EYE.

AND HE LOST HIS *FATHER*.

I CAN ALMOST UNDERSTAND IT...

...BUT NOW HE'S TRYING TO TAKE OUT A WHOLE *CITY*.

I DON'T THINK SO.

METROPO

YOU'VE GOT *TWO MINUTES* TO GET THE HELL *OUT* OF THIS SOLAR SYSTEM.

YOU WANT TO FIGHT? WONDERFUL.

BUT IF WE DO IT THIS WAY, HOW MANY OF THESE SOFT LITTLE HUMANS WILL DIE?

WHAT IS THIS?

SOME KIND OF *TEST*?

WHAT DO YOU WANT?

YOU AND YOUR *BATMAN* FRIEND TOOK DOWN MY *FATHER*.

I'D LIKE TO MEET *YOUR* FAMILIES.

YOU HAVE *ONE DAY*.

RETURN TO *WARWORLD* WITH *TWO* FROM EACH OF YOUR *CLANS*.

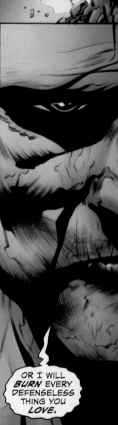

OR I WILL *BURN* EVERY DEFENSELESS THING YOU *LOVE*.

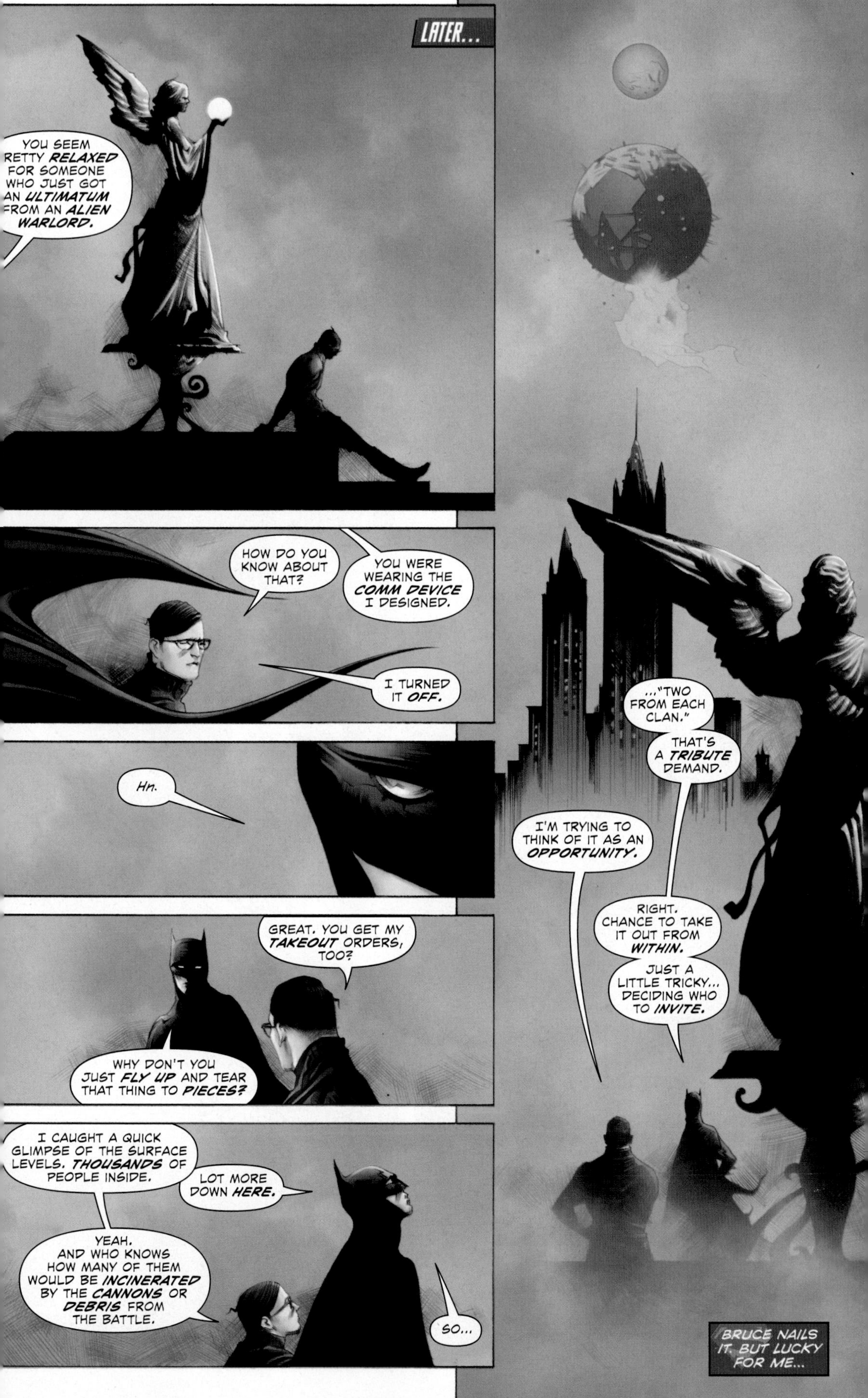

LATER...
YOU SEEM RETTY RELAXED FOR SOMEONE WHO JUST GOT AN ULTIMATUM FROM AN ALIEN WARLORD.
HOW DO YOU KNOW ABOUT THAT?
YOU WERE WEARING THE COMM DEVICE I DESIGNED.
I TURNED IT OFF.
Hn.
GREAT. YOU GET MY TAKEOUT ORDERS, TOO?
WHY DON'T YOU JUST FLY UP AND TEAR THAT THING TO PIECES?
I CAUGHT A QUICK GLIMPSE OF THE SURFACE LEVELS. THOUSANDS OF PEOPLE INSIDE.
LOT MORE DOWN HERE.
YEAH. AND WHO KNOWS HOW MANY OF THEM WOULD BE INCINERATED BY THE CANNONS OR DEBRIS FROM THE BATTLE.
SO...
..."TWO FROM EACH CLAN."
THAT'S A TRIBUTE DEMAND.
I'M TRYING TO THINK OF IT AS AN OPPORTUNITY.
RIGHT. CHANCE TO TAKE IT OUT FROM WITHIN.
JUST A LITTLE TRICKY... DECIDING WHO TO INVITE.
BRUCE NAILS IT. BUT LUCKY FOR ME...

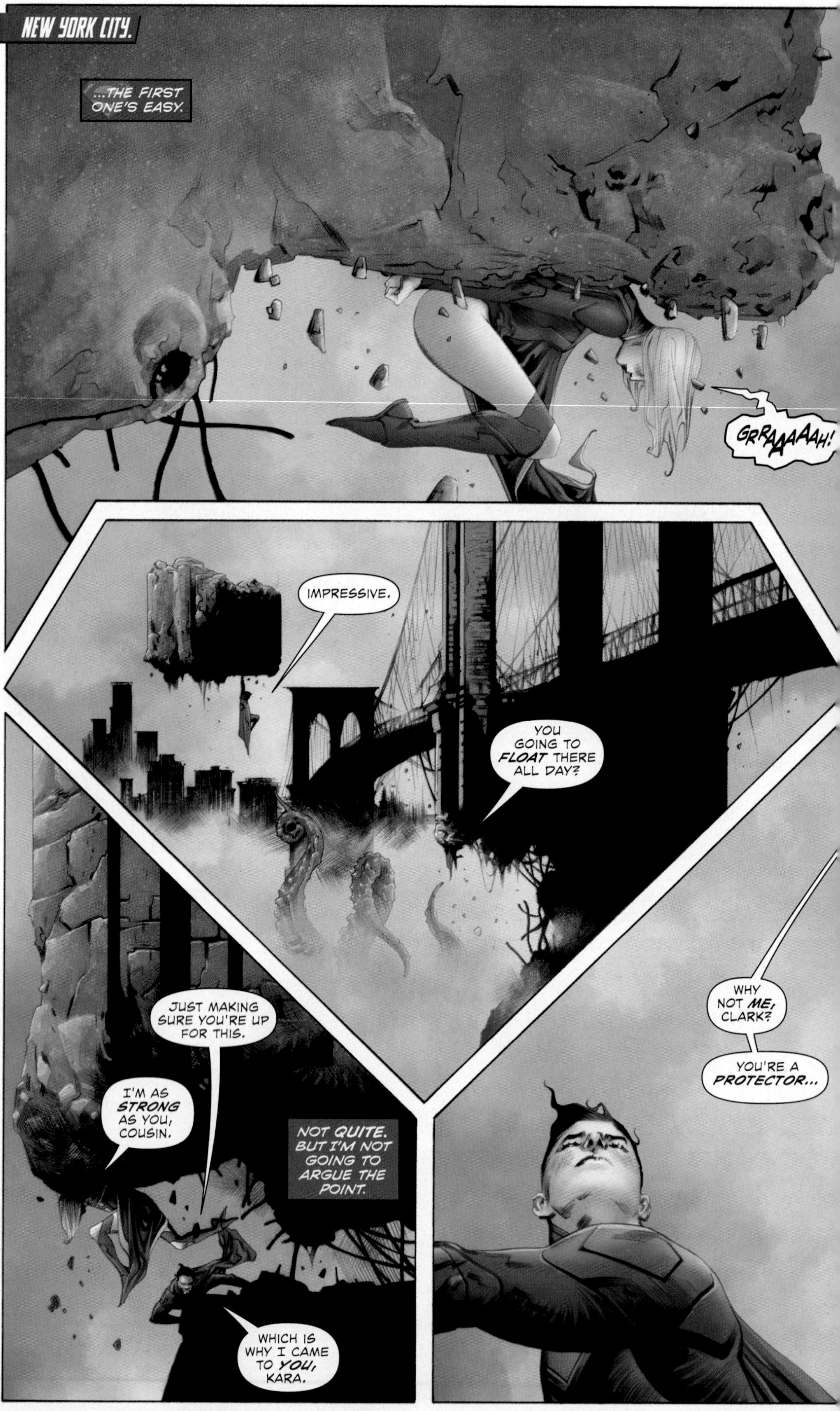
NEW YORK CITY.
...THE FIRST ONE'S EASY.
GRRAAAAAH!
IMPRESSIVE.
YOU GOING TO FLOAT THERE ALL DAY?
WHY NOT ME, CLARK?
YOU'RE A PROTECTOR...
JUST MAKING SURE YOU'RE UP FOR THIS.
I'M AS STRONG AS YOU, COUSIN.
NOT QUITE. BUT I'M NOT GOING TO ARGUE THE POINT.
WHICH IS WHY I CAME TO YOU, KARA.

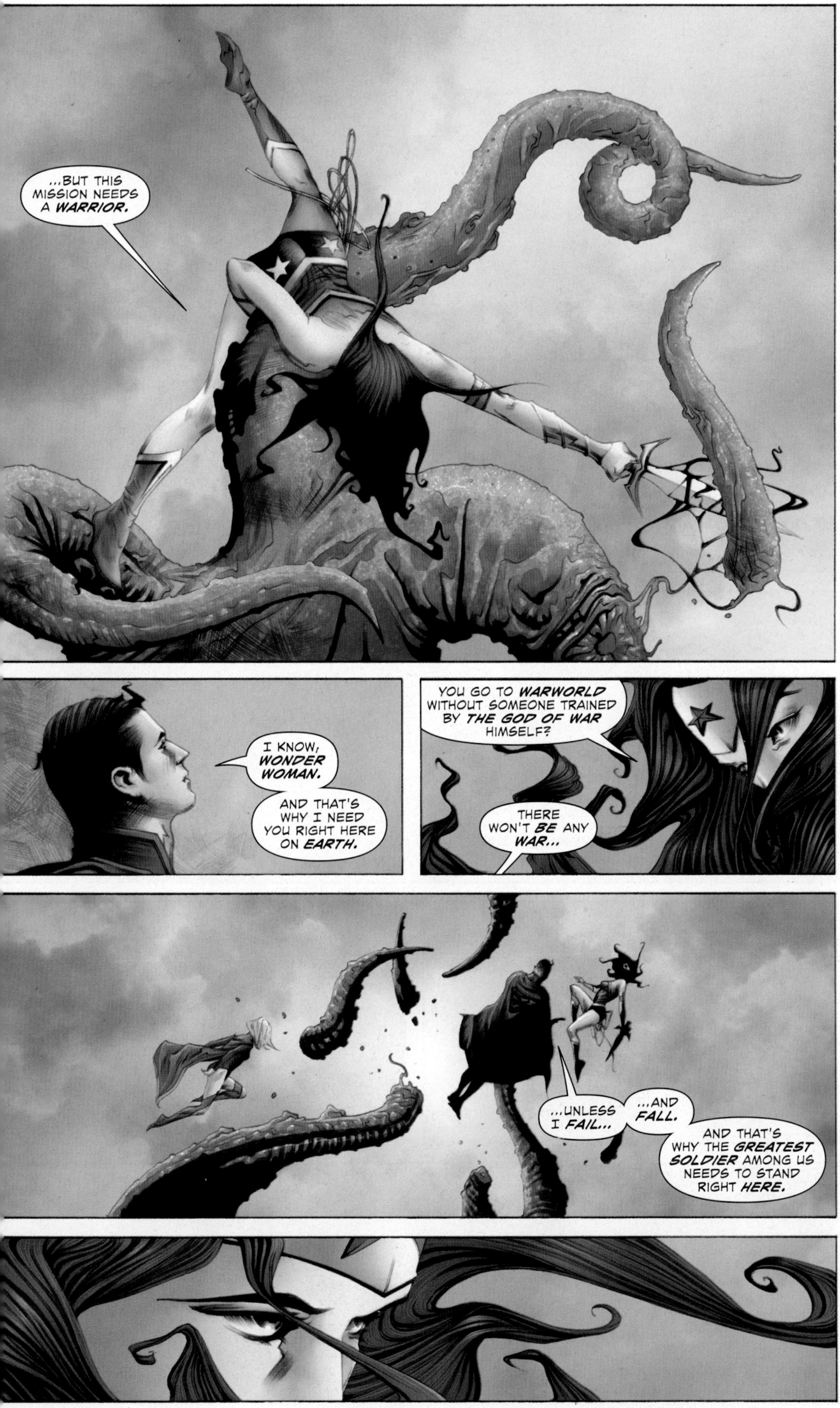
...BUT THIS MISSION NEEDS A WARRIOR.
I KNOW, WONDER WOMAN.
AND THAT'S WHY I NEED YOU RIGHT HERE ON EARTH.
YOU GO TO WARWORLD WITHOUT SOMEONE TRAINED BY THE GOD OF WAR HIMSELF?
THERE WON'T BE ANY WAR...
...UNLESS I FAIL...
...AND FALL.
AND THAT'S WHY THE GREATEST SOLDIER AMONG US NEEDS TO STAND RIGHT HERE.

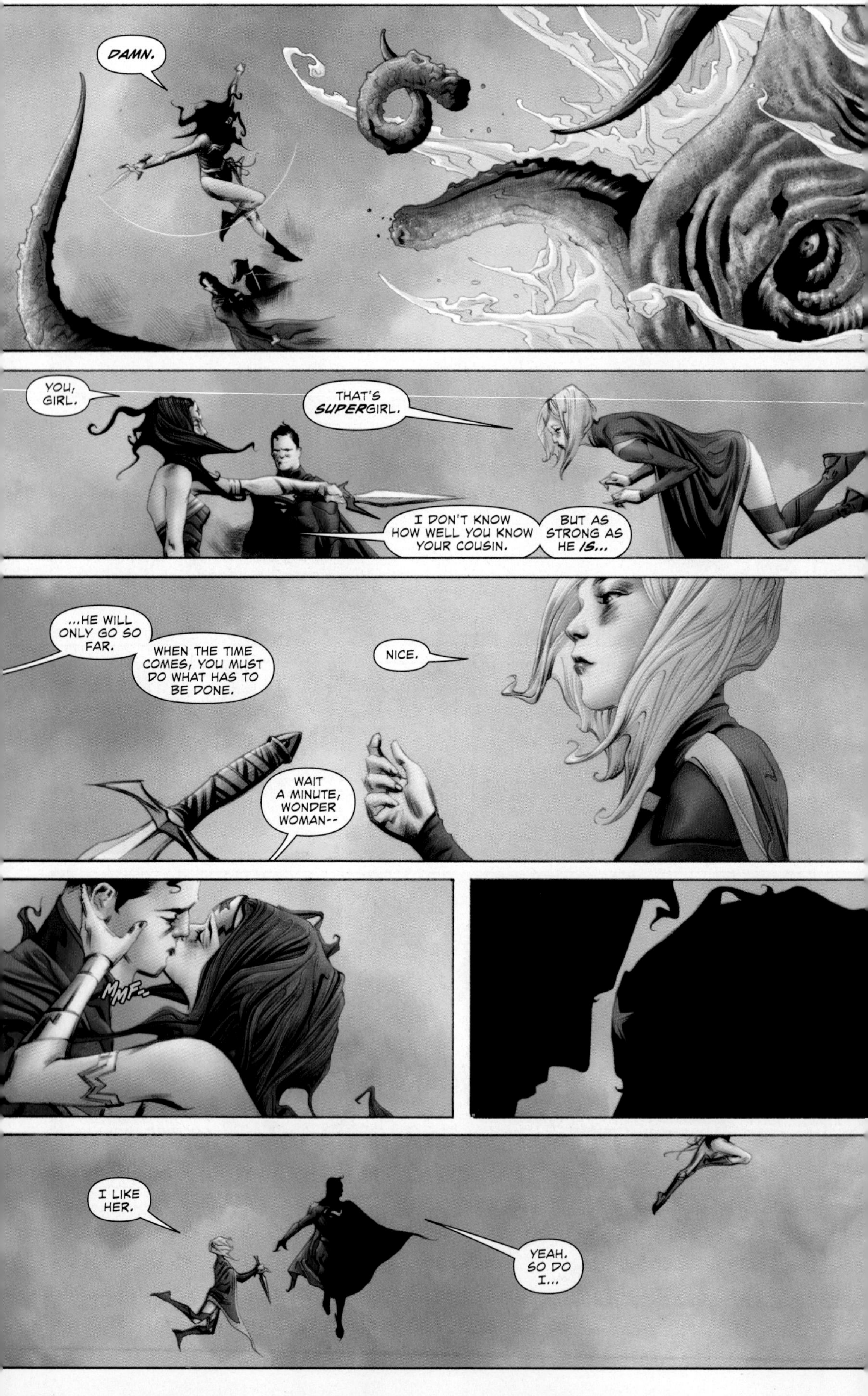
DAMN.
YOU, GIRL.
THAT'S SUPERGIRL.
I DON'T KNOW HOW WELL YOU KNOW YOUR COUSIN.
BUT AS STRONG AS HE IS...
...HE WILL ONLY GO SO FAR.
WHEN THE TIME COMES, YOU MUST DO WHAT HAS TO BE DONE.
NICE.
WAIT A MINUTE, WONDER WOMAN--
MMF--
I LIKE HER.
YEAH. SO DO I...

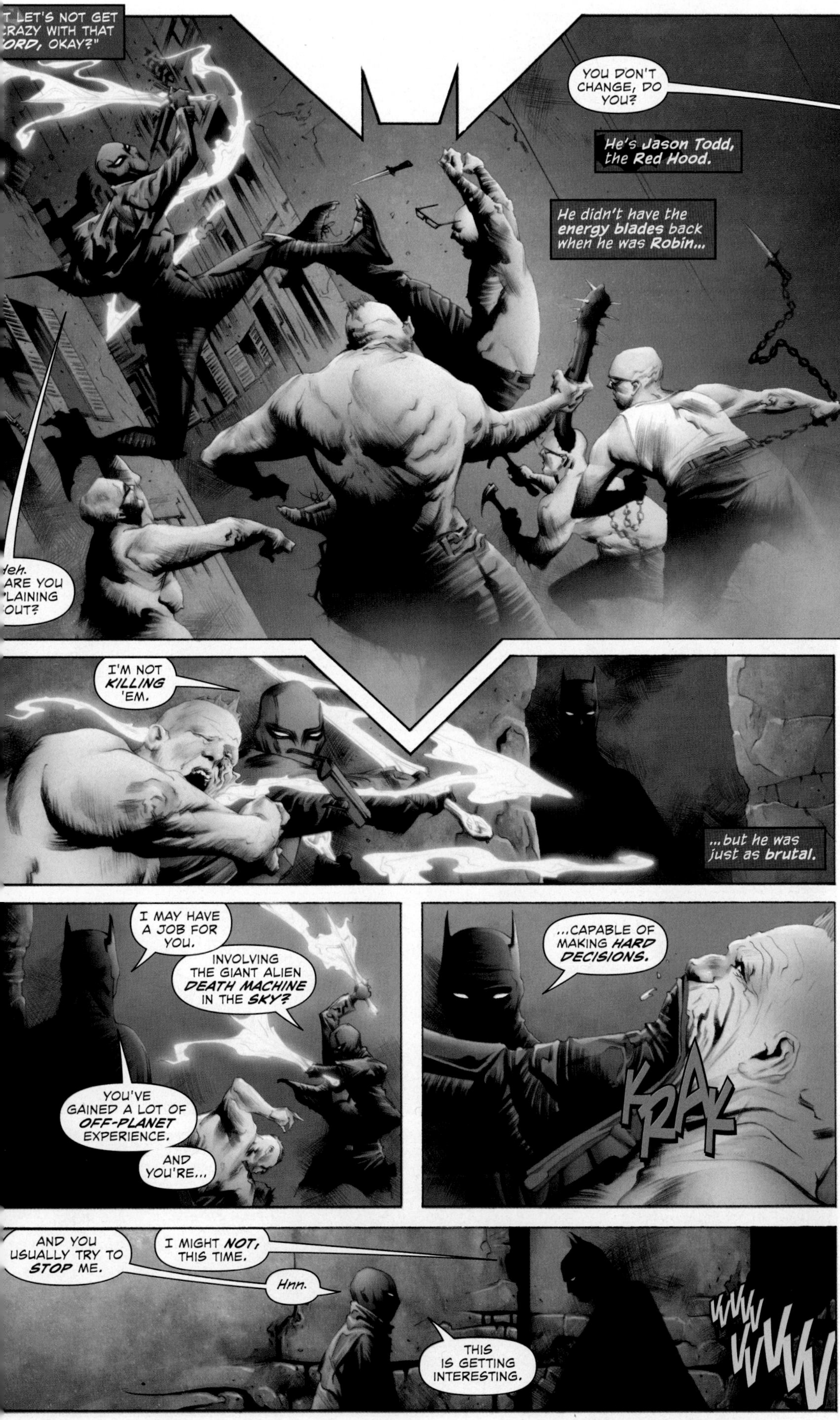

T LET'S NOT GET
CRAZY WITH THAT
ORD, OKAY?"
YOU DON'T CHANGE, DO YOU?
He's Jason Todd, the Red Hood.
He didn't have the energy blades back when he was Robin...
Heh. ARE YOU 'PLAINING OUT?
I'M NOT KILLING 'EM.
...but he was just as brutal.
I MAY HAVE A JOB FOR YOU.
INVOLVING THE GIANT ALIEN DEATH MACHINE IN THE SKY?
YOU'VE GAINED A LOT OF OFF-PLANET EXPERIENCE.
AND YOU'RE...
...CAPABLE OF MAKING HARD DECISIONS.
KRAK
AND YOU USUALLY TRY TO STOP ME.
I MIGHT NOT, THIS TIME.
Hnn.
THIS IS GETTING INTERESTING.
VVVVVVVVV

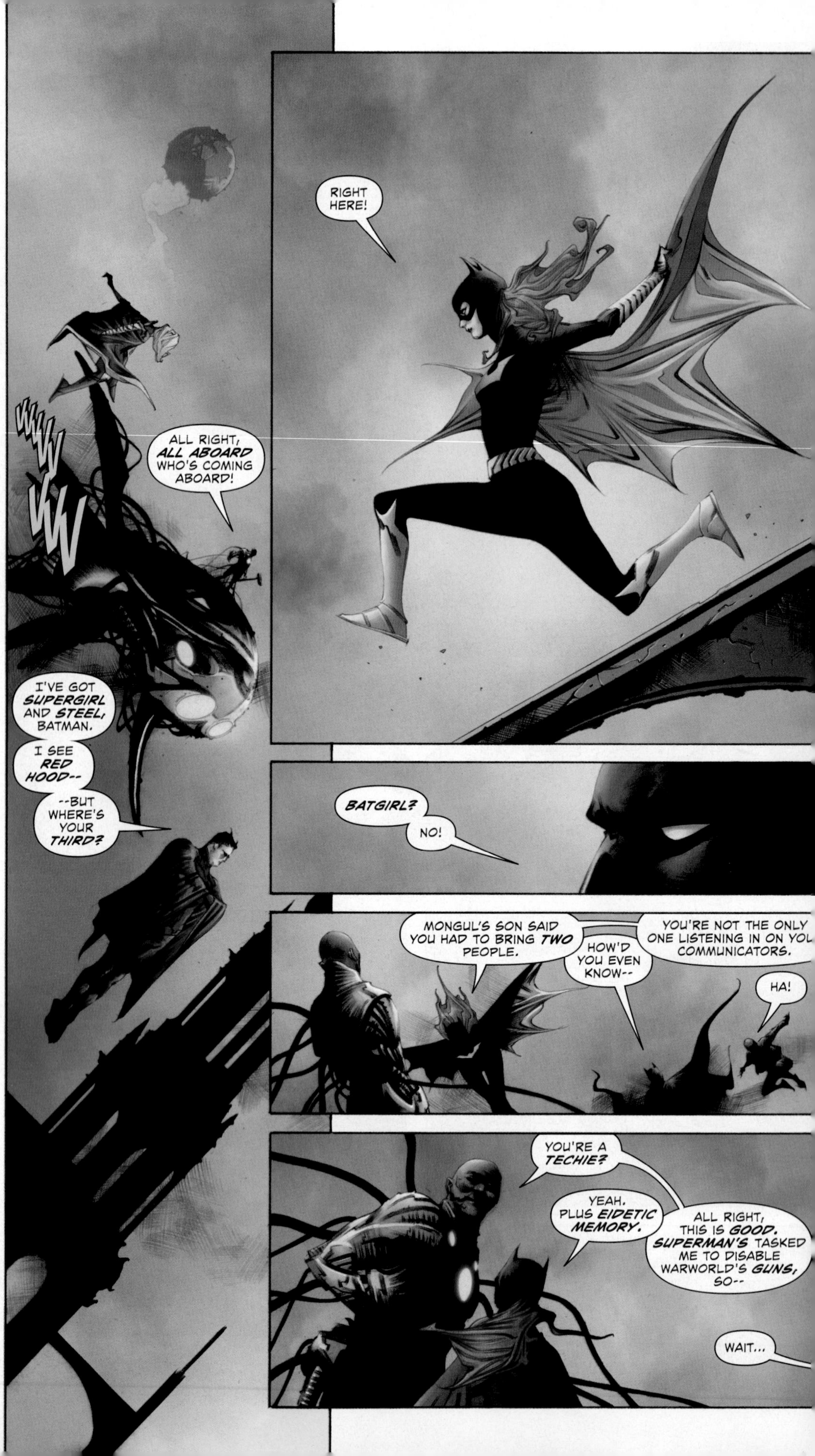
RIGHT HERE!
ALL RIGHT, ALL ABOARD WHO'S COMING ABOARD!
I'VE GOT SUPERGIRL AND STEEL, BATMAN.
I SEE RED HOOD--
--BUT WHERE'S YOUR THIRD?
BATGIRL?
NO!
MONGUL'S SON SAID YOU HAD TO BRING TWO PEOPLE.
HOW'D YOU EVEN KNOW--
YOU'RE NOT THE ONLY ONE LISTENING IN ON YOU COMMUNICATORS.
HA!
YOU'RE A TECHIE?
YEAH. PLUS EIDETIC MEMORY.
ALL RIGHT, THIS IS GOOD. SUPERMAN'S TASKED ME TO DISABLE WARWORLD'S GUNS, SO--
WAIT...

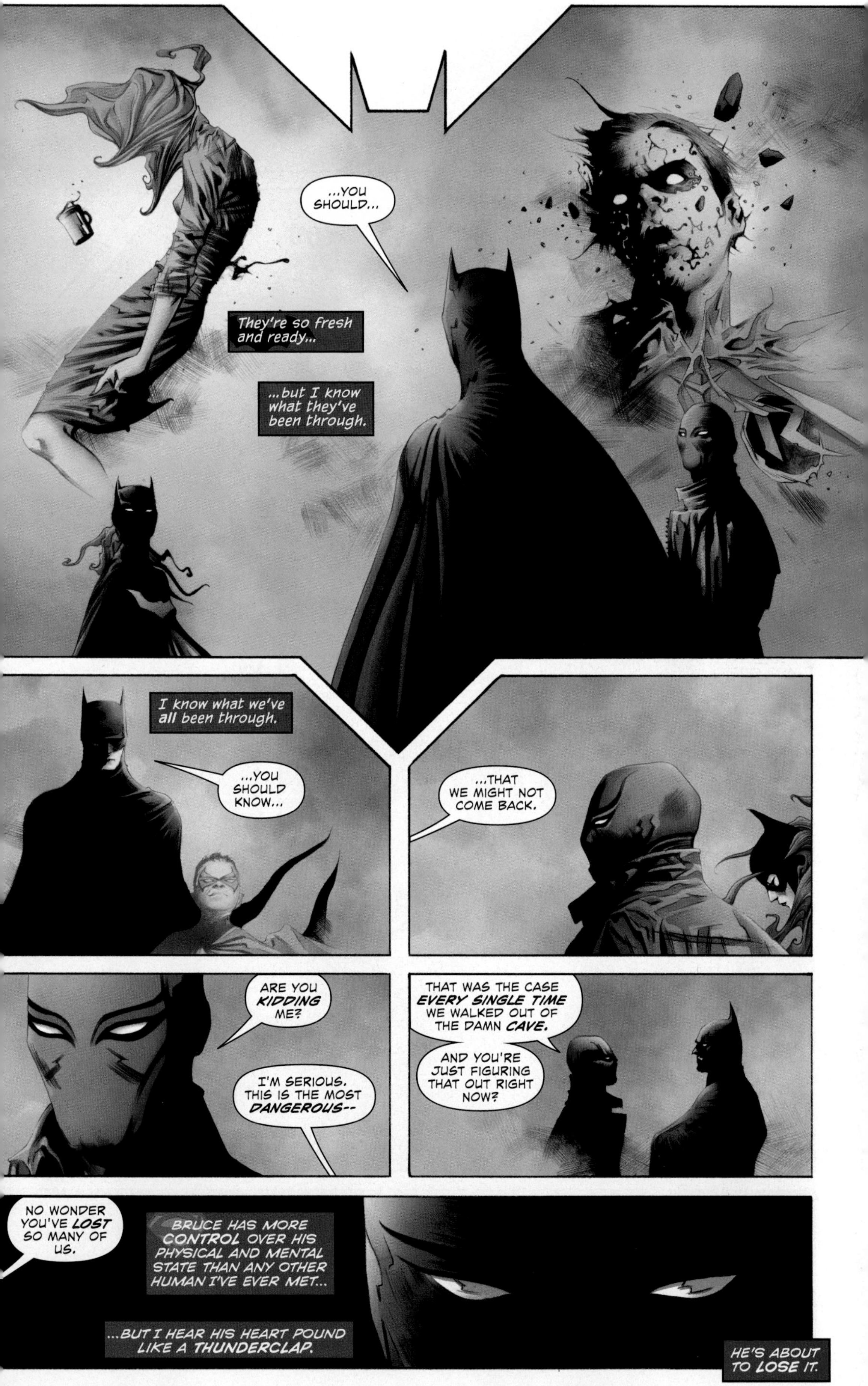
...YOU SHOULD...
They're so fresh and ready...
...but I know what they've been through.
I know what we've all been through.
...YOU SHOULD KNOW...
...THAT WE MIGHT NOT COME BACK.
ARE YOU KIDDING ME?
I'M SERIOUS. THIS IS THE MOST DANGEROUS--
THAT WAS THE CASE EVERY SINGLE TIME WE WALKED OUT OF THE DAMN CAVE.
AND YOU'RE JUST FIGURING THAT OUT RIGHT NOW?
NO WONDER YOU'VE LOST SO MANY OF US.
BRUCE HAS MORE CONTROL OVER HIS PHYSICAL AND MENTAL STATE THAN ANY OTHER HUMAN I'VE EVER MET...
...BUT I HEAR HIS HEART POUND LIKE A THUNDERCLAP.
HE'S ABOUT TO LOSE IT.

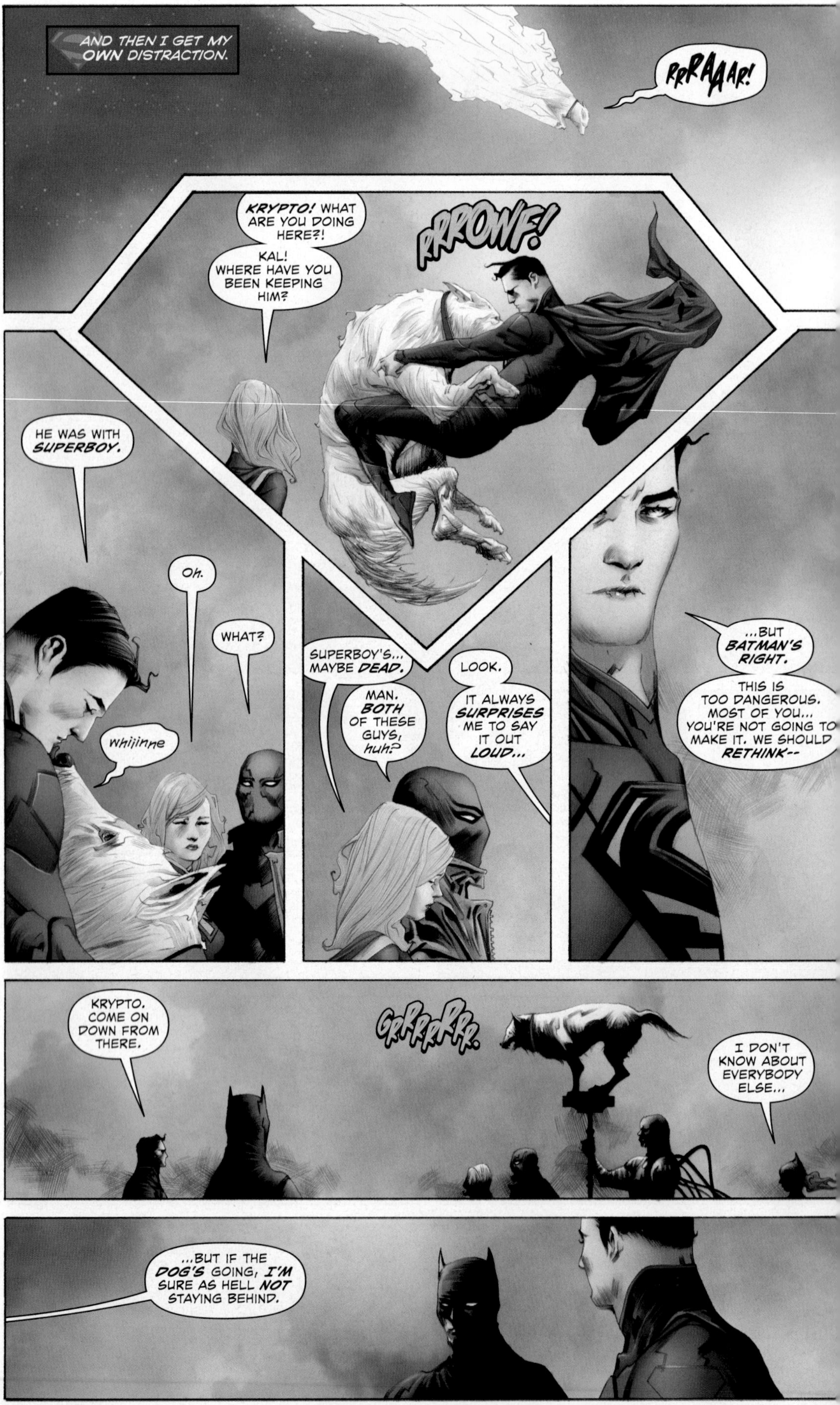

AND THEN I GET MY OWN DISTRACTION.
RRRAAAAR!
KRYPTO! WHAT ARE YOU DOING HERE?!
KAL! WHERE HAVE YOU BEEN KEEPING HIM?
RRROWF!
HE WAS WITH SUPERBOY.
Oh.
WHAT?
whiiinne
SUPERBOY'S... MAYBE DEAD.
MAN. BOTH OF THESE GUYS, huh?
LOOK.
IT ALWAYS SURPRISES ME TO SAY IT OUT LOUD...
...BUT BATMAN'S RIGHT.
THIS IS TOO DANGEROUS. MOST OF YOU... YOU'RE NOT GOING TO MAKE IT. WE SHOULD RETHINK--
KRYPTO. COME ON DOWN FROM THERE.
GRRRRRR.
I DON'T KNOW ABOUT EVERYBODY ELSE...
...BUT IF THE DOG'S GOING, I'M SURE AS HELL NOT STAYING BEHIND.

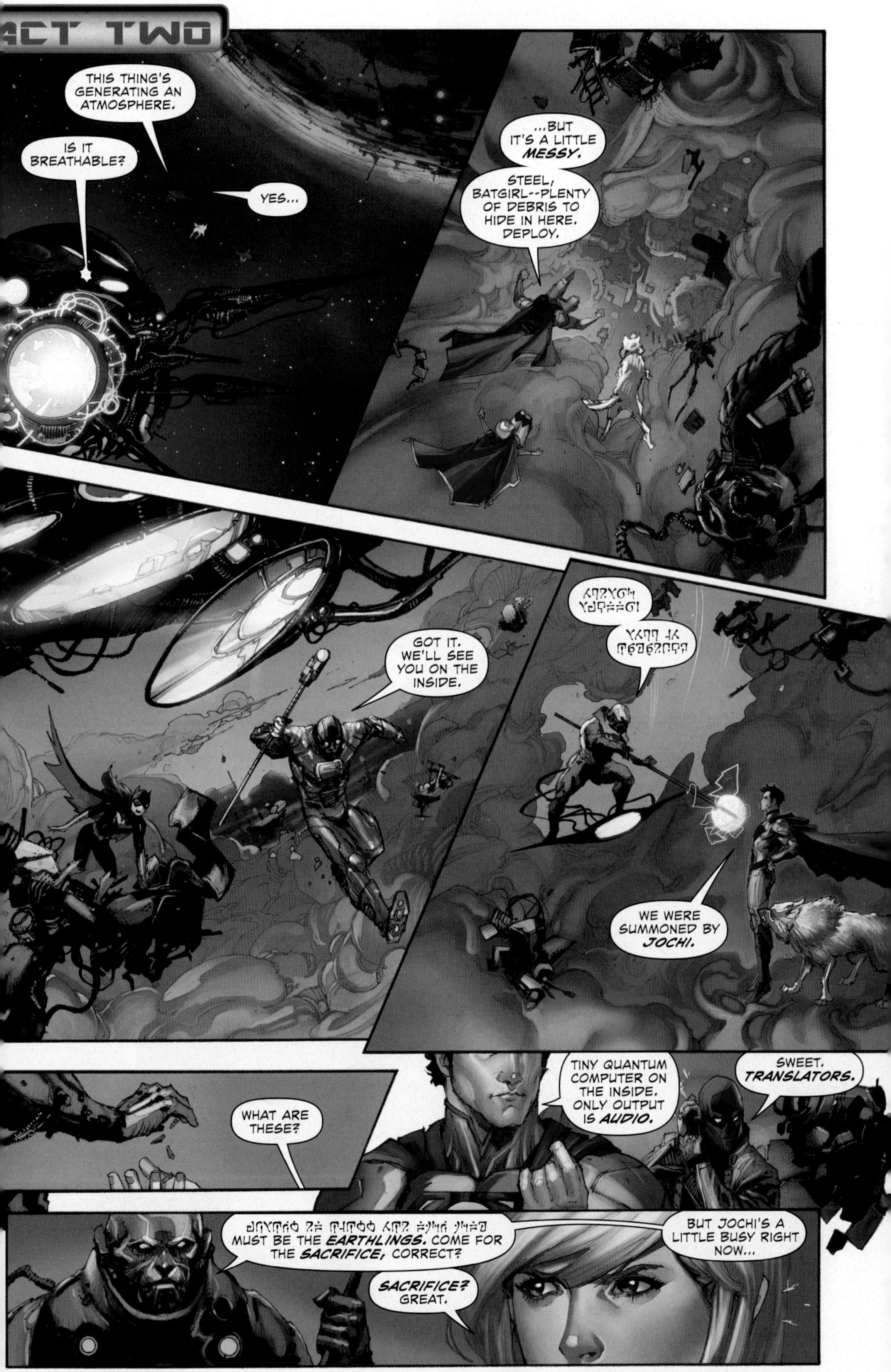
ACT TWO
THIS THING'S GENERATING AN ATMOSPHERE.
IS IT BREATHABLE?
YES...
...BUT IT'S A LITTLE MESSY.
STEEL, BATGIRL--PLENTY OF DEBRIS TO HIDE IN HERE. DEPLOY.
GOT IT. WE'LL SEE YOU ON THE INSIDE.
WE WERE SUMMONED BY JOCHI.
WHAT ARE THESE?
TINY QUANTUM COMPUTER ON THE INSIDE. ONLY OUTPUT IS AUDIO.
SWEET. TRANSLATORS.
MUST BE THE EARTHLINGS. COME FOR THE SACRIFICE, CORRECT?
BUT JOCHI'S A LITTLE BUSY RIGHT NOW...
SACRIFICE? GREAT.

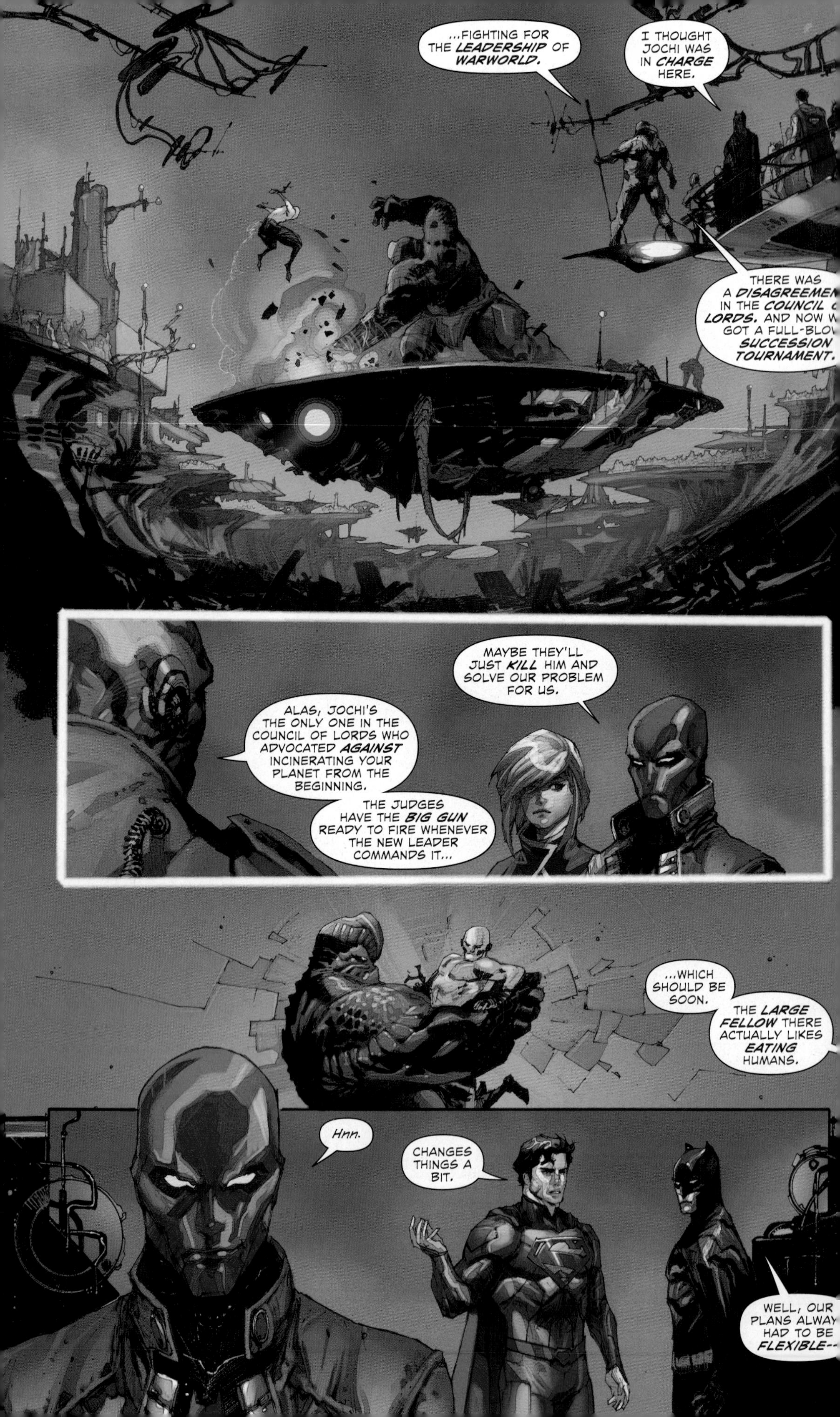
...FIGHTING FOR THE LEADERSHIP OF WARWORLD.
I THOUGHT JOCHI WAS IN CHARGE HERE.
THERE WAS A DISAGREEMEN IN THE COUNCIL LORDS. AND NOW W GOT A FULL-BLOW SUCCESSION TOURNAMENT.
MAYBE THEY'LL JUST KILL HIM AND SOLVE OUR PROBLEM FOR US.
ALAS, JOCHI'S THE ONLY ONE IN THE COUNCIL OF LORDS WHO ADVOCATED AGAINST INCINERATING YOUR PLANET FROM THE BEGINNING.
THE JUDGES HAVE THE BIG GUN READY TO FIRE WHENEVER THE NEW LEADER COMMANDS IT...
...WHICH SHOULD BE SOON.
THE LARGE FELLOW THERE ACTUALLY LIKES EATING HUMANS.
Hnn.
CHANGES THINGS A BIT.
WELL, OUR PLANS ALWAY HAD TO BE FLEXIBLE--

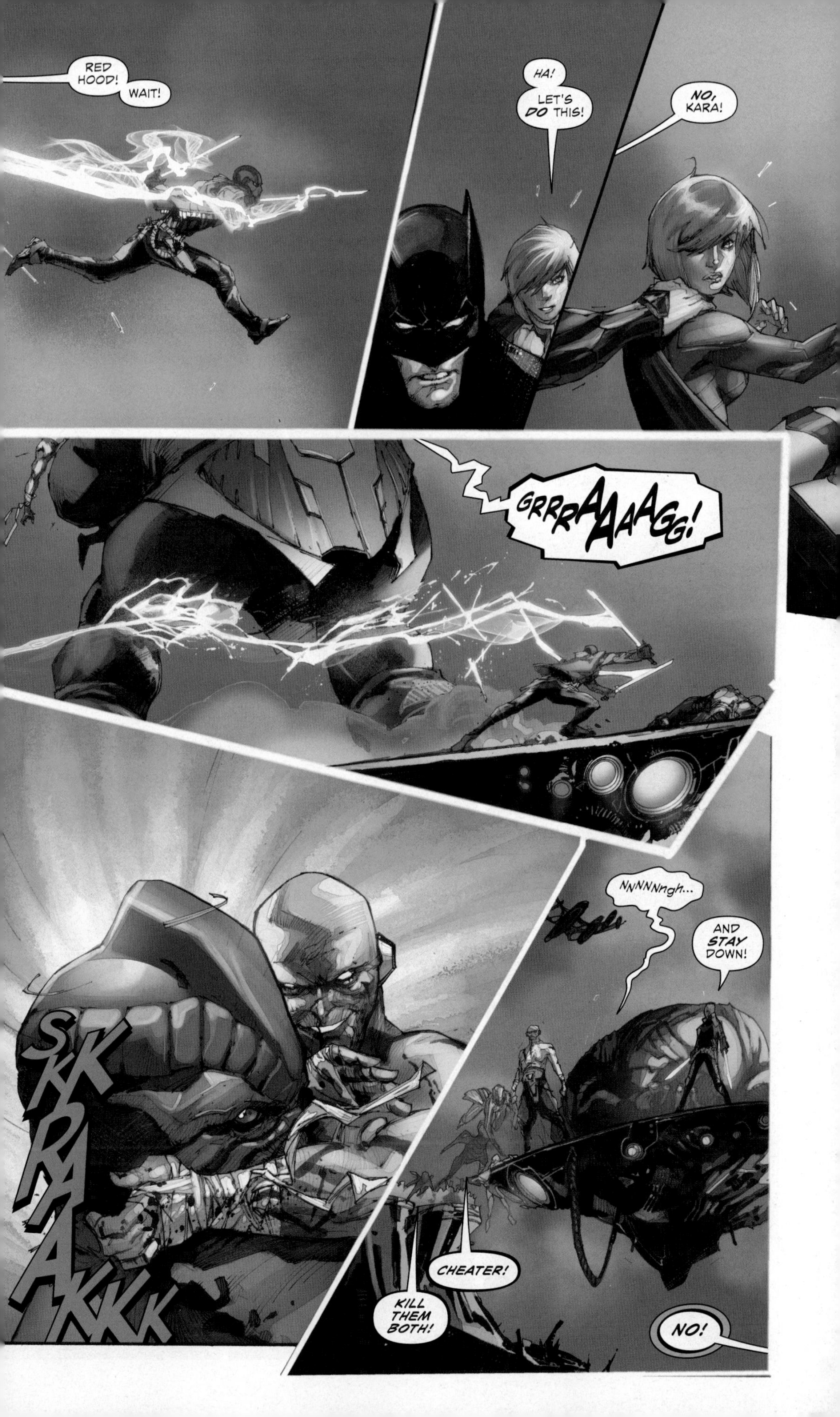
RED HOOD!
WAIT!
HA!
LET'S DO THIS!
NO, KARA!
GRRRAAAAGG!
NNNNNngh...
AND STAY DOWN!
SKRAKKK
CHEATER!
KILL THEM BOTH!
NO!

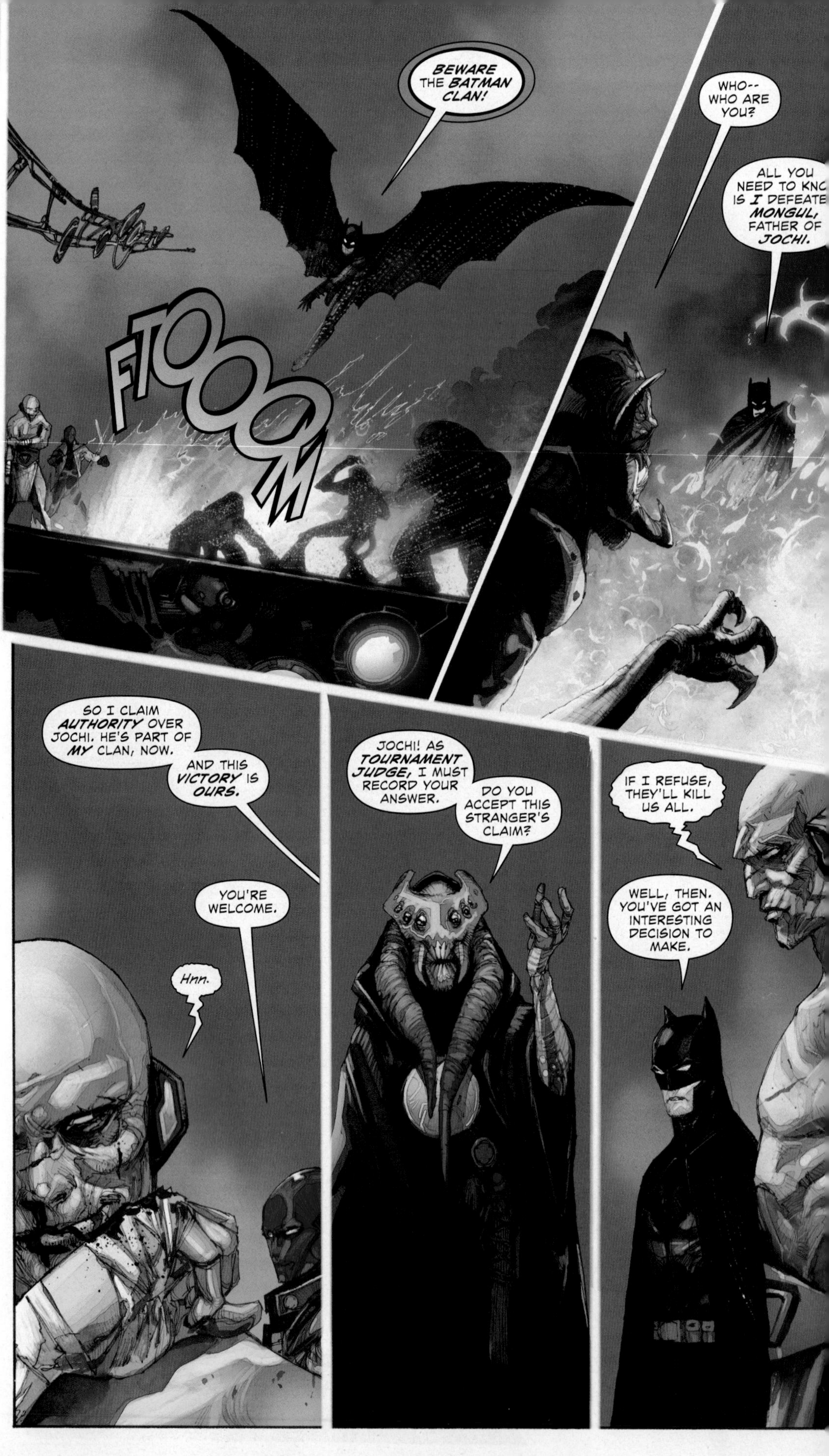
BEWARE THE BATMAN CLAN!
FTOOOM
WHO-- WHO ARE YOU?
ALL YOU NEED TO KNO IS I DEFEATE MONGUL, FATHER OF JOCHI.
SO I CLAIM AUTHORITY OVER JOCHI. HE'S PART OF MY CLAN, NOW.
AND THIS VICTORY IS OURS.
YOU'RE WELCOME.
Hnn.
JOCHI! AS TOURNAMENT JUDGE, I MUST RECORD YOUR ANSWER.
DO YOU ACCEPT THIS STRANGER'S CLAIM?
IF I REFUSE, THEY'LL KILL US ALL.
WELL, THEN. YOU'VE GOT AN INTERESTING DECISION TO MAKE.

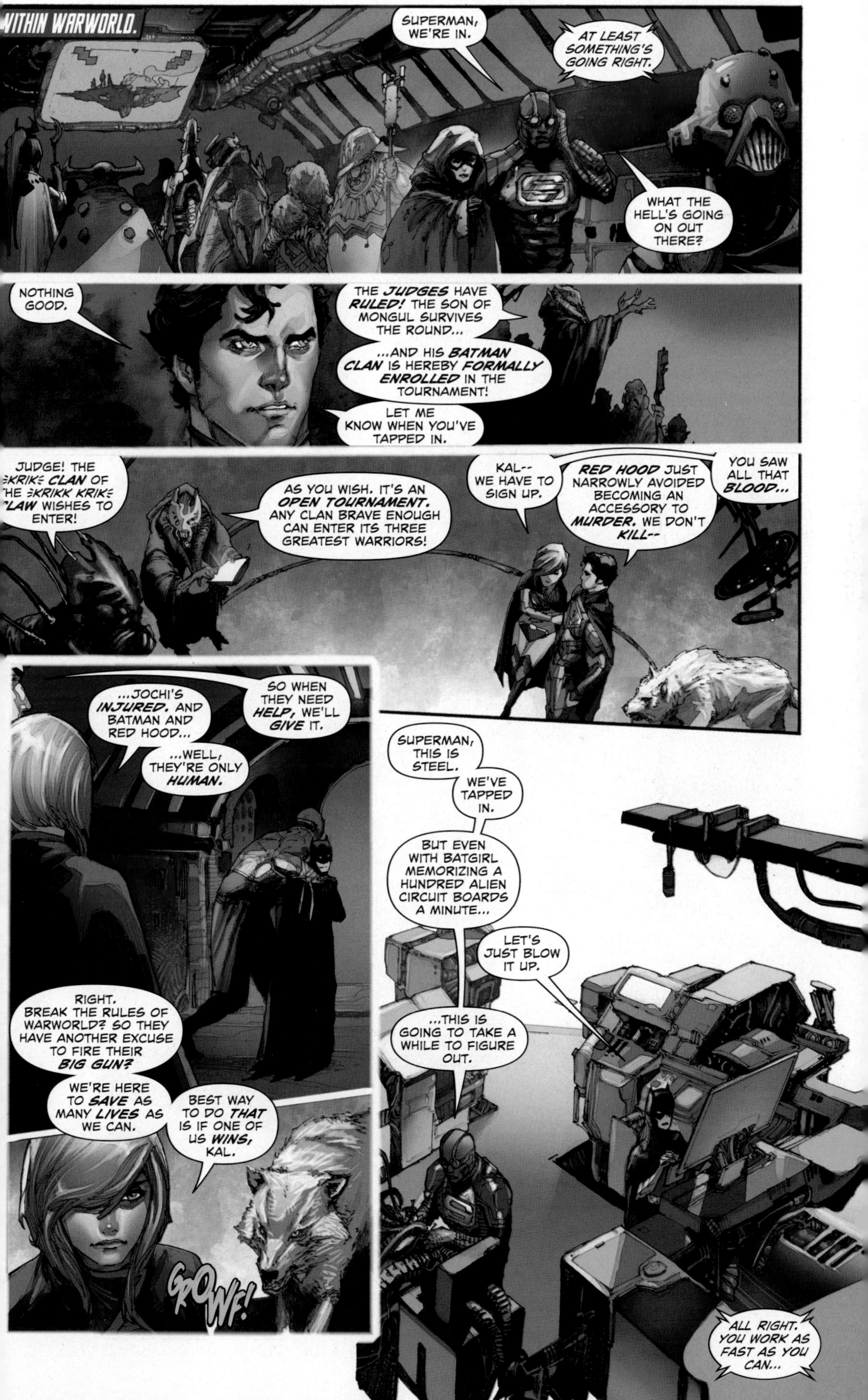
WITHIN WARWORLD.
SUPERMAN, WE'RE IN.
AT LEAST SOMETHING'S GOING RIGHT.
WHAT THE HELL'S GOING ON OUT THERE?
NOTHING GOOD.
THE JUDGES HAVE RULED! THE SON OF MONGUL SURVIVES THE ROUND...
...AND HIS BATMAN CLAN IS HEREBY FORMALLY ENROLLED IN THE TOURNAMENT!
LET ME KNOW WHEN YOU'VE TAPPED IN.
JUDGE! THE ƎKRIKƎ CLAN OF THE ƎKRIKK KRIKƎ CLAW WISHES TO ENTER!
AS YOU WISH. IT'S AN OPEN TOURNAMENT. ANY CLAN BRAVE ENOUGH CAN ENTER ITS THREE GREATEST WARRIORS!
KAL-- WE HAVE TO SIGN UP.
RED HOOD JUST NARROWLY AVOIDED BECOMING AN ACCESSORY TO MURDER. WE DON'T KILL--
YOU SAW ALL THAT BLOOD...
...JOCHI'S INJURED. AND BATMAN AND RED HOOD...
SO WHEN THEY NEED HELP, WE'LL GIVE IT.
...WELL, THEY'RE ONLY HUMAN.
RIGHT. BREAK THE RULES OF WARWORLD? SO THEY HAVE ANOTHER EXCUSE TO FIRE THEIR BIG GUN?
WE'RE HERE TO SAVE AS MANY LIVES AS WE CAN.
BEST WAY TO DO THAT IS IF ONE OF US WINS, KAL.
GROWF!
SUPERMAN, THIS IS STEEL.
WE'VE TAPPED IN.
BUT EVEN WITH BATGIRL MEMORIZING A HUNDRED ALIEN CIRCUIT BOARDS A MINUTE...
LET'S JUST BLOW IT UP.
...THIS IS GOING TO TAKE A WHILE TO FIGURE OUT.
ALL RIGHT. YOU WORK AS FAST AS YOU CAN...

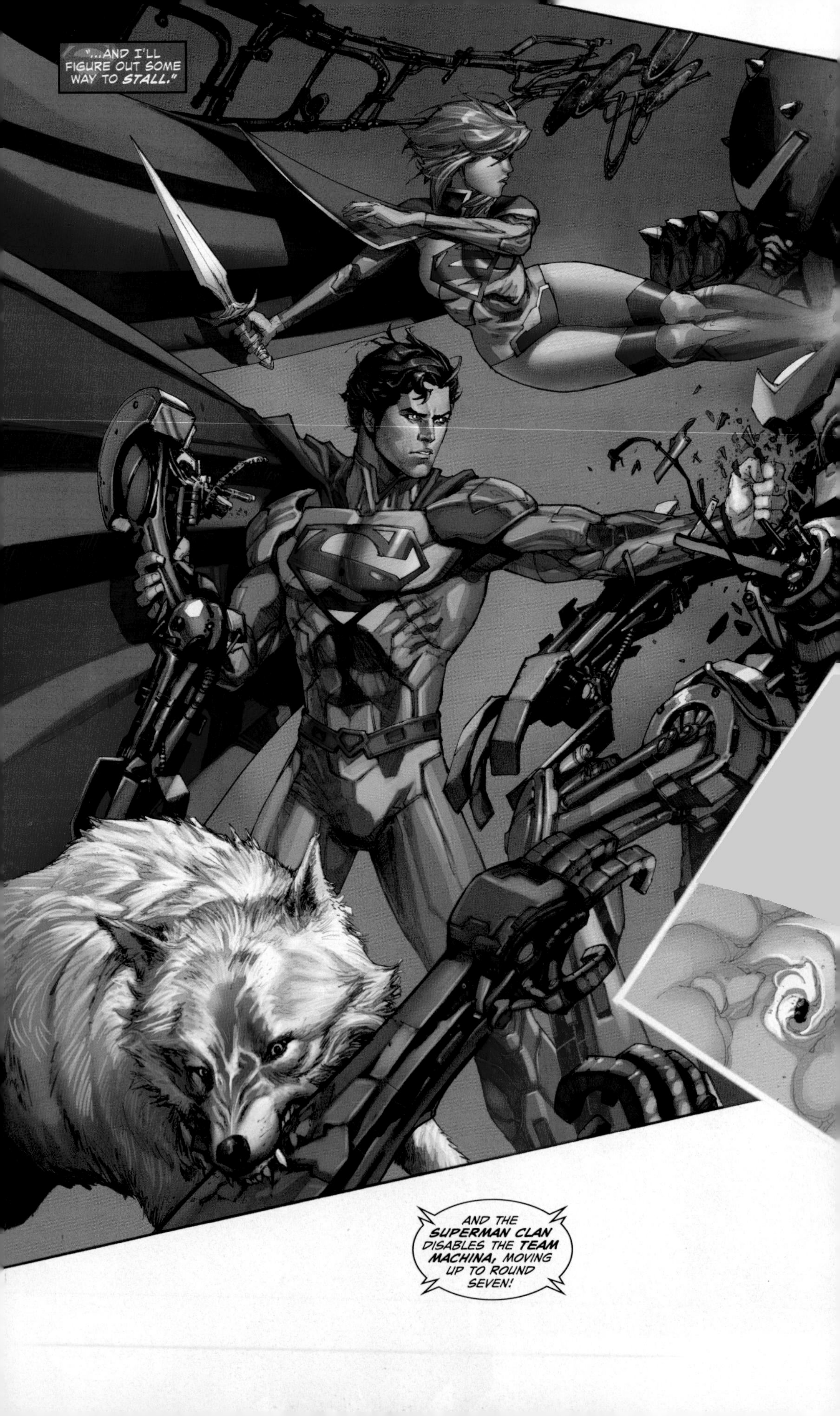
"...AND I'LL FIGURE OUT SOME WAY TO STALL."
AND THE SUPERMAN CLAN DISABLES THE TEAM MACHINA, MOVING UP TO ROUND SEVEN!

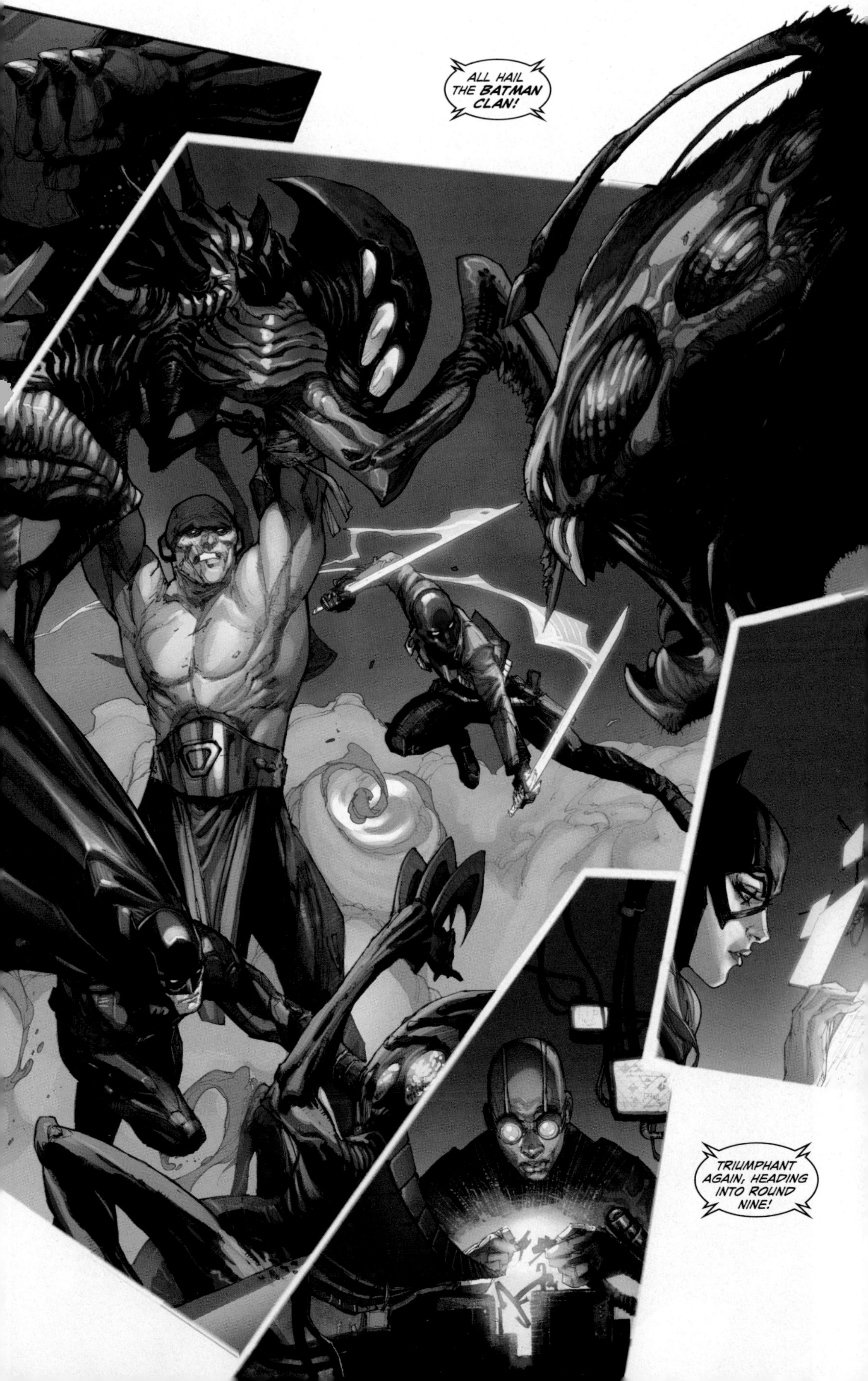
ALL HAIL THE BATMAN CLAN!
TRIUMPHANT AGAIN, HEADING INTO ROUND NINE!

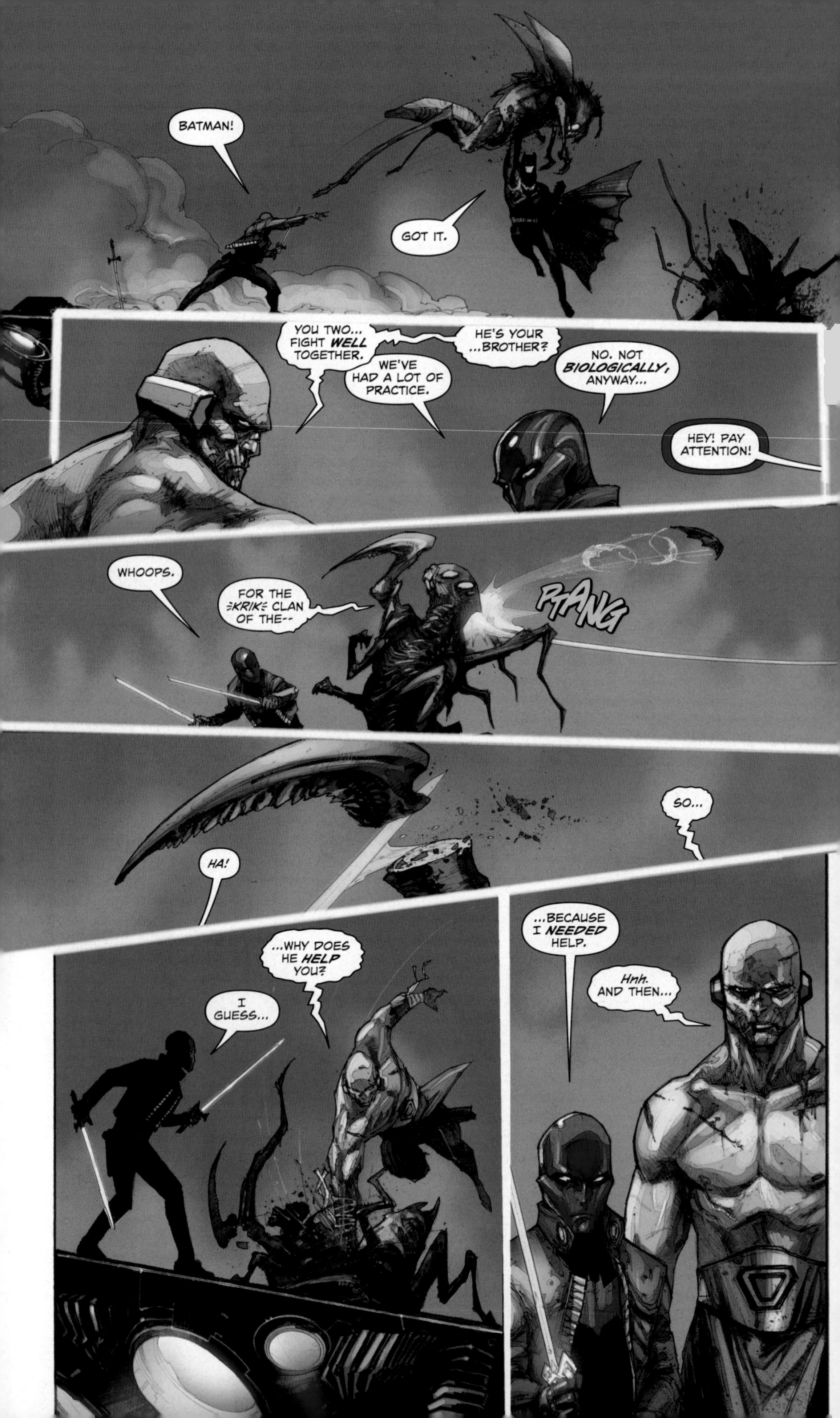
BATMAN!
GOT IT.
YOU TWO... FIGHT WELL TOGETHER.
HE'S YOUR ...BROTHER?
WE'VE HAD A LOT OF PRACTICE.
NO. NOT BIOLOGICALLY, ANYWAY...
HEY! PAY ATTENTION!
WHOOPS.
FOR THE ≡KRIK≡ CLAN OF THE--
PTANG
HA!
SO...
...WHY DOES HE HELP YOU?
I GUESS...
...BECAUSE I NEEDED HELP.
Hnh. AND THEN...

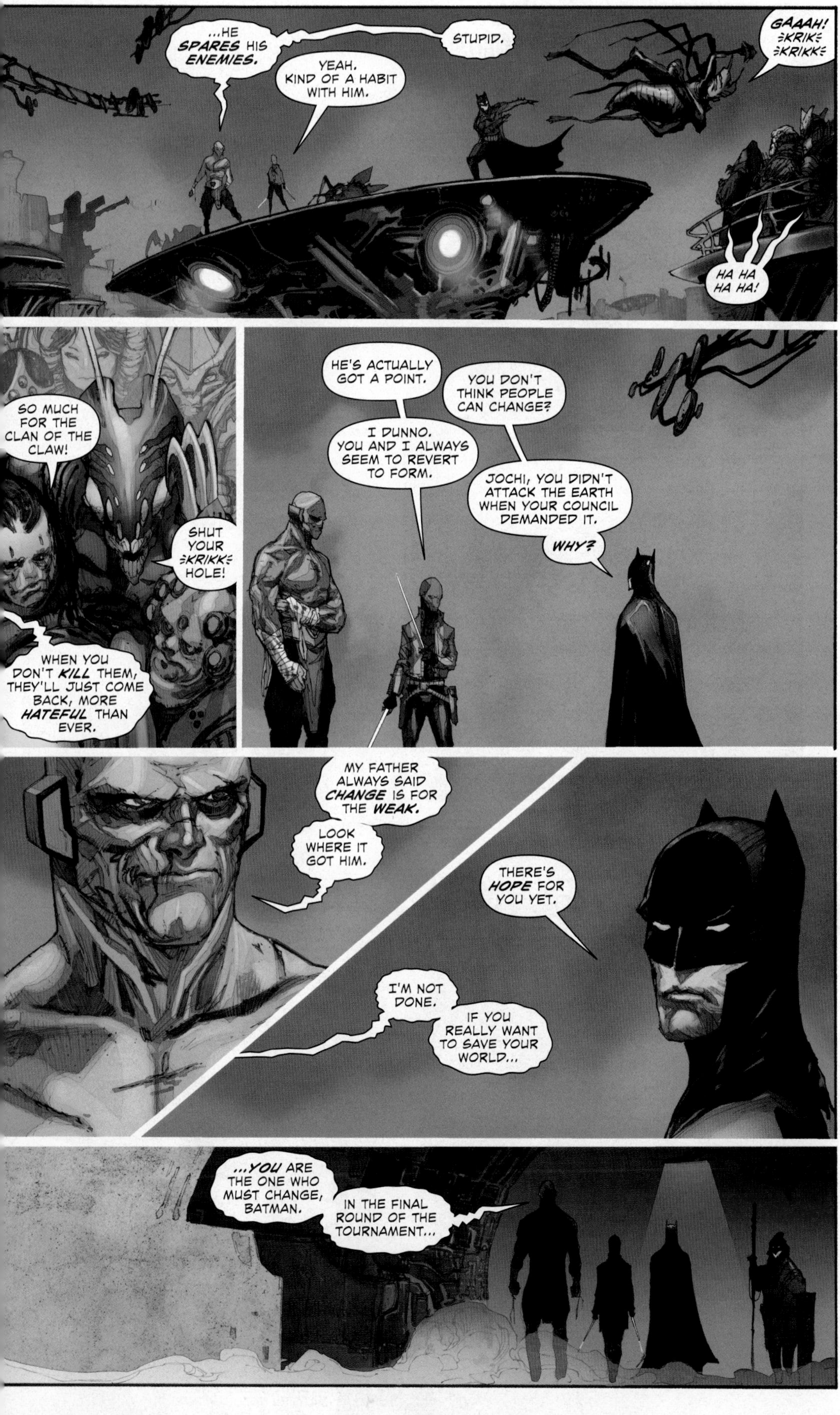
...HE SPARES HIS ENEMIES.
STUPID.
YEAH. KIND OF A HABIT WITH HIM.
GAAAH! ≶KRIK≶ ≶KRIKK≶
HA HA HA HA!
SO MUCH FOR THE CLAN OF THE CLAW!
SHUT YOUR ≶KRIKK≶ HOLE!
WHEN YOU DON'T KILL THEM, THEY'LL JUST COME BACK, MORE HATEFUL THAN EVER.
HE'S ACTUALLY GOT A POINT.
YOU DON'T THINK PEOPLE CAN CHANGE?
I DUNNO. YOU AND I ALWAYS SEEM TO REVERT TO FORM.
JOCHI, YOU DIDN'T ATTACK THE EARTH WHEN YOUR COUNCIL DEMANDED IT.
WHY?
MY FATHER ALWAYS SAID CHANGE IS FOR THE WEAK.
LOOK WHERE IT GOT HIM.
THERE'S HOPE FOR YOU YET.
I'M NOT DONE.
IF YOU REALLY WANT TO SAVE YOUR WORLD...
...YOU ARE THE ONE WHO MUST CHANGE, BATMAN.
IN THE FINAL ROUND OF THE TOURNAMENT...

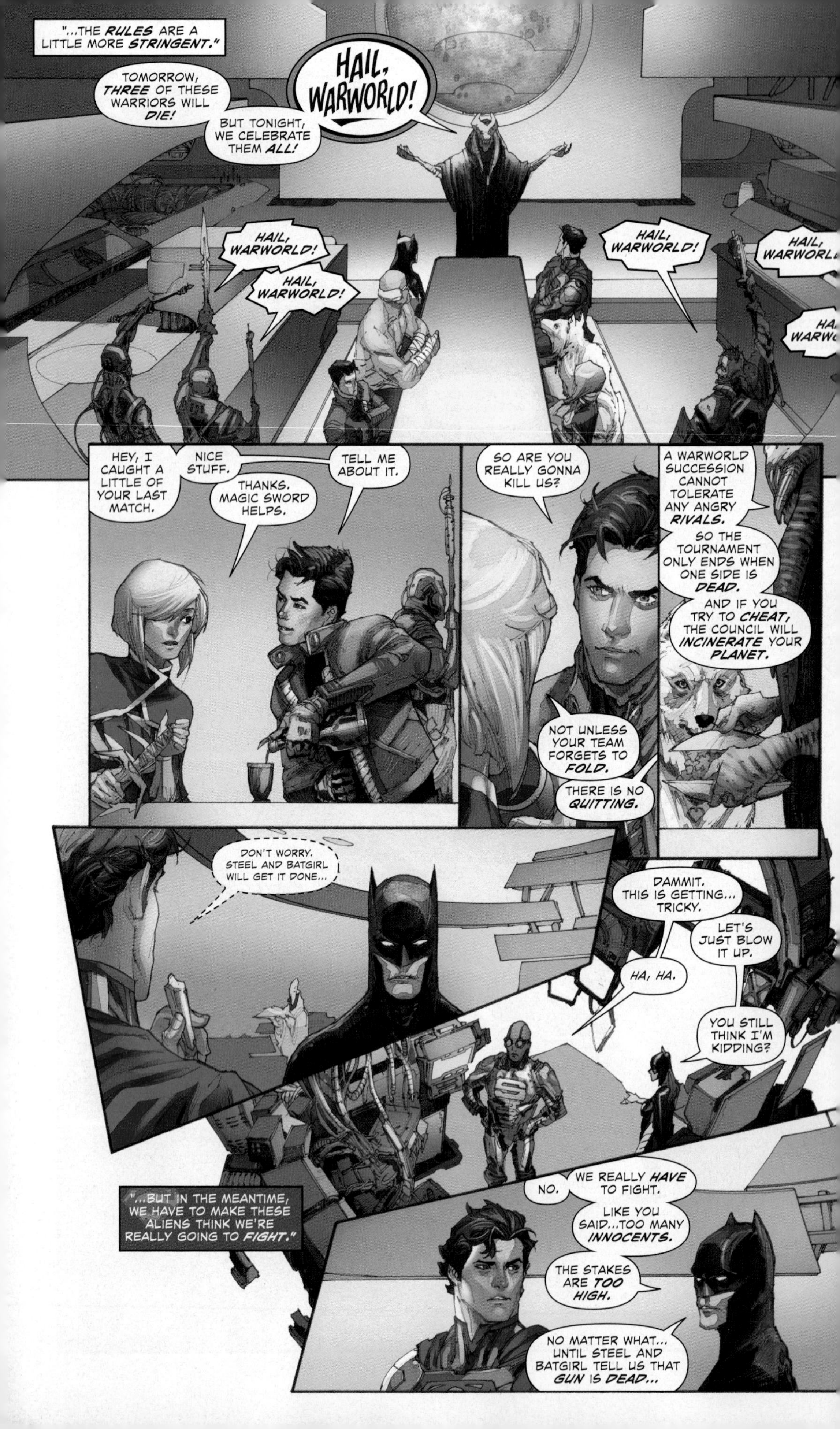
"...THE RULES ARE A LITTLE MORE STRINGENT."
TOMORROW, THREE OF THESE WARRIORS WILL DIE!
BUT TONIGHT, WE CELEBRATE THEM ALL!
HAIL, WARWORLD!
HAIL, WARWORLD!
HAIL, WARWORLD!
HAIL, WARWORLD!
HAIL, WARWORL
HAIL, WARWO
HEY, I CAUGHT A LITTLE OF YOUR LAST MATCH.
NICE STUFF.
THANKS. MAGIC SWORD HELPS.
TELL ME ABOUT IT.
SO ARE YOU REALLY GONNA KILL US?
A WARWORLD SUCCESSION CANNOT TOLERATE ANY ANGRY RIVALS.
SO THE TOURNAMENT ONLY ENDS WHEN ONE SIDE IS DEAD.
AND IF YOU TRY TO CHEAT, THE COUNCIL WILL INCINERATE YOUR PLANET.
NOT UNLESS YOUR TEAM FORGETS TO FOLD.
THERE IS NO QUITTING.
DON'T WORRY. STEEL AND BATGIRL WILL GET IT DONE...
DAMMIT. THIS IS GETTING... TRICKY.
LET'S JUST BLOW IT UP.
HA, HA.
YOU STILL THINK I'M KIDDING?
"...BUT IN THE MEANTIME, WE HAVE TO MAKE THESE ALIENS THINK WE'RE REALLY GOING TO FIGHT."
NO.
WE REALLY HAVE TO FIGHT.
LIKE YOU SAID...TOO MANY INNOCENTS.
THE STAKES ARE TOO HIGH.
NO MATTER WHAT... UNTIL STEEL AND BATGIRL TELL US THAT GUN IS DEAD...

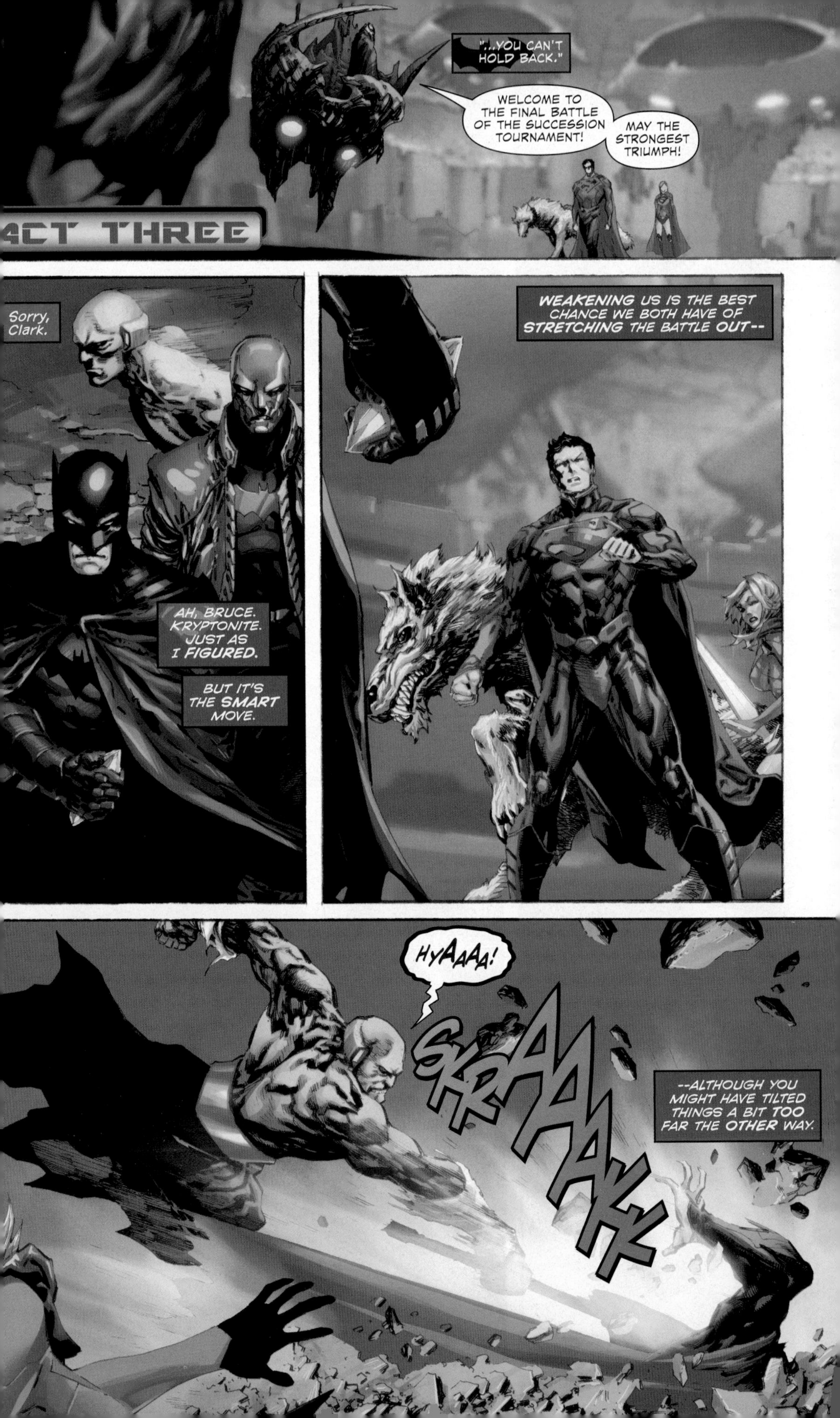
"...YOU CAN'T HOLD BACK."
WELCOME TO THE FINAL BATTLE OF THE SUCCESSION TOURNAMENT!
MAY THE STRONGEST TRIUMPH!
ACT THREE
Sorry, Clark.
AH, BRUCE. KRYPTONITE. JUST AS I FIGURED.
BUT IT'S THE SMART MOVE.
WEAKENING US IS THE BEST CHANCE WE BOTH HAVE OF STRETCHING THE BATTLE OUT--
HYAAAA!
SKRAAAAKK
--ALTHOUGH YOU MIGHT HAVE TILTED THINGS A BIT TOO FAR THE OTHER WAY.

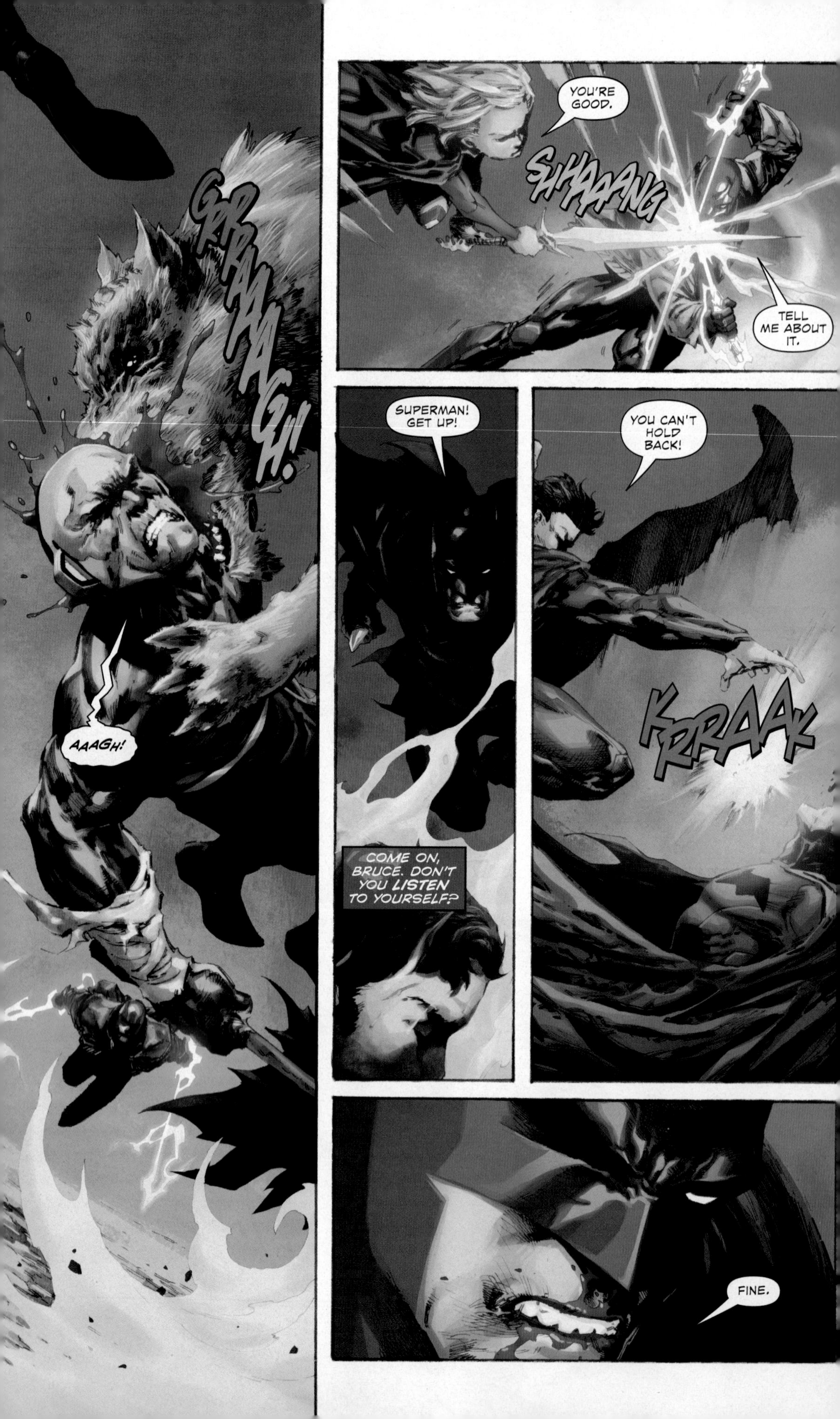
GRRAAAAAAAGH!!
AAAGH!
YOU'RE GOOD.
SHHAAAANG
TELL ME ABOUT IT.
SUPERMAN! GET UP!
COME ON, BRUCE. DON'T YOU LISTEN TO YOURSELF?
YOU CAN'T HOLD BACK!
KRAAK
FINE.

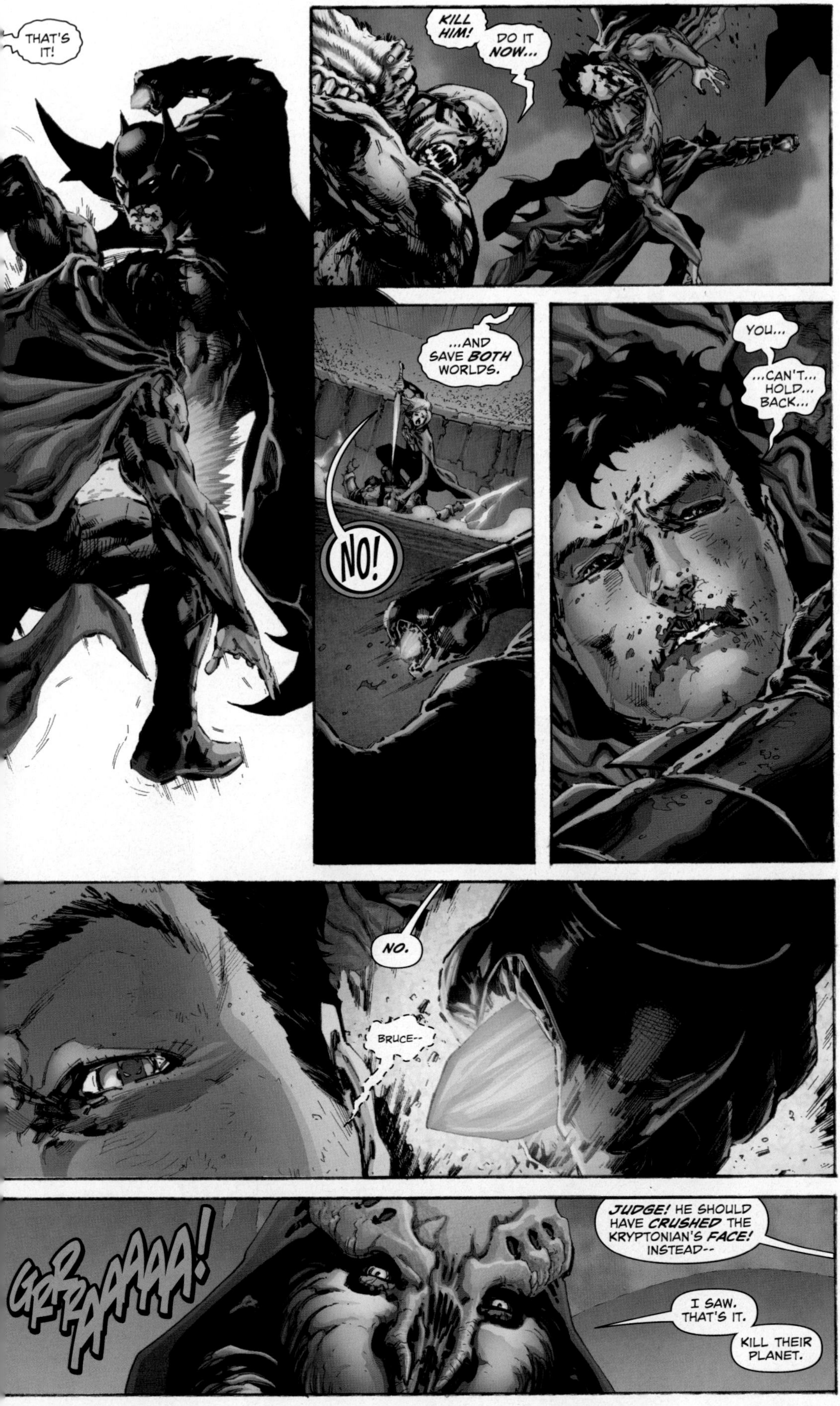

THAT'S IT!
KILL HIM!
DO IT NOW...
...AND SAVE BOTH WORLDS.
NO!
YOU...
...CAN'T... HOLD... BACK...
NO.
BRUCE--
GRRAAAAA!
JUDGE! HE SHOULD HAVE CRUSHED THE KRYPTONIAN'S FACE! INSTEAD--
I SAW. THAT'S IT.
KILL THEIR PLANET.

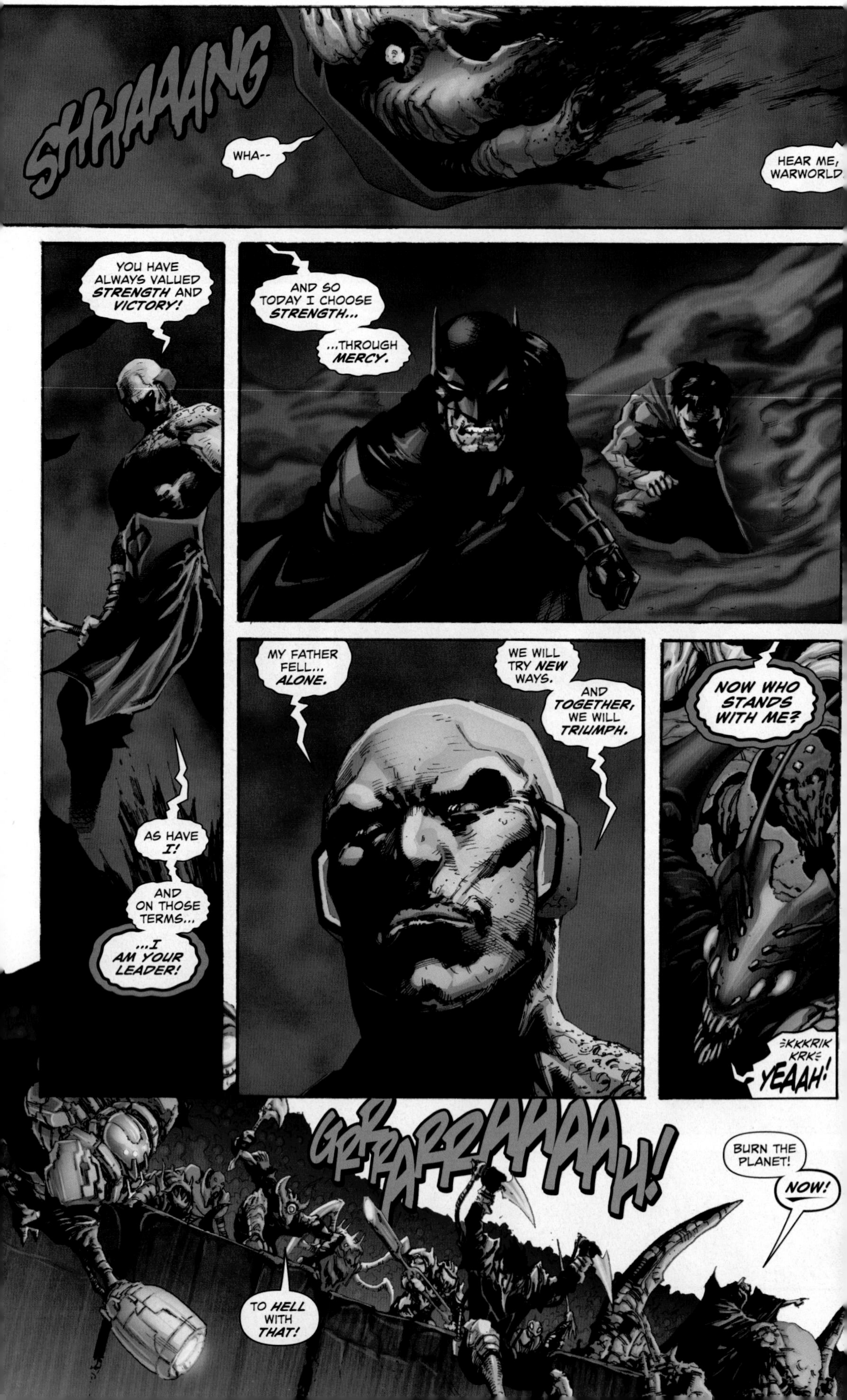
SHHAAANG
WHA--
HEAR ME, WARWORLD.
YOU HAVE ALWAYS VALUED STRENGTH AND VICTORY!
AND SO TODAY I CHOOSE STRENGTH...
...THROUGH MERCY.
AS HAVE I!
AND ON THOSE TERMS...
...I AM YOUR LEADER!
MY FATHER FELL... ALONE.
WE WILL TRY NEW WAYS.
AND TOGETHER, WE WILL TRIUMPH.
NOW WHO STANDS WITH ME?
KKKRIK KRK YEAAH!
GRRARRAAAAAH!
BURN THE PLANET!
NOW!
TO HELL WITH THAT!

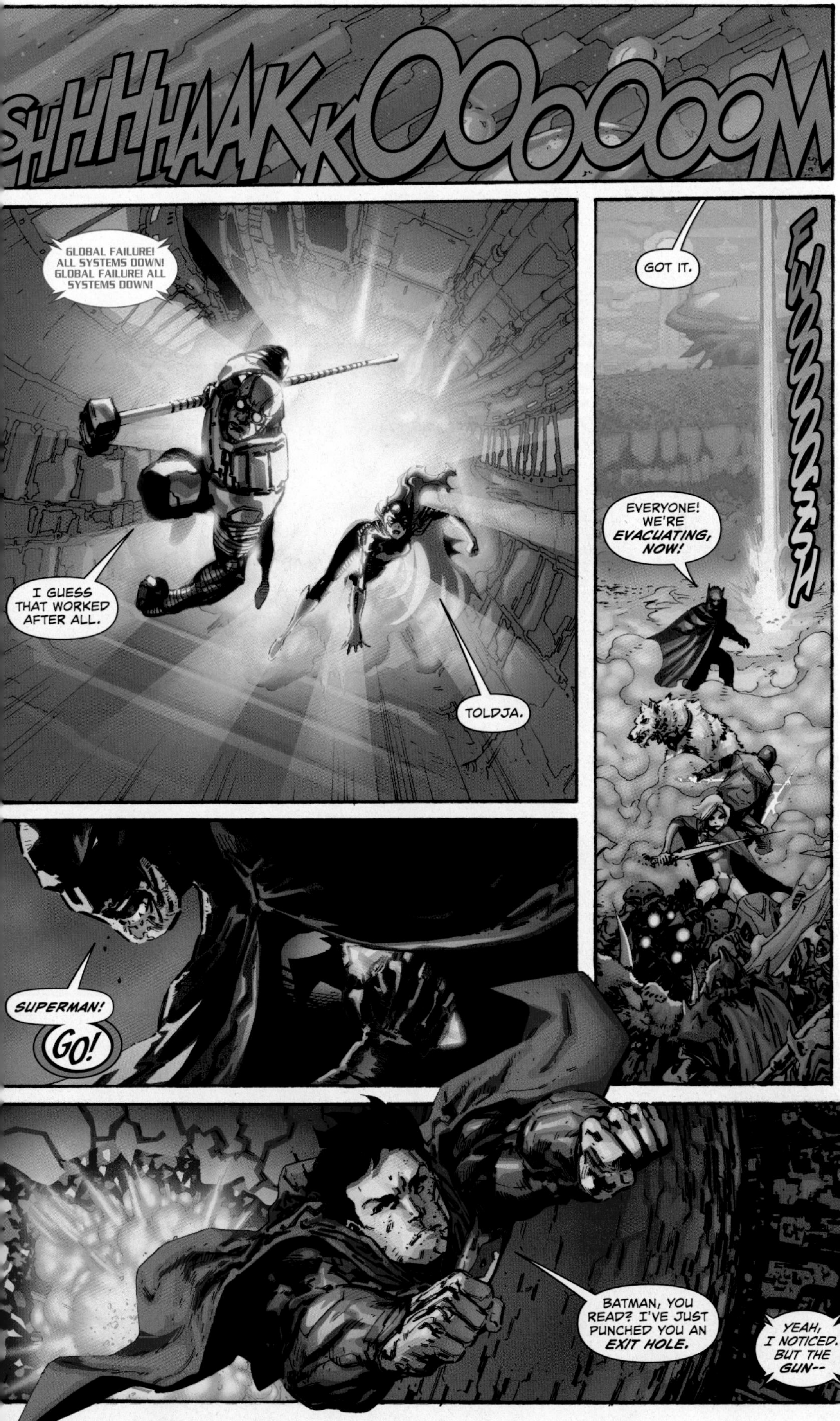
SHHHAAKKOOOOOOOM
GLOBAL FAILURE! ALL SYSTEMS DOWN! GLOBAL FAILURE! ALL SYSTEMS DOWN!
I GUESS THAT WORKED AFTER ALL.
TOLDJA.
GOT IT.
EVERYONE! WE'RE EVACUATING, NOW!
SUPERMAN!
GO!
BATMAN, YOU READ? I'VE JUST PUNCHED YOU AN EXIT HOLE.
YEAH, I NOTICED. BUT THE GUN--

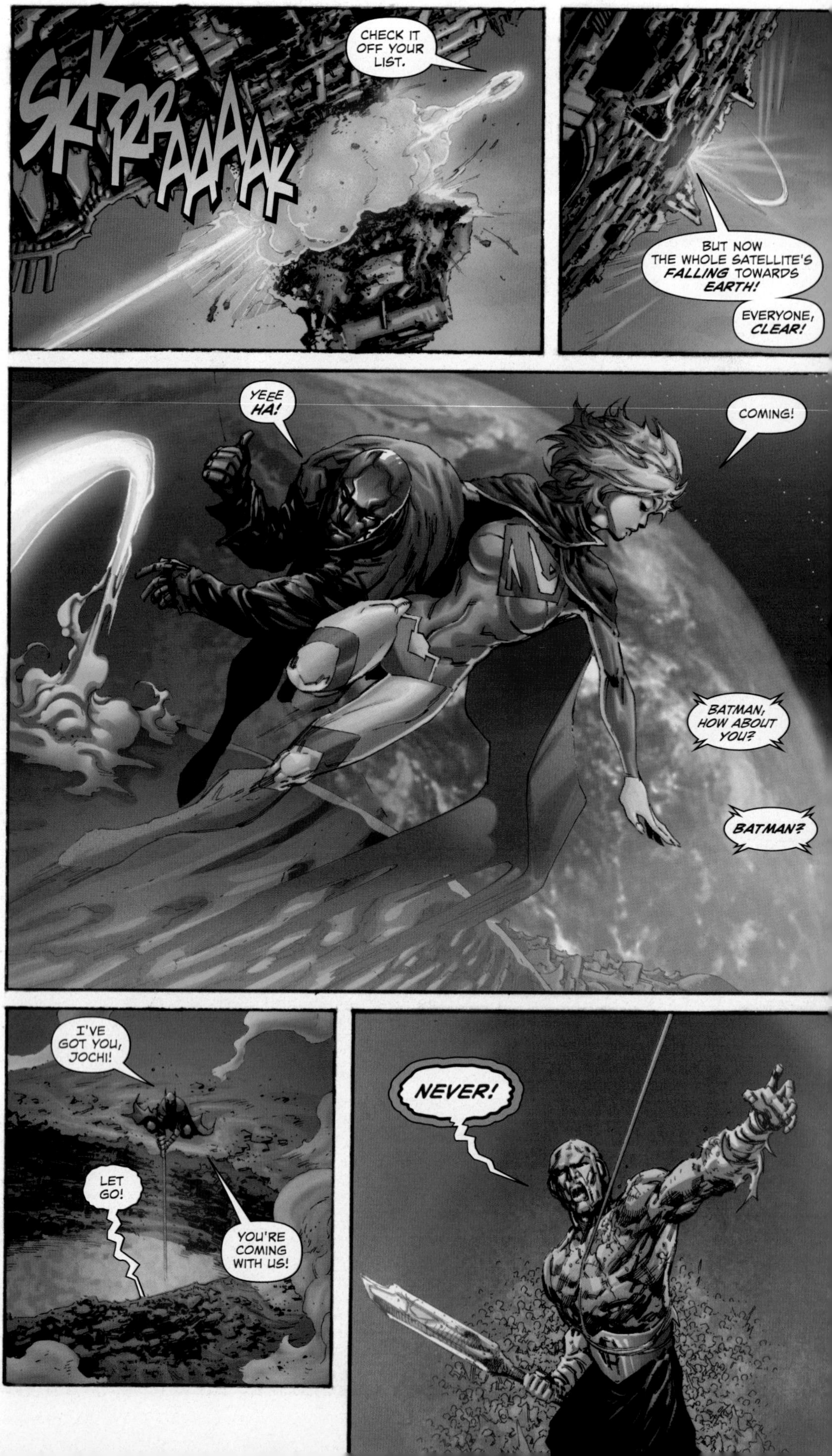
SKKRRRAAAAK
CHECK IT OFF YOUR LIST.
BUT NOW THE WHOLE SATELLITE'S FALLING TOWARDS EARTH!
EVERYONE, CLEAR!
YEEE HA!
COMING!
BATMAN, HOW ABOUT YOU?
BATMAN?
I'VE GOT YOU, JOCHI!
LET GO!
YOU'RE COMING WITH US!
NEVER!

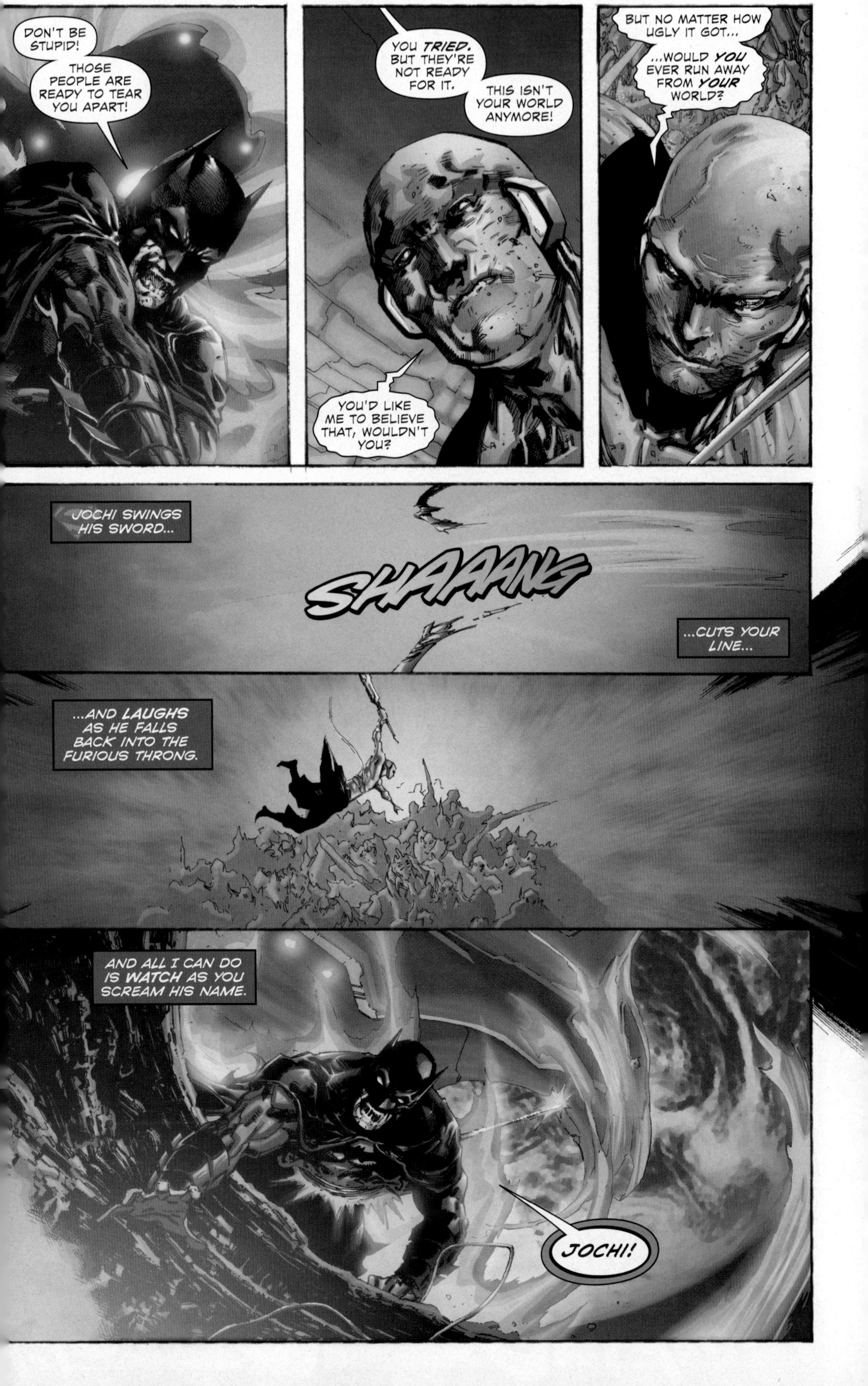
DON'T BE STUPID!
THOSE PEOPLE ARE READY TO TEAR YOU APART!
YOU TRIED. BUT THEY'RE NOT READY FOR IT.
THIS ISN'T YOUR WORLD ANYMORE!
YOU'D LIKE ME TO BELIEVE THAT, WOULDN'T YOU?
BUT NO MATTER HOW UGLY IT GOT...
...WOULD YOU EVER RUN AWAY FROM YOUR WORLD?
JOCHI SWINGS HIS SWORD...
SHAAANG
...CUTS YOUR LINE...
...AND LAUGHS AS HE FALLS BACK INTO THE FURIOUS THRONG.
AND ALL I CAN DO IS WATCH AS YOU SCREAM HIS NAME.
JOCHI!

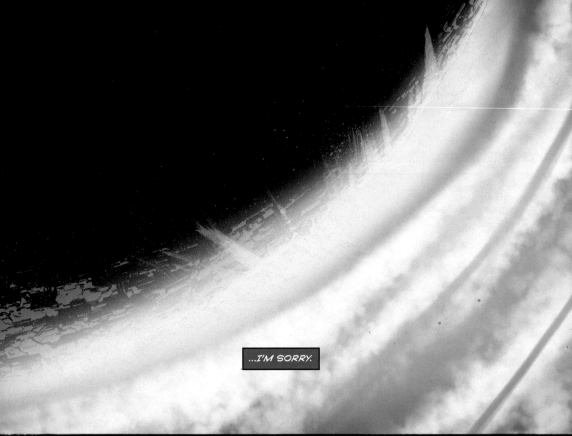

I'M SORRY, BRUCE...

...I'M SORRY.

MY GOD...

IT'S GOING TO *CRASH* RIGHT INTO THE *ARCTIC!*

MAYBE. BUT WE GOT *SUPERMAN* ON THE JOB...

KRRRAKOOOOSH!

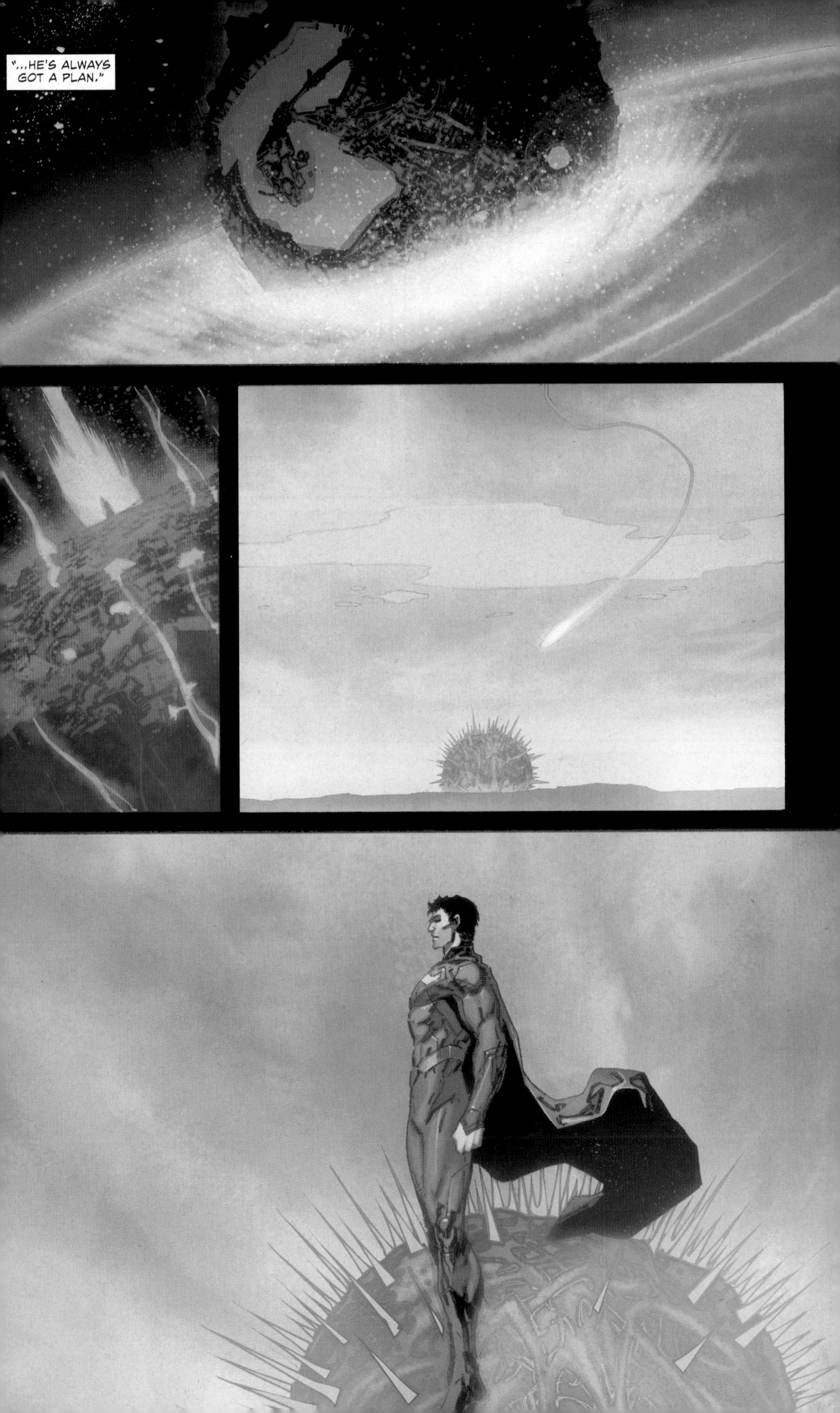
"...HE'S ALWAYS GOT A PLAN."

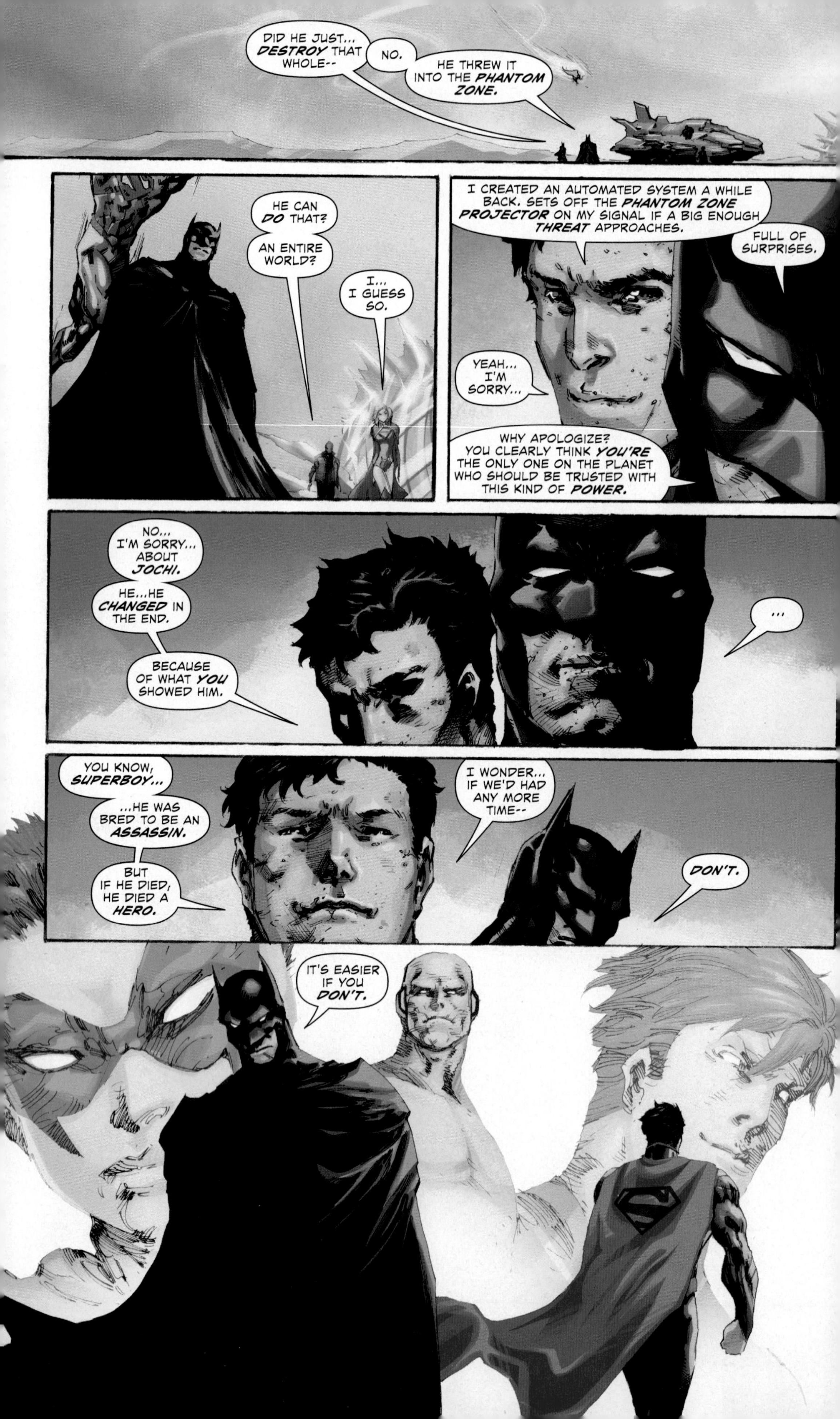
DID HE JUST... DESTROY THAT WHOLE--
NO.
HE THREW IT INTO THE PHANTOM ZONE.
HE CAN DO THAT?
AN ENTIRE WORLD?
I... I GUESS SO.
I CREATED AN AUTOMATED SYSTEM A WHILE BACK. SETS OFF THE PHANTOM ZONE PROJECTOR ON MY SIGNAL IF A BIG ENOUGH THREAT APPROACHES.
FULL OF SURPRISES.
YEAH... I'M SORRY...
WHY APOLOGIZE? YOU CLEARLY THINK YOU'RE THE ONLY ONE ON THE PLANET WHO SHOULD BE TRUSTED WITH THIS KIND OF POWER.
NO... I'M SORRY... ABOUT JOCHI.
HE...HE CHANGED IN THE END.
BECAUSE OF WHAT YOU SHOWED HIM.
...
YOU KNOW, SUPERBOY...
...HE WAS BRED TO BE AN ASSASSIN.
BUT IF HE DIED, HE DIED A HERO.
I WONDER... IF WE'D HAD ANY MORE TIME--
DON'T.
IT'S EASIER IF YOU DON'T.

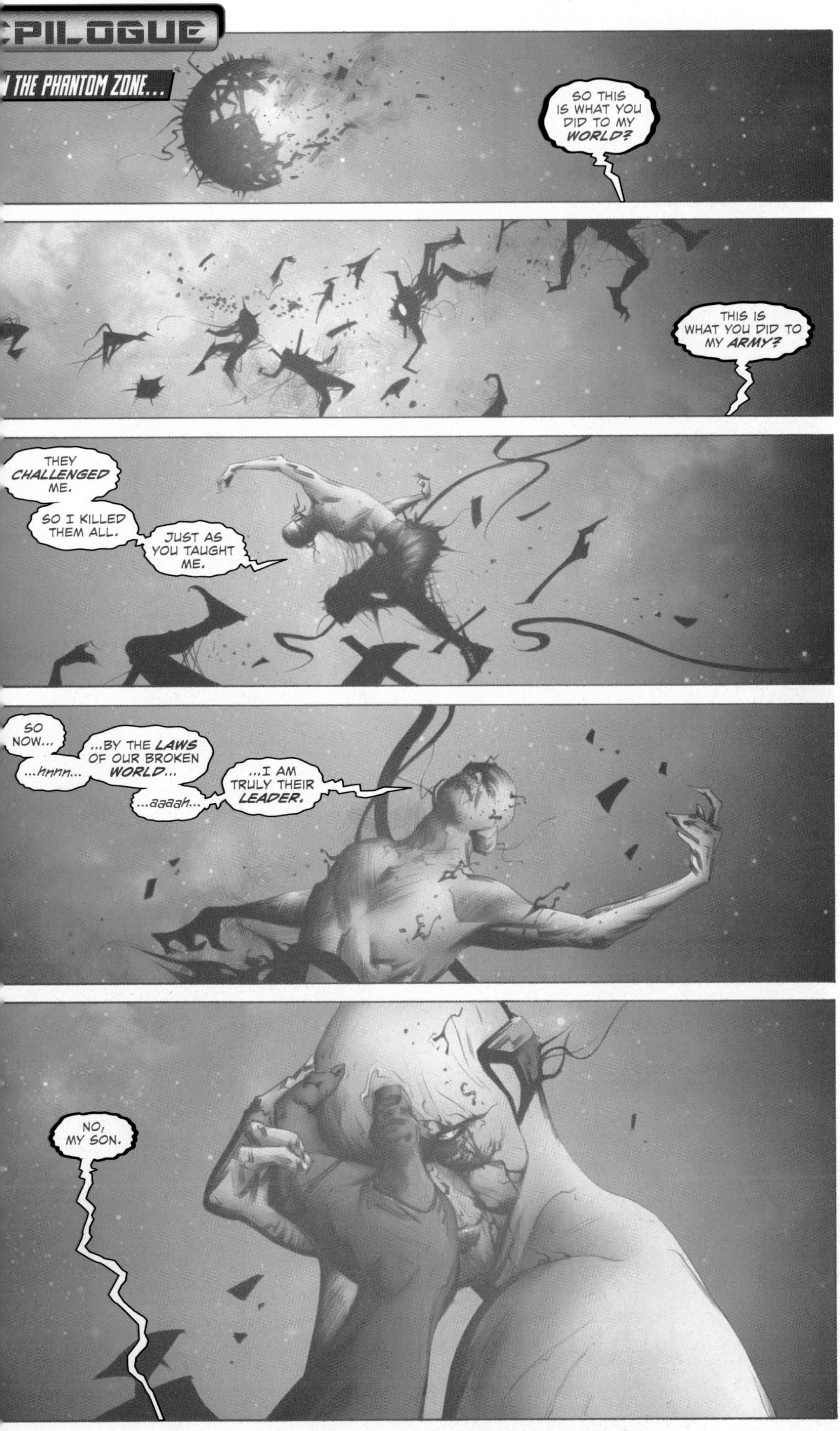
EPILOGUE
IN THE PHANTOM ZONE...
SO THIS IS WHAT YOU DID TO MY WORLD?
THIS IS WHAT YOU DID TO MY ARMY?
THEY CHALLENGED ME.
SO I KILLED THEM ALL.
JUST AS YOU TAUGHT ME.
SO NOW...
...hnnn...
...BY THE LAWS OF OUR BROKEN WORLD...
...aaaah...
...I AM TRULY THEIR LEADER.
NO, MY SON.

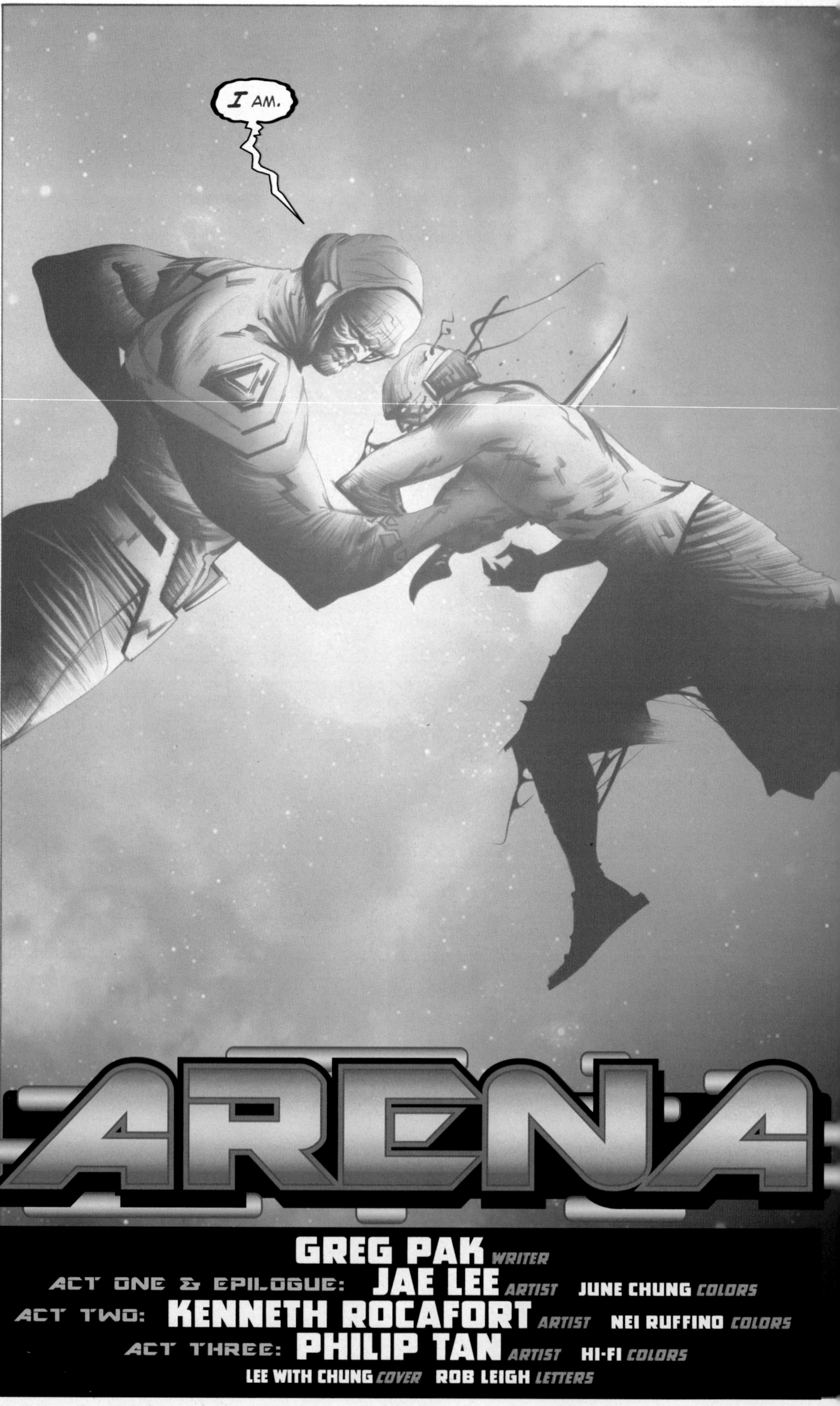
I AM.
ARENA

GREG PAK *WRITER*

ACT ONE & EPILOGUE: **JAE LEE** *ARTIST* **JUNE CHUNG** *COLORS*

ACT TWO: **KENNETH ROCAFORT** *ARTIST* **NEI RUFFINO** *COLORS*

ACT THREE: **PHILIP TAN** *ARTIST* **HI-FI** *COLORS*

LEE WITH CHUNG *COVER* **ROB LEIGH** *LETTERS*

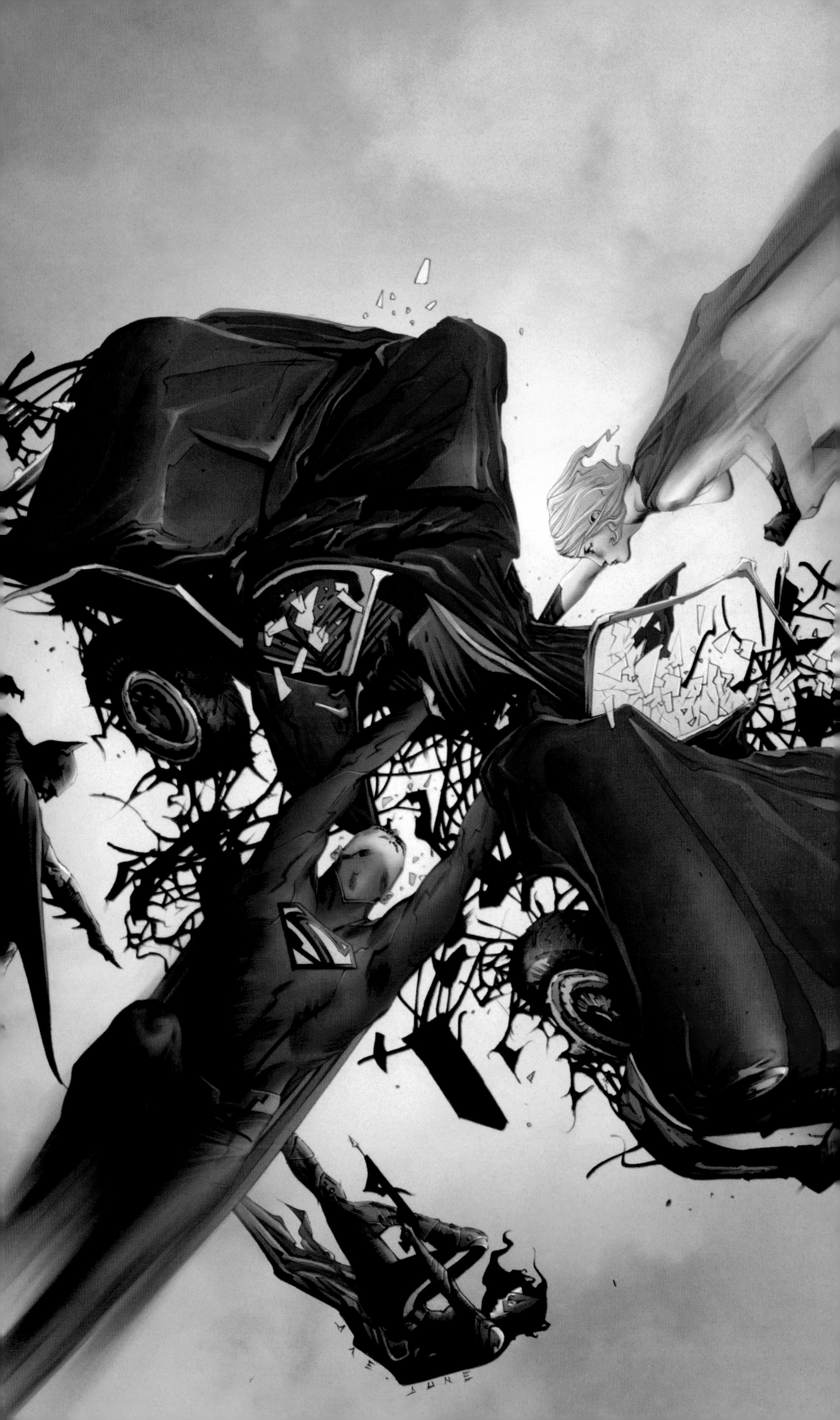

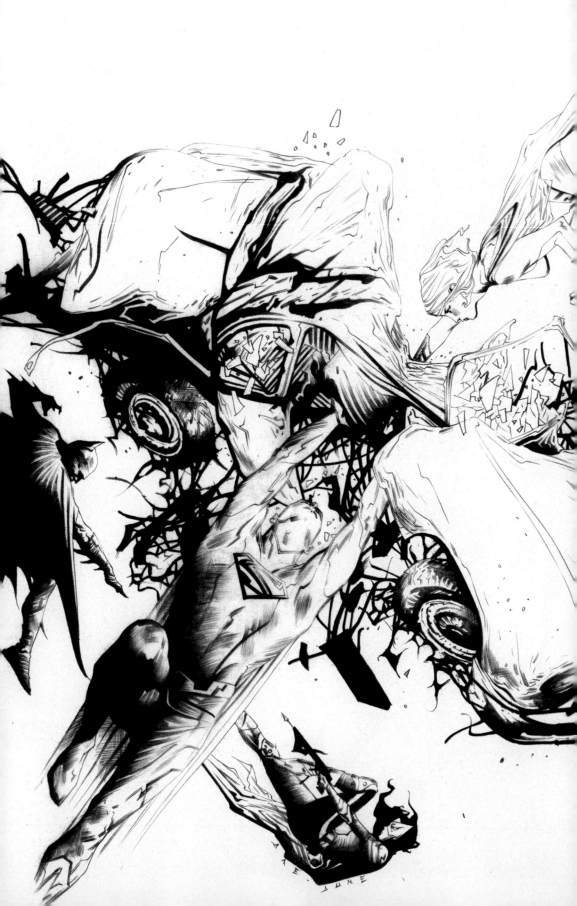

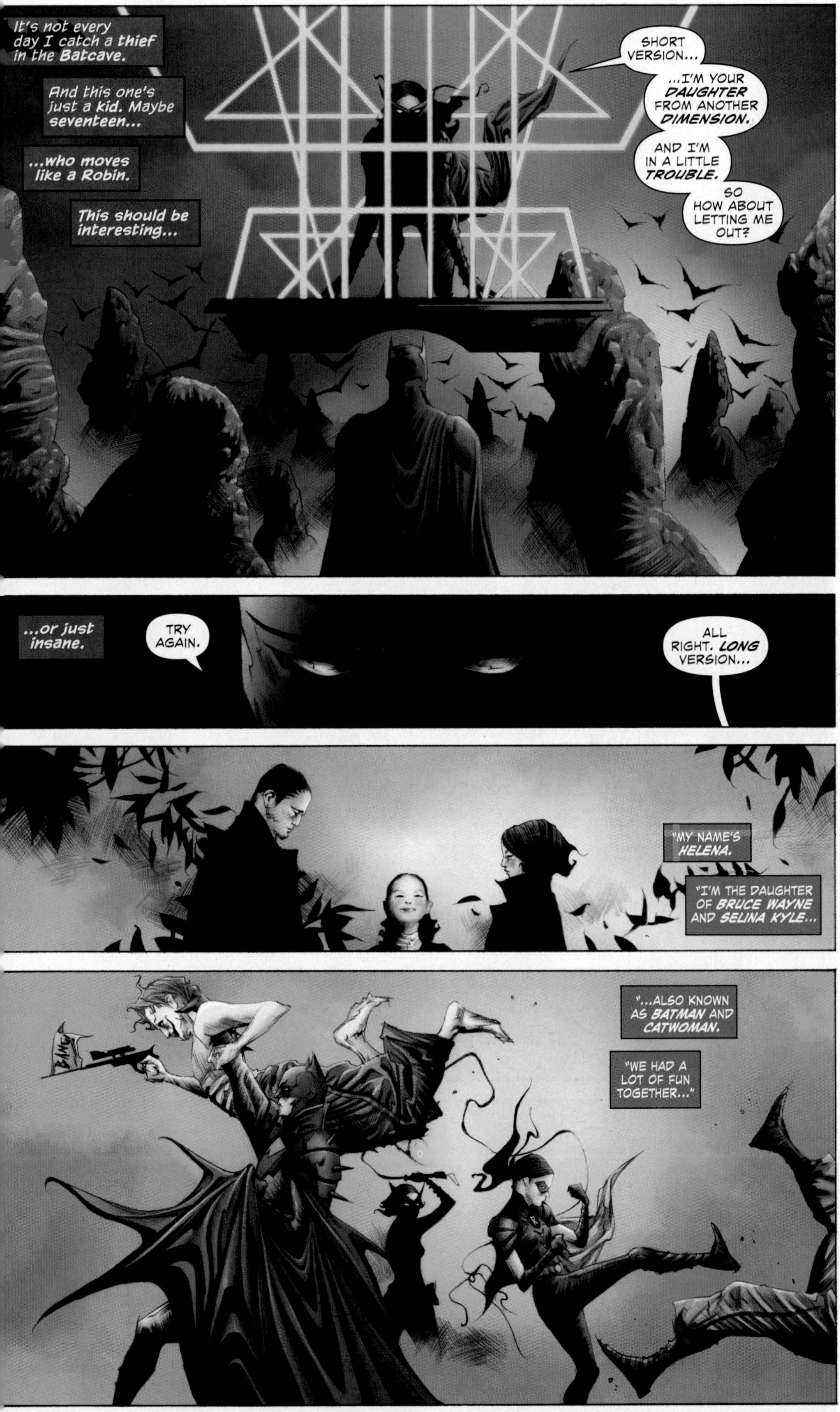
It's not every day I catch a thief in the Batcave.
And this one's just a kid. Maybe seventeen...
...who moves like a Robin.
This should be interesting...
SHORT VERSION...
...I'M YOUR DAUGHTER FROM ANOTHER DIMENSION.
AND I'M IN A LITTLE TROUBLE.
SO HOW ABOUT LETTING ME OUT?
...or just insane.
TRY AGAIN.
ALL RIGHT. LONG VERSION...
"MY NAME'S HELENA.
"I'M THE DAUGHTER OF BRUCE WAYNE AND SELINA KYLE...
"...ALSO KNOWN AS BATMAN AND CATWOMAN.
"WE HAD A LOT OF FUN TOGETHER..."
BANG

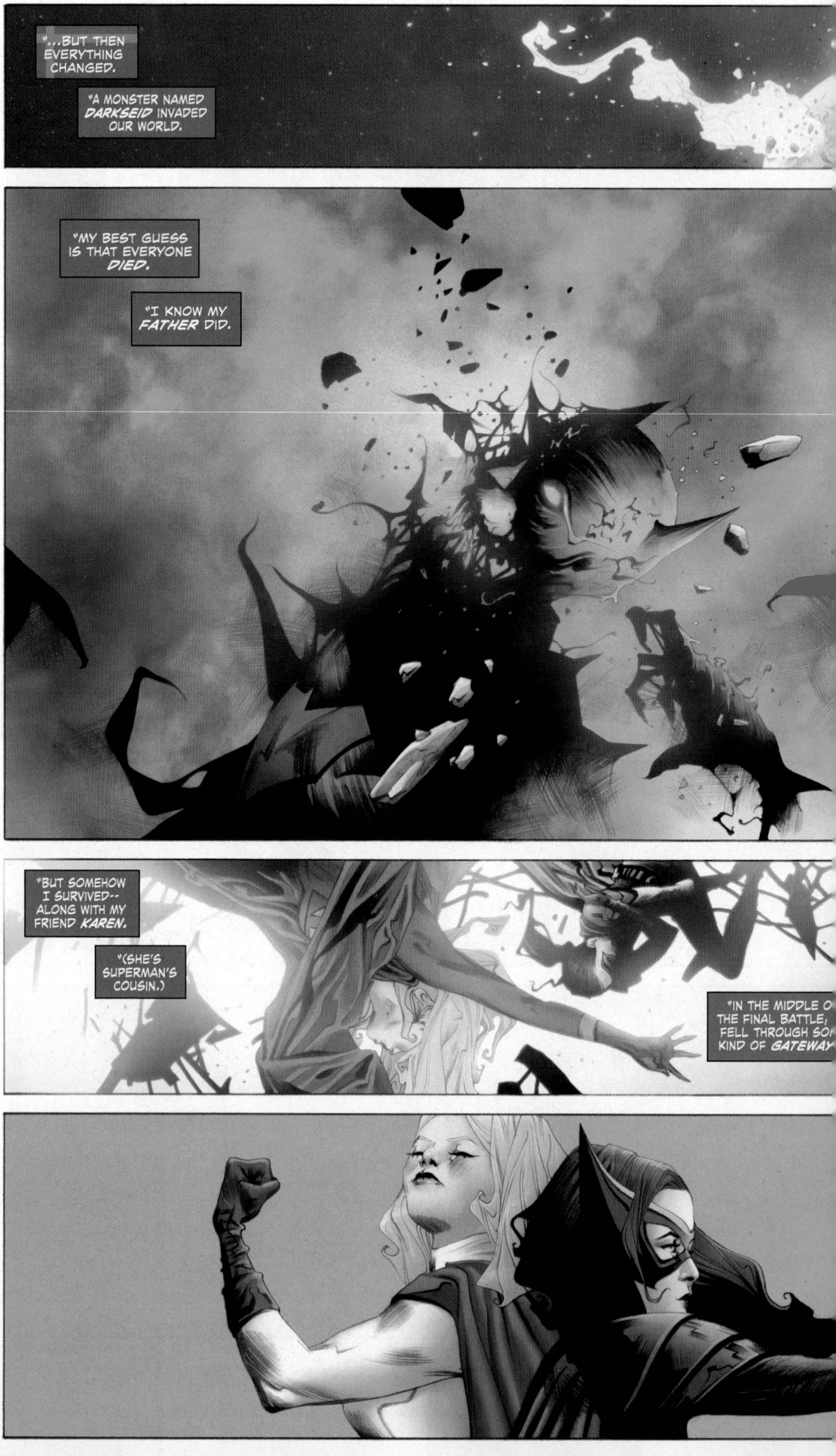
"...BUT THEN EVERYTHING CHANGED.
"A MONSTER NAMED *DARKSEID* INVADED OUR WORLD.
"MY BEST GUESS IS THAT EVERYONE *DIED*.
"I KNOW MY *FATHER* DID.
"BUT SOMEHOW I SURVIVED-- ALONG WITH MY FRIEND *KAREN*.
"(SHE'S SUPERMAN'S COUSIN.)
"IN THE MIDDLE O THE FINAL BATTLE, FELL THROUGH SO KIND OF *GATEWAY*

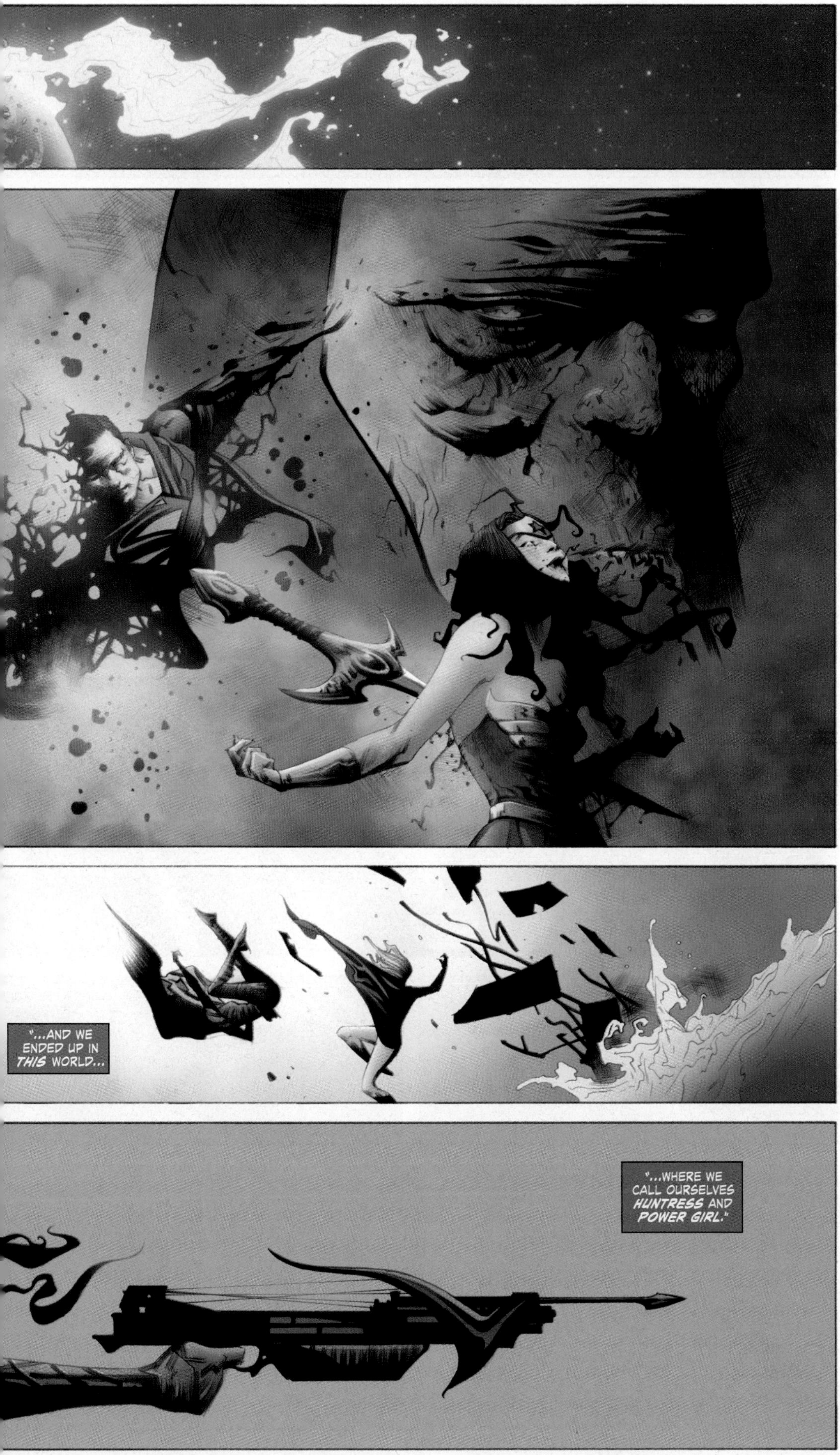
"...AND WE ENDED UP IN *THIS* WORLD...
"...WHERE WE CALL OURSELVES *HUNTRESS* AND *POWER GIRL*."

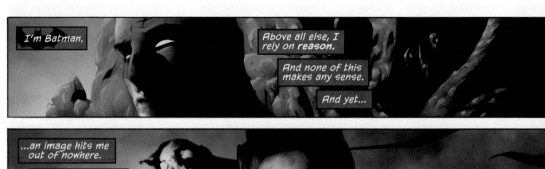

I'm Batman.

Above all else, I rely on *reason*.

And none of this makes any sense.

And yet...

...an image hits me out of nowhere.

I'm standing with *Clark* on another *world*, facing our *doubles*.

It's as vivid as a *memory*...

...but how can you *remember* something you've never *seen*?

YOU OKAY?

I'M FINE.

SO... ...YOU BELIEVE ME?

The problem is...I *do*.

In my *heart*, I believe every *word* she says.

PAF

HEY!

HNNN...

KLONK

But I know better than to trust my heart.

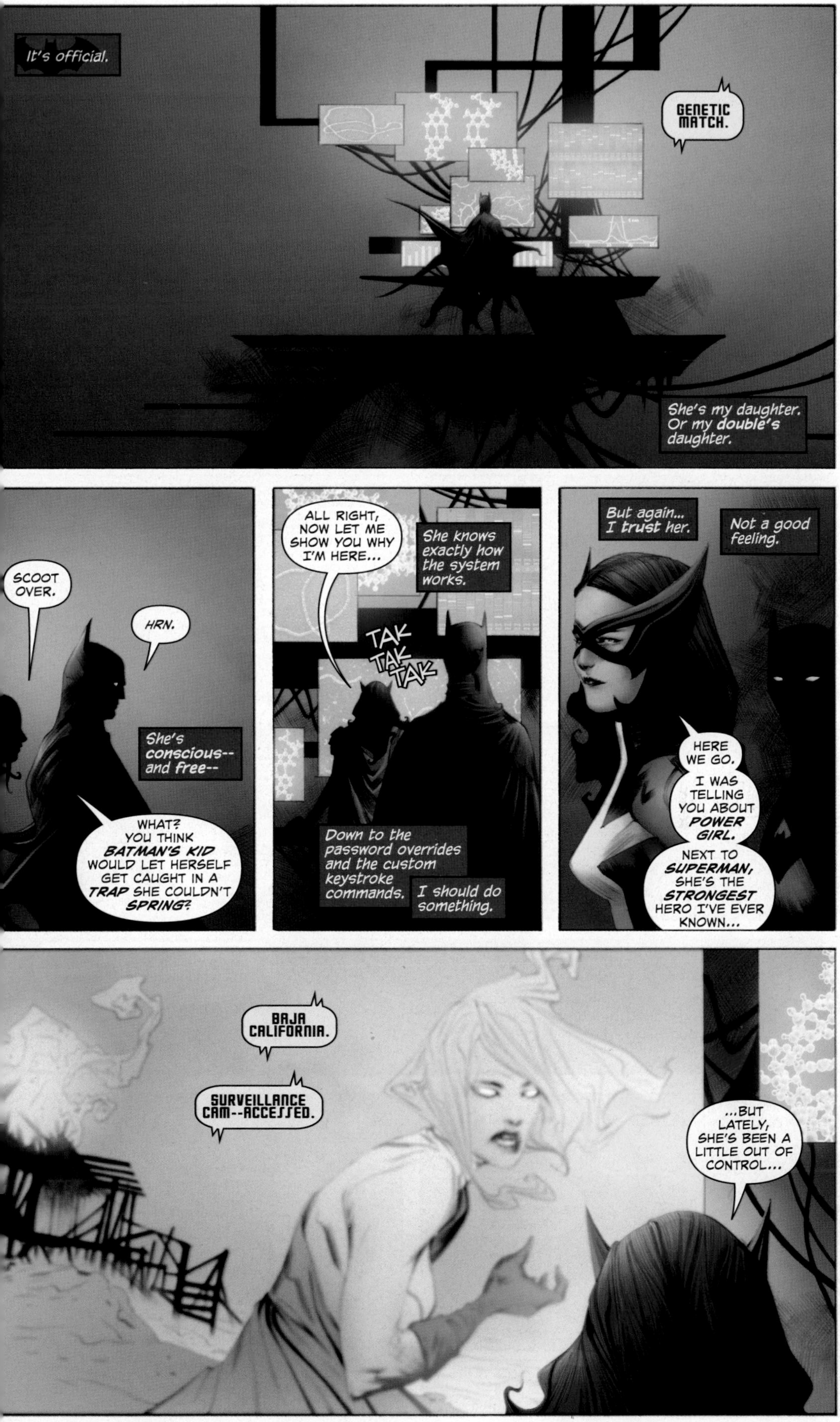
It's official.
GENETIC MATCH.
She's my daughter. Or my double's daughter.
SCOOT OVER.
HRN.
She's conscious--and free--
WHAT? YOU THINK BATMAN'S KID WOULD LET HERSELF GET CAUGHT IN A TRAP SHE COULDN'T SPRING?
ALL RIGHT, NOW LET ME SHOW YOU WHY I'M HERE...
She knows exactly how the system works.
TAK TAK TAK
Down to the password overrides and the custom keystroke commands.
I should do something.
But again... I trust her.
Not a good feeling.
HERE WE GO.
I WAS TELLING YOU ABOUT POWER GIRL.
NEXT TO SUPERMAN, SHE'S THE STRONGEST HERO I'VE EVER KNOWN...
BAJA CALIFORNIA.
SURVEILLANCE CAM--ACCESSED.
...BUT LATELY, SHE'S BEEN A LITTLE OUT OF CONTROL...

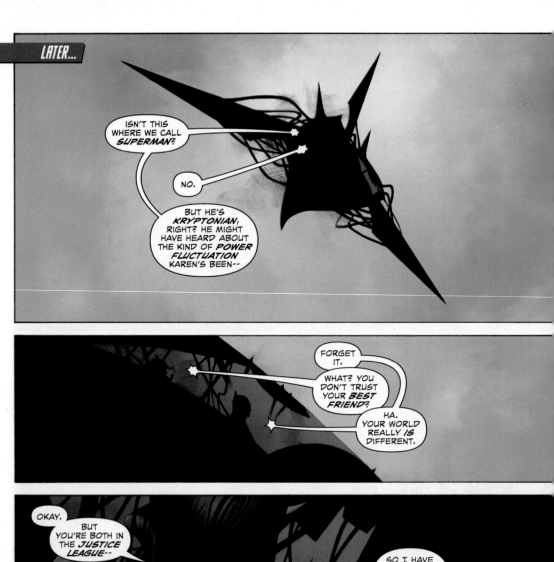

ISN'T THIS WHERE WE CALL *SUPERMAN?*

NO.

BUT HE'S *KRYPTONIAN,* RIGHT? HE MIGHT HAVE HEARD ABOUT THE KIND OF *POWER FLUCTUATION* KAREN'S BEEN--

FORGET IT.

WHAT? YOU DON'T TRUST YOUR *BEST FRIEND?*

HA. YOUR WORLD REALLY *IS* DIFFERENT.

OKAY. YOU'RE BOTH IN THE *JUSTICE LEAGUE--*

SO I HAVE PLENTY OF *EXPERIENCE* TO BASE THIS DECISION ON.

SUPERMAN HAS A HABIT OF RUNNING OFF AND DOING THINGS HIS WAY, WITHOUT THINKING THINGS THROUGH.

BETTER TO INVESTIGATE ON OUR OWN AND DECIDE IF WE NEED HIS HELP LATER.

THAT'S NUTS.

DIDN'T YOUR FATHER TEACH YOU TO BE *CAREFUL?*

SURE. BUT MY MOTHER *ALSO* TAUGHT ME THAT THE ONLY WAY WE MAKE IT IN THE WORLD...

...IS IF WE *TRUST* OUR *FRIENDS.*

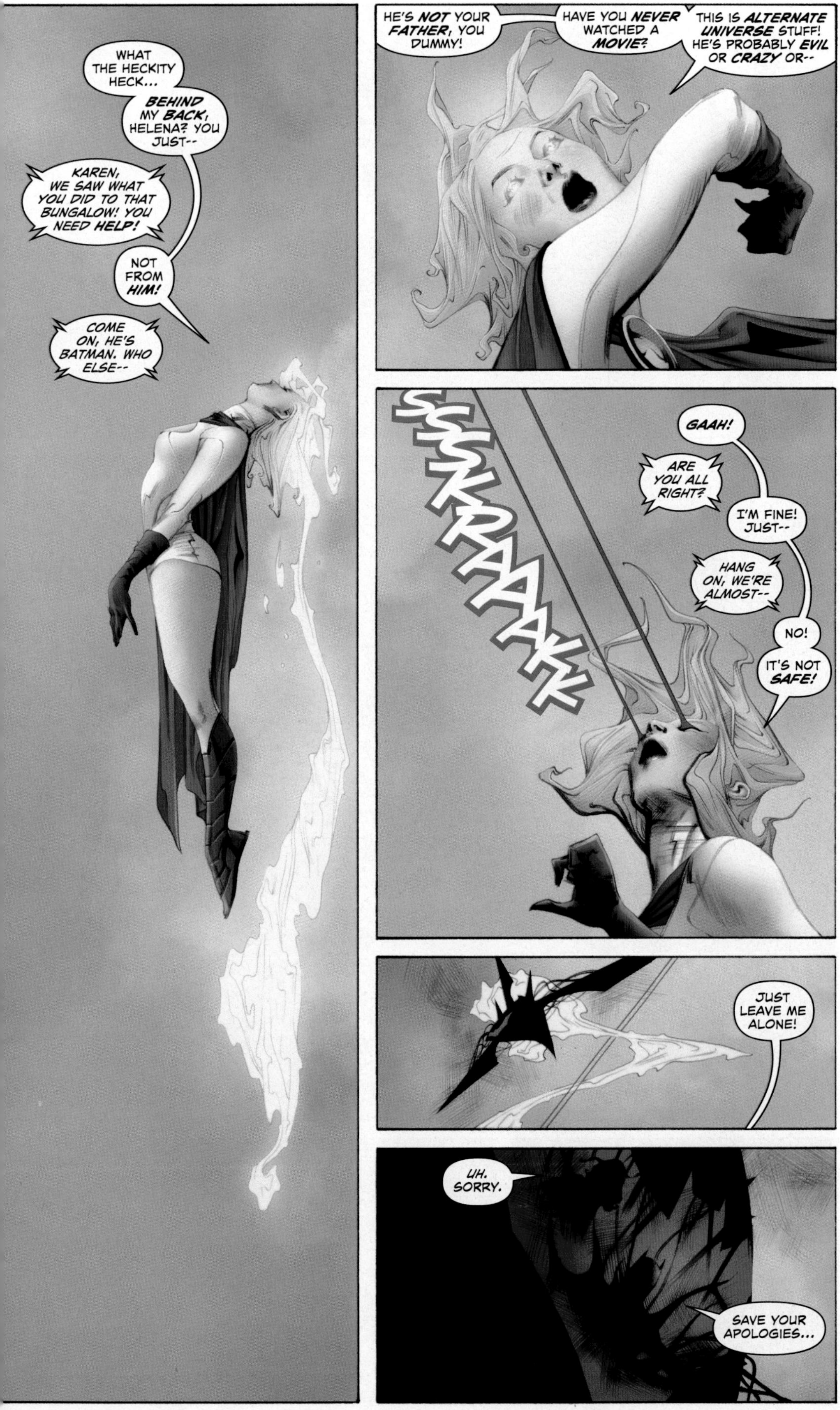

WHAT THE HECKITY HECK...
BEHIND MY BACK, HELENA? YOU JUST--
KAREN, WE SAW WHAT YOU DID TO THAT BUNGALOW! YOU NEED HELP!
NOT FROM HIM!
COME ON, HE'S BATMAN. WHO ELSE--
HE'S NOT YOUR FATHER, YOU DUMMY!
HAVE YOU NEVER WATCHED A MOVIE?
THIS IS ALTERNATE UNIVERSE STUFF! HE'S PROBABLY EVIL OR CRAZY OR--
SSSKRAAAK
GAAH!
ARE YOU ALL RIGHT?
I'M FINE! JUST--
HANG ON, WE'RE ALMOST--
NO!
IT'S NOT SAFE!
JUST LEAVE ME ALONE!
UH. SORRY.
SAVE YOUR APOLOGIES...

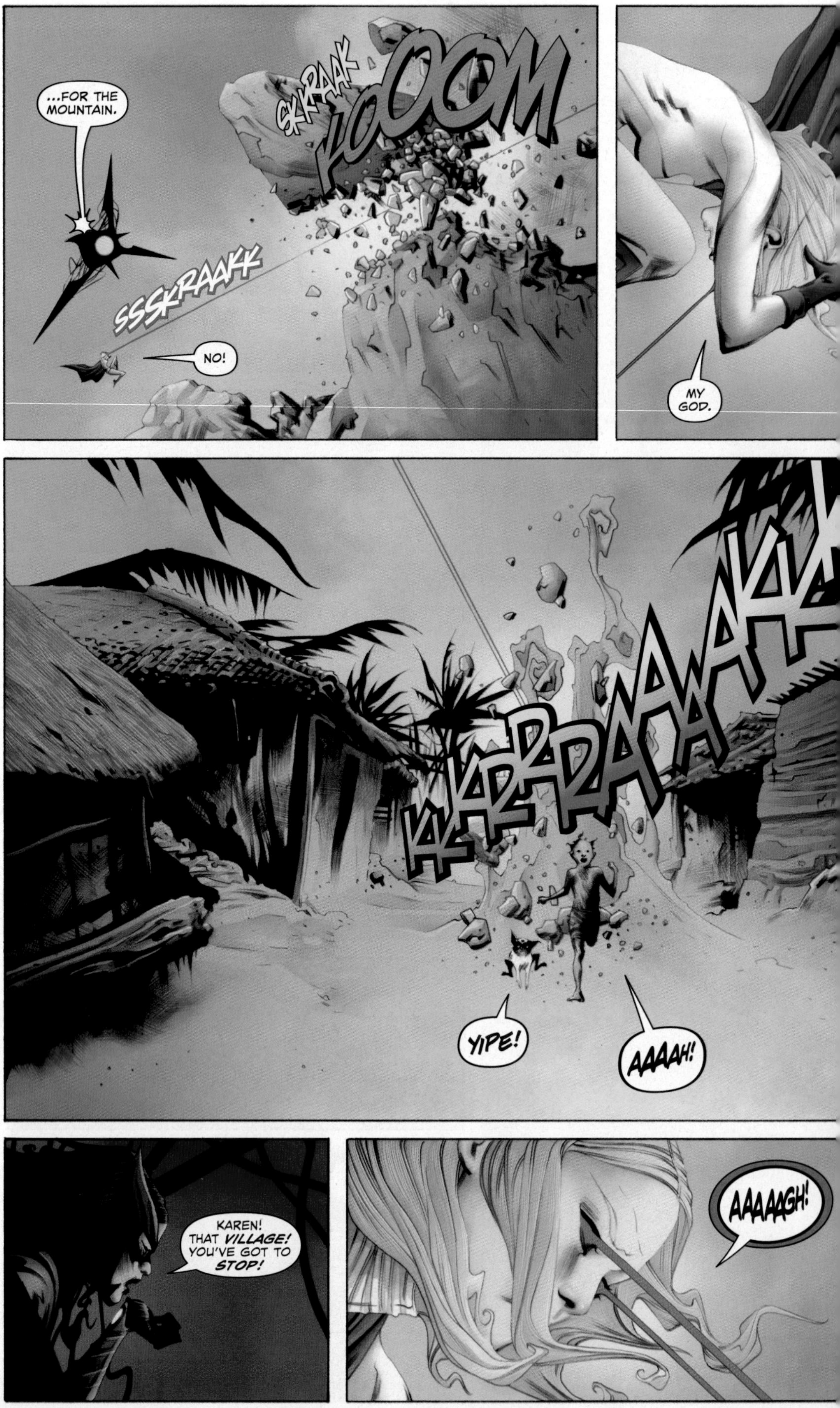
...FOR THE MOUNTAIN.
SKKRAAK
KOOOOM
SSSKRAAKK
NO!
MY GOD.
KKARRRAAAAKK
YIPE!
AAAAH!
KAREN! THAT *VILLAGE!* YOU'VE GOT TO *STOP!*
AAAAAGH!

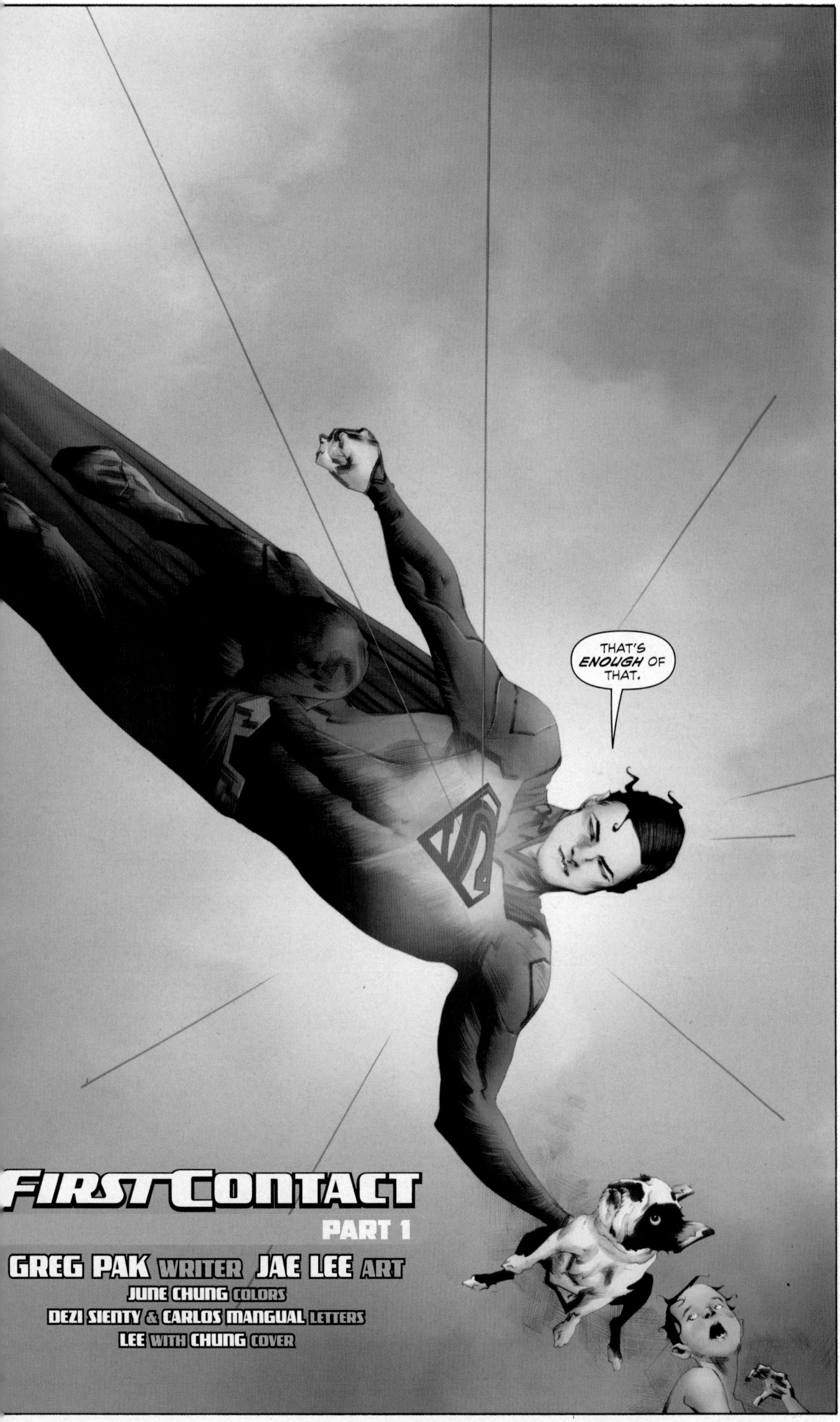

THAT'S *ENOUGH* OF THAT.
FIRST CONTACT
PART 1
GREG PAK WRITER JAE LEE ART
JUNE CHUNG COLORS
DEZI SIENTY & CARLOS MANGUAL LETTERS
LEE WITH CHUNG COVER

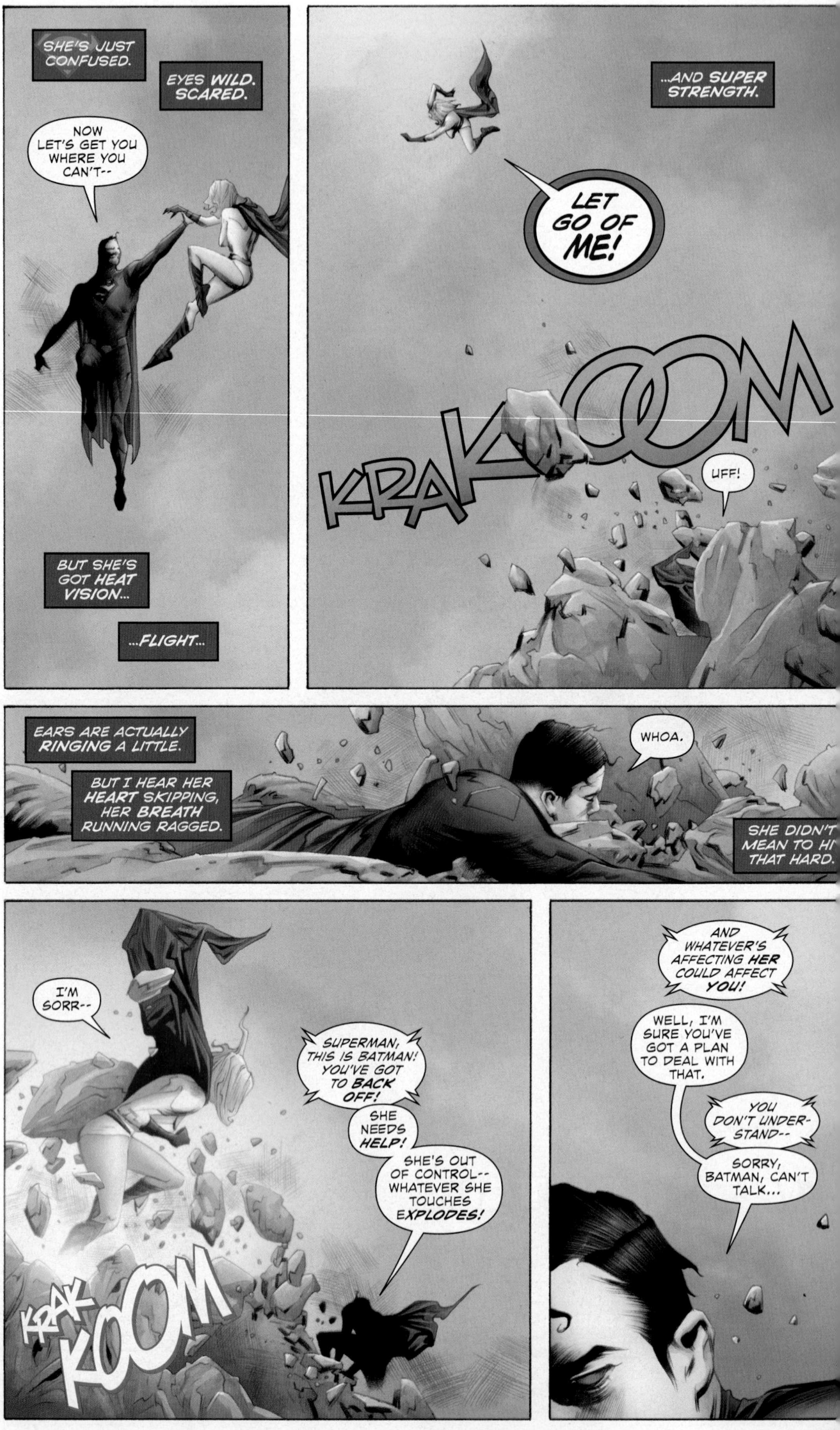
SHE'S JUST CONFUSED.
EYES WILD. SCARED.
NOW LET'S GET YOU WHERE YOU CAN'T--
BUT SHE'S GOT HEAT VISION...
...FLIGHT...
...AND SUPER STRENGTH.
LET GO OF ME!
KRAKOOM
UFF!
EARS ARE ACTUALLY RINGING A LITTLE.
BUT I HEAR HER HEART SKIPPING, HER BREATH RUNNING RAGGED.
WHOA.
SHE DIDN'T MEAN TO HI THAT HARD.
I'M SORR--
SUPERMAN, THIS IS BATMAN! YOU'VE GOT TO BACK OFF!
SHE NEEDS HELP!
SHE'S OUT OF CONTROL-- WHATEVER SHE TOUCHES EXPLODES!
KRAK KOOM
AND WHATEVER'S AFFECTING HER COULD AFFECT YOU!
WELL, I'M SURE YOU'VE GOT A PLAN TO DEAL WITH THAT.
YOU DON'T UNDER-STAND--
SORRY, BATMAN, CAN'T TALK...

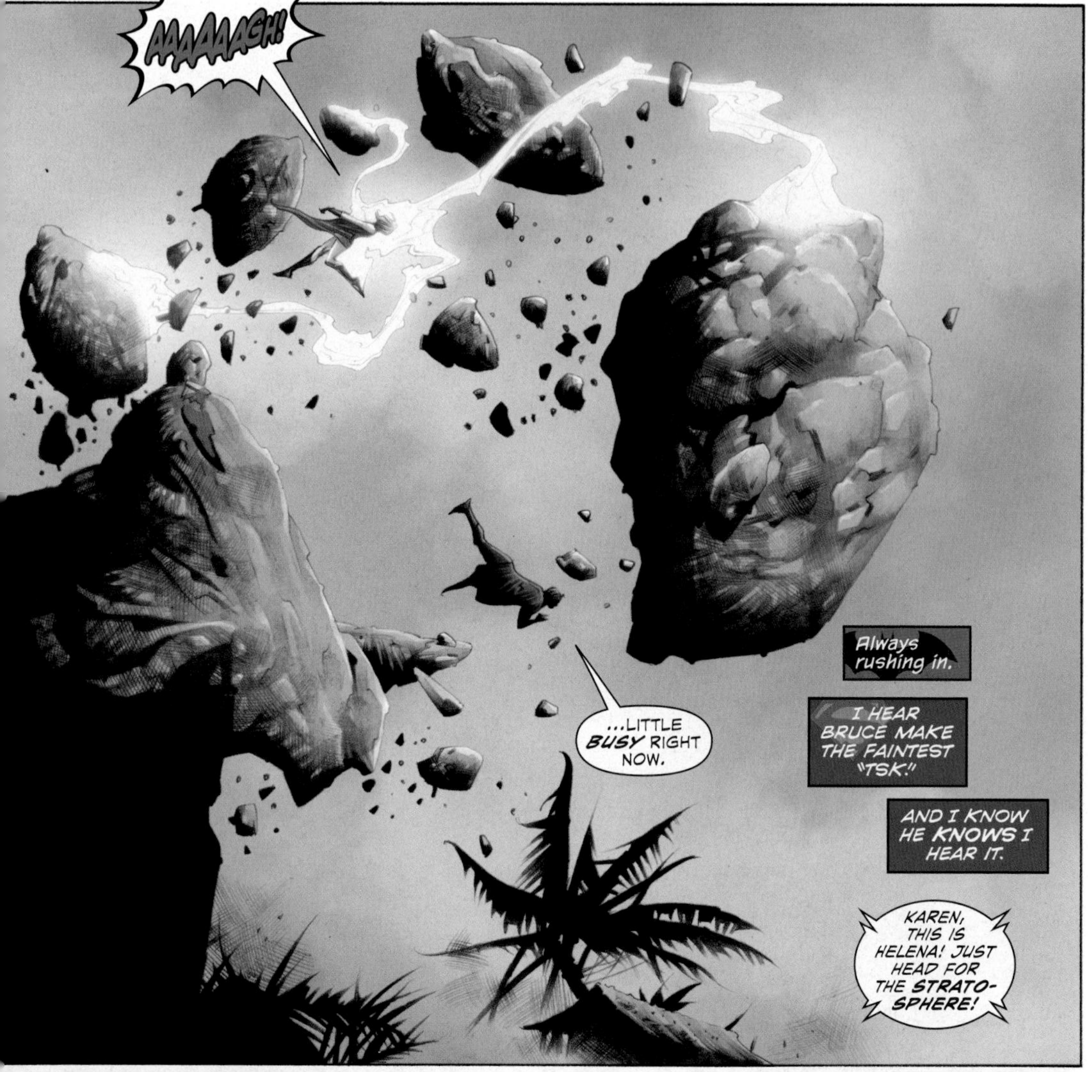
AAAAAAACH!
...LITTLE BUSY RIGHT NOW.
Always rushing in.
I HEAR BRUCE MAKE THE FAINTEST "TSK."
AND I KNOW HE KNOWS I HEAR IT.
KAREN, THIS IS HELENA! JUST HEAD FOR THE STRATO-SPHERE!

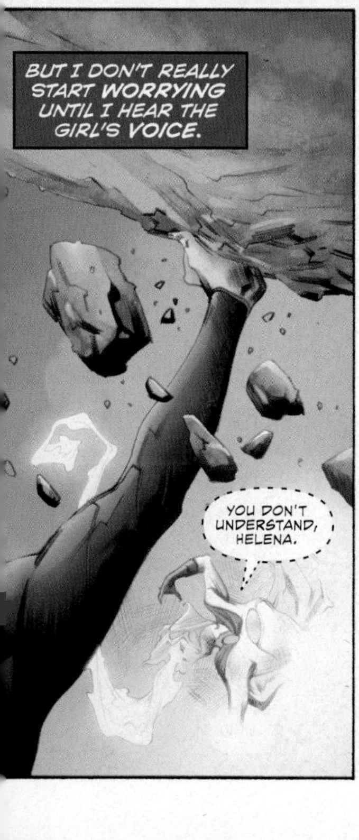
BUT I DON'T REALLY START WORRYING UNTIL I HEAR THE GIRL'S VOICE.
YOU DON'T UNDERSTAND, HELENA.

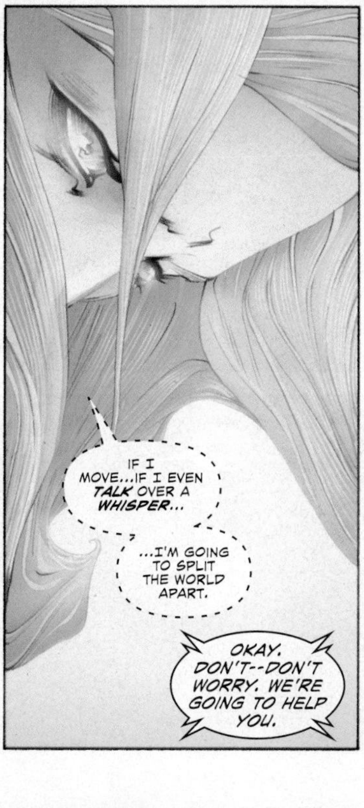
IF I MOVE...IF I EVEN TALK OVER A WHISPER...
...I'M GOING TO SPLIT THE WORLD APART.
OKAY. DON'T--DON'T WORRY. WE'RE GOING TO HELP YOU.

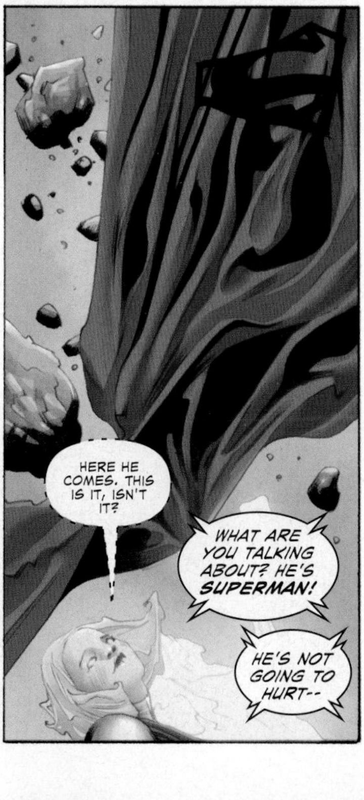
HERE HE COMES. THIS IS IT, ISN'T IT?
WHAT ARE YOU TALKING ABOUT? HE'S SUPERMAN!
HE'S NOT GOING TO HURT--

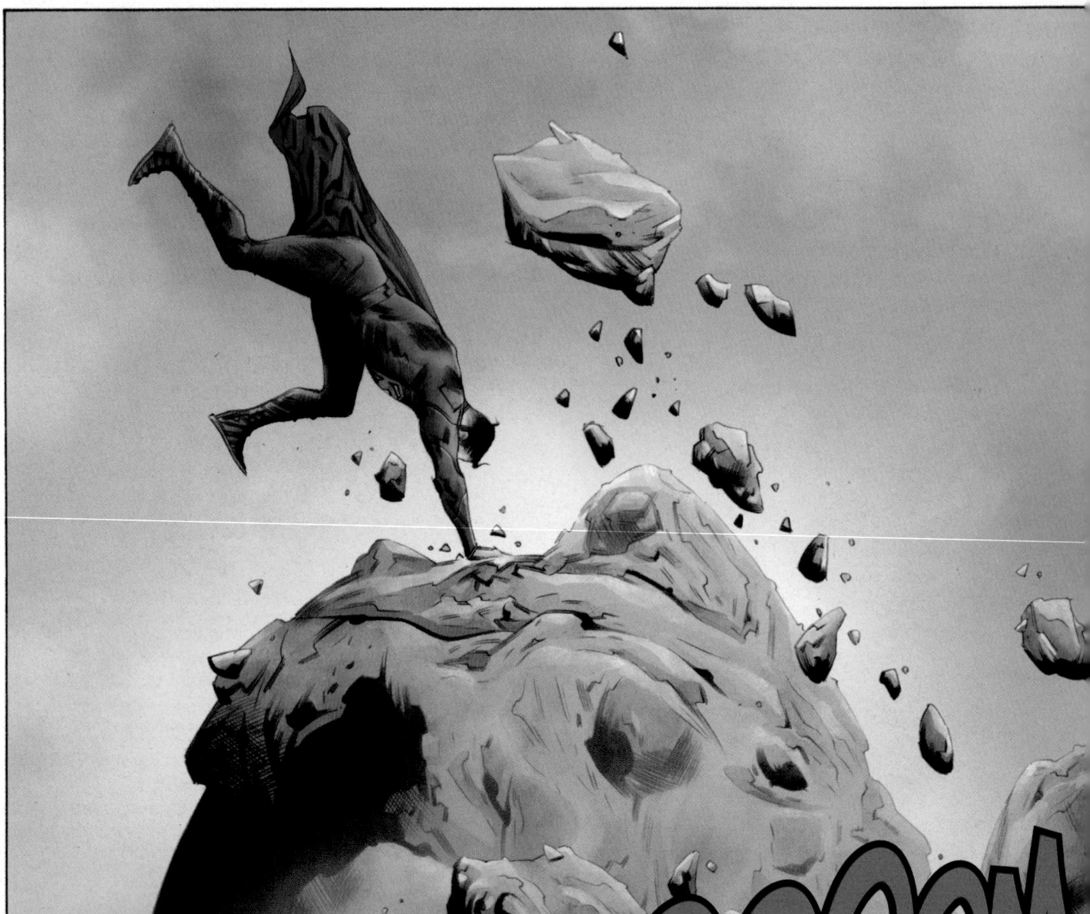
KRRRAKOOOOOM

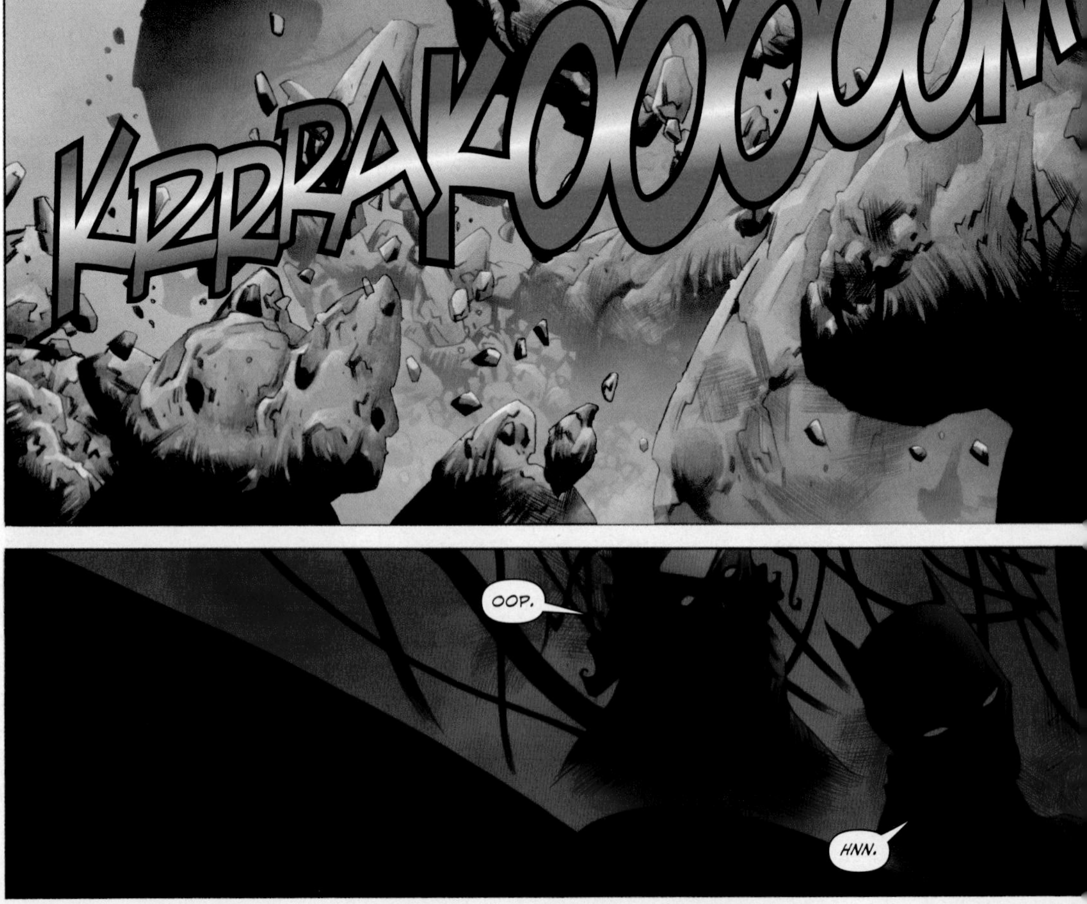
OOP.
HNN.

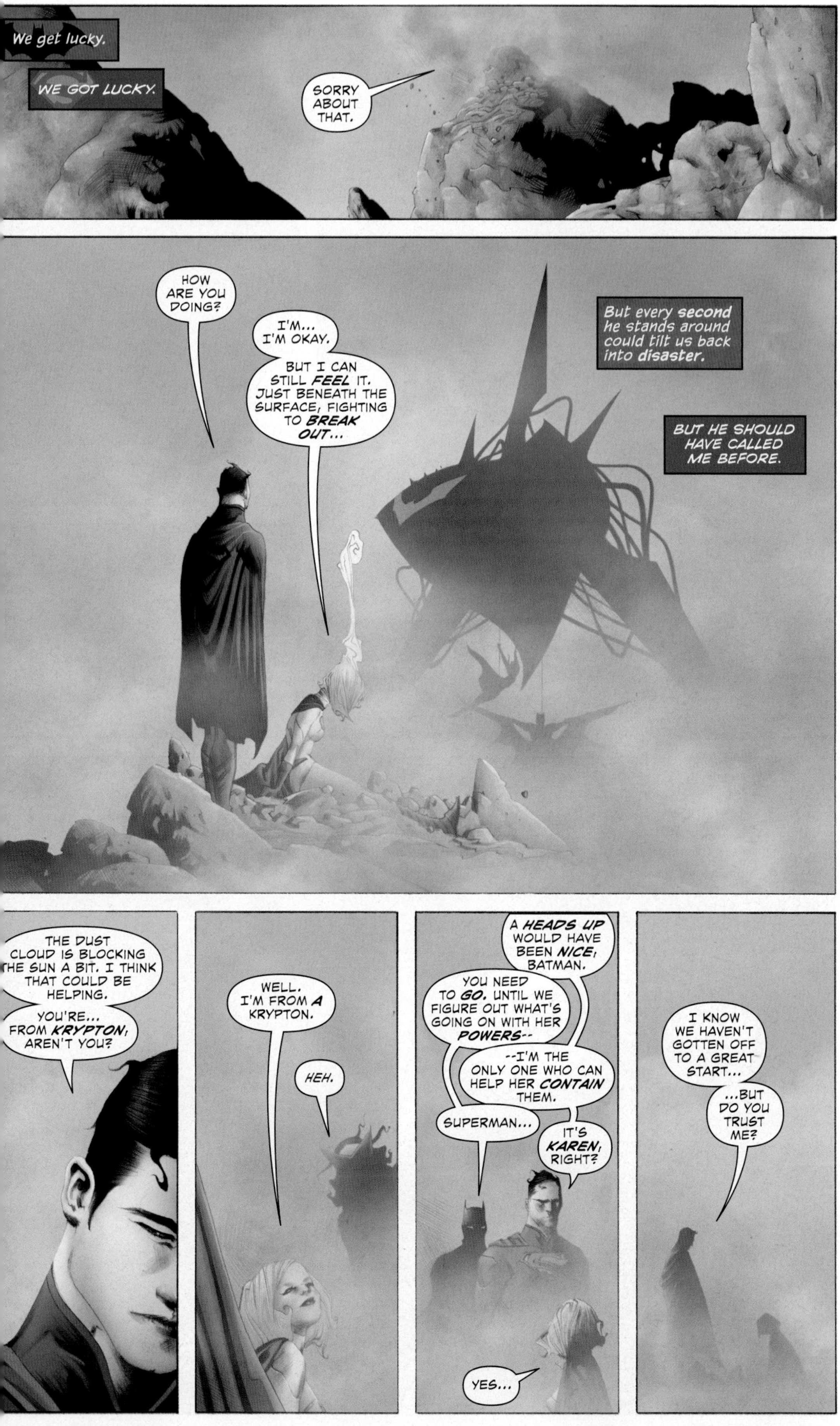
We get lucky.
WE GOT LUCKY.
SORRY ABOUT THAT.
HOW ARE YOU DOING?
I'M... I'M OKAY.
BUT I CAN STILL FEEL IT. JUST BENEATH THE SURFACE, FIGHTING TO BREAK OUT...
But every second he stands around could tilt us back into disaster.
BUT HE SHOULD HAVE CALLED ME BEFORE.
THE DUST CLOUD IS BLOCKING THE SUN A BIT. I THINK THAT COULD BE HELPING.
YOU'RE... FROM KRYPTON, AREN'T YOU?
WELL. I'M FROM A KRYPTON.
HEH.
A HEADS UP WOULD HAVE BEEN NICE, BATMAN.
YOU NEED TO GO. UNTIL WE FIGURE OUT WHAT'S GOING ON WITH HER POWERS--
--I'M THE ONLY ONE WHO CAN HELP HER CONTAIN THEM.
SUPERMAN...
IT'S KAREN, RIGHT?
YES...
I KNOW WE HAVEN'T GOTTEN OFF TO A GREAT START...
...BUT DO YOU TRUST ME?

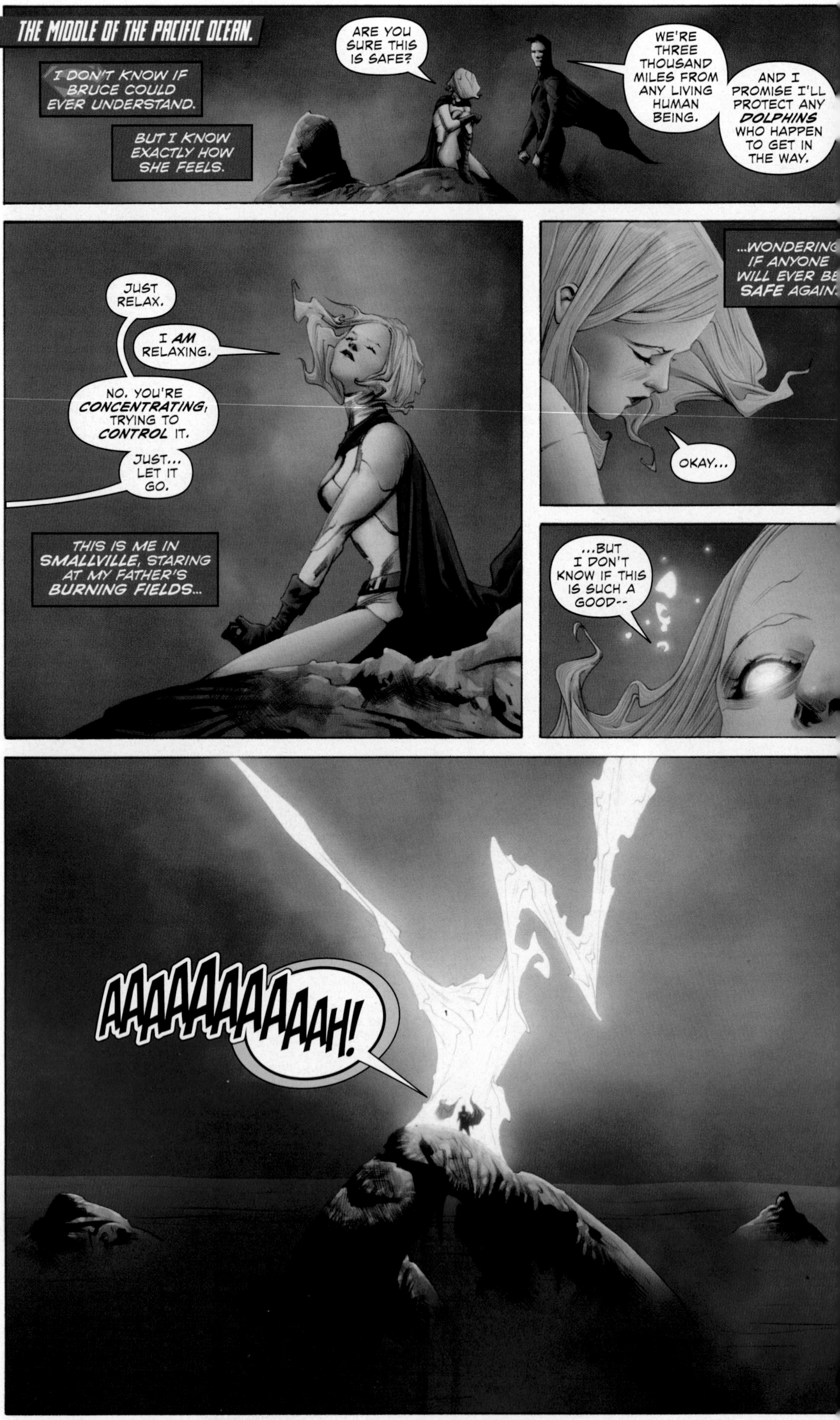
THE MIDDLE OF THE PACIFIC OCEAN.
I DON'T KNOW IF BRUCE COULD EVER UNDERSTAND.
BUT I KNOW EXACTLY HOW SHE FEELS.
ARE YOU SURE THIS IS SAFE?
WE'RE THREE THOUSAND MILES FROM ANY LIVING HUMAN BEING.
AND I PROMISE I'LL PROTECT ANY DOLPHINS WHO HAPPEN TO GET IN THE WAY.
JUST RELAX.
I AM RELAXING.
NO. YOU'RE CONCENTRATING, TRYING TO CONTROL IT.
JUST... LET IT GO.
THIS IS ME IN SMALLVILLE, STARING AT MY FATHER'S BURNING FIELDS...
...WONDERING IF ANYONE WILL EVER BE SAFE AGAIN.
OKAY...
...BUT I DON'T KNOW IF THIS IS SUCH A GOOD--
AAAAAAAAAAAH!

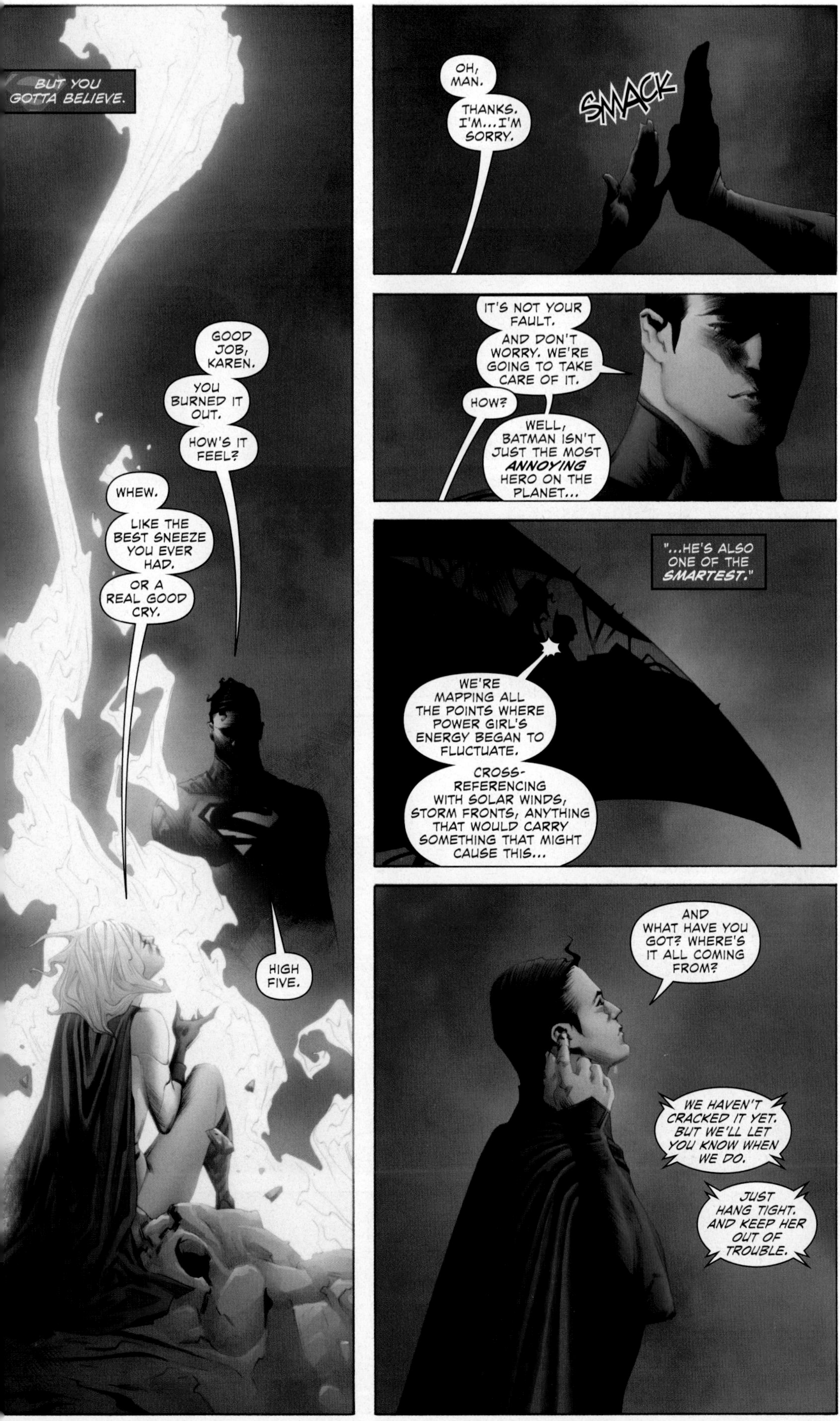
BUT YOU GOTTA BELIEVE.
GOOD JOB, KAREN.
YOU BURNED IT OUT.
HOW'S IT FEEL?
WHEW.
LIKE THE BEST SNEEZE YOU EVER HAD.
OR A REAL GOOD CRY.
HIGH FIVE.
OH, MAN.
THANKS. I'M...I'M SORRY.
SMACK
IT'S NOT YOUR FAULT.
AND DON'T WORRY. WE'RE GOING TO TAKE CARE OF IT.
HOW?
WELL, BATMAN ISN'T JUST THE MOST ANNOYING HERO ON THE PLANET...
"...HE'S ALSO ONE OF THE SMARTEST."
WE'RE MAPPING ALL THE POINTS WHERE POWER GIRL'S ENERGY BEGAN TO FLUCTUATE.
CROSS-REFERENCING WITH SOLAR WINDS, STORM FRONTS, ANYTHING THAT WOULD CARRY SOMETHING THAT MIGHT CAUSE THIS...
AND WHAT HAVE YOU GOT? WHERE'S IT ALL COMING FROM?
WE HAVEN'T CRACKED IT YET. BUT WE'LL LET YOU KNOW WHEN WE DO.
JUST HANG TIGHT. AND KEEP HER OUT OF TROUBLE.

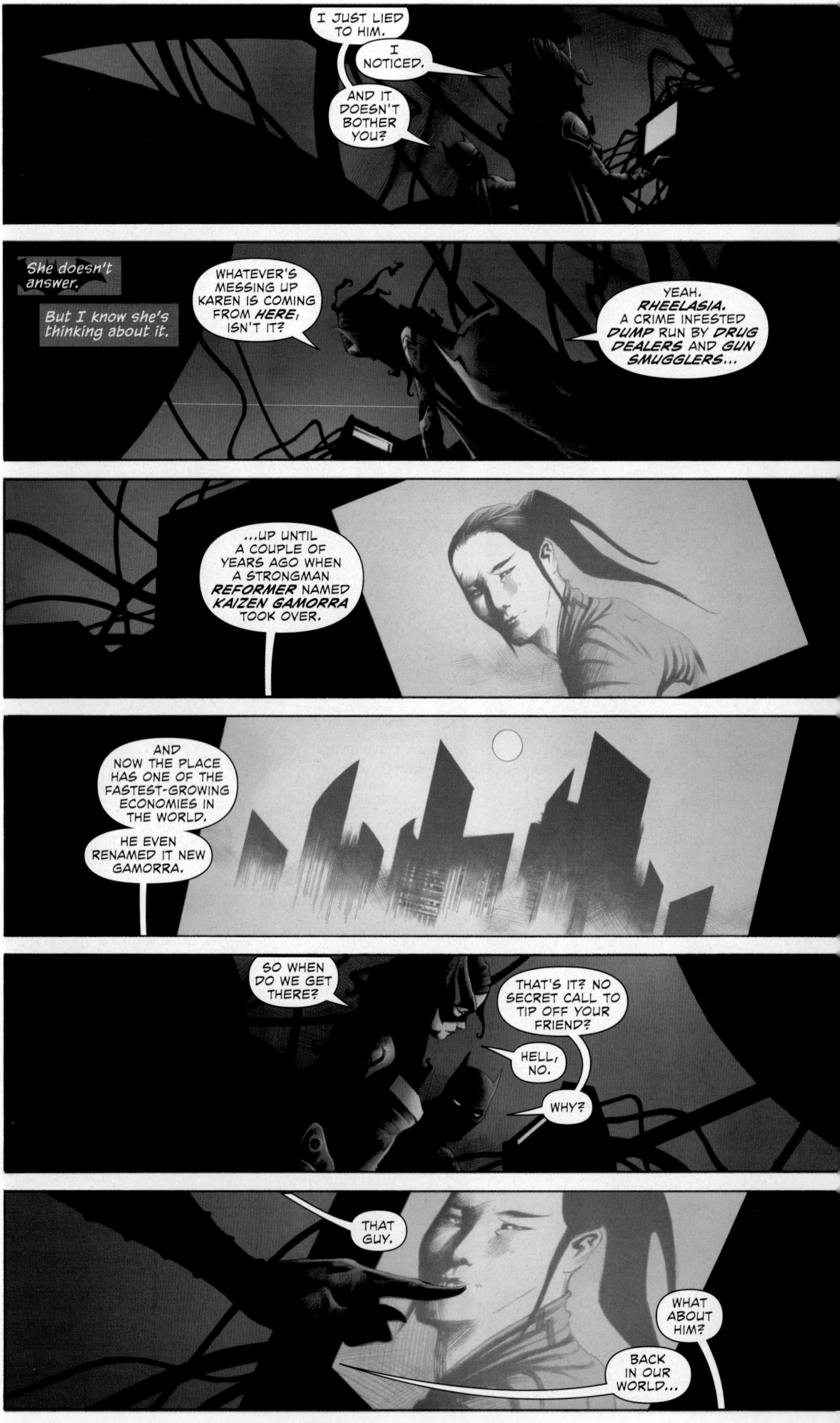
I JUST LIED TO HIM.
I NOTICED.
AND IT DOESN'T BOTHER YOU?
She doesn't answer.
But I know she's thinking about it.
WHATEVER'S MESSING UP KAREN IS COMING FROM HERE, ISN'T IT?
YEAH. RHEELASIA. A CRIME INFESTED DUMP RUN BY DRUG DEALERS AND GUN SMUGGLERS...
...UP UNTIL A COUPLE OF YEARS AGO WHEN A STRONGMAN REFORMER NAMED KAIZEN GAMORRA TOOK OVER.
AND NOW THE PLACE HAS ONE OF THE FASTEST-GROWING ECONOMIES IN THE WORLD.
HE EVEN RENAMED IT NEW GAMORRA.
SO WHEN DO WE GET THERE?
THAT'S IT? NO SECRET CALL TO TIP OFF YOUR FRIEND?
HELL, NO.
WHY?
THAT GUY.
WHAT ABOUT HIM?
BACK IN OUR WORLD...

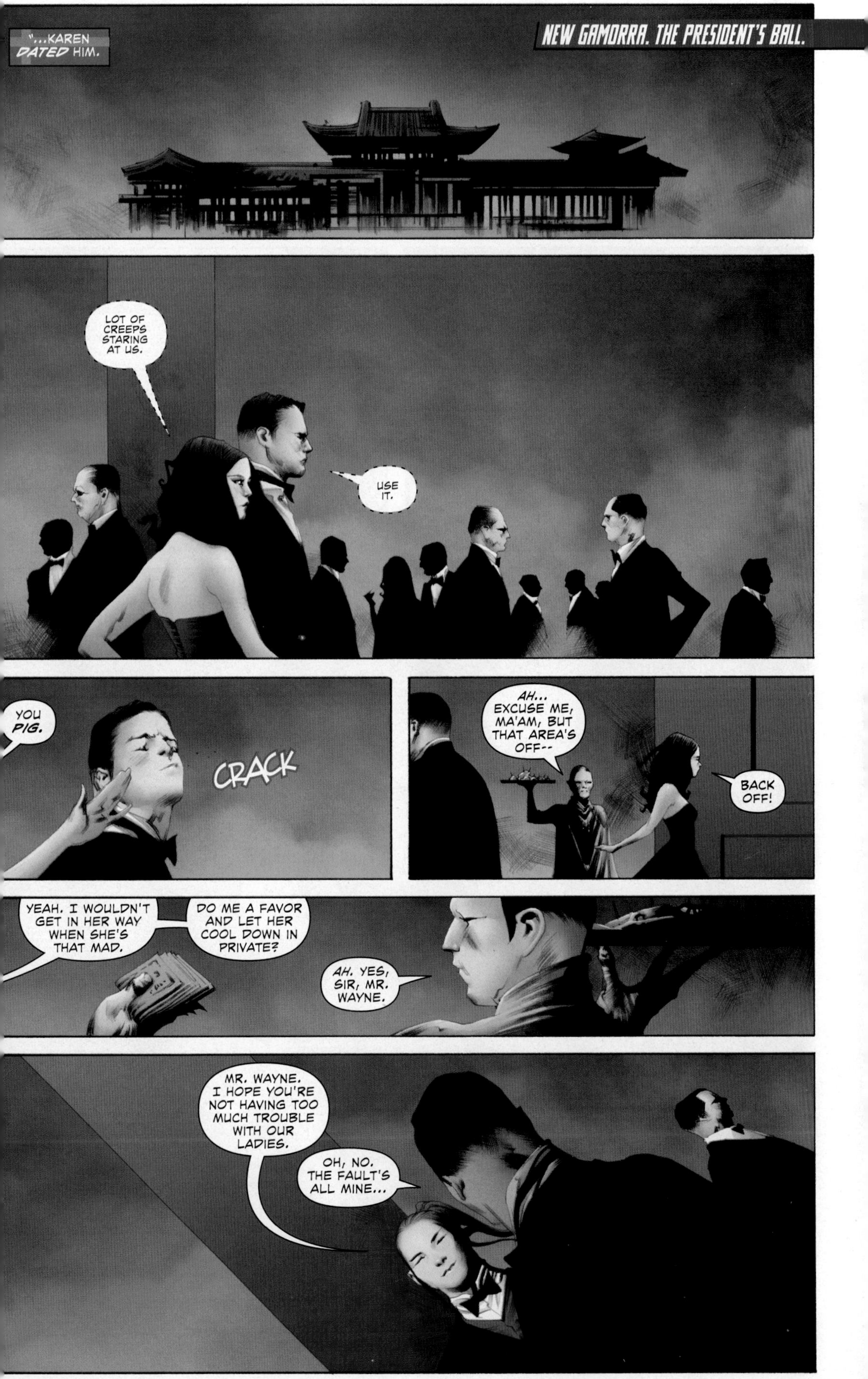
"...KAREN DATED HIM.
NEW GAMORRA. THE PRESIDENT'S BALL.
LOT OF CREEPS STARING AT US.
USE IT.
YOU PIG.
CRACK
AH... EXCUSE ME, MA'AM, BUT THAT AREA'S OFF--
BACK OFF!
YEAH. I WOULDN'T GET IN HER WAY WHEN SHE'S THAT MAD.
DO ME A FAVOR AND LET HER COOL DOWN IN PRIVATE?
AH. YES, SIR, MR. WAYNE.
MR. WAYNE. I HOPE YOU'RE NOT HAVING TOO MUCH TROUBLE WITH OUR LADIES.
OH, NO. THE FAULT'S ALL MINE...

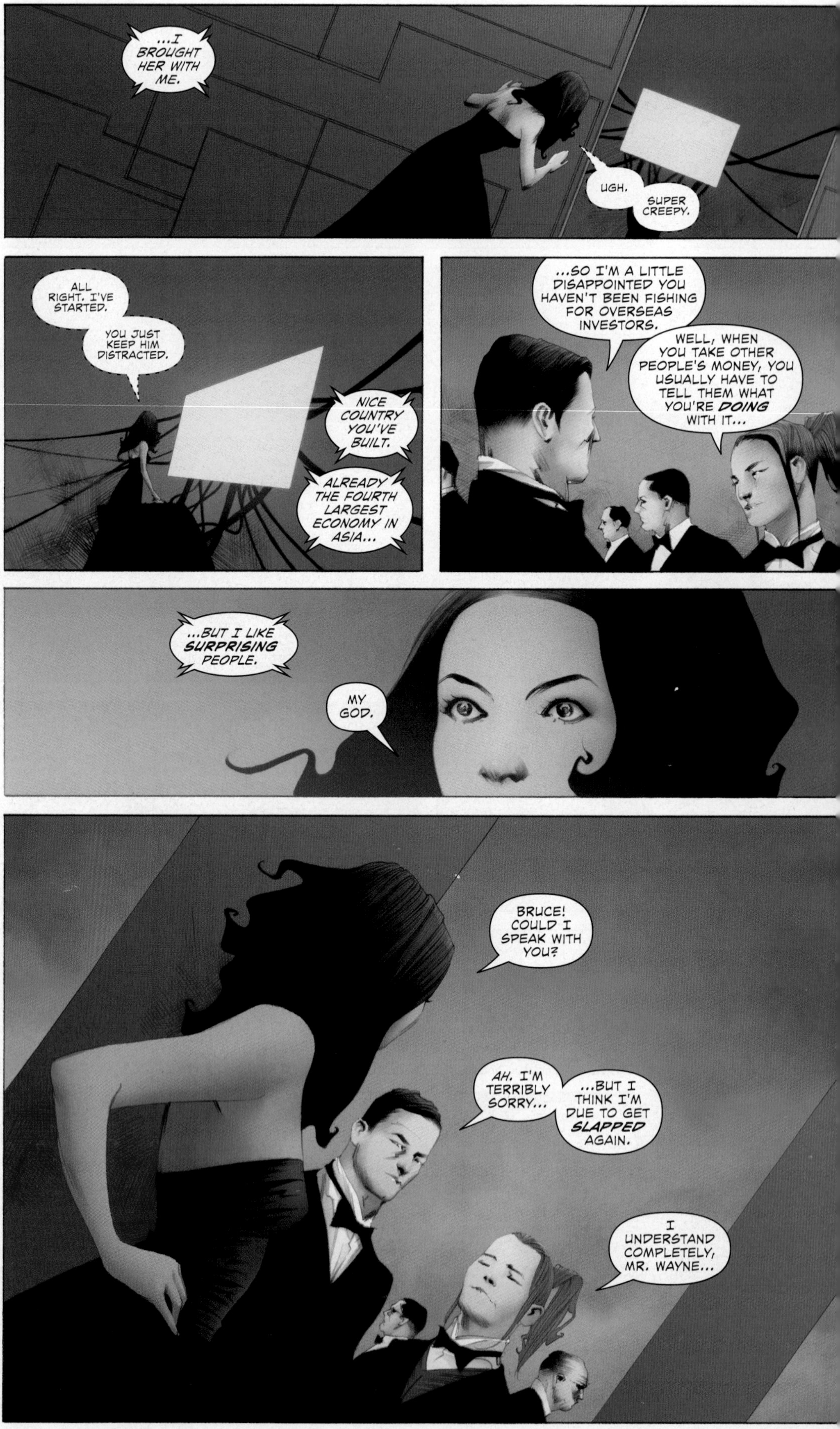
...I BROUGHT HER WITH ME.
UGH.
SUPER CREEPY.
ALL RIGHT. I'VE STARTED.
YOU JUST KEEP HIM DISTRACTED.
NICE COUNTRY YOU'VE BUILT.
ALREADY THE FOURTH LARGEST ECONOMY IN ASIA...
...SO I'M A LITTLE DISAPPOINTED YOU HAVEN'T BEEN FISHING FOR OVERSEAS INVESTORS.
WELL, WHEN YOU TAKE OTHER PEOPLE'S MONEY, YOU USUALLY HAVE TO TELL THEM WHAT YOU'RE DOING WITH IT...
...BUT I LIKE SURPRISING PEOPLE.
MY GOD.
BRUCE! COULD I SPEAK WITH YOU?
AH. I'M TERRIBLY SORRY...
...BUT I THINK I'M DUE TO GET SLAPPED AGAIN.
I UNDERSTAND COMPLETELY, MR. WAYNE...

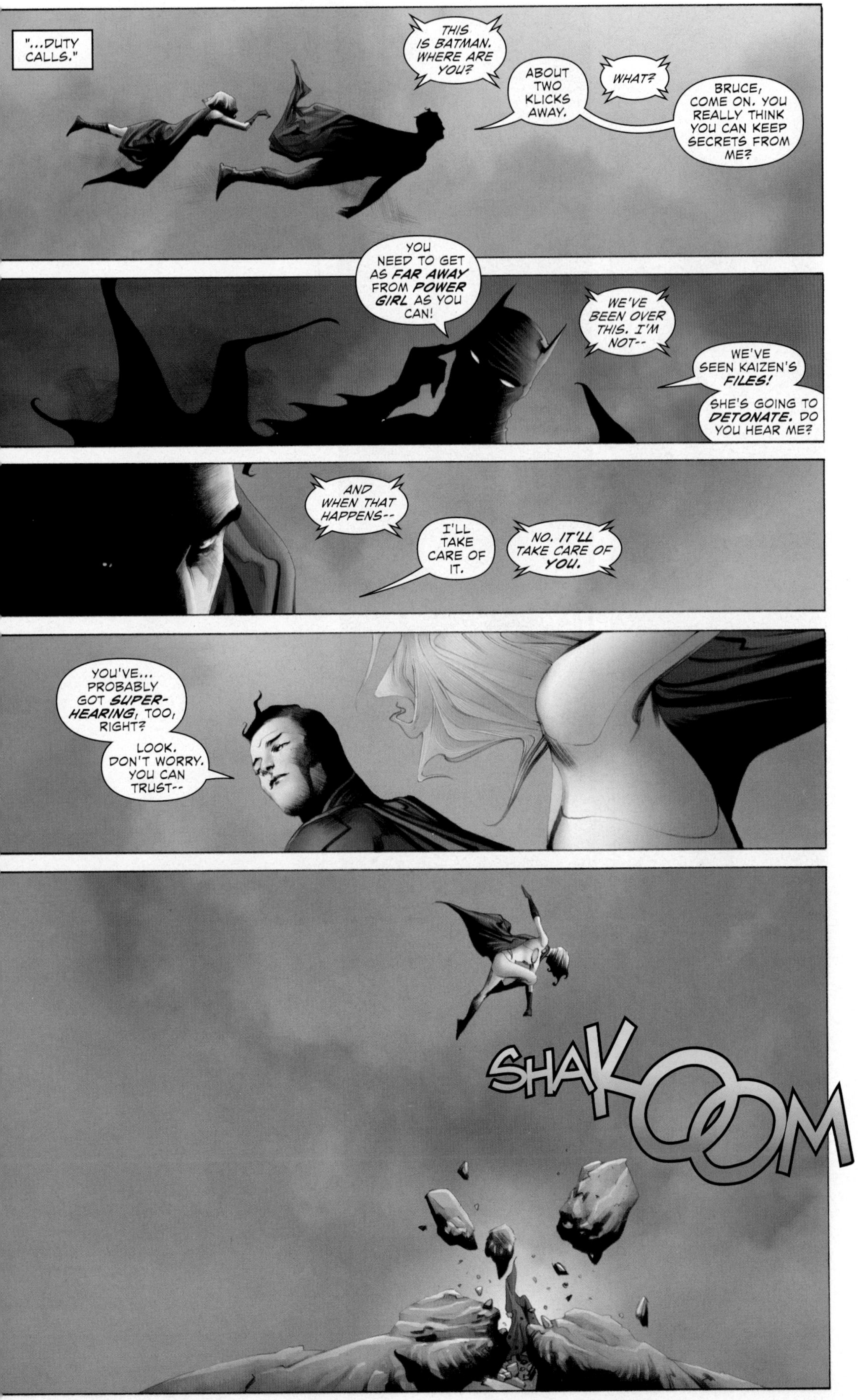

"...DUTY CALLS."
THIS IS BATMAN. WHERE ARE YOU?
ABOUT TWO KLICKS AWAY.
WHAT?
BRUCE, COME ON. YOU REALLY THINK YOU CAN KEEP SECRETS FROM ME?
YOU NEED TO GET AS FAR AWAY FROM POWER GIRL AS YOU CAN!
WE'VE BEEN OVER THIS. I'M NOT--
WE'VE SEEN KAIZEN'S FILES!
SHE'S GOING TO DETONATE. DO YOU HEAR ME?
AND WHEN THAT HAPPENS--
I'LL TAKE CARE OF IT.
NO. IT'LL TAKE CARE OF YOU.
YOU'VE... PROBABLY GOT SUPER-HEARING, TOO, RIGHT?
LOOK. DON'T WORRY. YOU CAN TRUST--
SHAKOOM

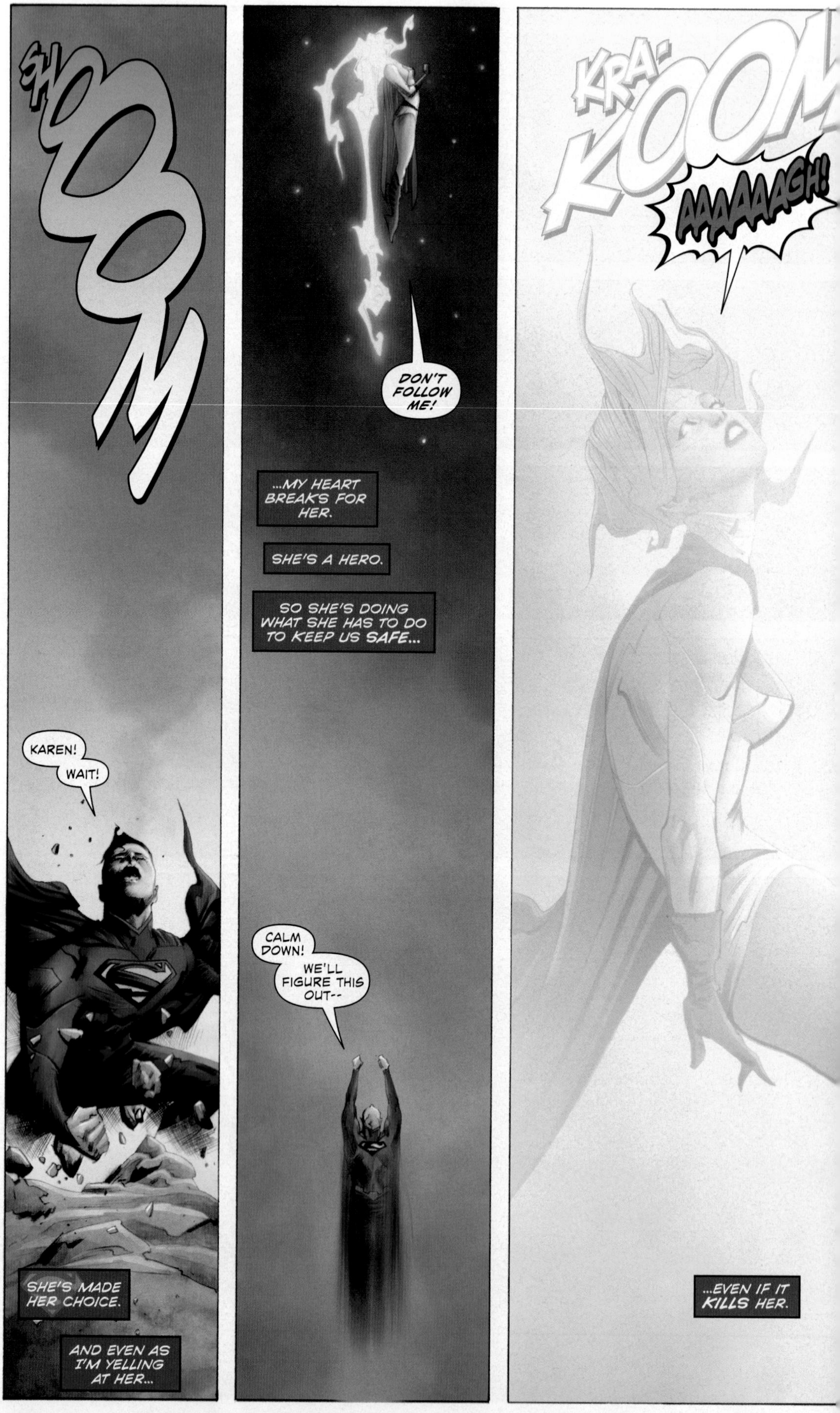
SHOOOM
KAREN!
WAIT!
SHE'S MADE HER CHOICE.
AND EVEN AS I'M YELLING AT HER...
DON'T FOLLOW ME!
...MY HEART BREAKS FOR HER.
SHE'S A HERO.
SO SHE'S DOING WHAT SHE HAS TO DO TO KEEP US SAFE...
CALM DOWN!
WE'LL FIGURE THIS OUT--
KRA-KOOOM
AAAAAAGH!
...EVEN IF IT KILLS HER.

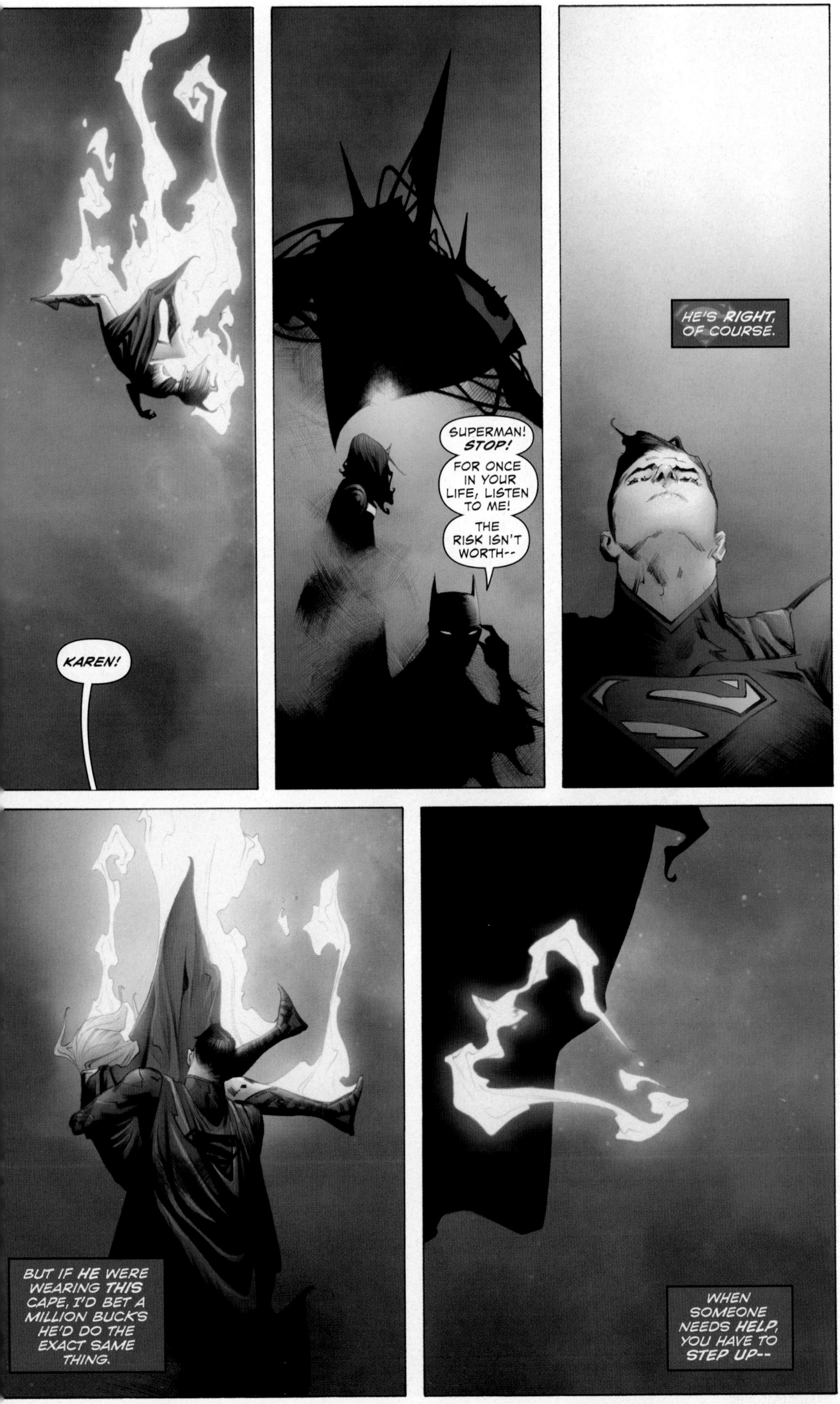
KAREN!
SUPERMAN! STOP!
FOR ONCE IN YOUR LIFE, LISTEN TO ME!
THE RISK ISN'T WORTH--
HE'S RIGHT, OF COURSE.
BUT IF HE WERE WEARING THIS CAPE, I'D BET A MILLION BUCKS HE'D DO THE EXACT SAME THING.
WHEN SOMEONE NEEDS HELP, YOU HAVE TO STEP UP--

--AND DEAL WITH THE CONSEQUENCES LATER.
KKKRAAAKOOOOOM
AAAAAAAAGH

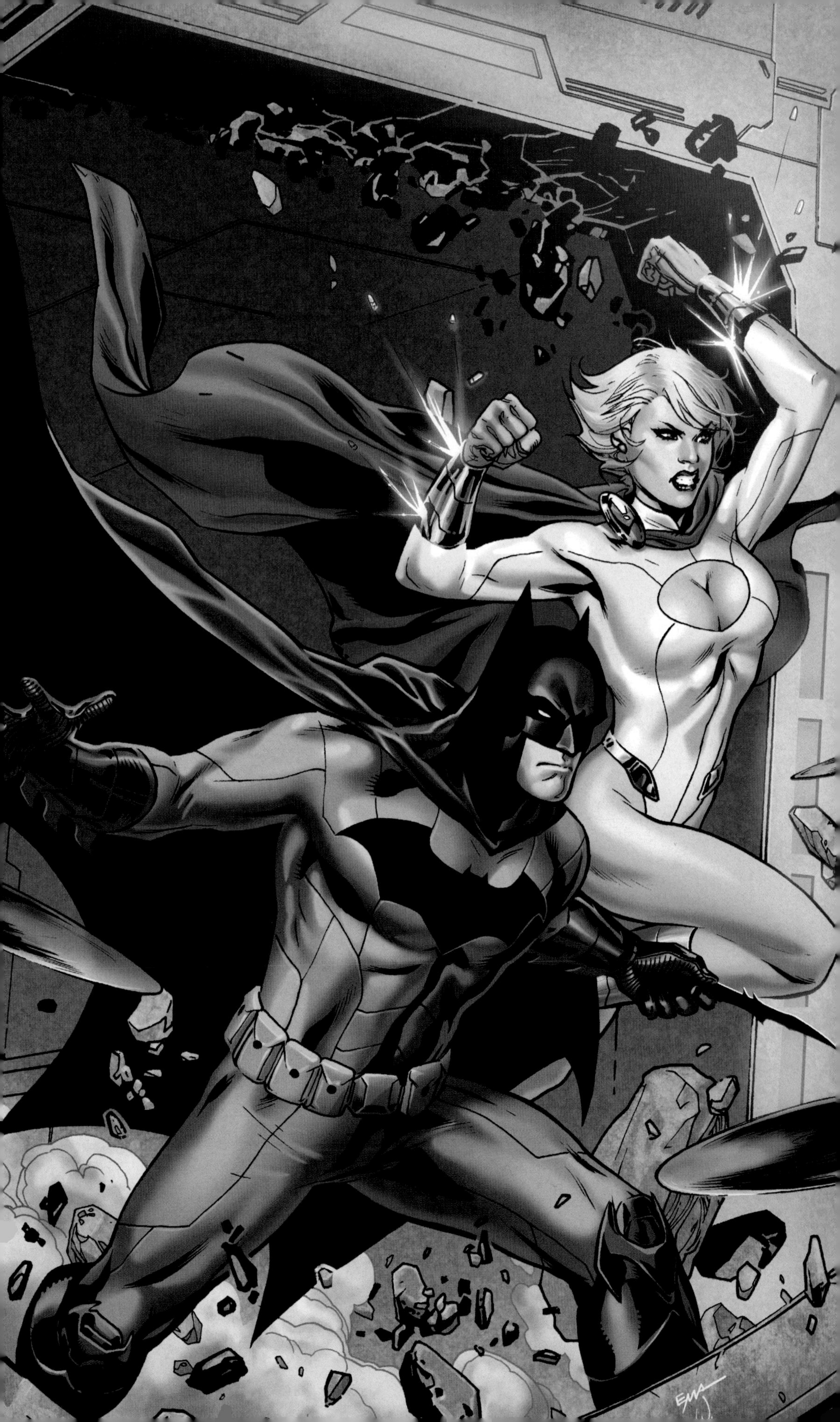

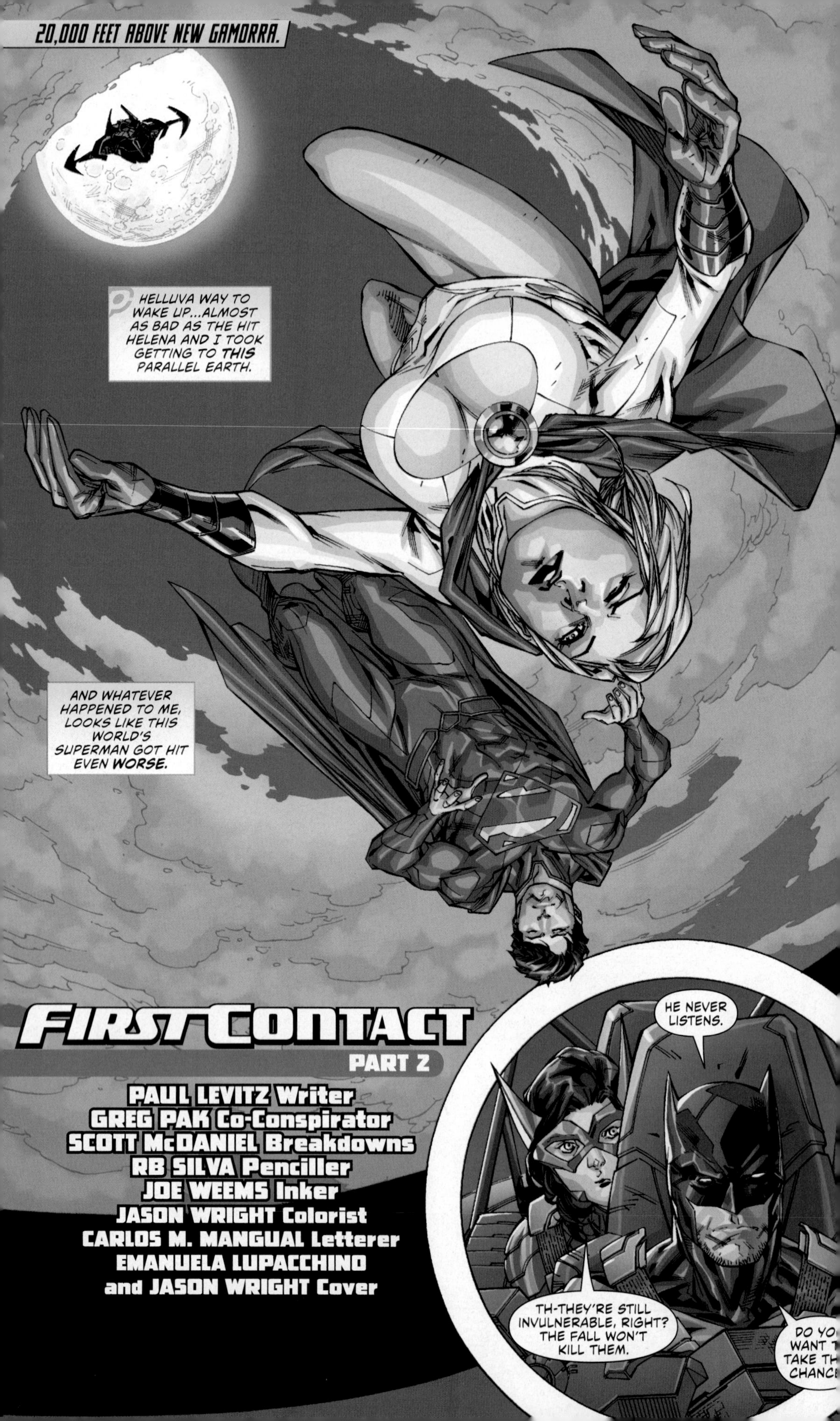
20,000 FEET ABOVE NEW GAMORRA.
HELLUVA WAY TO WAKE UP...ALMOST AS BAD AS THE HIT HELENA AND I TOOK GETTING TO THIS PARALLEL EARTH.
AND WHATEVER HAPPENED TO ME, LOOKS LIKE THIS WORLD'S SUPERMAN GOT HIT EVEN WORSE.
FIRST CONTACT
PART 2
PAUL LEVITZ Writer
GREG PAK Co-Conspirator
SCOTT McDANIEL Breakdowns
RB SILVA Penciller
JOE WEEMS Inker
JASON WRIGHT Colorist
CARLOS M. MANGUAL Letterer
EMANUELA LUPACCHINO
and JASON WRIGHT Cover
HE NEVER LISTENS.
TH-THEY'RE STILL INVULNERABLE, RIGHT? THE FALL WON'T KILL THEM.

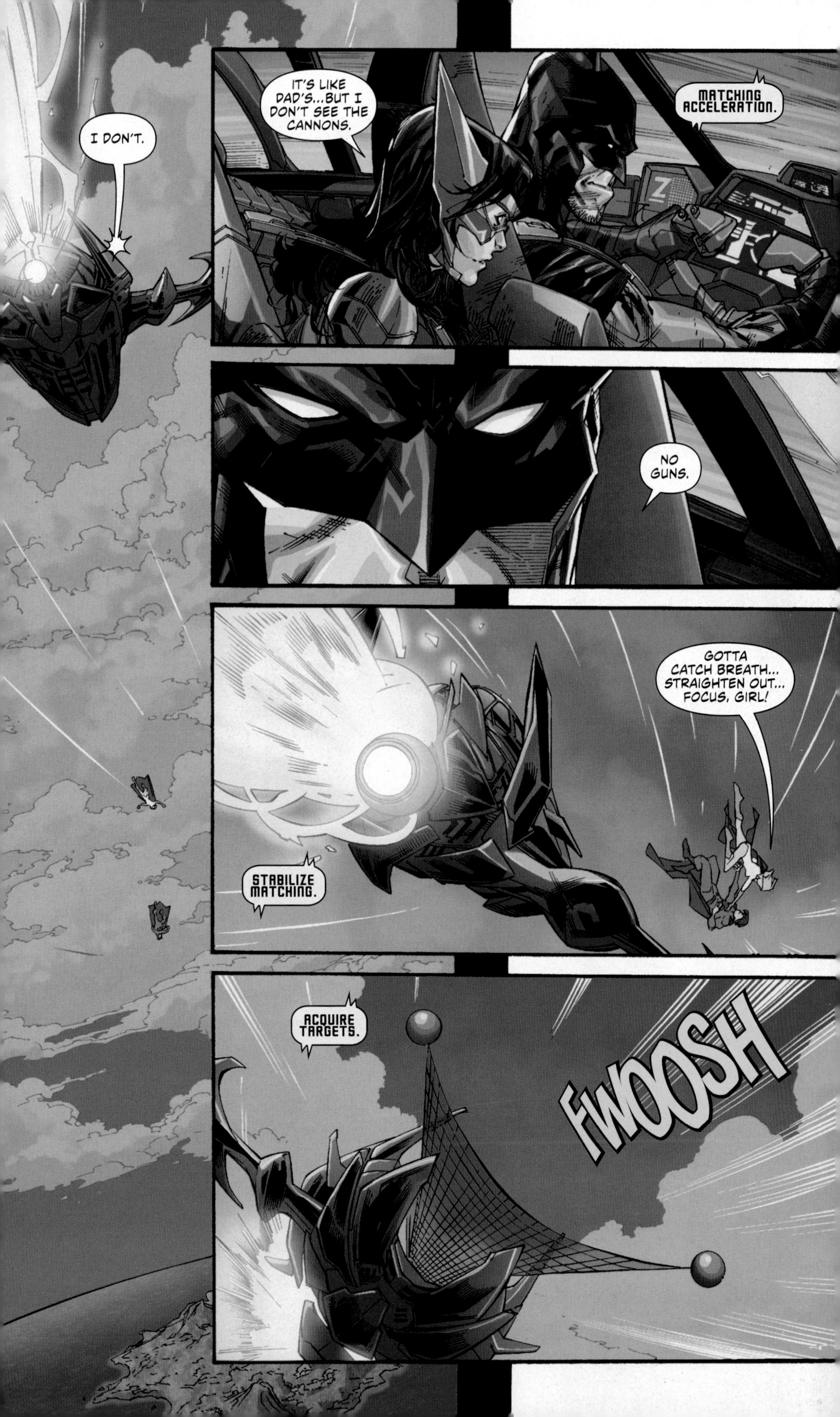
I DON'T.
IT'S LIKE DAD'S...BUT I DON'T SEE THE CANNONS.
MATCHING ACCELERATION.
NO GUNS.
GOTTA CATCH BREATH... STRAIGHTEN OUT... FOCUS, GIRL!
STABILIZE MATCHING.
ACQUIRE TARGETS.
FWOOSH

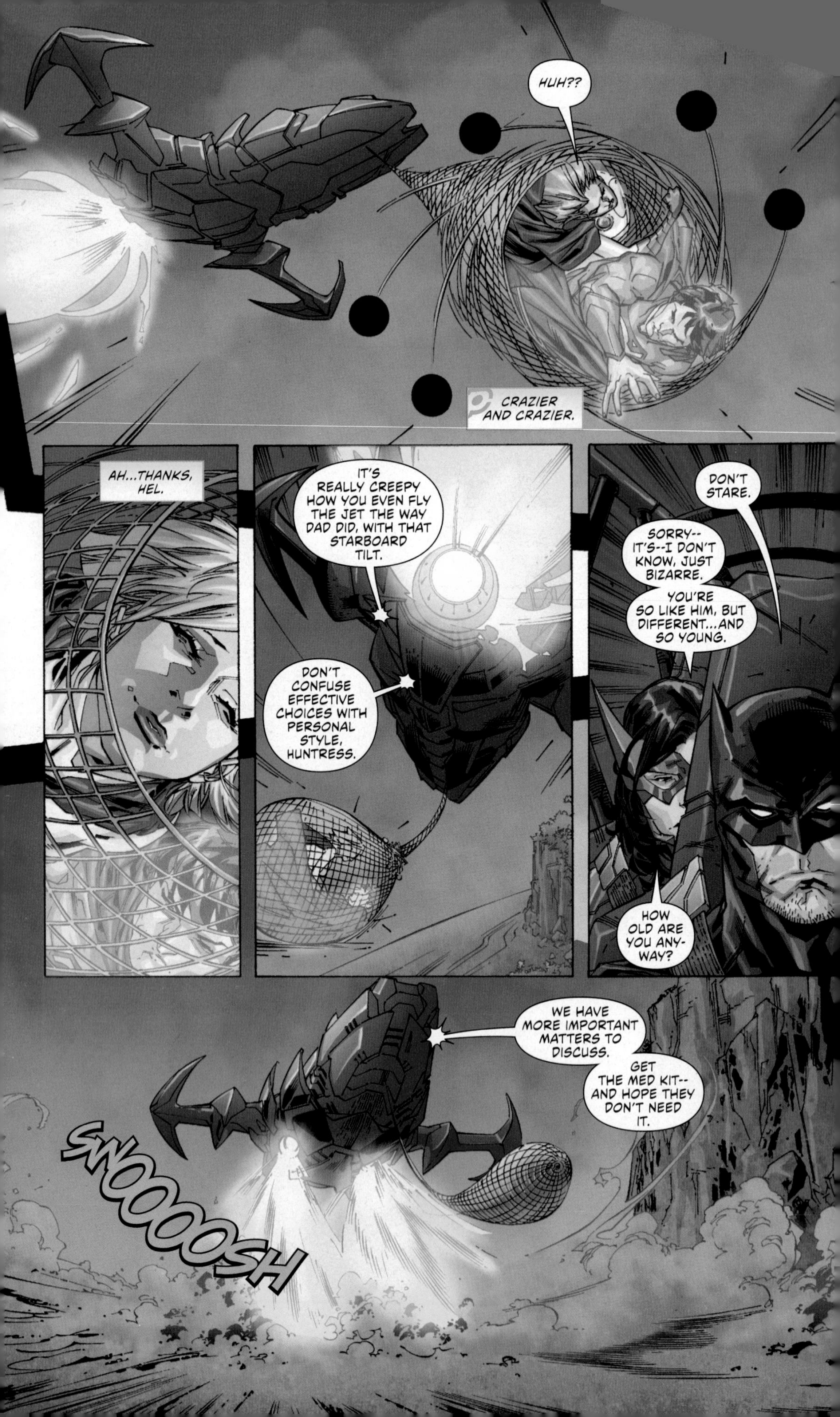
HUH??
CRAZIER AND CRAZIER.
AH...THANKS, HEL.
IT'S REALLY CREEPY HOW YOU EVEN FLY THE JET THE WAY DAD DID, WITH THAT STARBOARD TILT.
DON'T CONFUSE EFFECTIVE CHOICES WITH PERSONAL STYLE, HUNTRESS.
DON'T STARE.
SORRY-- IT'S--I DON'T KNOW, JUST BIZARRE.
YOU'RE SO LIKE HIM, BUT DIFFERENT...AND SO YOUNG.
HOW OLD ARE YOU ANY-WAY?
WE HAVE MORE IMPORTANT MATTERS TO DISCUSS.
GET THE MED KIT-- AND HOPE THEY DON'T NEED IT.
SNOOOOSH

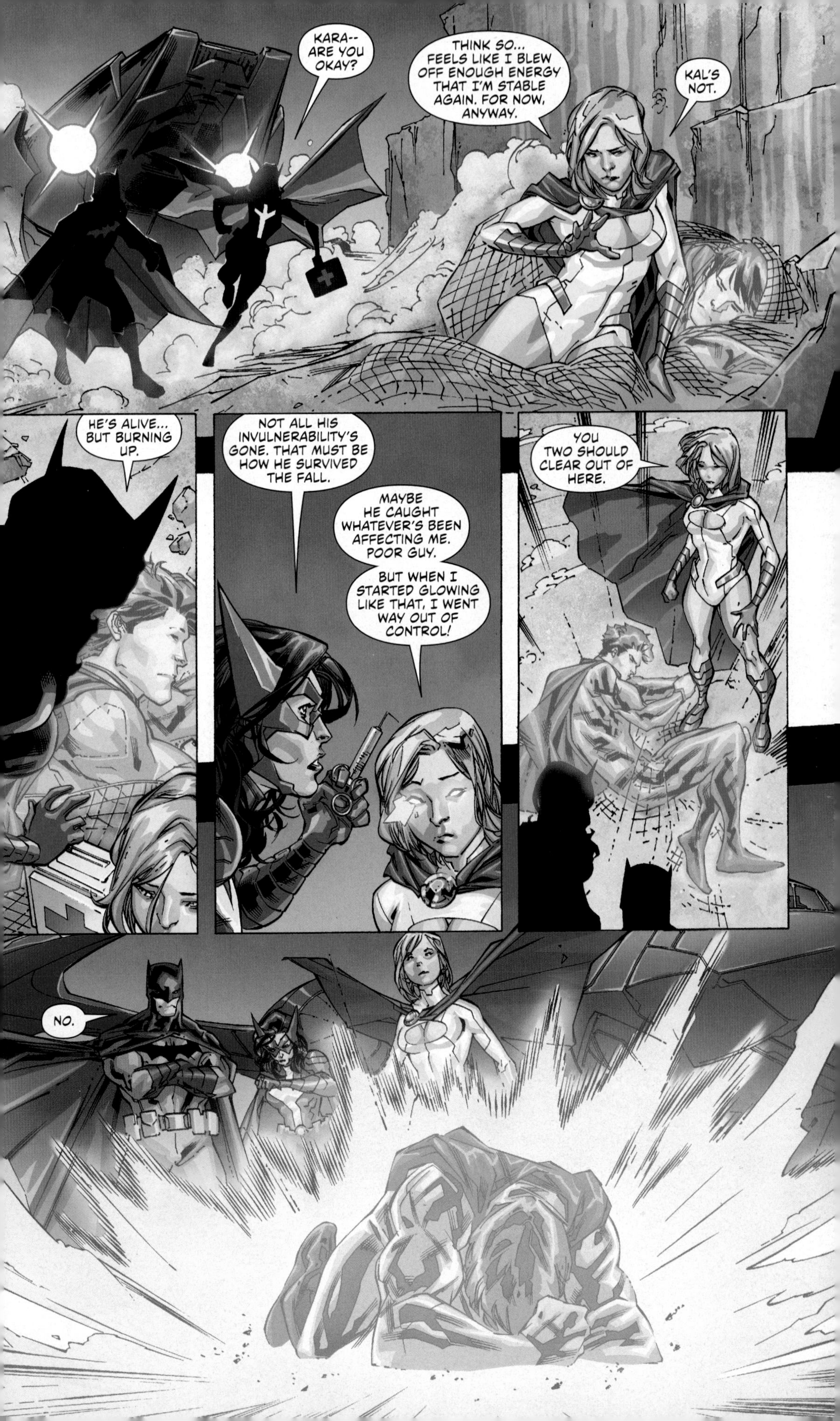
KARA-- ARE YOU OKAY?
THINK SO... FEELS LIKE I BLEW OFF ENOUGH ENERGY THAT I'M STABLE AGAIN. FOR NOW, ANYWAY.
KAL'S NOT.
HE'S ALIVE... BUT BURNING UP.
NOT ALL HIS INVULNERABILITY'S GONE. THAT MUST BE HOW HE SURVIVED THE FALL.
MAYBE HE CAUGHT WHATEVER'S BEEN AFFECTING ME. POOR GUY.
BUT WHEN I STARTED GLOWING LIKE THAT, I WENT WAY OUT OF CONTROL!
YOU TWO SHOULD CLEAR OUT OF HERE.
NO.

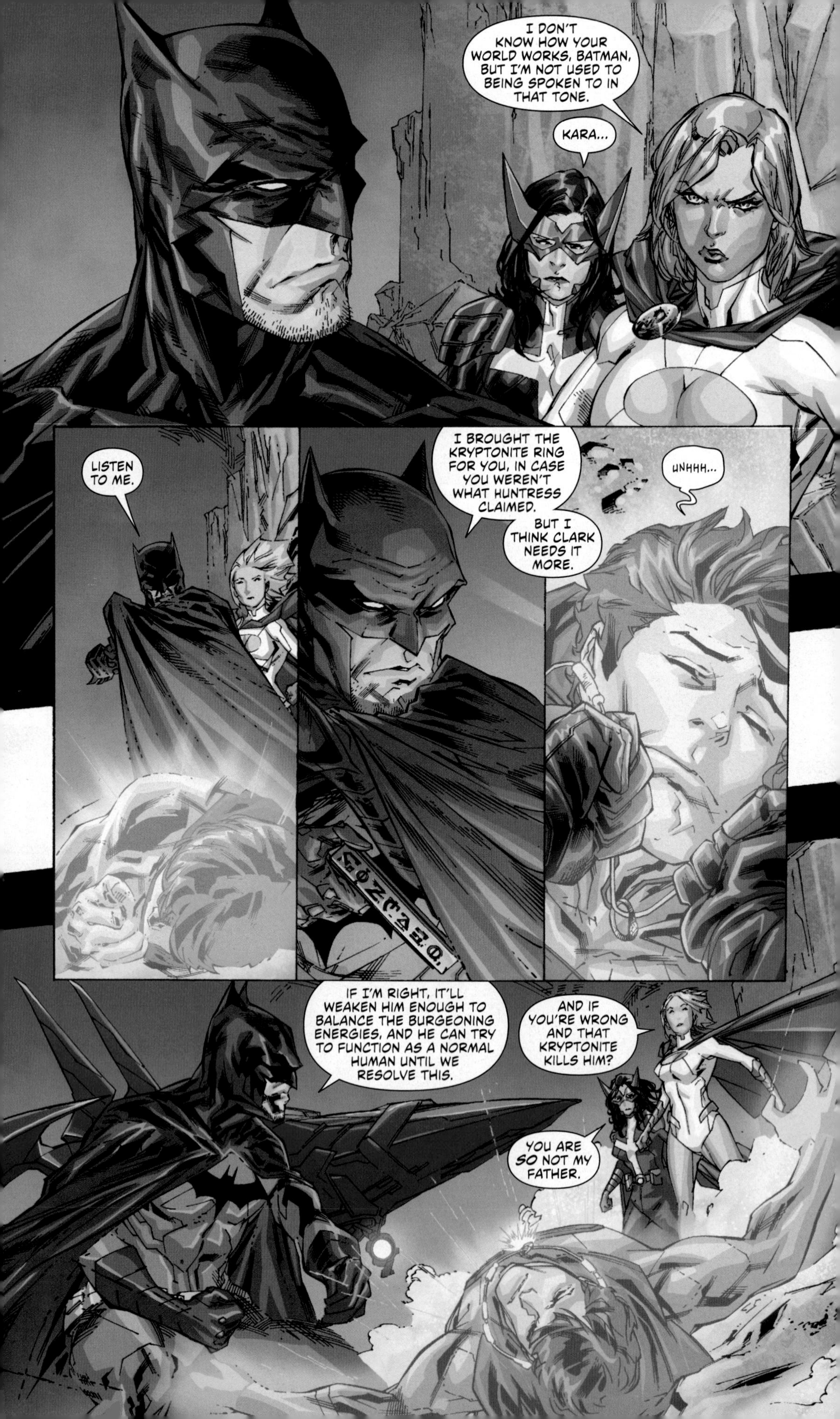
I DON'T KNOW HOW YOUR WORLD WORKS, BATMAN, BUT I'M NOT USED TO BEING SPOKEN TO IN THAT TONE.
KARA...
LISTEN TO ME.
I BROUGHT THE KRYPTONITE RING FOR YOU, IN CASE YOU WEREN'T WHAT HUNTRESS CLAIMED.
BUT I THINK CLARK NEEDS IT MORE.
UNHHH...
IF I'M RIGHT, IT'LL WEAKEN HIM ENOUGH TO BALANCE THE BURGEONING ENERGIES, AND HE CAN TRY TO FUNCTION AS A NORMAL HUMAN UNTIL WE RESOLVE THIS.
AND IF YOU'RE WRONG AND THAT KRYPTONITE KILLS HIM?
YOU ARE SO NOT MY FATHER.

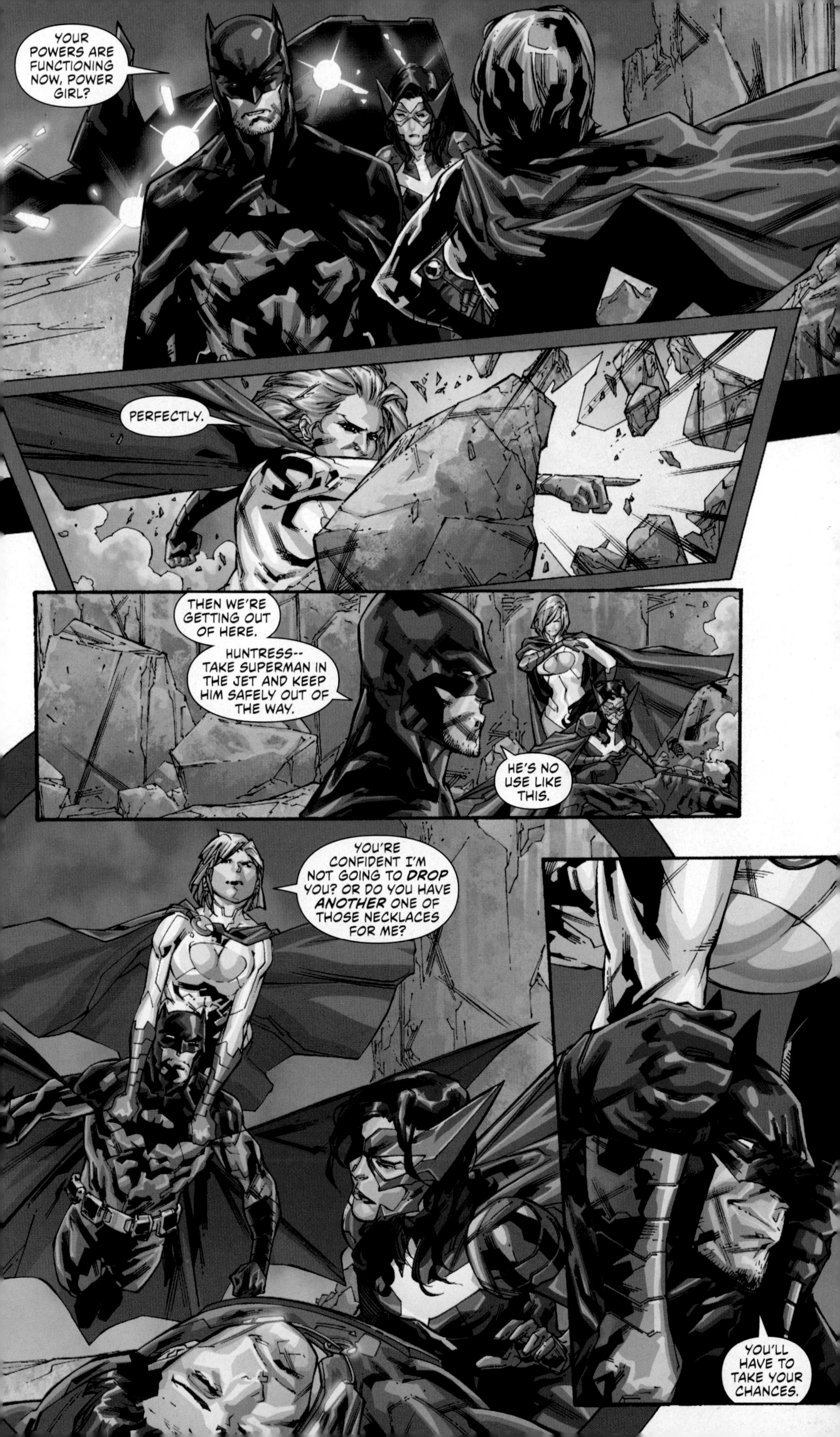
YOUR POWERS ARE FUNCTIONING NOW, POWER GIRL?
PERFECTLY.
THEN WE'RE GETTING OUT OF HERE.
HUNTRESS-- TAKE SUPERMAN IN THE JET AND KEEP HIM SAFELY OUT OF THE WAY.
HE'S NO USE LIKE THIS.
YOU'RE CONFIDENT I'M NOT GOING TO *DROP* YOU? OR DO YOU HAVE *ANOTHER* ONE OF THOSE NECKLACES FOR ME?
YOU'LL HAVE TO TAKE YOUR CHANCES.

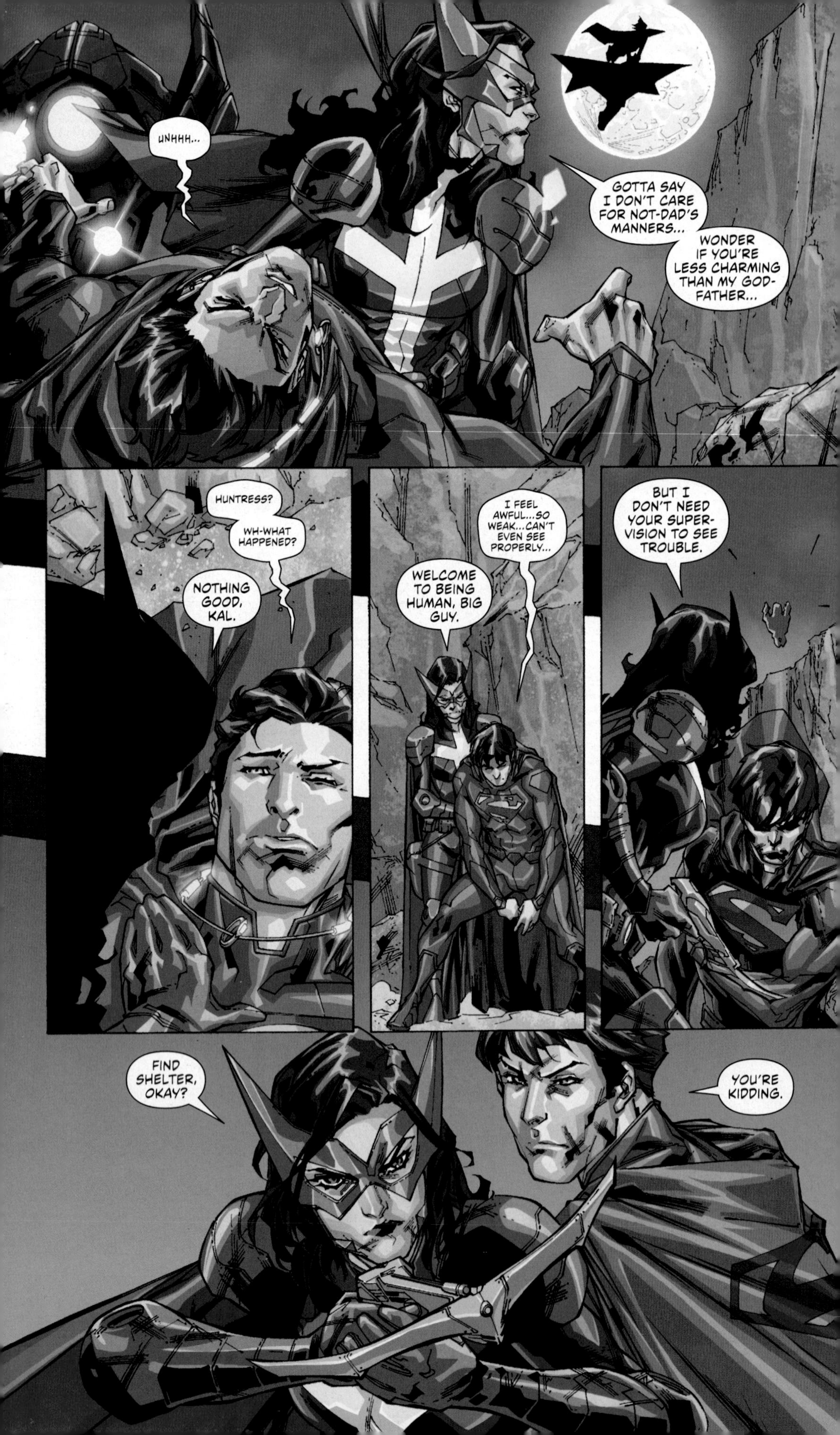
UNHHH...
GOTTA SAY I DON'T CARE FOR NOT-DAD'S MANNERS...
WONDER IF YOU'RE LESS CHARMING THAN MY GOD-FATHER...
HUNTRESS?
WH-WHAT HAPPENED?
NOTHING GOOD, KAL.
I FEEL AWFUL...SO WEAK...CAN'T EVEN SEE PROPERLY...
WELCOME TO BEING HUMAN, BIG GUY.
BUT I DON'T NEED YOUR SUPER-VISION TO SEE TROUBLE.
FIND SHELTER, OKAY?
YOU'RE KIDDING.

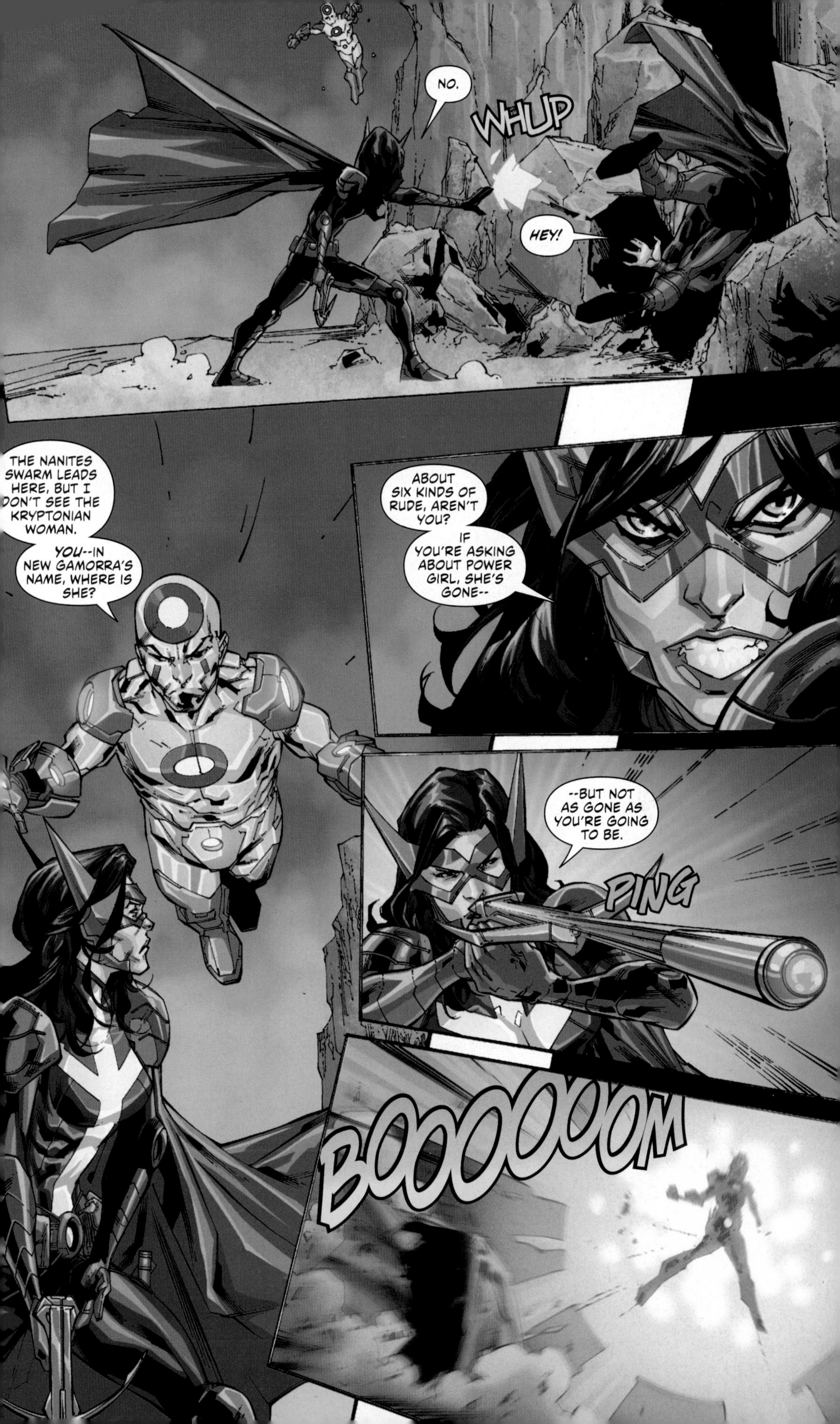
NO.
WHUP
HEY!
THE NANITES SWARM LEADS HERE, BUT I DON'T SEE THE KRYPTONIAN WOMAN.
YOU--IN NEW GAMORRA'S NAME, WHERE IS SHE?
ABOUT SIX KINDS OF RUDE, AREN'T YOU?
IF YOU'RE ASKING ABOUT POWER GIRL, SHE'S GONE--
--BUT NOT AS GONE AS YOU'RE GOING TO BE.
PING
BOOOOOOM

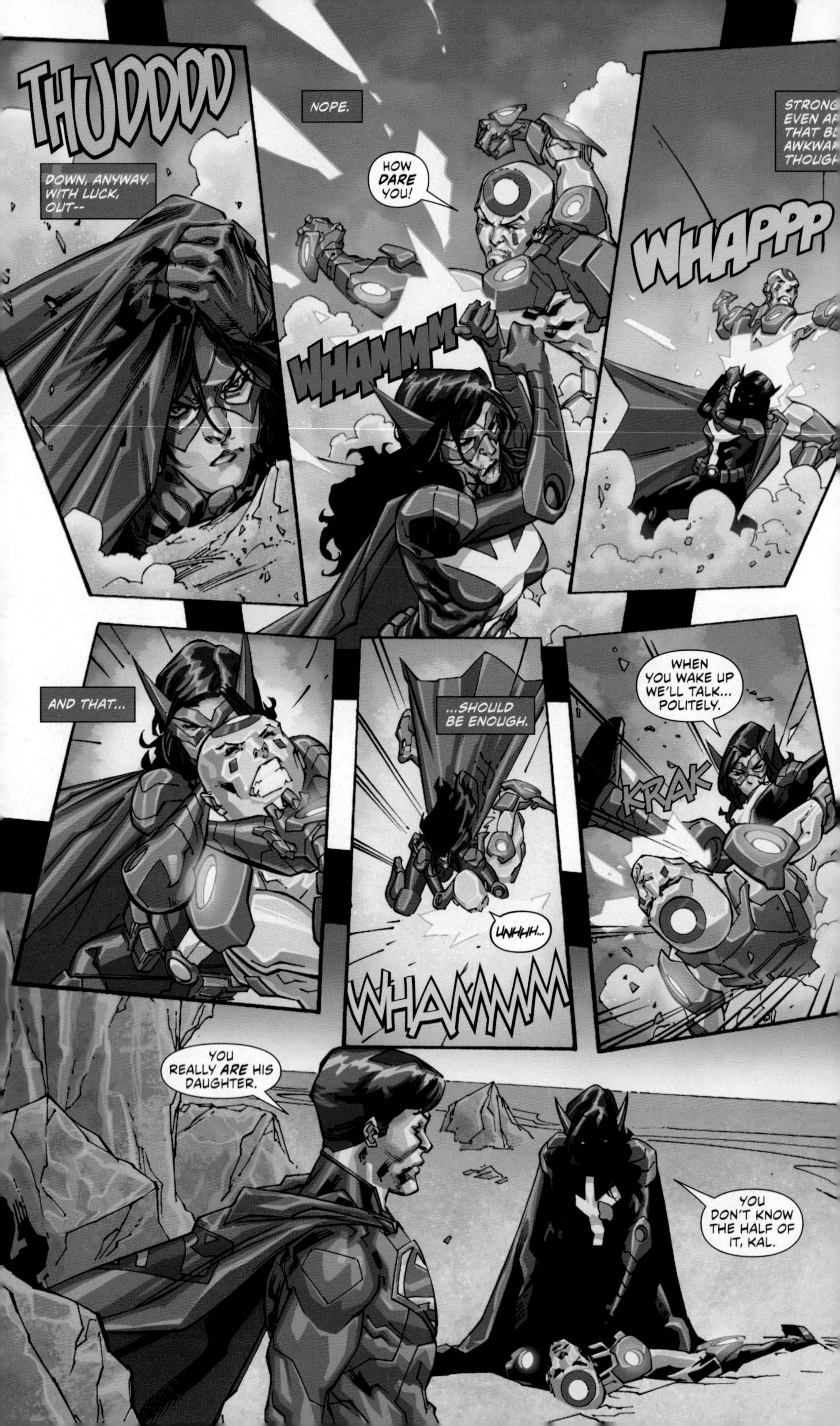
THUDDDD
DOWN, ANYWAY. WITH LUCK, OUT--
NOPE.
HOW DARE YOU!
WHAMMM
STRONG EVEN A THAT B AWKWA THOUGH
WHAPPP
AND THAT...
...SHOULD BE ENOUGH.
UNHHH...
WHAMMM
WHEN YOU WAKE UP WE'LL TALK... POLITELY.
KRAK
YOU REALLY ARE HIS DAUGHTER.
YOU DON'T KNOW THE HALF OF IT, KAL.

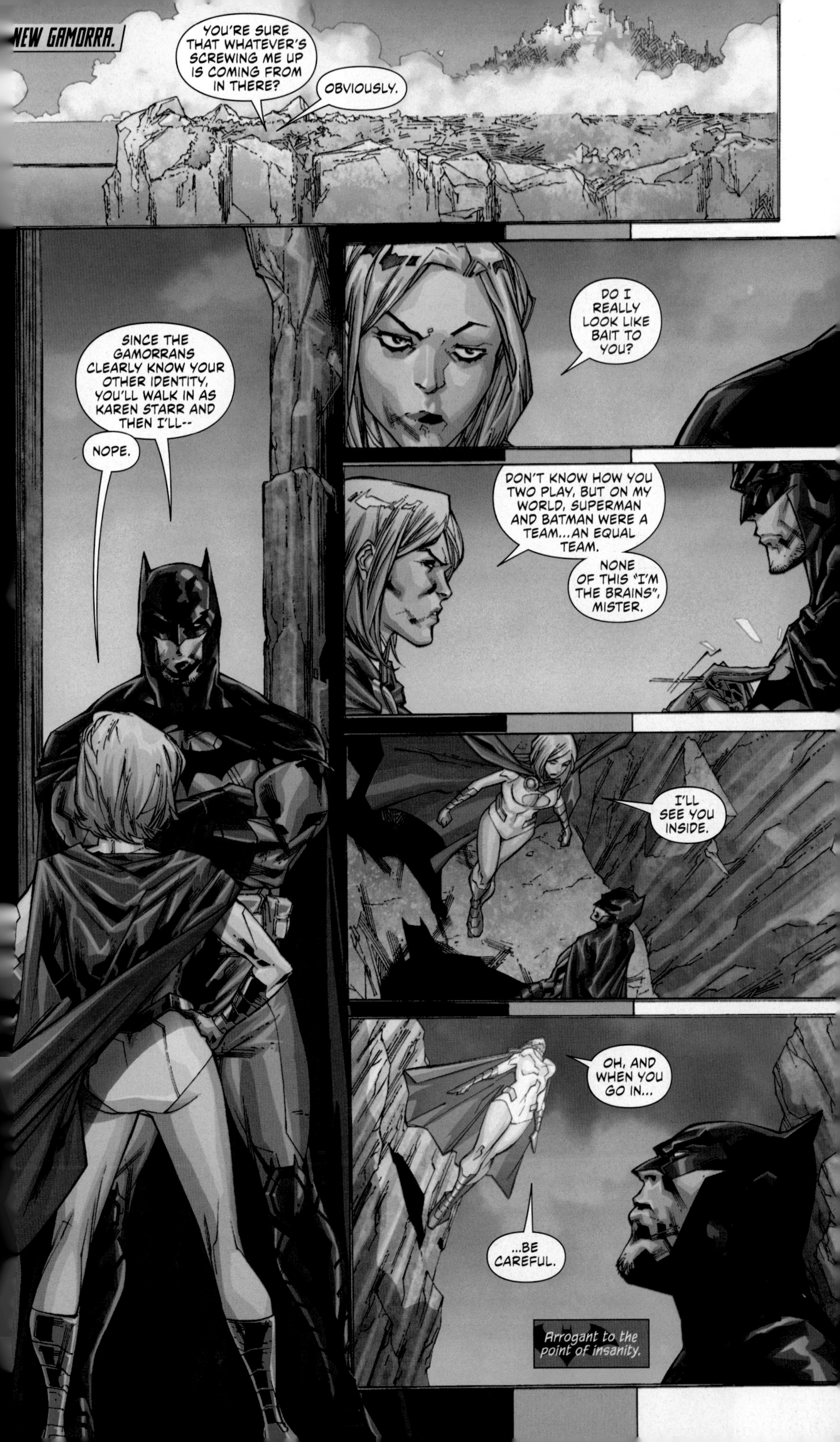
NEW GAMORRA.
YOU'RE SURE THAT WHATEVER'S SCREWING ME UP IS COMING FROM IN THERE?
OBVIOUSLY.
SINCE THE GAMORRANS CLEARLY KNOW YOUR OTHER IDENTITY, YOU'LL WALK IN AS KAREN STARR AND THEN I'LL--
NOPE.
DO I REALLY LOOK LIKE BAIT TO YOU?
DON'T KNOW HOW YOU TWO PLAY, BUT ON MY WORLD, SUPERMAN AND BATMAN WERE A TEAM...AN EQUAL TEAM.
NONE OF THIS "I'M THE BRAINS", MISTER.
I'LL SEE YOU INSIDE.
OH, AND WHEN YOU GO IN...
...BE CAREFUL.
Arrogant to the point of insanity.

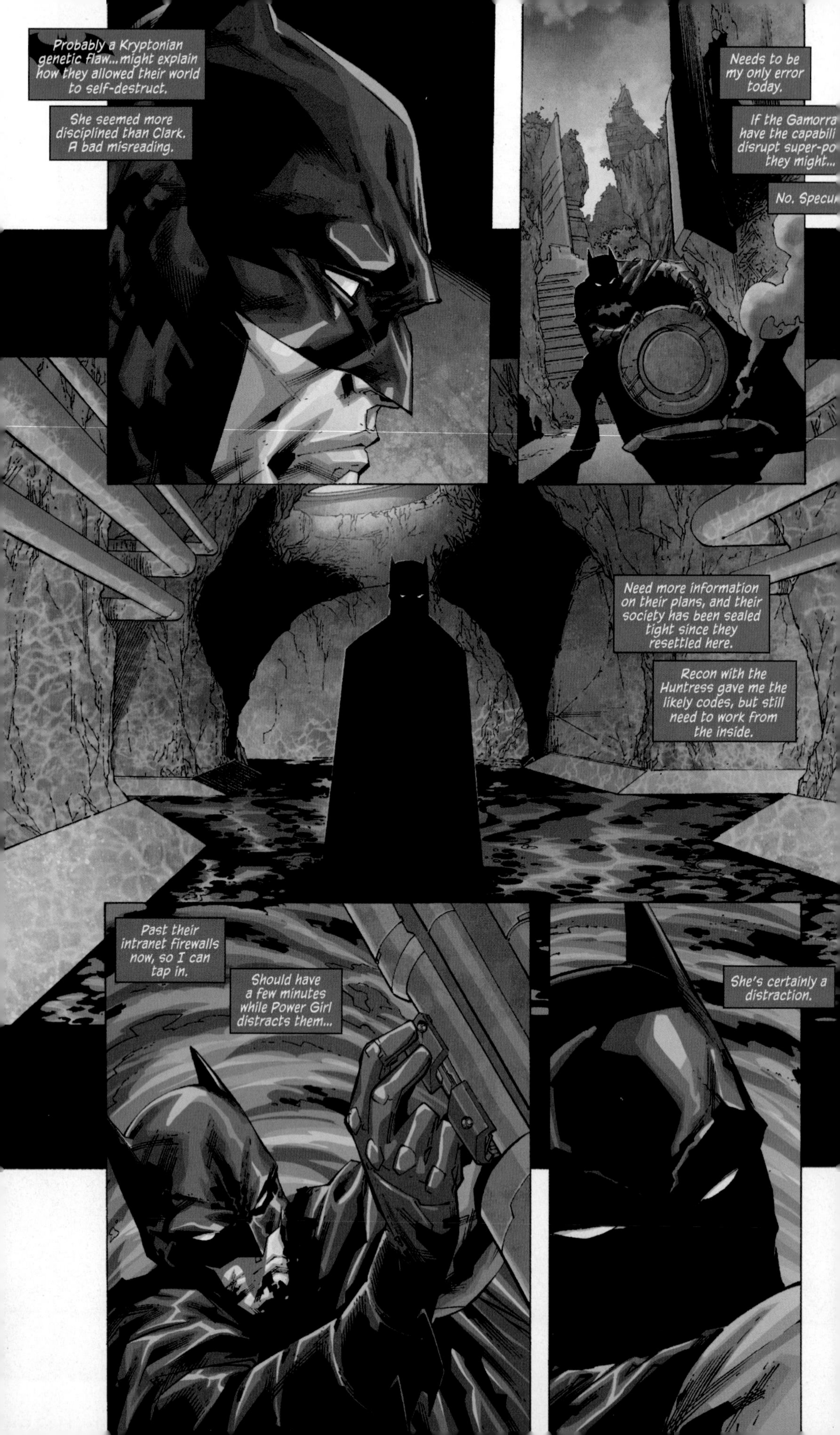

Probably a Kryptonian genetic flaw...might explain how they allowed their world to self-destruct.
She seemed more disciplined than Clark. A bad misreading.
Needs to be my only error today.
If the Gamorra have the capabili disrupt super-po they might...
No. Specu
Need more information on their plans, and their society has been sealed tight since they resettled here.
Recon with the Huntress gave me the likely codes, but still need to work from the inside.
Past their intranet firewalls now, so I can tap in.
Should have a few minutes while Power Girl distracts them...
She's certainly a distraction.

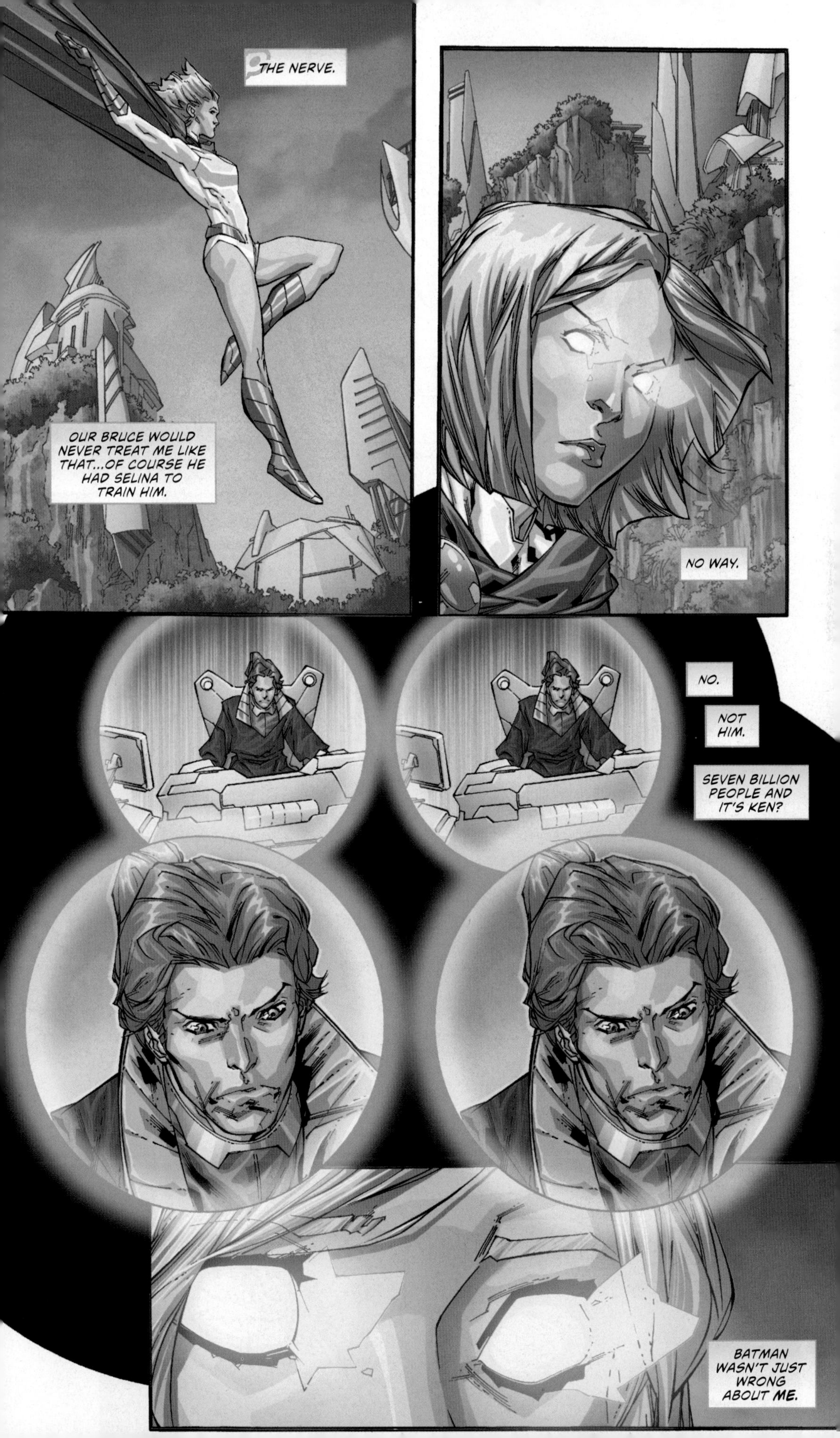
THE NERVE.
OUR BRUCE WOULD NEVER TREAT ME LIKE THAT...OF COURSE HE HAD SELINA TO TRAIN HIM.
NO WAY.
NO.
NOT HIM.
SEVEN BILLION PEOPLE AND IT'S KEN?
BATMAN WASN'T JUST WRONG ABOUT ME.

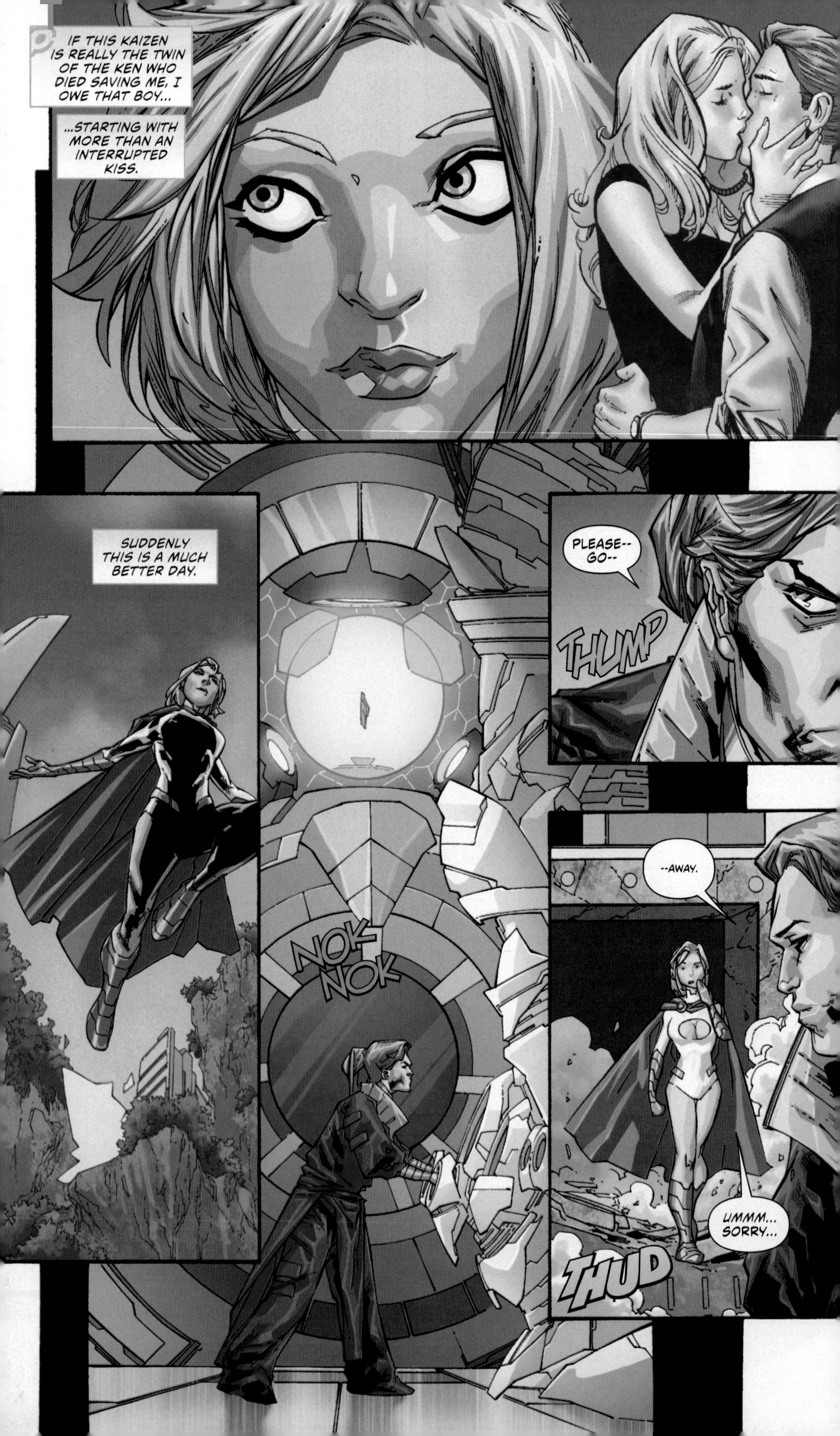
IF THIS KAIZEN IS REALLY THE TWIN OF THE KEN WHO DIED SAVING ME, I OWE THAT BOY...
...STARTING WITH MORE THAN AN INTERRUPTED KISS.
SUDDENLY THIS IS A MUCH BETTER DAY.
NOK NOK
PLEASE-- GO--
THUMP
--AWAY.
UMMM... SORRY...
THUD

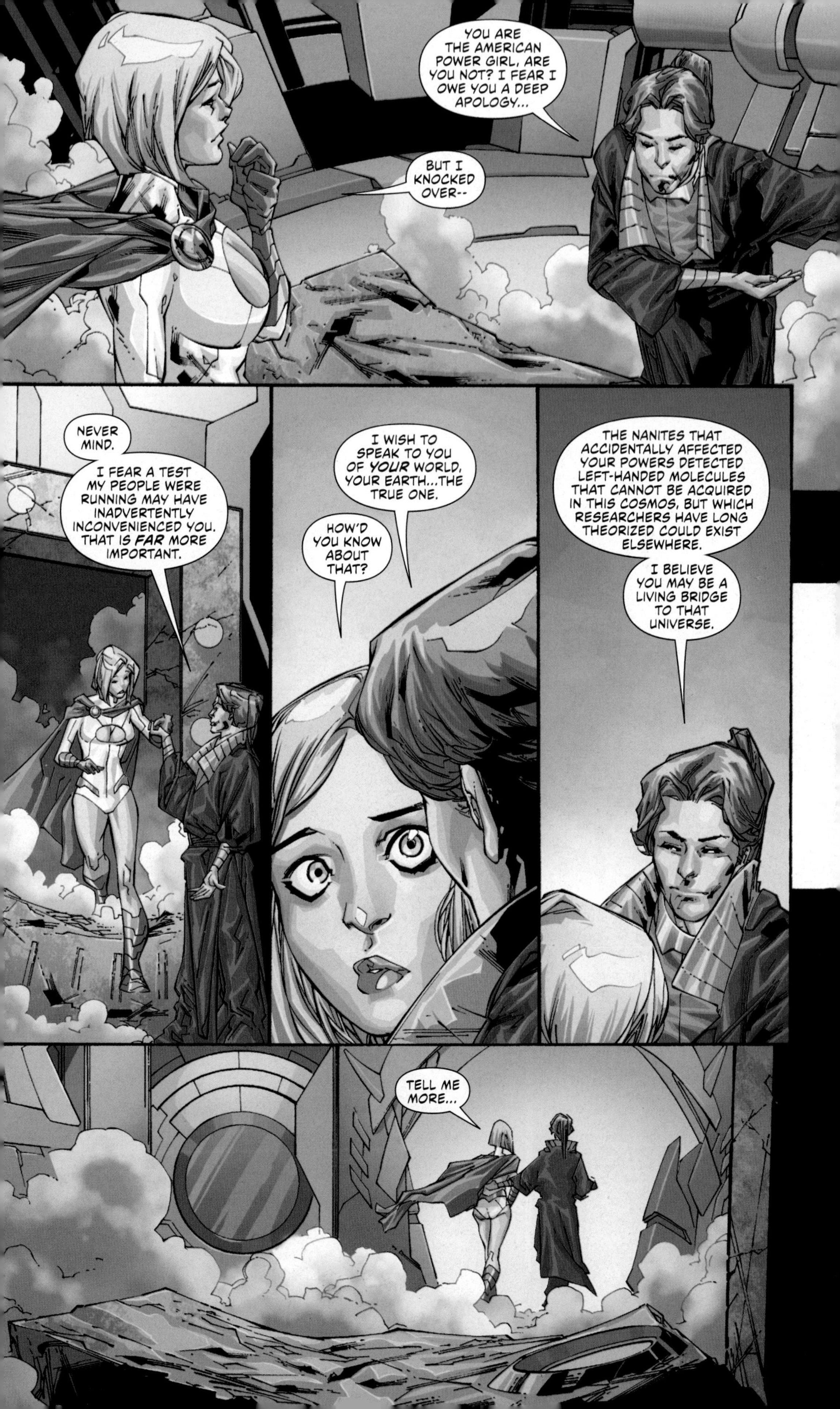

YOU ARE THE AMERICAN POWER GIRL, ARE YOU NOT? I FEAR I OWE YOU A DEEP APOLOGY...
BUT I KNOCKED OVER--
NEVER MIND.
I FEAR A TEST MY PEOPLE WERE RUNNING MAY HAVE INADVERTENTLY INCONVENIENCED YOU. THAT IS *FAR* MORE IMPORTANT.
I WISH TO SPEAK TO YOU OF *YOUR* WORLD, YOUR EARTH...THE TRUE ONE.
HOW'D YOU KNOW ABOUT THAT?
THE NANITES THAT ACCIDENTALLY AFFECTED YOUR POWERS DETECTED LEFT-HANDED MOLECULES THAT CANNOT BE ACQUIRED IN THIS COSMOS, BUT WHICH RESEARCHERS HAVE LONG THEORIZED COULD EXIST ELSEWHERE.
I BELIEVE YOU MAY BE A LIVING BRIDGE TO THAT UNIVERSE.
TELL ME MORE...

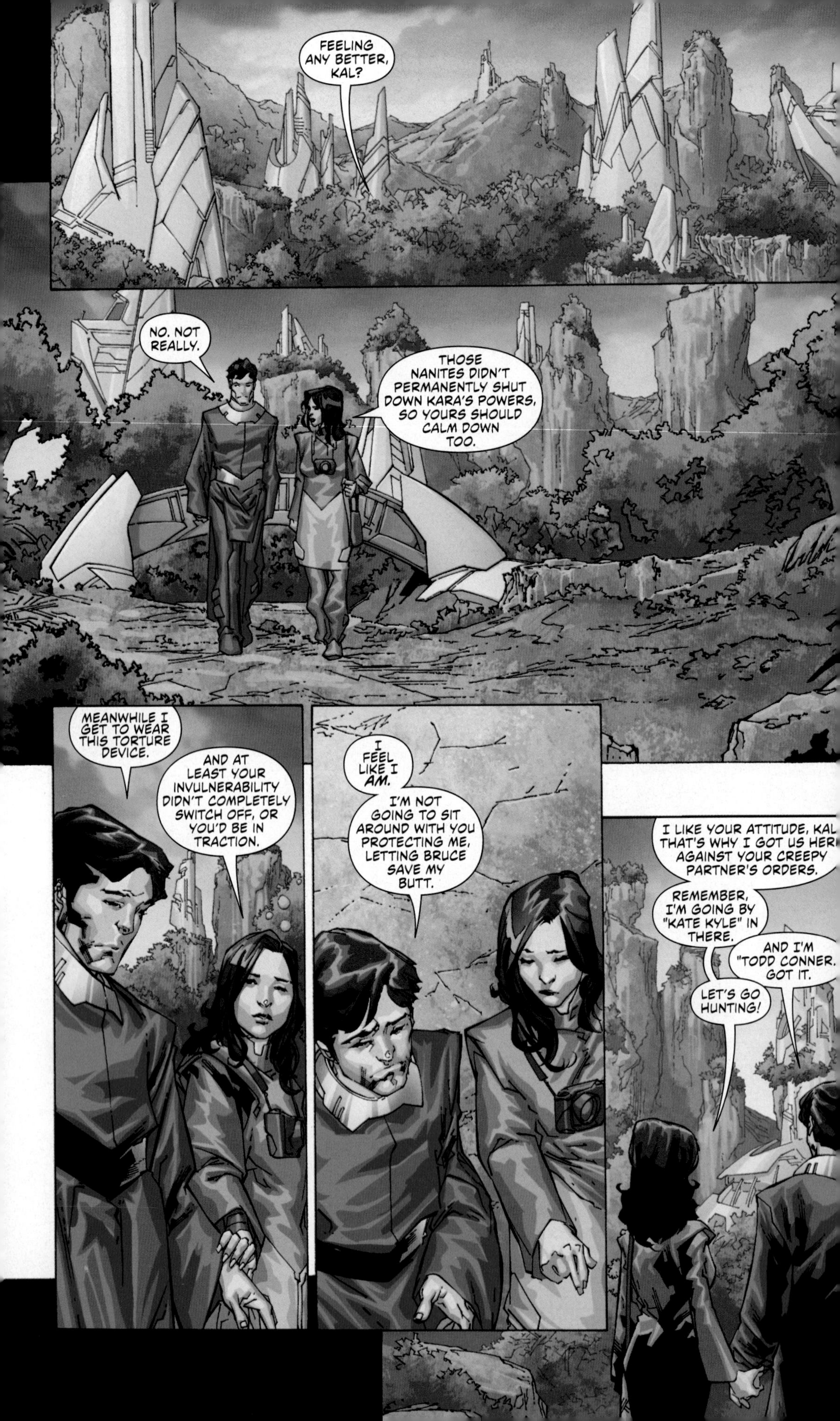
FEELING ANY BETTER, KAL?
NO. NOT REALLY.
THOSE NANITES DIDN'T PERMANENTLY SHUT DOWN KARA'S POWERS, SO YOURS SHOULD CALM DOWN TOO.
MEANWHILE I GET TO WEAR THIS TORTURE DEVICE.
AND AT LEAST YOUR INVULNERABILITY DIDN'T COMPLETELY SWITCH OFF, OR YOU'D BE IN TRACTION.
I FEEL LIKE I AM.
I'M NOT GOING TO SIT AROUND WITH YOU PROTECTING ME, LETTING BRUCE SAVE MY BUTT.
I LIKE YOUR ATTITUDE, KAL THAT'S WHY I GOT US HER AGAINST YOUR CREEPY PARTNER'S ORDERS.
REMEMBER, I'M GOING BY "KATE KYLE" IN THERE.
AND I'M "TODD CONNER. GOT IT.
LET'S GO HUNTING!

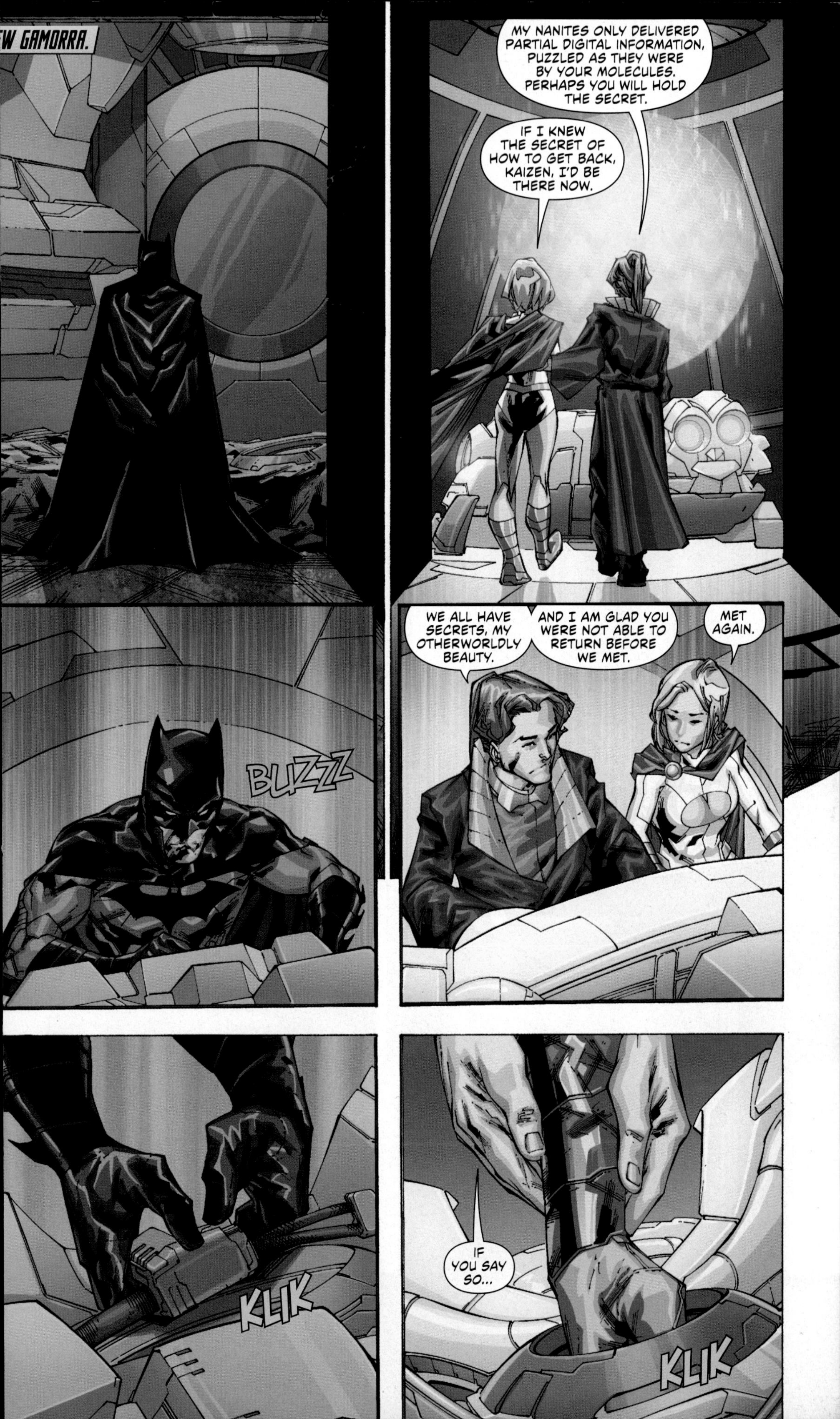

...EW GAMORRA.
MY NANITES ONLY DELIVERED PARTIAL DIGITAL INFORMATION, PUZZLED AS THEY WERE BY YOUR MOLECULES. PERHAPS YOU WILL HOLD THE SECRET.
IF I KNEW THE SECRET OF HOW TO GET BACK, KAIZEN, I'D BE THERE NOW.
BUZZZ
WE ALL HAVE SECRETS, MY OTHERWORLDLY BEAUTY.
AND I AM GLAD YOU WERE NOT ABLE TO RETURN BEFORE WE MET.
MET AGAIN.
KLIK
IF YOU SAY SO...
KLIK

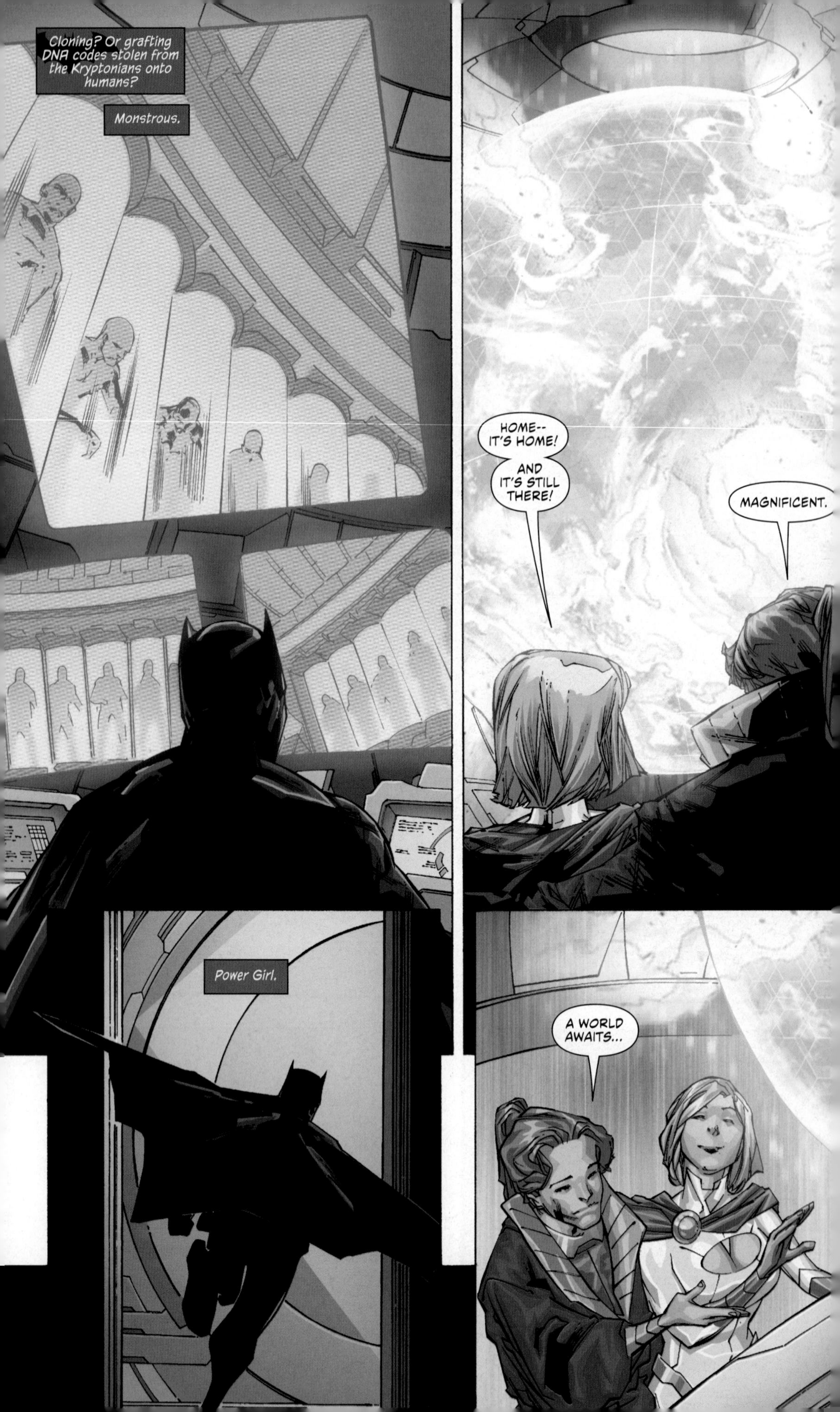
Cloning? Or grafting DNA codes stolen from the Kryptonians onto humans?
Monstrous.
HOME-- IT'S HOME!
AND IT'S STILL THERE!
MAGNIFICENT.
Power Girl.
A WORLD AWAITS...

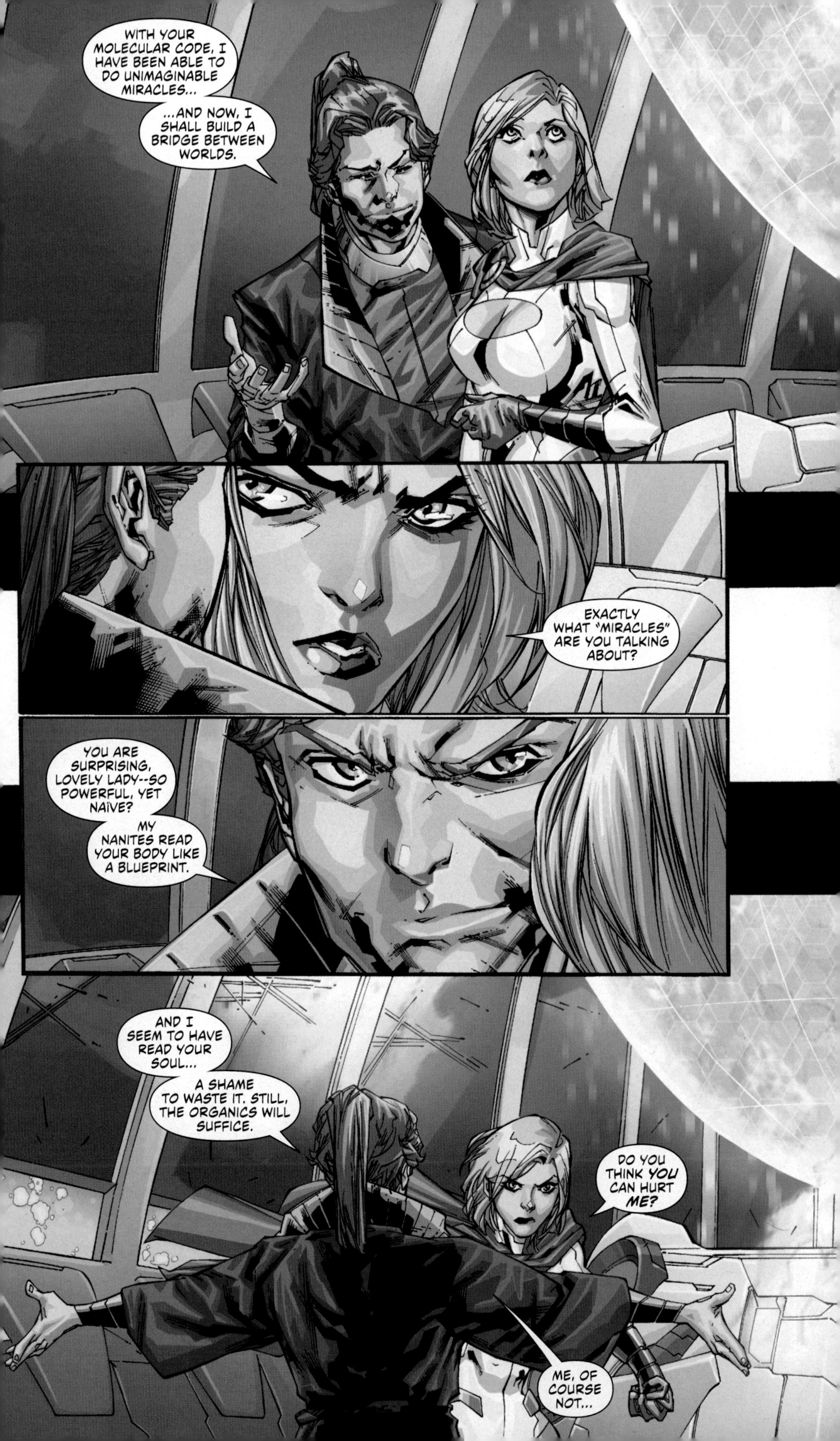
WITH YOUR MOLECULAR CODE, I HAVE BEEN ABLE TO DO UNIMAGINABLE MIRACLES...
...AND NOW, I SHALL BUILD A BRIDGE BETWEEN WORLDS.
EXACTLY WHAT "MIRACLES" ARE YOU TALKING ABOUT?
YOU ARE SURPRISING, LOVELY LADY--SO POWERFUL, YET NAÏVE?
MY NANITES READ YOUR BODY LIKE A BLUEPRINT.
AND I SEEM TO HAVE READ YOUR SOUL...
A SHAME TO WASTE IT. STILL, THE ORGANICS WILL SUFFICE.
DO YOU THINK YOU CAN HURT ME?
ME, OF COURSE NOT...

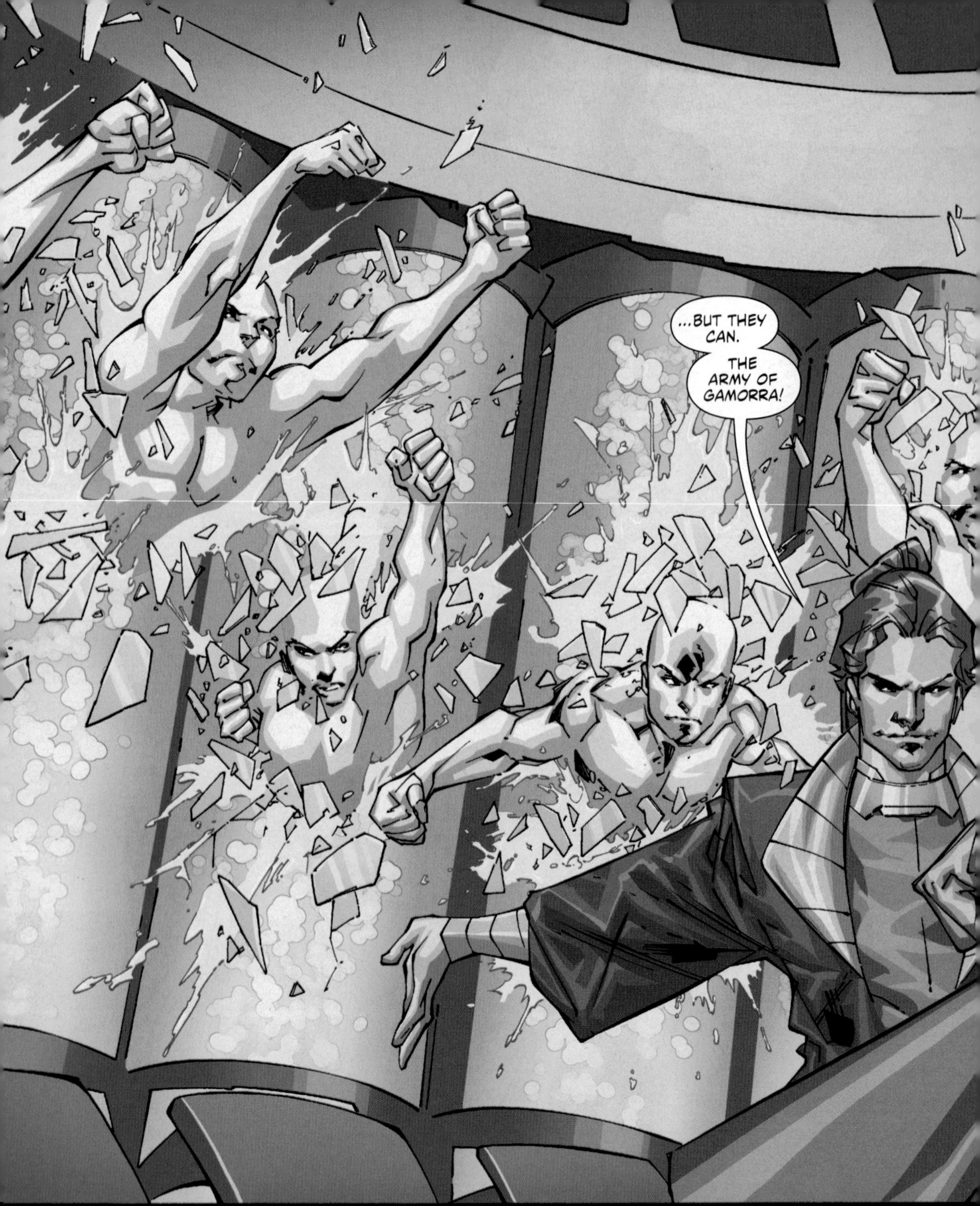
...BUT THEY CAN.
THE ARMY OF GAMORRA!

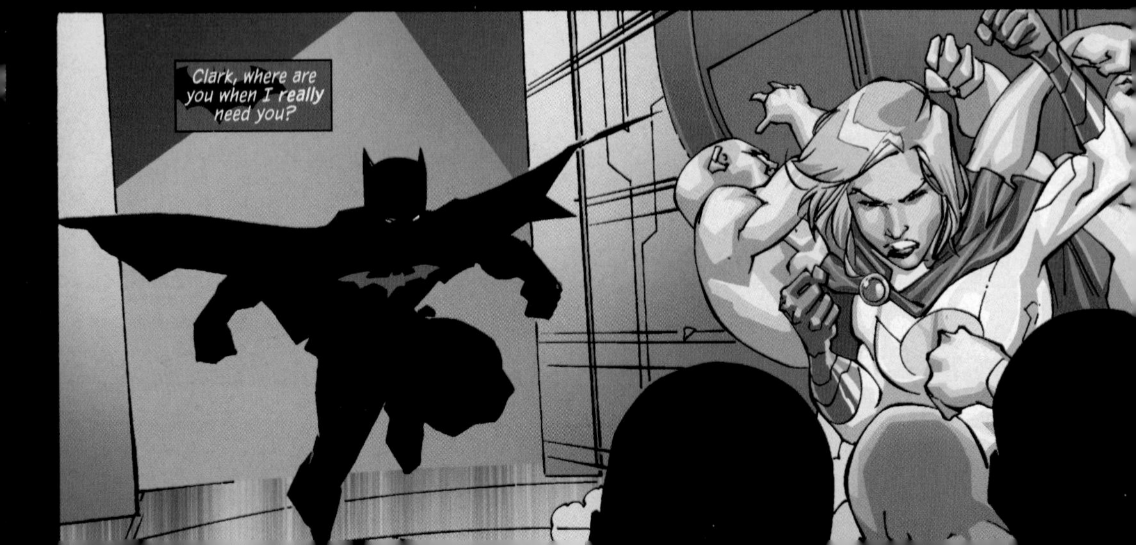
Clark, where are you when I really need you?

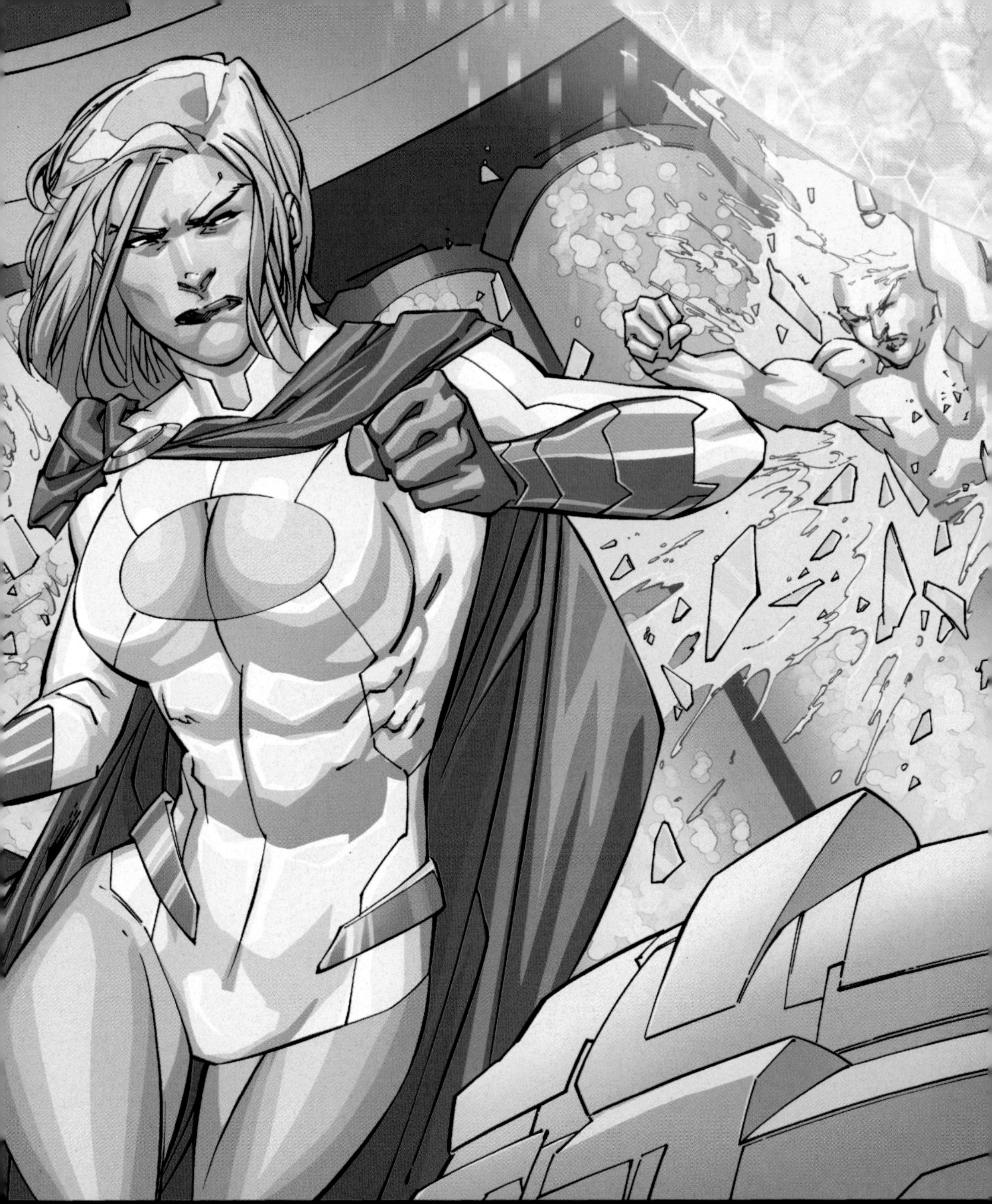

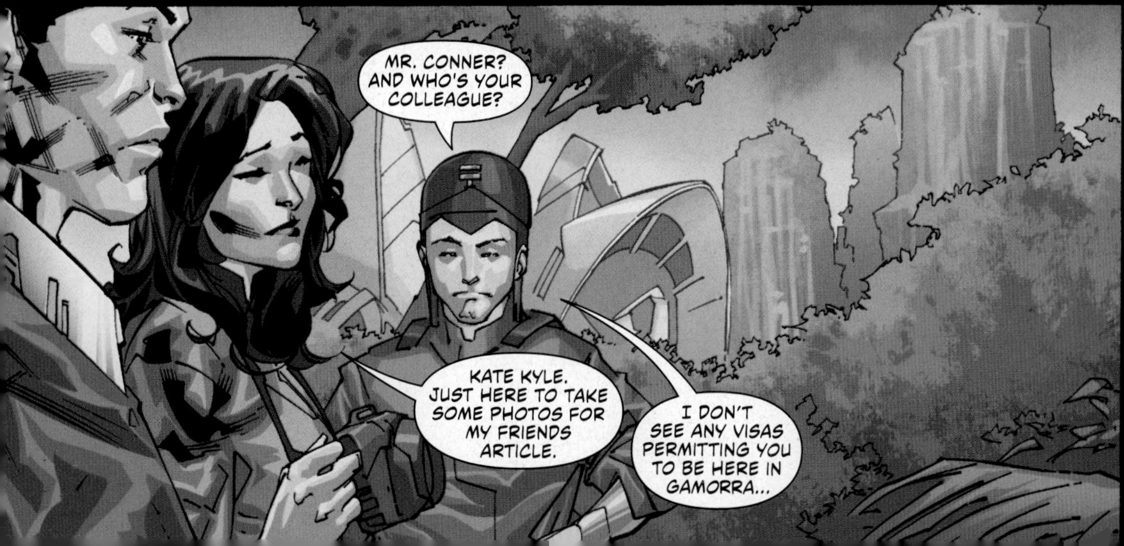
MR. CONNER? AND WHO'S YOUR COLLEAGUE?
KATE KYLE. JUST HERE TO TAKE SOME PHOTOS FOR MY FRIENDS ARTICLE.
I DON'T SEE ANY VISAS PERMITTING YOU TO BE HERE IN GAMORRA...

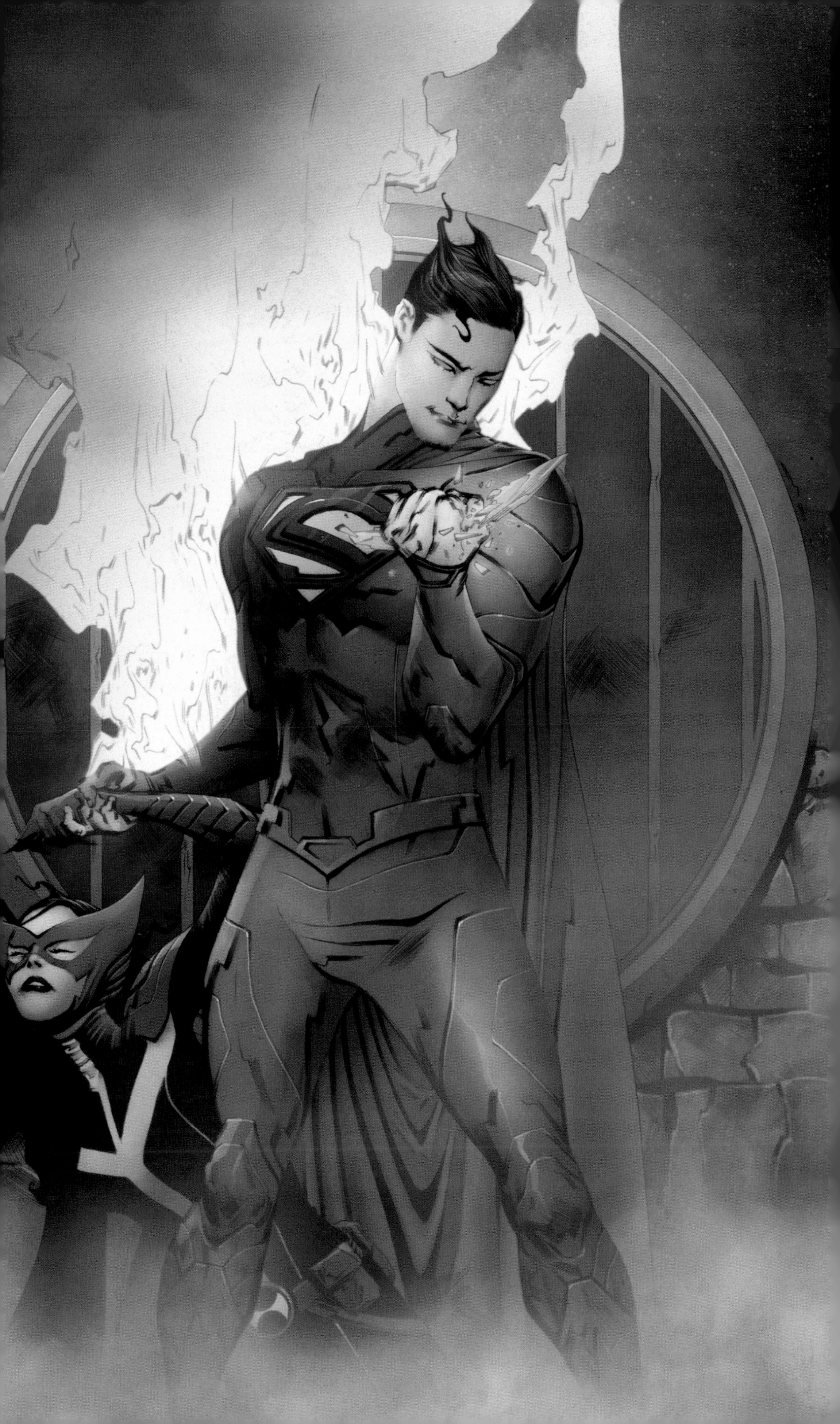

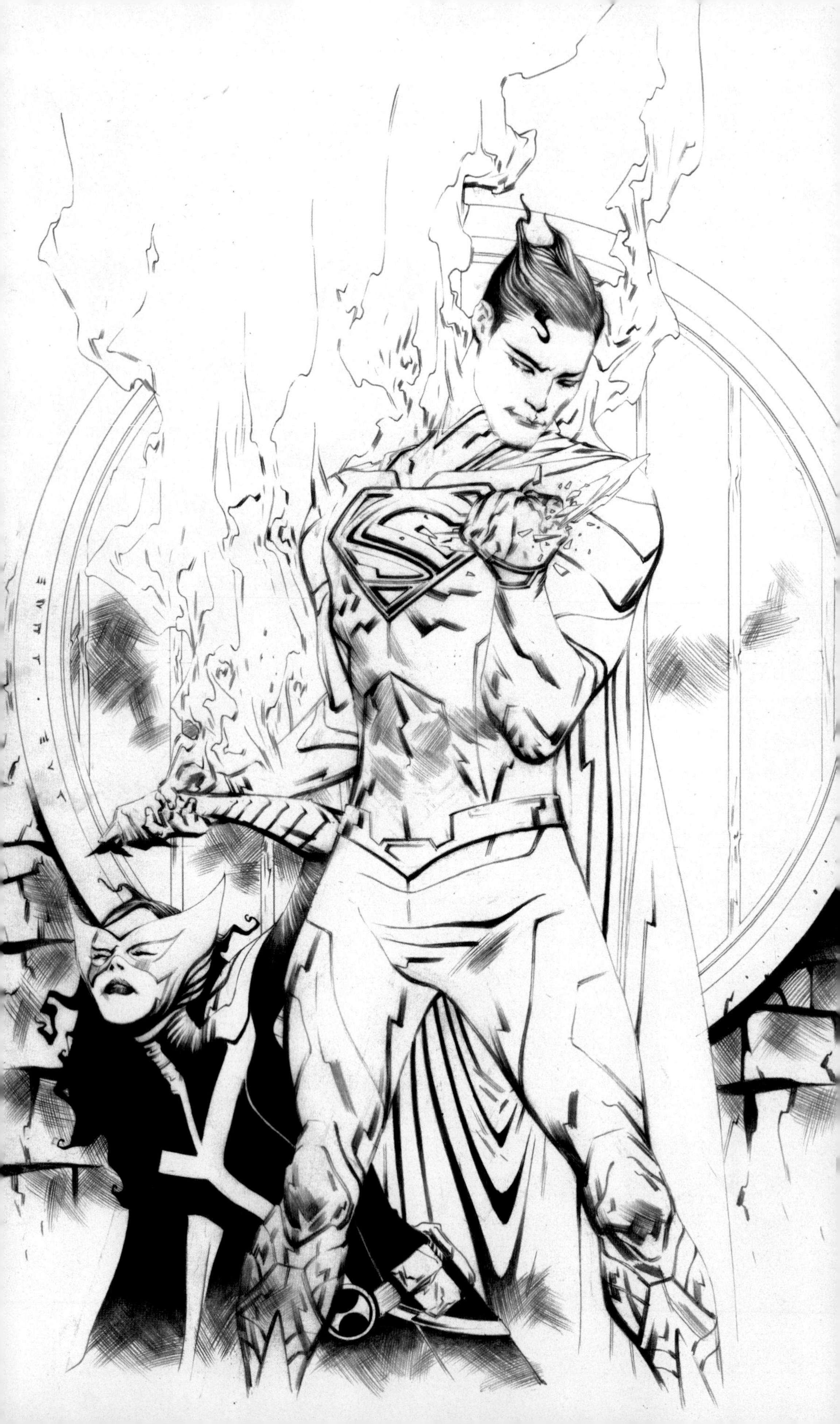

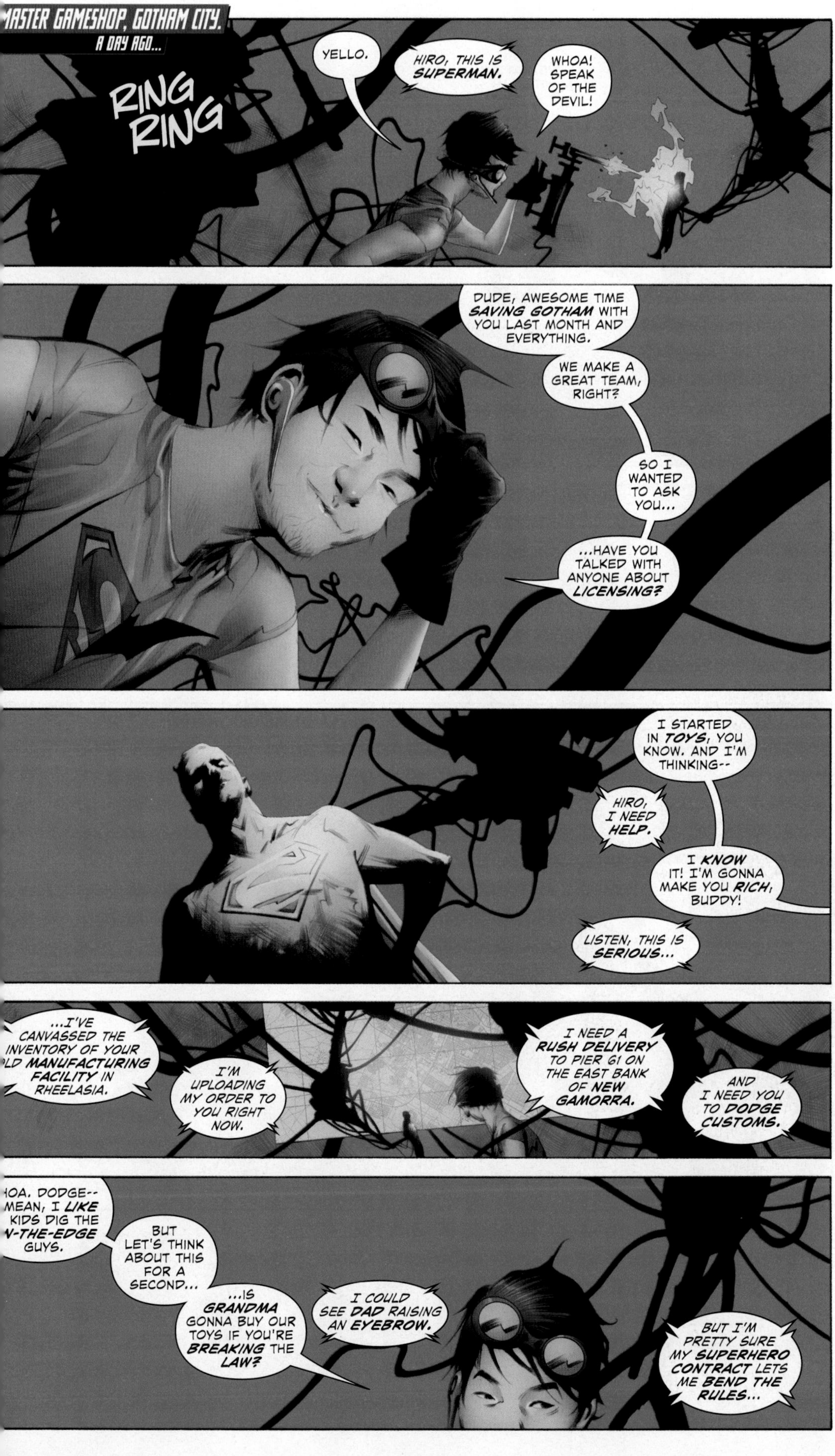

MASTER GAMESHOP, GOTHAM CITY.
A DAY AGO...
RING RING
YELLO.
HIRO, THIS IS SUPERMAN.
WHOA! SPEAK OF THE DEVIL!
DUDE, AWESOME TIME SAVING GOTHAM WITH YOU LAST MONTH AND EVERYTHING.
WE MAKE A GREAT TEAM, RIGHT?
SO I WANTED TO ASK YOU...
...HAVE YOU TALKED WITH ANYONE ABOUT LICENSING?
I STARTED IN TOYS, YOU KNOW. AND I'M THINKING--
HIRO, I NEED HELP.
I KNOW IT! I'M GONNA MAKE YOU RICH, BUDDY!
LISTEN, THIS IS SERIOUS...
...I'VE CANVASSED THE INVENTORY OF YOUR OLD MANUFACTURING FACILITY IN RHEELASIA.
I'M UPLOADING MY ORDER TO YOU RIGHT NOW.
I NEED A RUSH DELIVERY TO PIER 61 ON THE EAST BANK OF NEW GAMORRA.
AND I NEED YOU TO DODGE CUSTOMS.
WHOA. DODGE-- I MEAN, I LIKE KIDS DIG THE ON-THE-EDGE GUYS.
BUT LET'S THINK ABOUT THIS FOR A SECOND...
...IS GRANDMA GONNA BUY OUR TOYS IF YOU'RE BREAKING THE LAW?
I COULD SEE DAD RAISING AN EYEBROW.
BUT I'M PRETTY SURE MY SUPERHERO CONTRACT LETS ME BEND THE RULES...

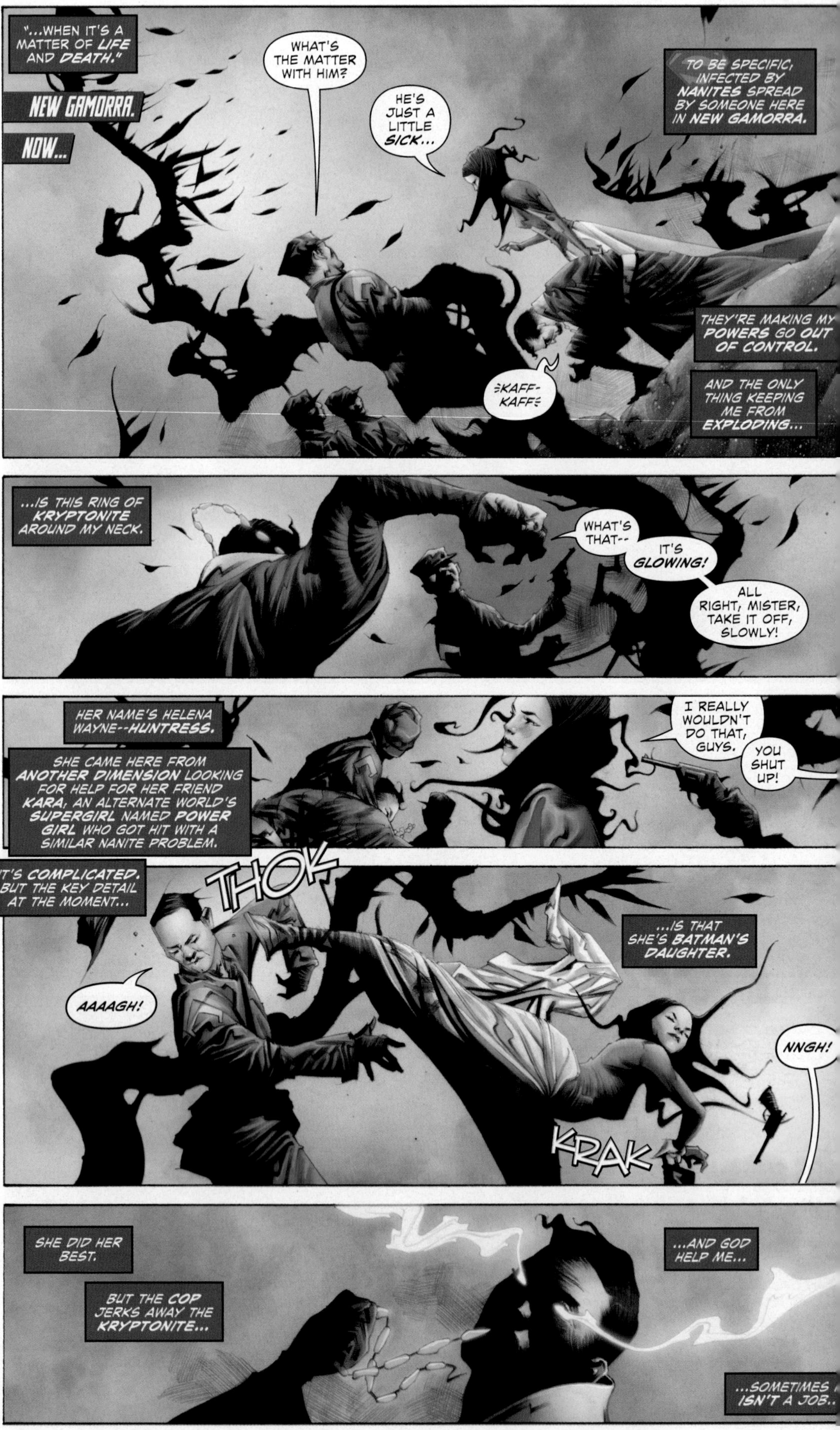
"...WHEN IT'S A MATTER OF LIFE AND DEATH."
NEW GAMORRA.
NOW...
WHAT'S THE MATTER WITH HIM?
HE'S JUST A LITTLE SICK...
TO BE SPECIFIC, INFECTED BY NANITES SPREAD BY SOMEONE HERE IN NEW GAMORRA.
THEY'RE MAKING MY POWERS GO OUT OF CONTROL.
KAFF-KAFF
AND THE ONLY THING KEEPING ME FROM EXPLODING...
...IS THIS RING OF KRYPTONITE AROUND MY NECK.
WHAT'S THAT--
IT'S GLOWING!
ALL RIGHT, MISTER, TAKE IT OFF, SLOWLY!
HER NAME'S HELENA WAYNE--HUNTRESS.
SHE CAME HERE FROM ANOTHER DIMENSION LOOKING FOR HELP FOR HER FRIEND KARA, AN ALTERNATE WORLD'S SUPERGIRL NAMED POWER GIRL WHO GOT HIT WITH A SIMILAR NANITE PROBLEM.
I REALLY WOULDN'T DO THAT, GUYS.
YOU SHUT UP!
IT'S COMPLICATED. BUT THE KEY DETAIL AT THE MOMENT...
THOK
...IS THAT SHE'S BATMAN'S DAUGHTER.
AAAAGH!
NNGH!
KRAK
SHE DID HER BEST.
BUT THE COP JERKS AWAY THE KRYPTONITE...
...AND GOD HELP ME...
...SOMETIMES IT ISN'T A JOB...

FIRST CONTACT

PART 3

GREG PAK - WRITER JAE LEE - ART
JUNE CHUNG - COLORS DC LETTERING - LETTERS
LEE WITH CHUNG - COVER

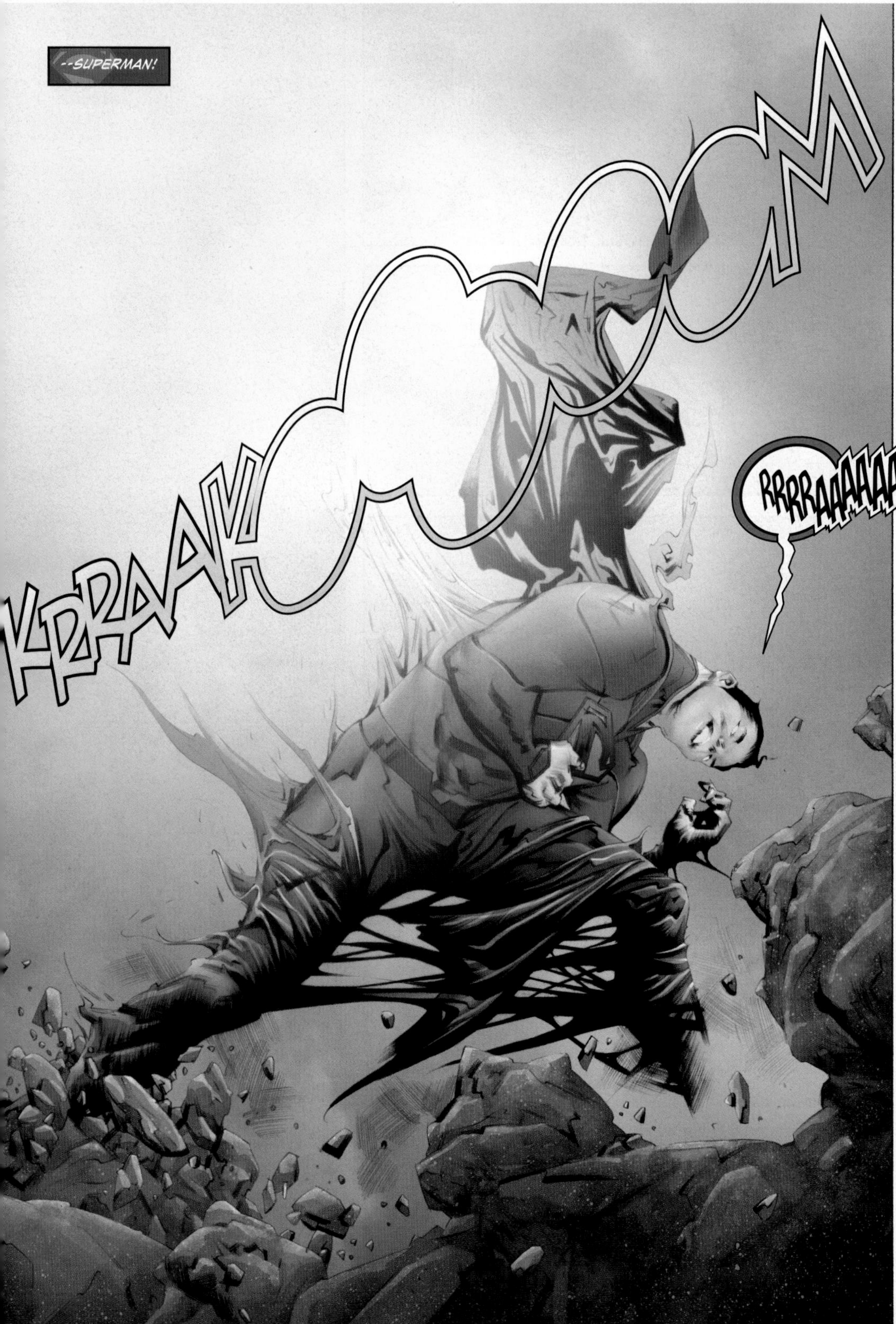
--SUPERMAN!
KRRAAKOOOOOM
RRRRAAAAAA!

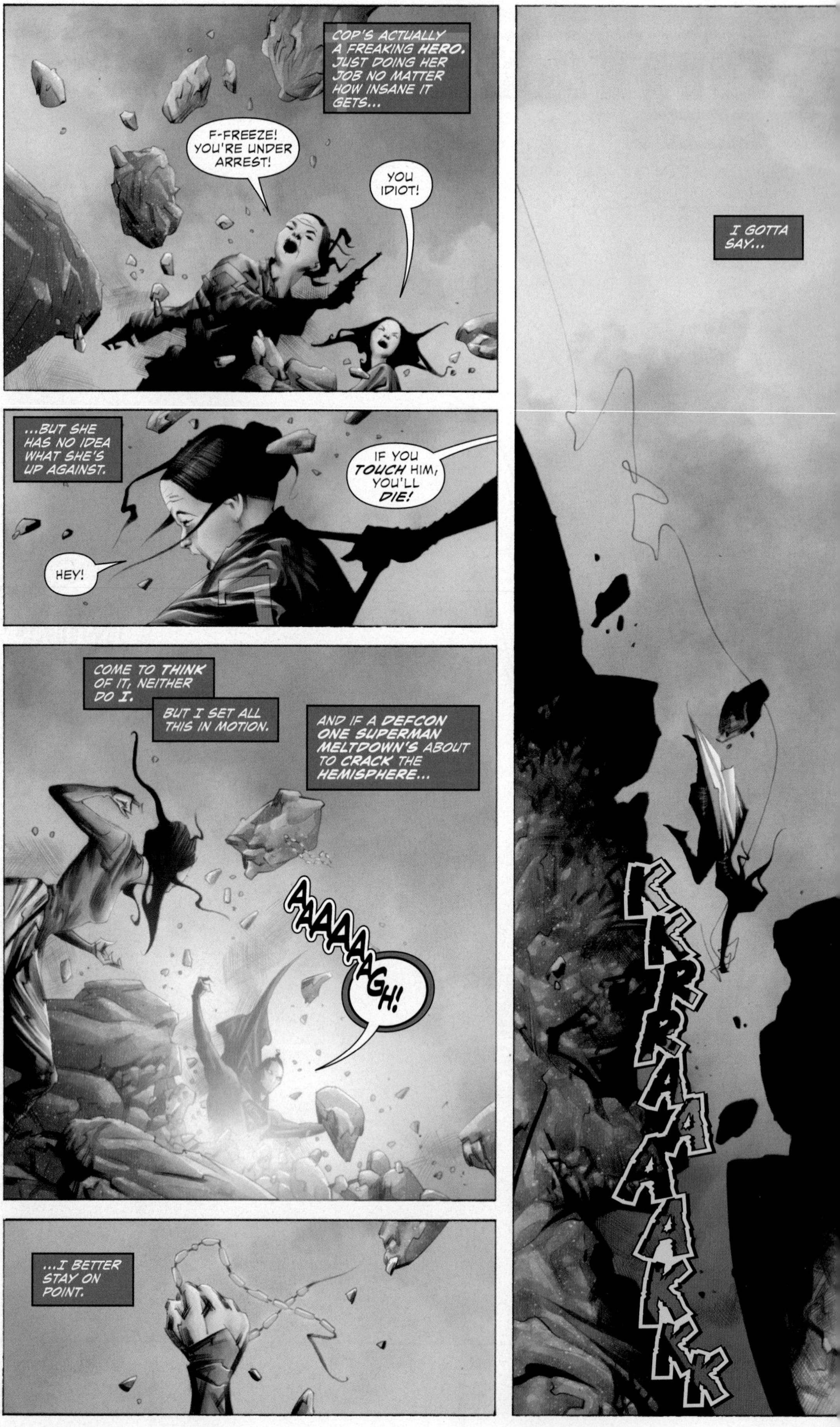
COP'S ACTUALLY A FREAKING HERO. JUST DOING HER JOB NO MATTER HOW INSANE IT GETS...
F-FREEZE! YOU'RE UNDER ARREST!
YOU IDIOT!
...BUT SHE HAS NO IDEA WHAT SHE'S UP AGAINST.
IF YOU TOUCH HIM, YOU'LL DIE!
HEY!
COME TO THINK OF IT, NEITHER DO I.
BUT I SET ALL THIS IN MOTION.
AND IF A DEFCON ONE SUPERMAN MELTDOWN'S ABOUT TO CRACK THE HEMISPHERE...
AAAAAAAGH!
...I BETTER STAY ON POINT.
I GOTTA SAY...
KKRRAAAAKK

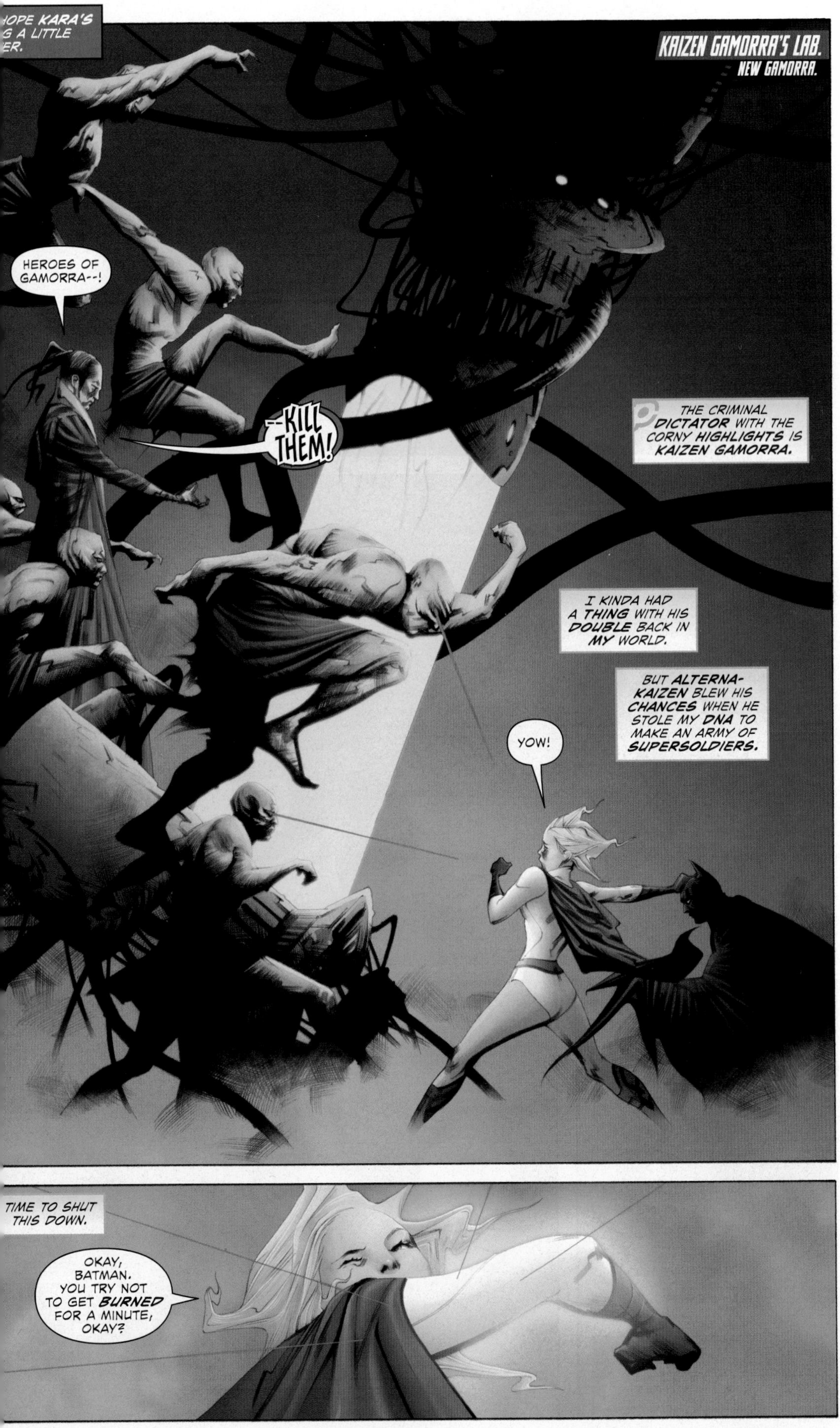

...HOPE KARA'S ...G A LITTLE ...ER.
KAIZEN GAMORRA'S LAB. NEW GAMORRA.
HEROES OF GAMORRA--!
--KILL THEM!
THE CRIMINAL DICTATOR WITH THE CORNY HIGHLIGHTS IS KAIZEN GAMORRA.
I KINDA HAD A THING WITH HIS DOUBLE BACK IN MY WORLD.
BUT ALTERNA-KAIZEN BLEW HIS CHANCES WHEN HE STOLE MY DNA TO MAKE AN ARMY OF SUPERSOLDIERS.
YOW!
TIME TO SHUT THIS DOWN.
OKAY, BATMAN. YOU TRY NOT TO GET BURNED FOR A MINUTE, OKAY?

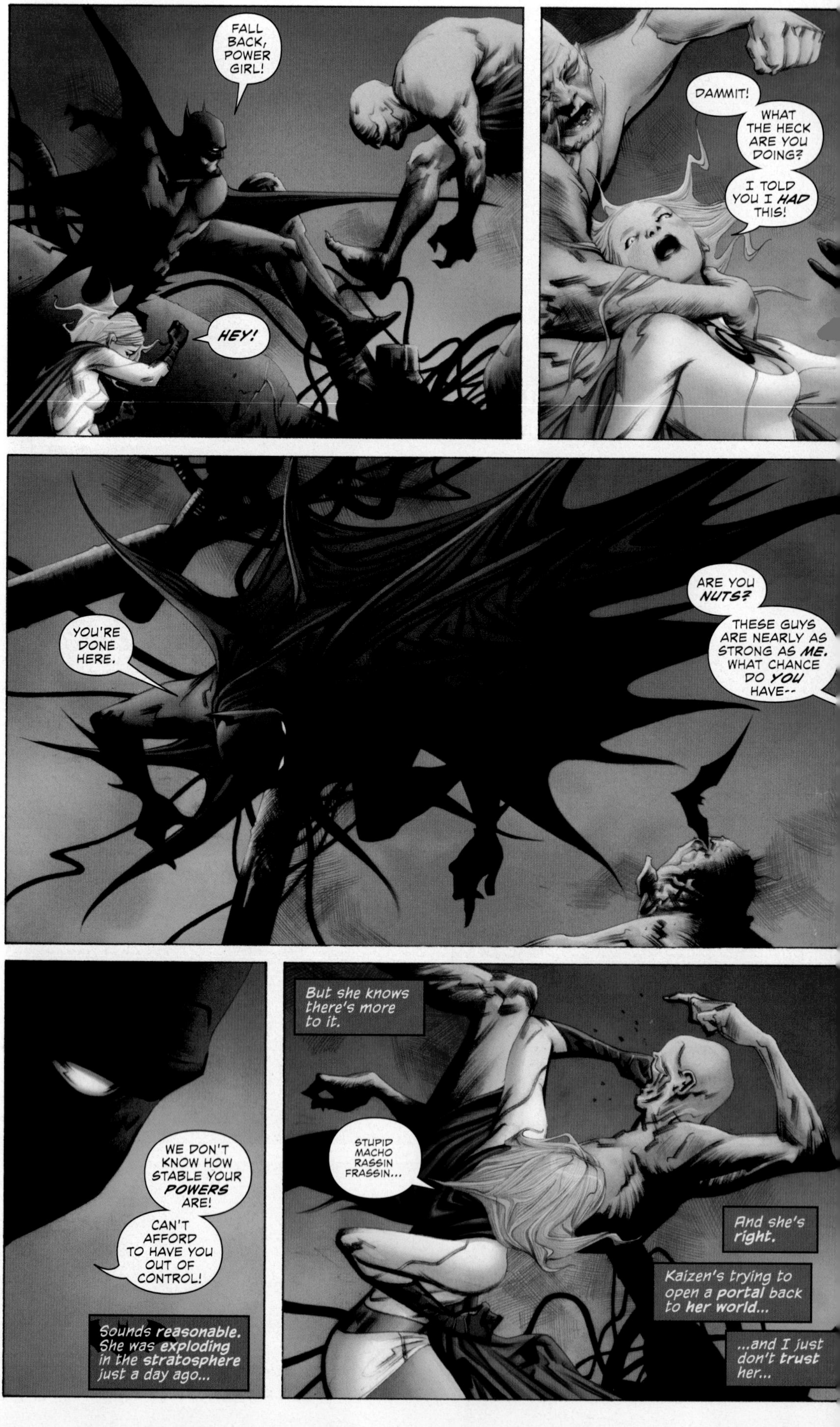
FALL BACK, POWER GIRL!
HEY!
DAMMIT!
WHAT THE HECK ARE YOU DOING?
I TOLD YOU I HAD THIS!
YOU'RE DONE HERE.
ARE YOU NUTS?
THESE GUYS ARE NEARLY AS STRONG AS ME. WHAT CHANCE DO YOU HAVE--
WE DON'T KNOW HOW STABLE YOUR POWERS ARE!
CAN'T AFFORD TO HAVE YOU OUT OF CONTROL!
Sounds reasonable. She was exploding in the stratosphere just a day ago...
But she knows there's more to it.
STUPID MACHO RASSIN FRASSIN...
And she's right.
Kaizen's trying to open a portal back to her world...
...and I just don't trust her...

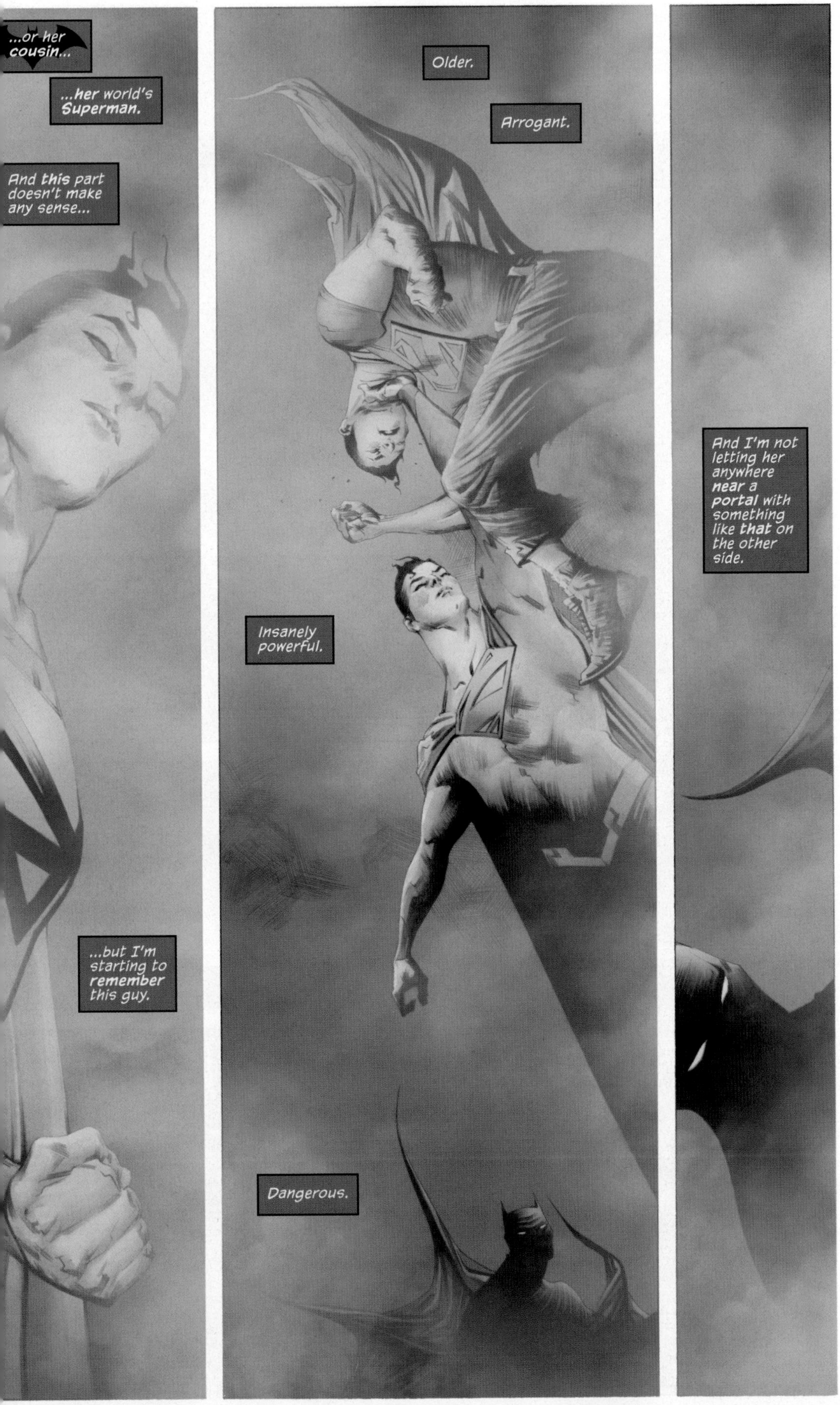

...or her cousin...
...her world's Superman.
And this part doesn't make any sense...
...but I'm starting to remember this guy.
Older.
Arrogant.
Insanely powerful.
Dangerous.
And I'm not letting her anywhere near a portal with something like that on the other side.

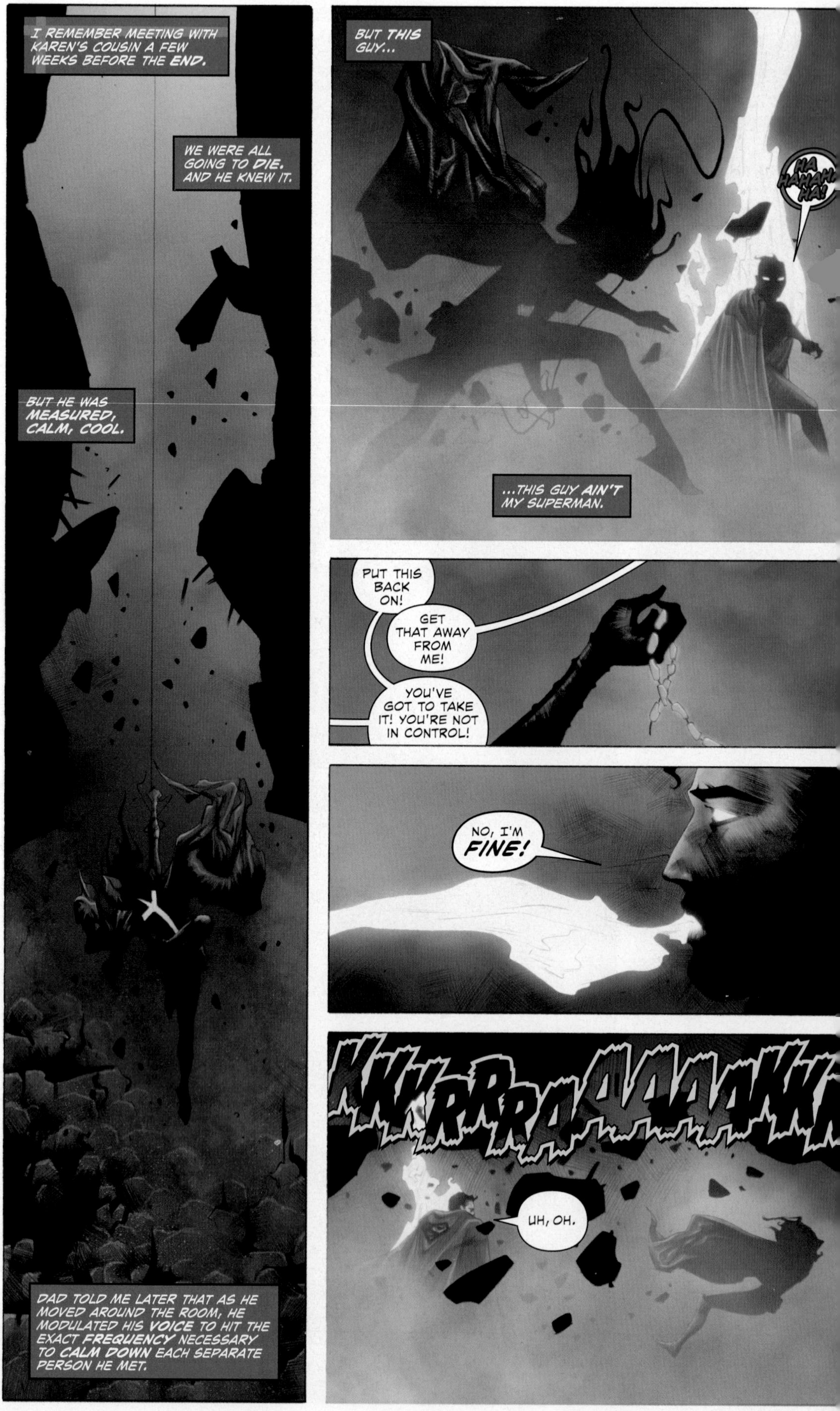
I REMEMBER MEETING WITH KAREN'S COUSIN A FEW WEEKS BEFORE THE END.
WE WERE ALL GOING TO DIE. AND HE KNEW IT.
BUT HE WAS MEASURED, CALM, COOL.
DAD TOLD ME LATER THAT AS HE MOVED AROUND THE ROOM, HE MODULATED HIS VOICE TO HIT THE EXACT FREQUENCY NECESSARY TO CALM DOWN EACH SEPARATE PERSON HE MET.
BUT THIS GUY...
HA HAHAHA HA!
...THIS GUY AIN'T MY SUPERMAN.
PUT THIS BACK ON!
GET THAT AWAY FROM ME!
YOU'VE GOT TO TAKE IT! YOU'RE NOT IN CONTROL!
NO, I'M FINE!
KKKRRRAAAAAKK
UH, OH.

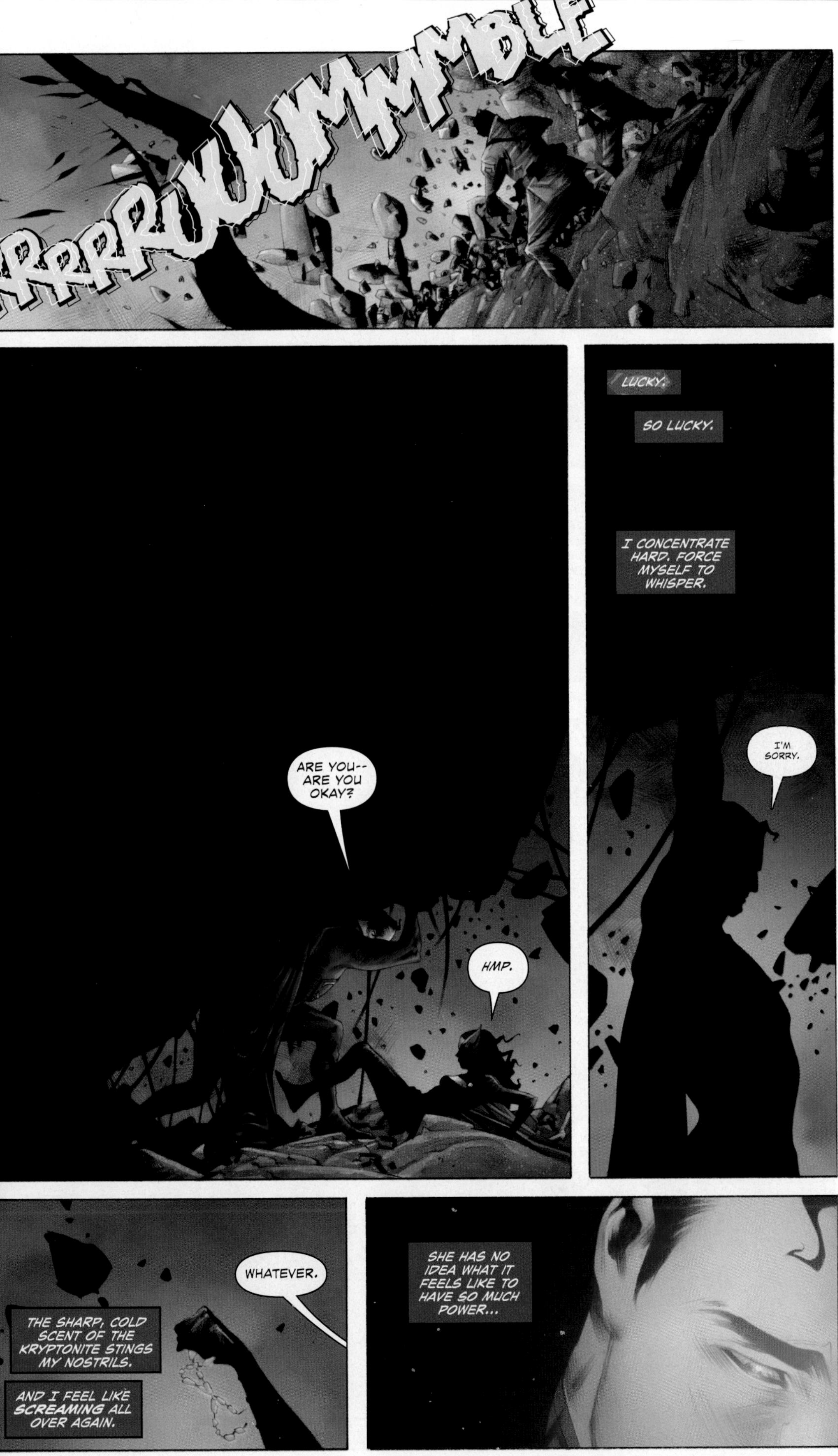
RRRRRUUMMMBLE
LUCKY.
SO LUCKY.
I CONCENTRATE HARD. FORCE MYSELF TO WHISPER.
ARE YOU-- ARE YOU OKAY?
HMP.
I'M SORRY.
THE SHARP, COLD SCENT OF THE KRYPTONITE STINGS MY NOSTRILS.
AND I FEEL LIKE SCREAMING ALL OVER AGAIN.
WHATEVER.
SHE HAS NO IDEA WHAT IT FEELS LIKE TO HAVE SO MUCH POWER...

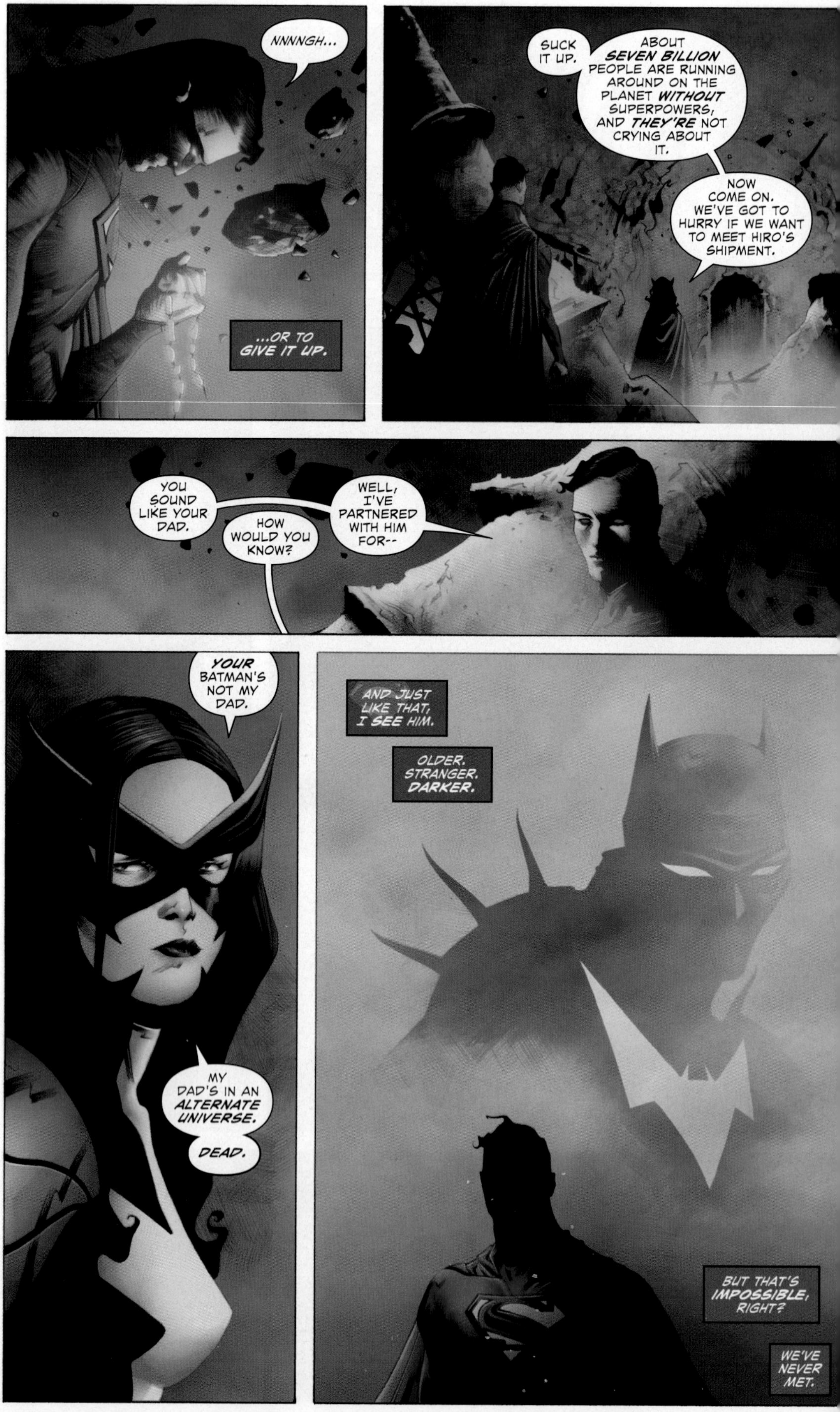
NNNNGH...
...OR TO GIVE IT UP.
SUCK IT UP.
ABOUT SEVEN BILLION PEOPLE ARE RUNNING AROUND ON THE PLANET WITHOUT SUPERPOWERS, AND THEY'RE NOT CRYING ABOUT IT.
NOW COME ON. WE'VE GOT TO HURRY IF WE WANT TO MEET HIRO'S SHIPMENT.
YOU SOUND LIKE YOUR DAD.
WELL, I'VE PARTNERED WITH HIM FOR--
HOW WOULD YOU KNOW?
YOUR BATMAN'S NOT MY DAD.
MY DAD'S IN AN ALTERNATE UNIVERSE.
DEAD.
AND JUST LIKE THAT, I SEE HIM.
OLDER. STRANGER. DARKER.
BUT THAT'S IMPOSSIBLE, RIGHT?
WE'VE NEVER MET.

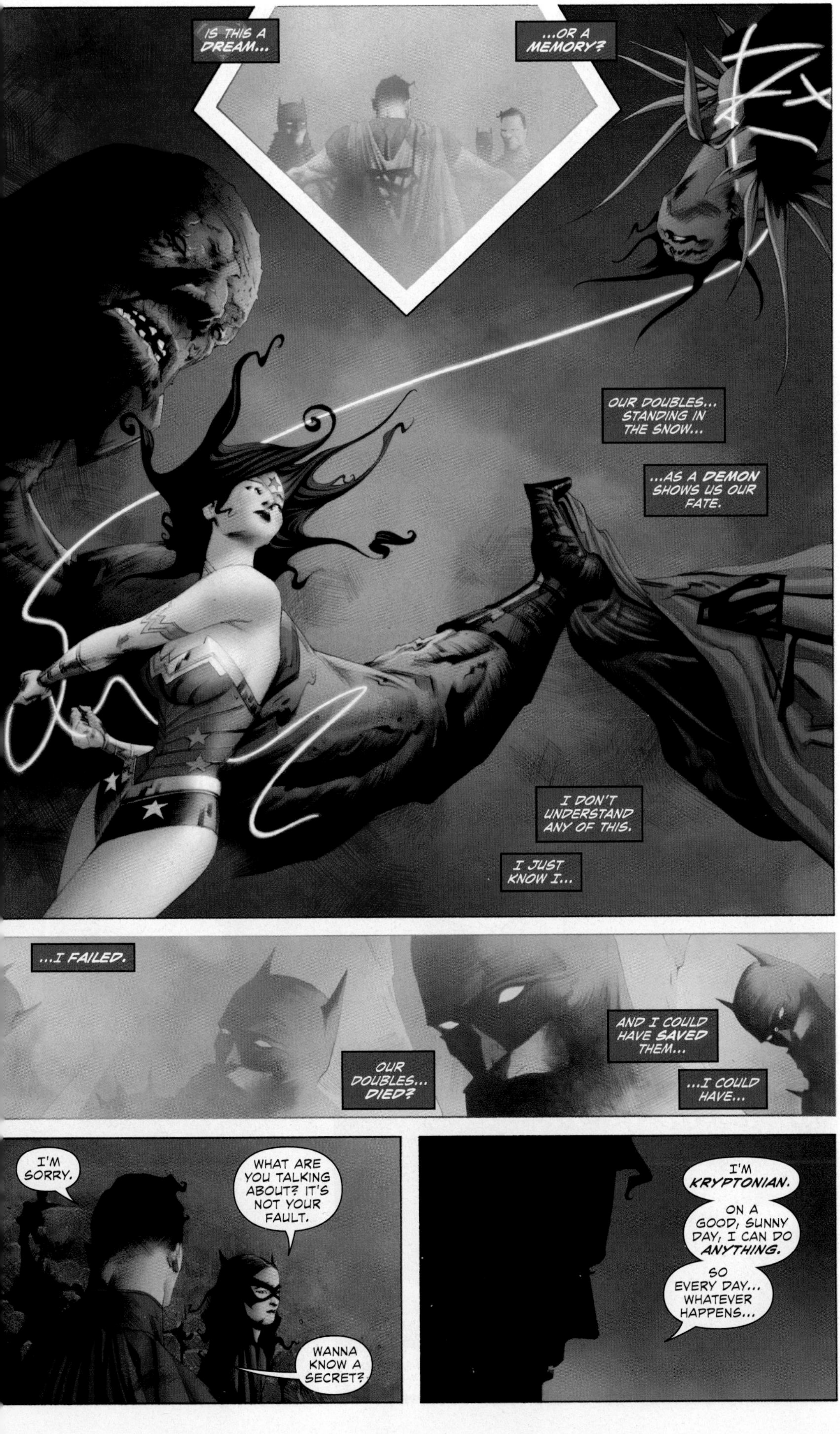
IS THIS A DREAM...
...OR A MEMORY?
OUR DOUBLES... STANDING IN THE SNOW...
...AS A DEMON SHOWS US OUR FATE.
I DON'T UNDERSTAND ANY OF THIS.
I JUST KNOW I...
...I FAILED.
OUR DOUBLES... DIED?
AND I COULD HAVE SAVED THEM...
...I COULD HAVE...
I'M SORRY.
WHAT ARE YOU TALKING ABOUT? IT'S NOT YOUR FAULT.
WANNA KNOW A SECRET?
I'M KRYPTONIAN.
ON A GOOD, SUNNY DAY, I CAN DO ANYTHING.
SO EVERY DAY... WHATEVER HAPPENS...

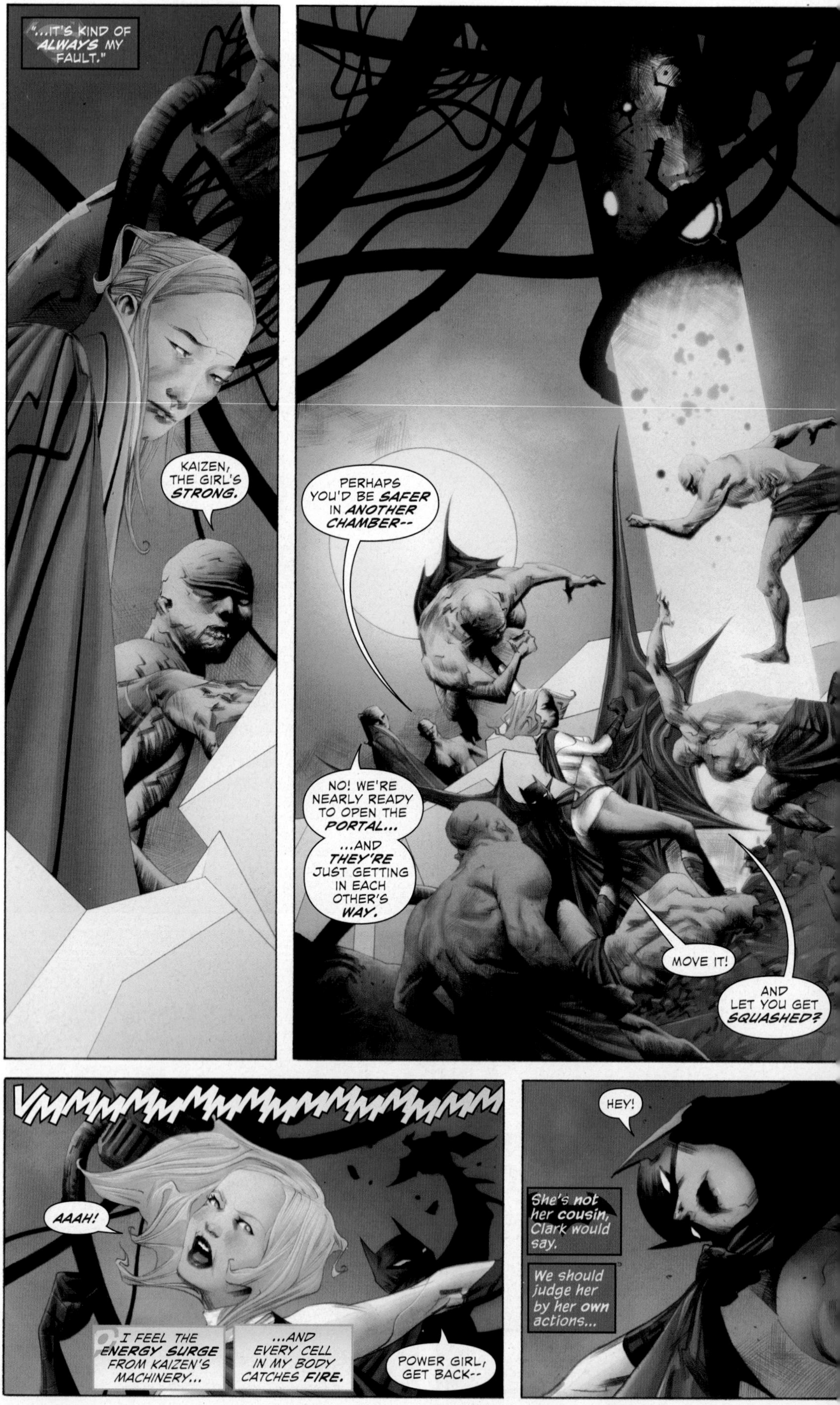
"...IT'S KIND OF ALWAYS MY FAULT."
KAIZEN, THE GIRL'S STRONG.
PERHAPS YOU'D BE SAFER IN ANOTHER CHAMBER--
NO! WE'RE NEARLY READY TO OPEN THE PORTAL...
...AND THEY'RE JUST GETTING IN EACH OTHER'S WAY.
MOVE IT!
AND LET YOU GET SQUASHED?
VMMMMMMMMMMMMMMMMMM
AAAH!
I FEEL THE ENERGY SURGE FROM KAIZEN'S MACHINERY...
...AND EVERY CELL IN MY BODY CATCHES FIRE.
POWER GIRL, GET BACK--
HEY!
She's not her cousin, Clark would say.
We should judge her by her own actions...

NNNGH!

...but even *Clark* might see the problem here.

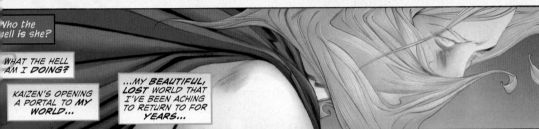

Who the hell *is* she?

WHAT THE HELL AM I *DOING?*

KAIZEN'S OPENING A PORTAL TO *MY WORLD*...

...MY *BEAUTIFUL, LOST* WORLD THAT I'VE BEEN ACHING TO RETURN TO FOR *YEARS*...

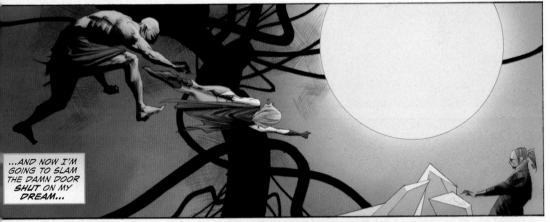

...AND NOW I'M GOING TO SLAM THE DAMN DOOR *SHUT* ON MY *DREAM*...

...BECAUSE IF *KAIZEN* WANTS IT, IT CAN'T BE GOOD.

DAMMIT!

ACTIVATE.

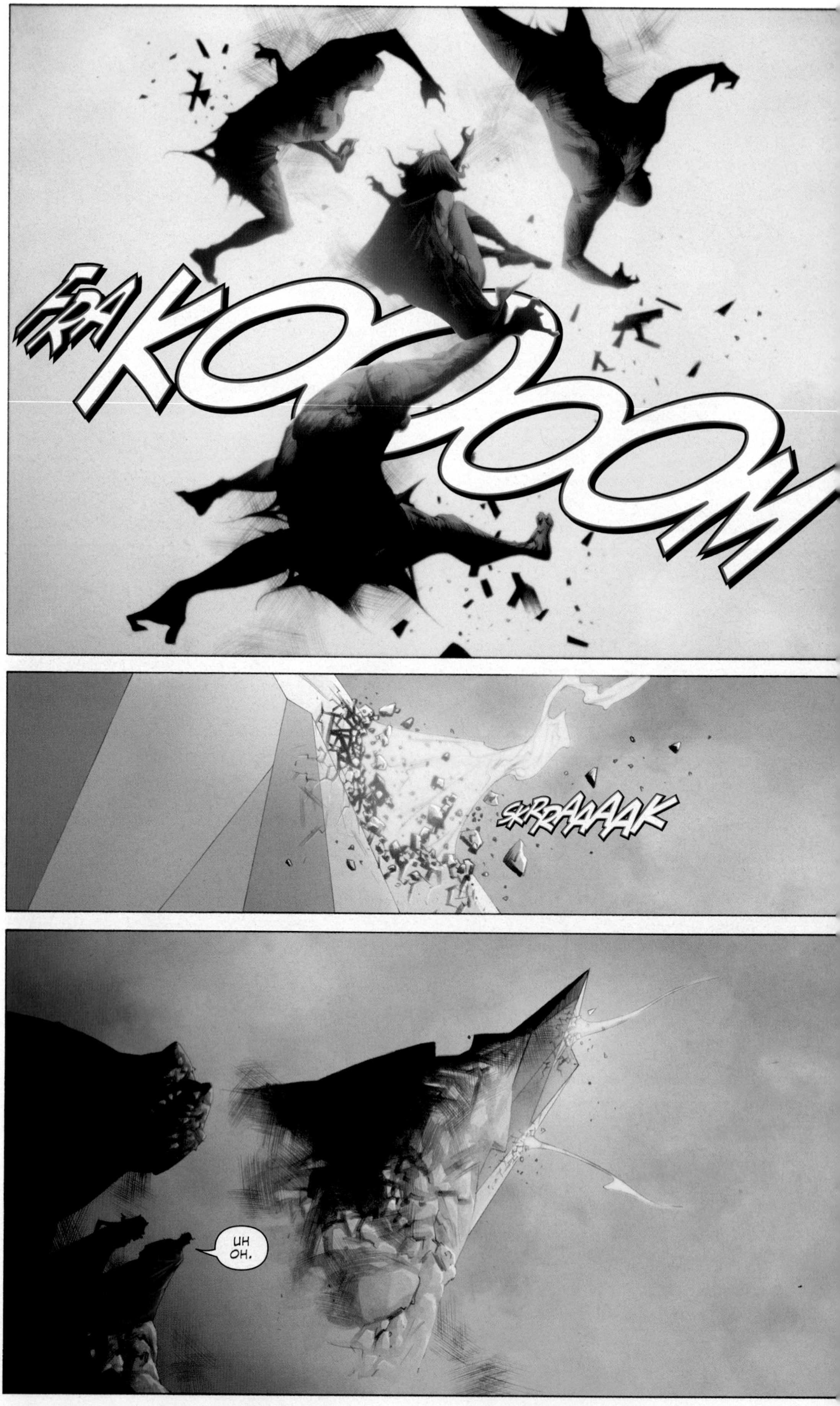
FRAKOOOOM
SKRRAAAAK
UH OH.

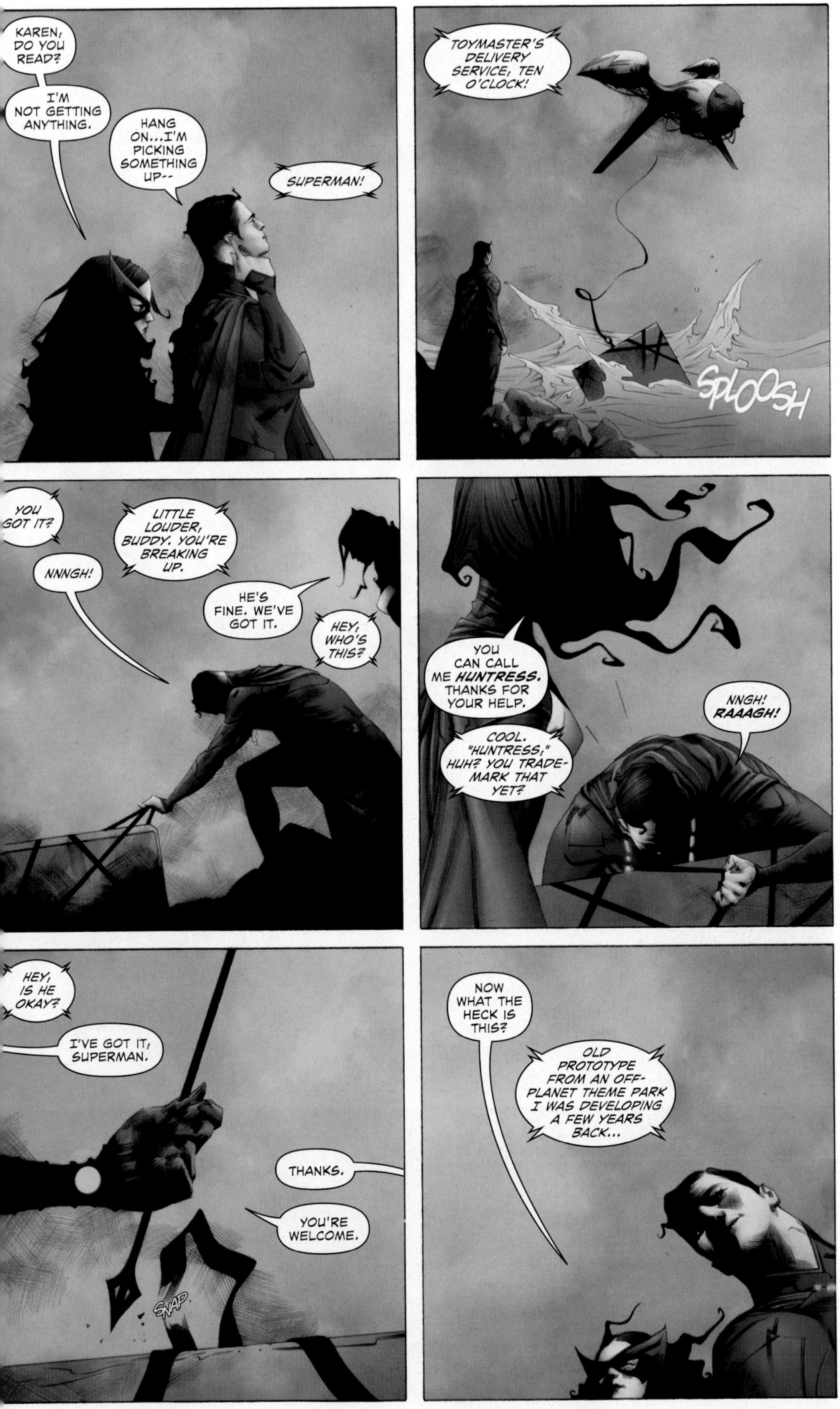
KAREN, DO YOU READ?
I'M NOT GETTING ANYTHING.
HANG ON...I'M PICKING SOMETHING UP--
SUPERMAN!
TOYMASTER'S DELIVERY SERVICE, TEN O'CLOCK!
SPLOOSH
YOU GOT IT?
LITTLE LOUDER, BUDDY. YOU'RE BREAKING UP.
NNNGH!
HE'S FINE. WE'VE GOT IT.
HEY, WHO'S THIS?
YOU CAN CALL ME HUNTRESS. THANKS FOR YOUR HELP.
NNGH! RAAAGH!
COOL. "HUNTRESS," HUH? YOU TRADE-MARK THAT YET?
HEY, IS HE OKAY?
I'VE GOT IT, SUPERMAN.
THANKS.
YOU'RE WELCOME.
SNAP
NOW WHAT THE HECK IS THIS?
OLD PROTOTYPE FROM AN OFF-PLANET THEME PARK I WAS DEVELOPING A FEW YEARS BACK...

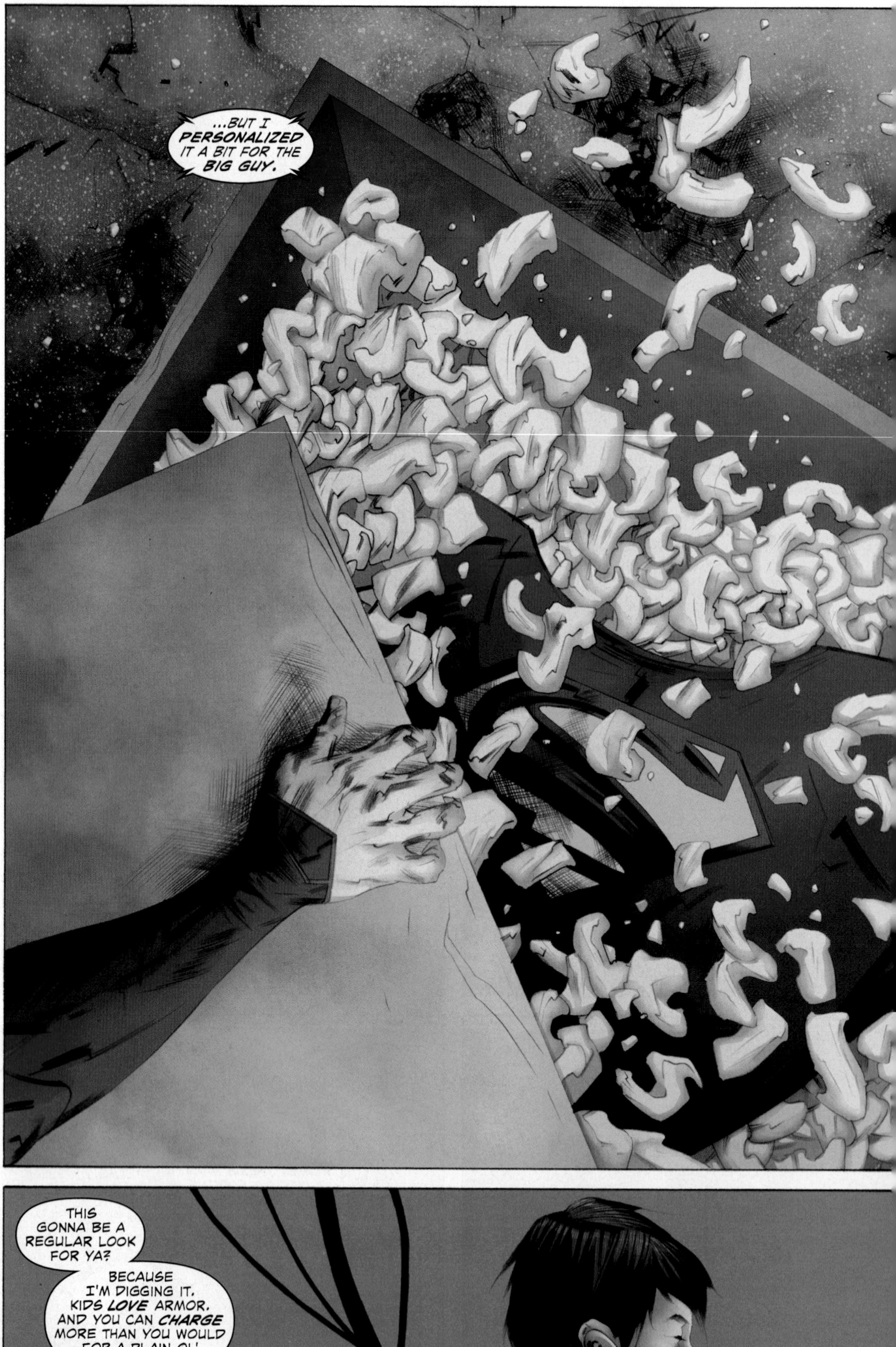
...BUT I PERSONALIZED IT A BIT FOR THE BIG GUY.

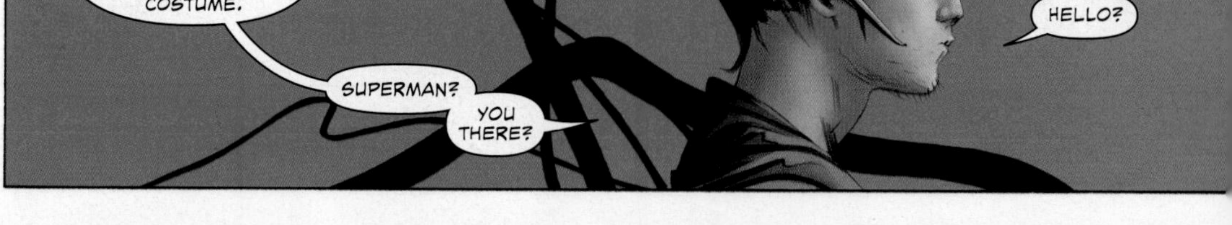
THIS GONNA BE A REGULAR LOOK FOR YA?
BECAUSE I'M DIGGING IT. KIDS LOVE ARMOR. AND YOU CAN CHARGE MORE THAN YOU WOULD FOR A PLAIN OL' COSTUME.
SUPERMAN?
YOU THERE?
HELLO?

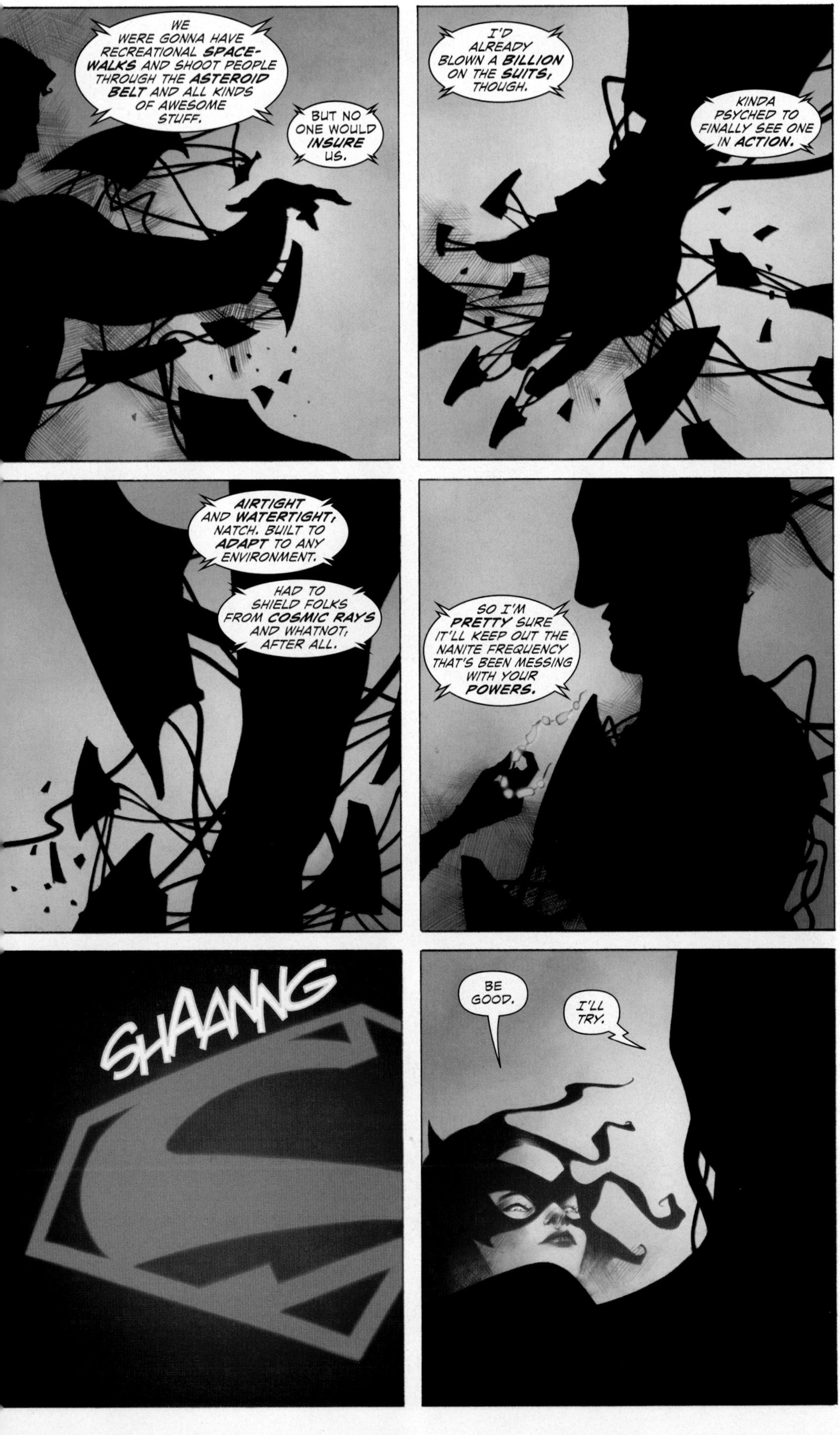
WE WERE GONNA HAVE RECREATIONAL SPACE-WALKS AND SHOOT PEOPLE THROUGH THE ASTEROID BELT AND ALL KINDS OF AWESOME STUFF.
BUT NO ONE WOULD INSURE US.
I'D ALREADY BLOWN A BILLION ON THE SUITS, THOUGH.
KINDA PSYCHED TO FINALLY SEE ONE IN ACTION.
AIRTIGHT AND WATERTIGHT, NATCH. BUILT TO ADAPT TO ANY ENVIRONMENT.
HAD TO SHIELD FOLKS FROM COSMIC RAYS AND WHATNOT, AFTER ALL.
SO I'M PRETTY SURE IT'LL KEEP OUT THE NANITE FREQUENCY THAT'S BEEN MESSING WITH YOUR POWERS.
SHAANNG
BE GOOD.
I'LL TRY.

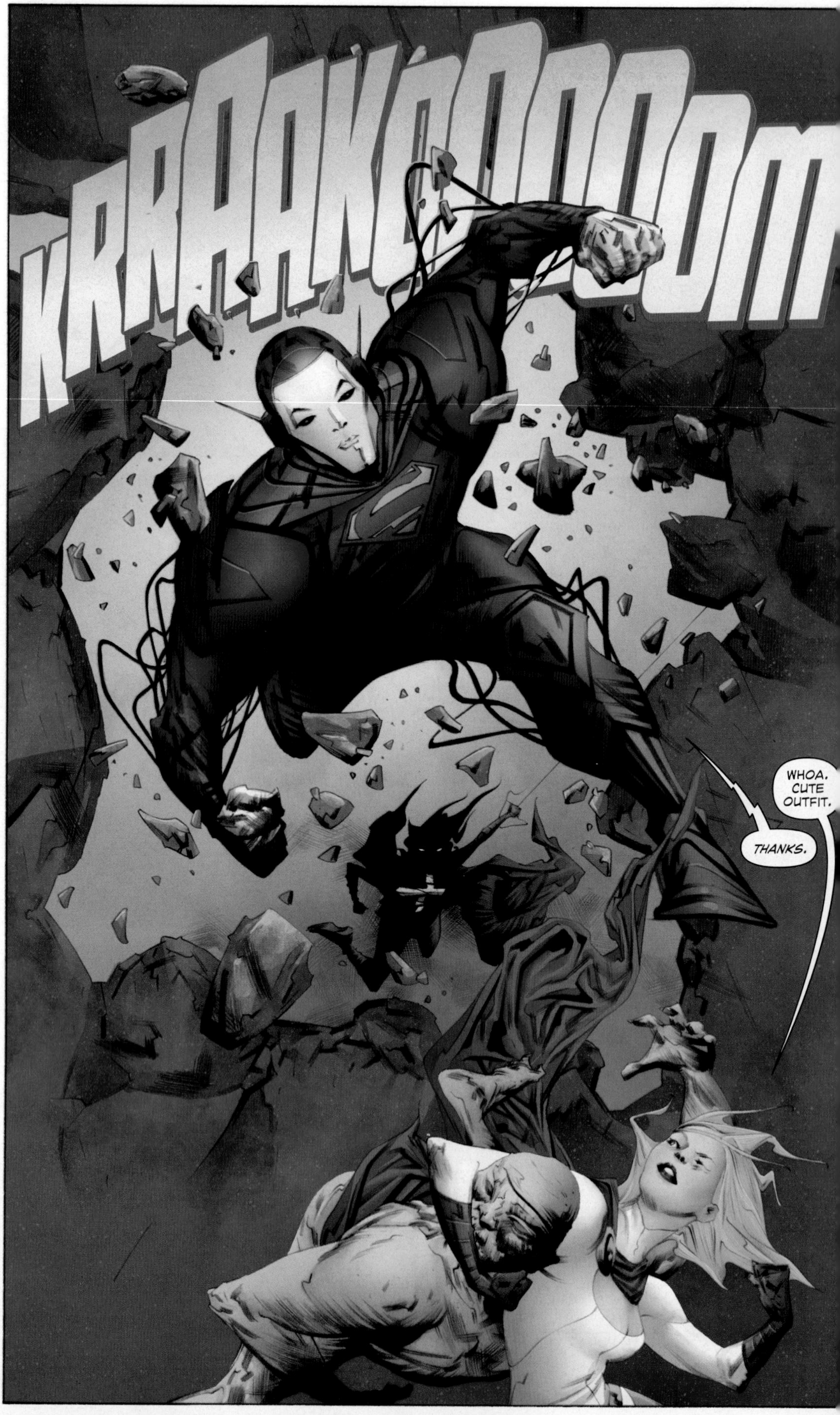
KRRAAKOOOOOOM
WHOA. CUTE OUTFIT.
THANKS.

WATCH YOUR BACK!

KAIZEN'S OPENED THE *PORTAL*, SUPERMAN! WE'VE GOT TO CLOSE IT!

IT'S EMITTING SOME KIND OF *ENERGY*--WE DON'T KNOW WHAT--

GOT IT.

HANG ON-- DON'T JUST *SMASH* EVERY- THING!

THAT'S MY *WORLD* ON THE OTHER SIDE! AND THIS IS OUR ONLY WAY TO *REACH* IT!

AND WE DON'T KNOW HOW THIS TECH *WORKS* YET!

BLOW IT UP, AND WHO *KNOWS* WHAT IT'LL DO!

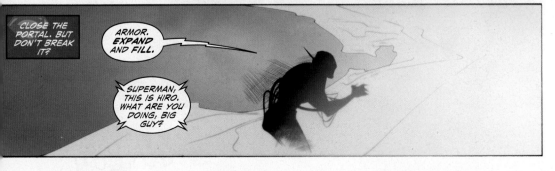

CLOSE THE PORTAL. BUT DON'T BREAK IT?

ARMOR. *EXPAND* AND *FILL*.

SUPERMAN, THIS IS HIRO. WHAT ARE YOU DOING, BIG GUY?

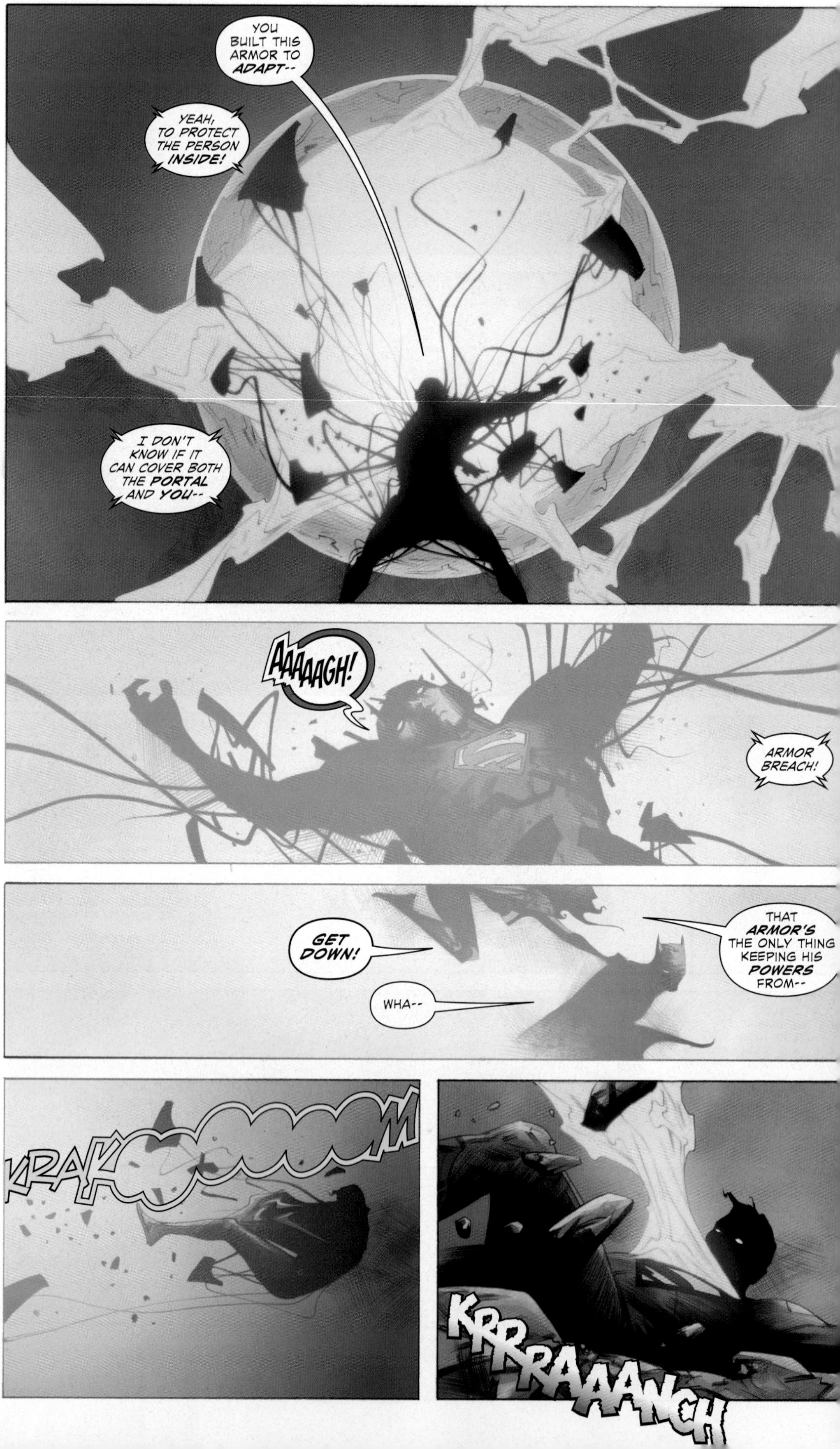

YOU BUILT THIS ARMOR TO ADAPT--
YEAH, TO PROTECT THE PERSON INSIDE!
I DON'T KNOW IF IT CAN COVER BOTH THE PORTAL AND YOU--
AAAAAGH!
ARMOR BREACH!
THAT ARMOR'S THE ONLY THING KEEPING HIS POWERS FROM--
GET DOWN!
WHA--
KRAKOOOOOOM
KRRRAAAANCH

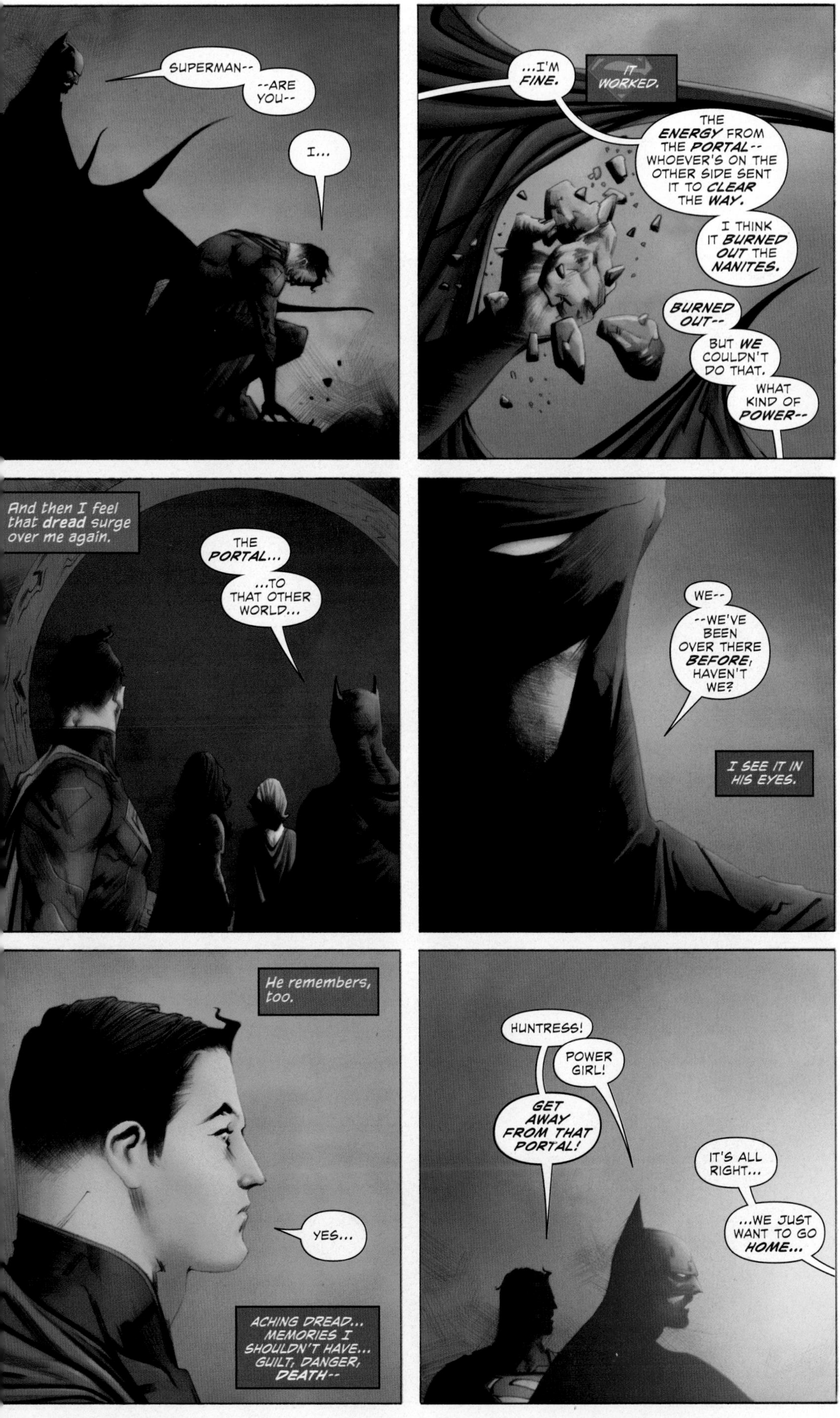
SUPERMAN--
--ARE YOU--
I...
...I'M FINE.
IT WORKED.
THE ENERGY FROM THE PORTAL--WHOEVER'S ON THE OTHER SIDE SENT IT TO CLEAR THE WAY.
I THINK IT BURNED OUT THE NANITES.
BURNED OUT--
BUT WE COULDN'T DO THAT.
WHAT KIND OF POWER--
And then I feel that dread surge over me again.
THE PORTAL...
...TO THAT OTHER WORLD...
WE--
--WE'VE BEEN OVER THERE BEFORE; HAVEN'T WE?
I SEE IT IN HIS EYES.
He remembers, too.
YES...
ACHING DREAD... MEMORIES I SHOULDN'T HAVE... GUILT, DANGER, DEATH--
HUNTRESS!
POWER GIRL!
GET AWAY FROM THAT PORTAL!
IT'S ALL RIGHT...
...WE JUST WANT TO GO HOME...

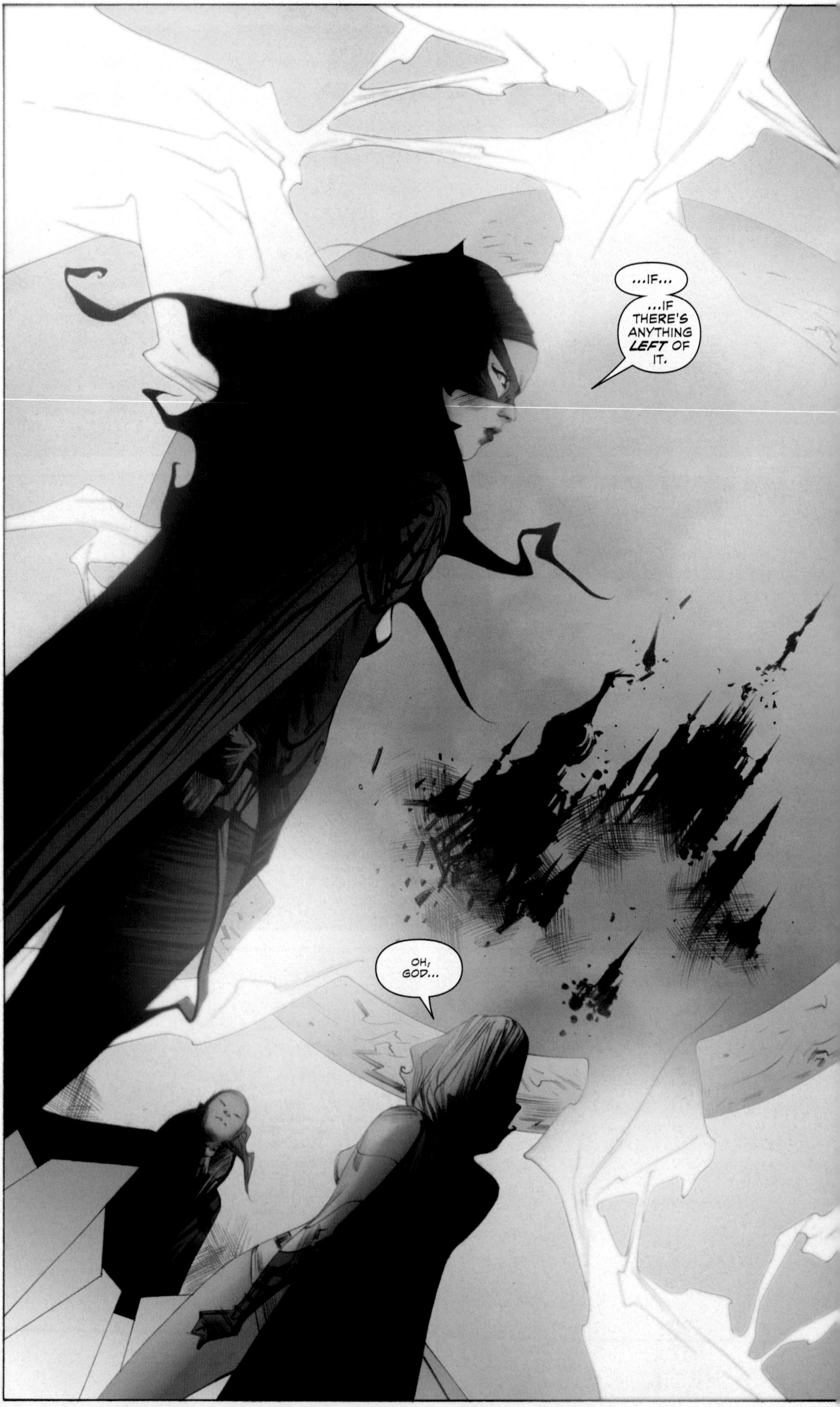
...IF...
...IF THERE'S ANYTHING *LEFT* OF IT.
OH, GOD...

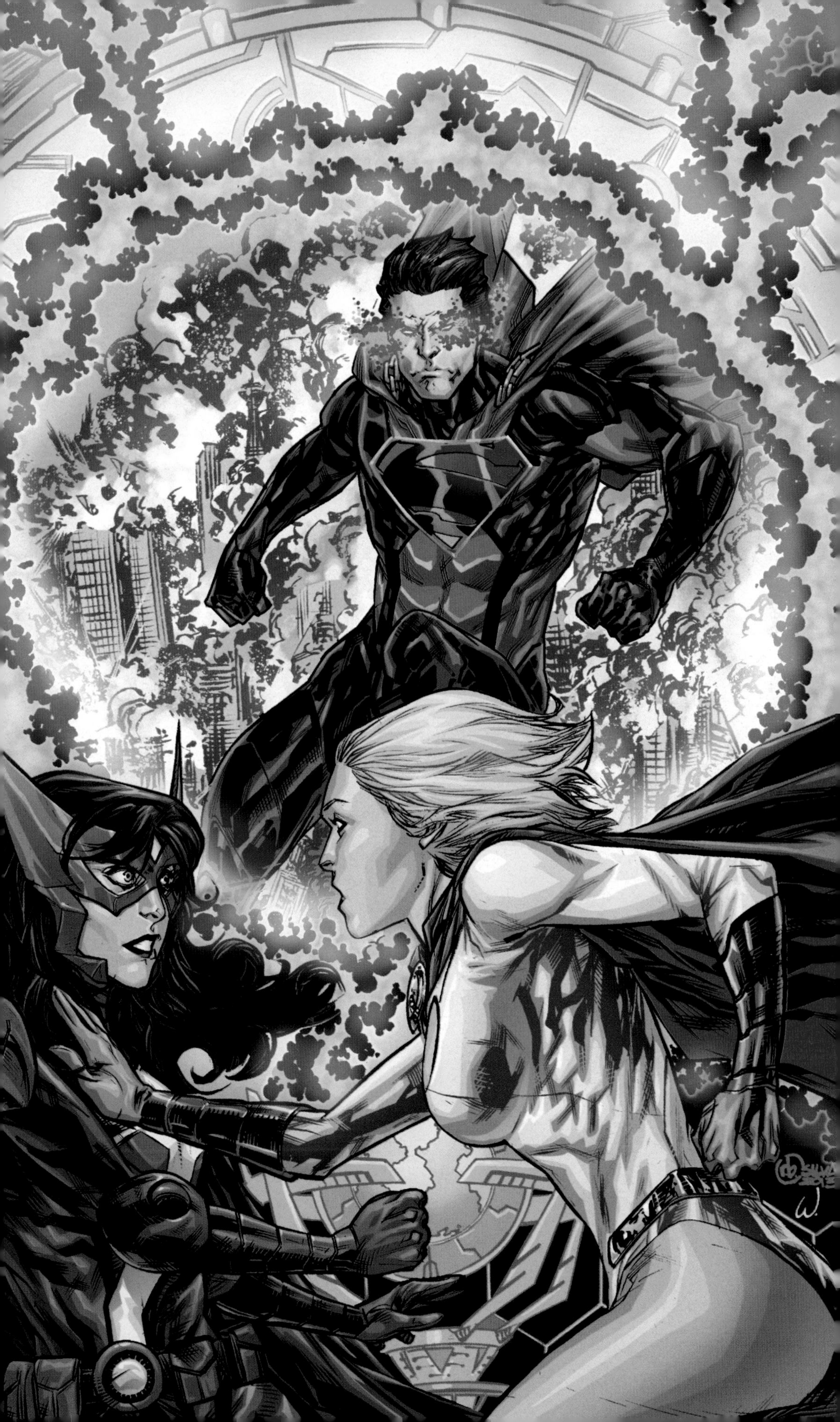

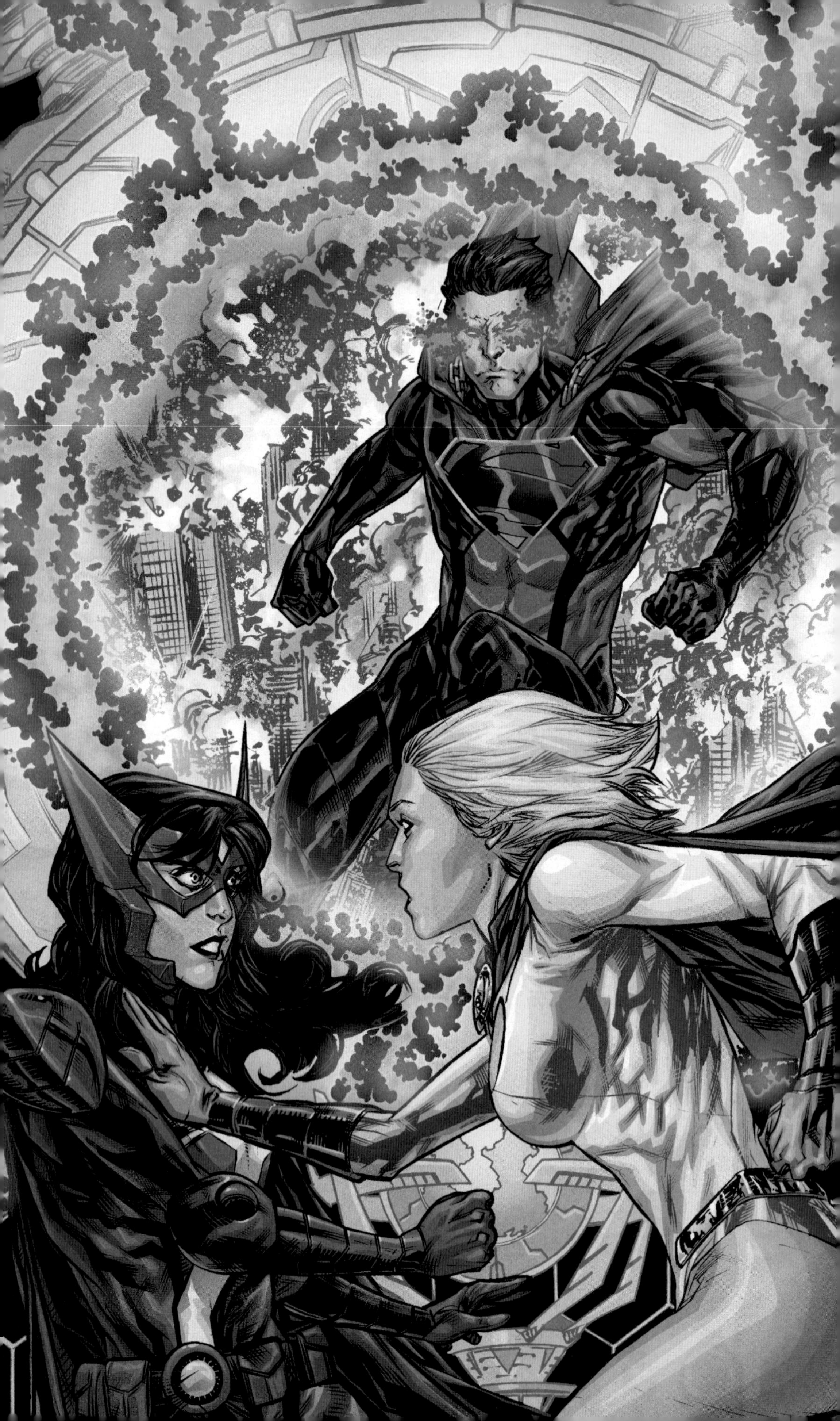

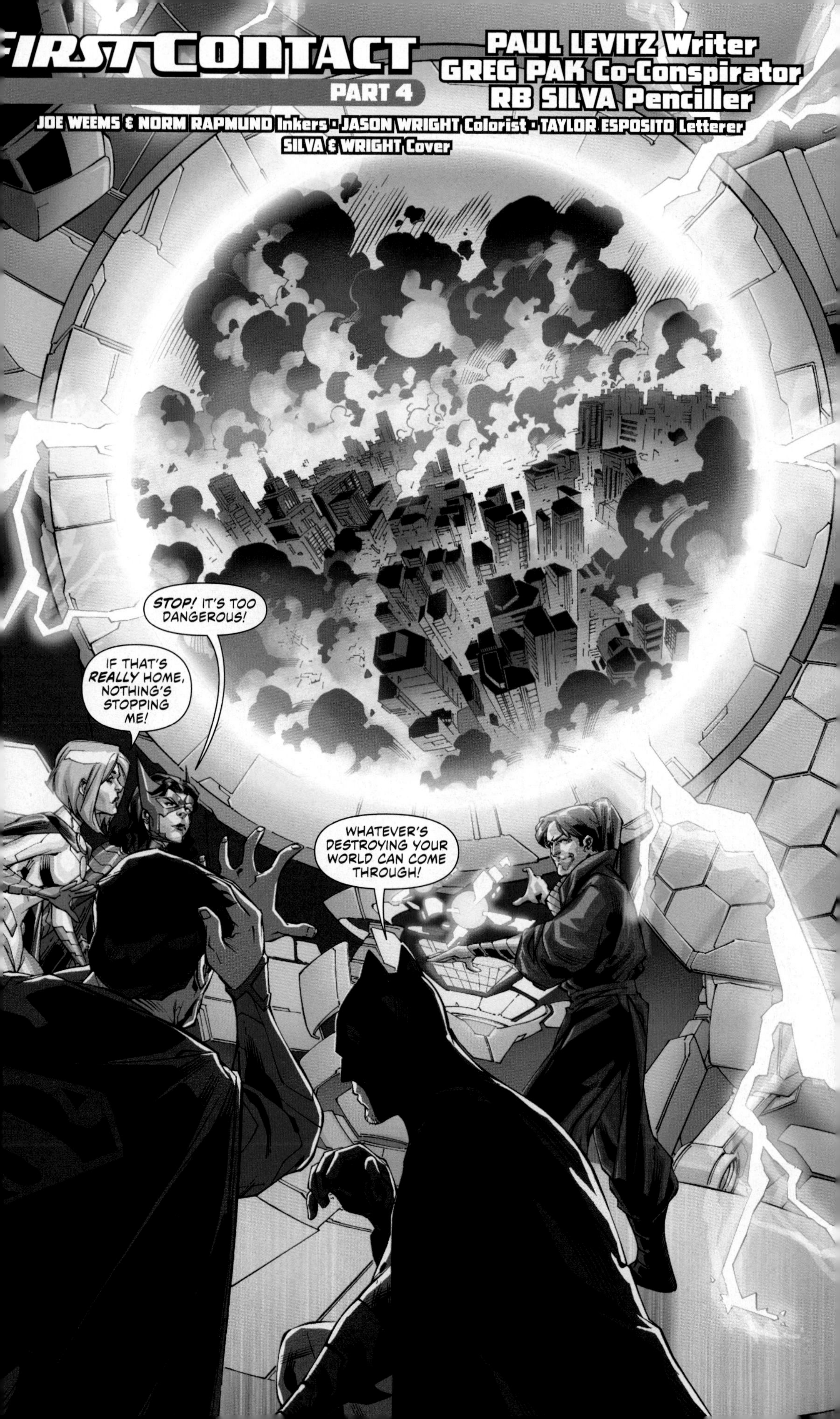
FIRST CONTACT
PART 4
PAUL LEVITZ Writer
GREG PAK Co-Conspirator
RB SILVA Penciller
JOE WEEMS & NORM RAPMUND Inkers · JASON WRIGHT Colorist · TAYLOR ESPOSITO Letterer
SILVA & WRIGHT Cover
STOP! IT'S TOO DANGEROUS!
IF THAT'S REALLY HOME, NOTHING'S STOPPING ME!
WHATEVER'S DESTROYING YOUR WORLD CAN COME THROUGH!

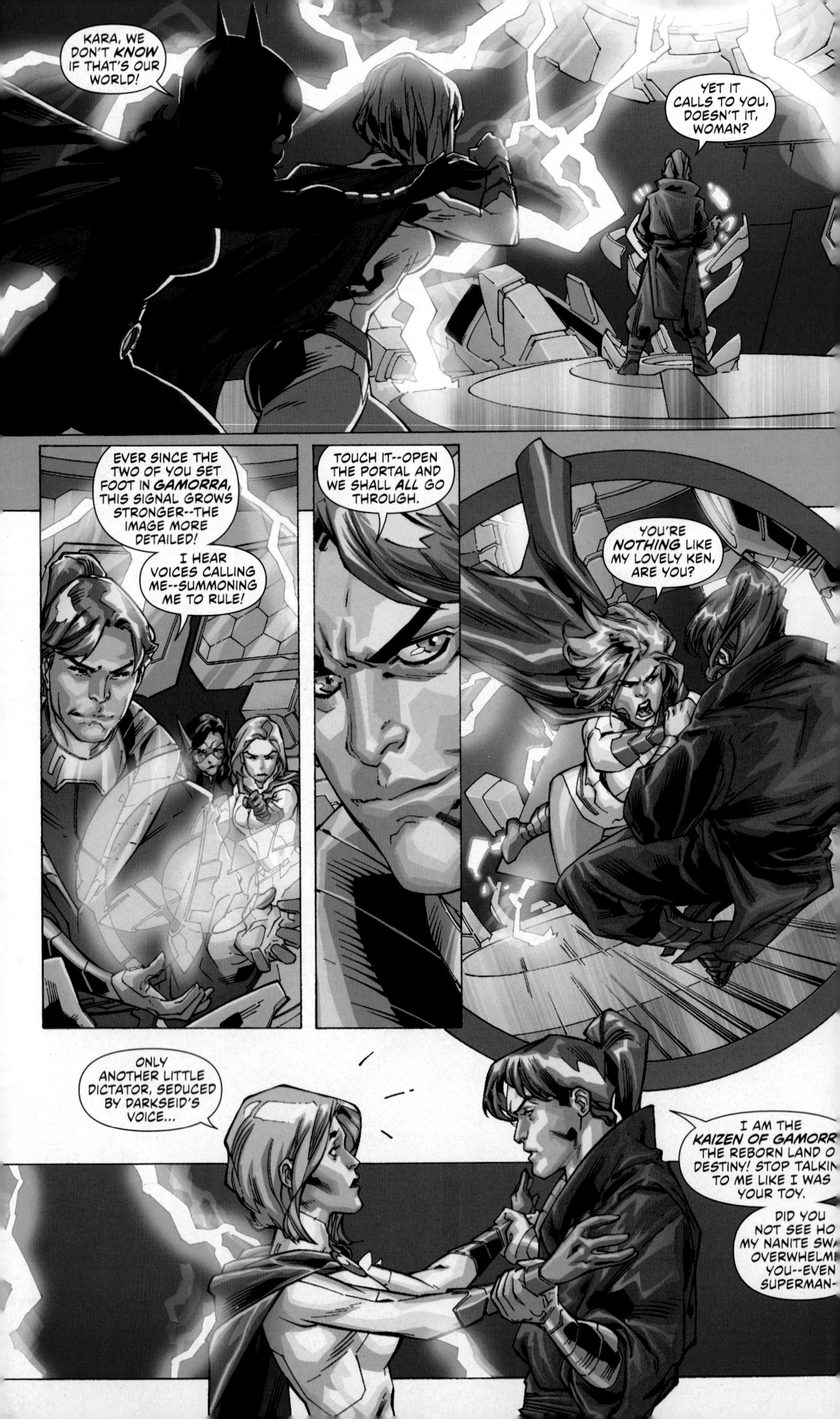

KARA, WE DON'T KNOW IF THAT'S OUR WORLD!
YET IT CALLS TO YOU, DOESN'T IT, WOMAN?
EVER SINCE THE TWO OF YOU SET FOOT IN GAMORRA, THIS SIGNAL GROWS STRONGER--THE IMAGE MORE DETAILED!
I HEAR VOICES CALLING ME--SUMMONING ME TO RULE!
TOUCH IT--OPEN THE PORTAL AND WE SHALL ALL GO THROUGH.
YOU'RE NOTHING LIKE MY LOVELY KEN, ARE YOU?
ONLY ANOTHER LITTLE DICTATOR, SEDUCED BY DARKSEID'S VOICE...
I AM THE KAIZEN OF GAMORR THE REBORN LAND O DESTINY! STOP TALKIN TO ME LIKE I WAS YOUR TOY.
DID YOU NOT SEE HO MY NANITE SW OVERWHELM YOU--EVEN SUPERMAN-

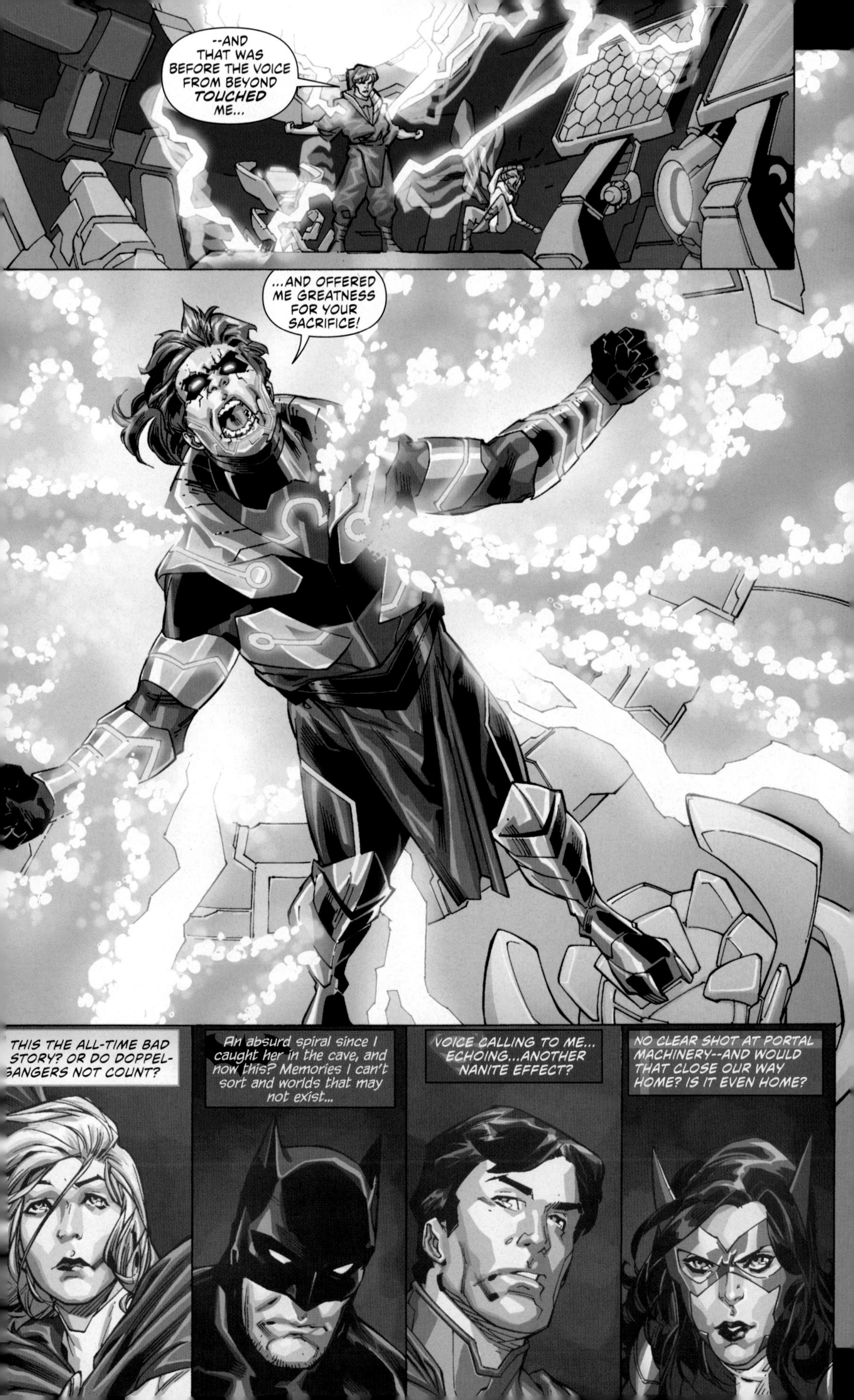
--AND THAT WAS BEFORE THE VOICE FROM BEYOND TOUCHED ME...
...AND OFFERED ME GREATNESS FOR YOUR SACRIFICE!
THIS THE ALL-TIME BAD STORY? OR DO DOPPEL-GANGERS NOT COUNT?
An absurd spiral since I caught her in the cave, and now this? Memories I can't sort and worlds that may not exist...
VOICE CALLING TO ME... ECHOING...ANOTHER NANITE EFFECT?
NO CLEAR SHOT AT PORTAL MACHINERY--AND WOULD THAT CLOSE OUR WAY HOME? IS IT EVEN HOME?

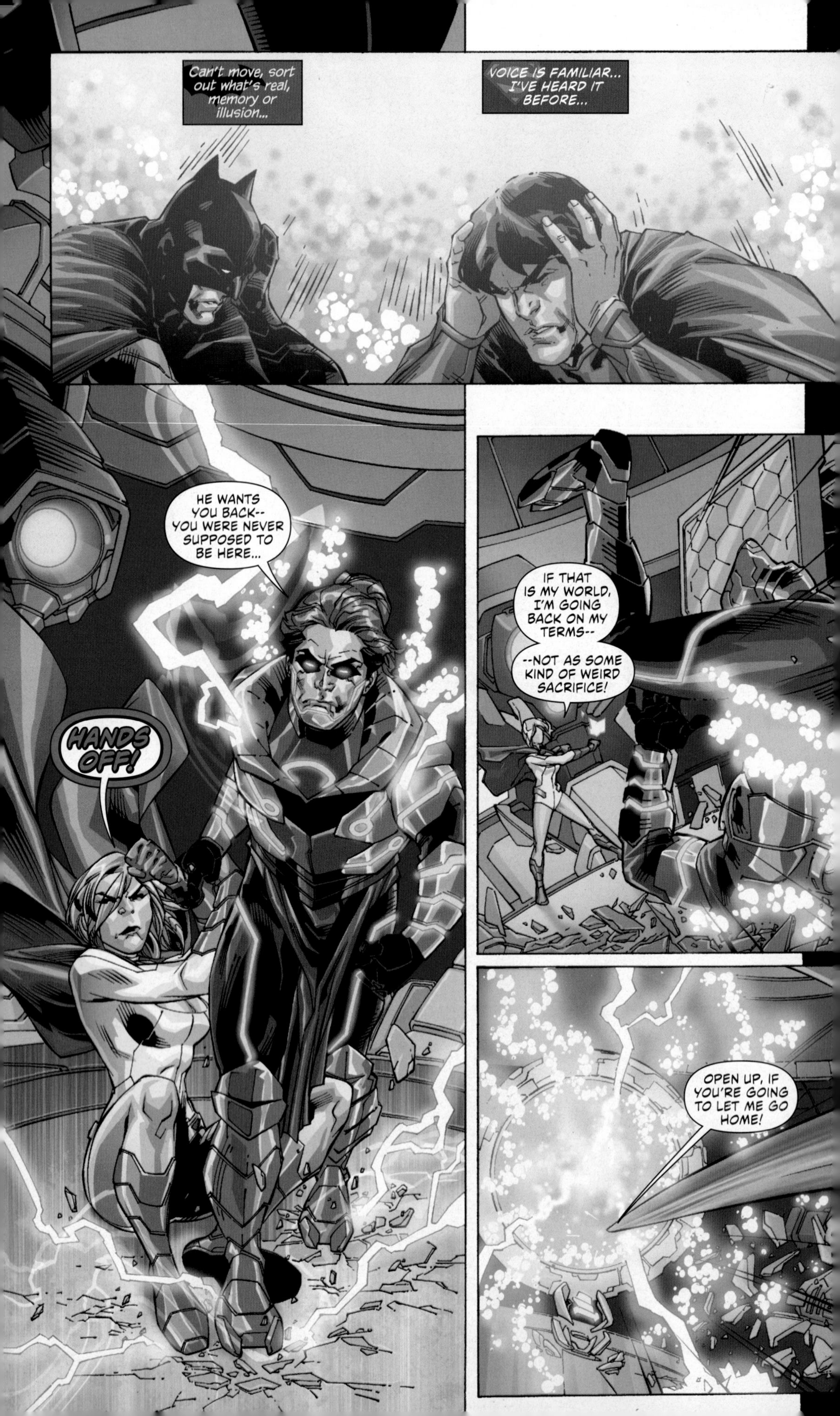
Can't move, sort out what's real, memory or illusion...
VOICE IS FAMILIAR... I'VE HEARD IT BEFORE...
HE WANTS YOU BACK-- YOU WERE NEVER SUPPOSED TO BE HERE...
HANDS OFF!
IF THAT IS MY WORLD, I'M GOING BACK ON MY TERMS--
--NOT AS SOME KIND OF WEIRD SACRIFICE!
OPEN UP, IF YOU'RE GOING TO LET ME GO HOME!

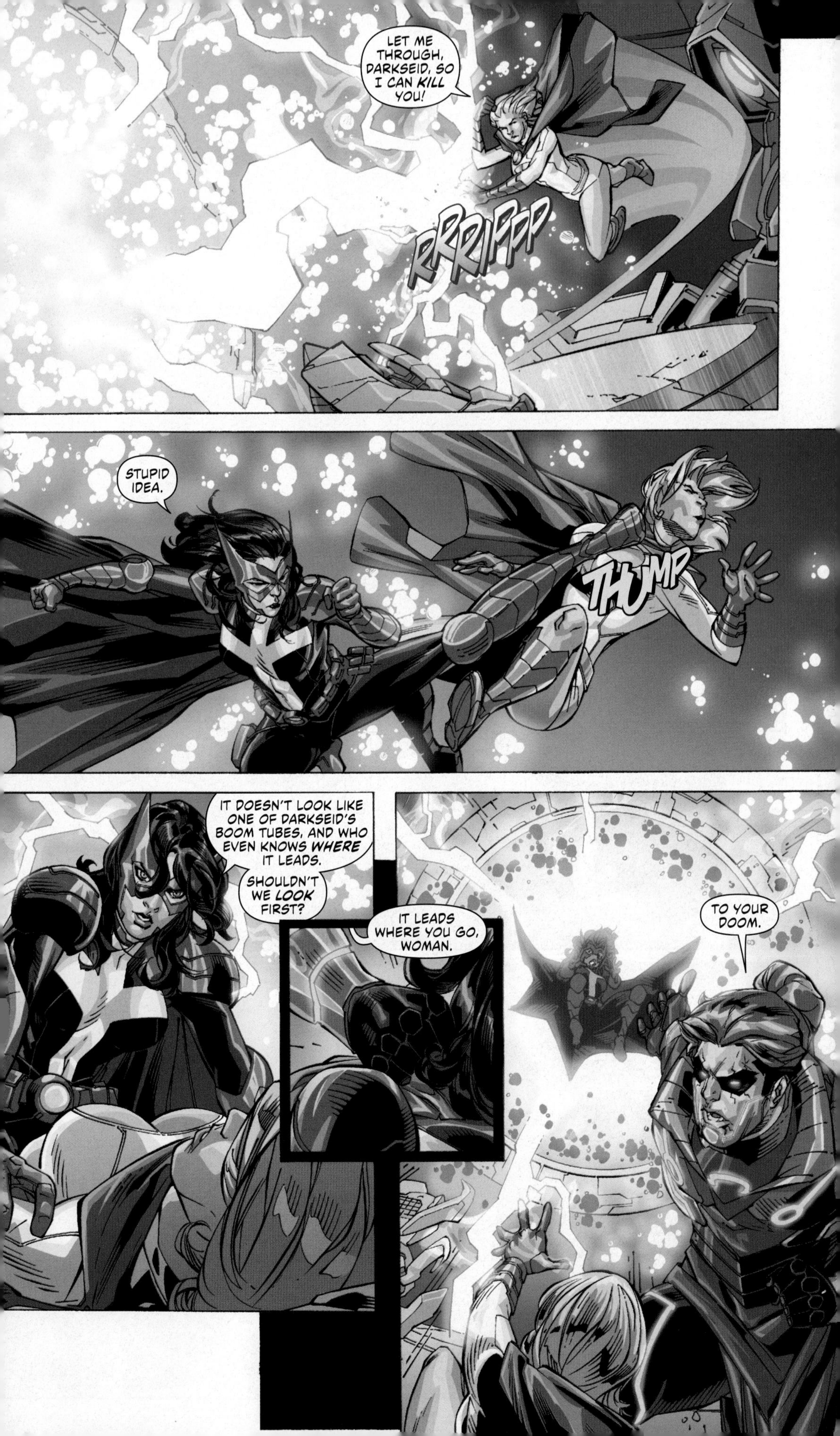
LET ME THROUGH, DARKSEID, SO I CAN KILL YOU!
RRRIPPP
STUPID IDEA.
THUMP
IT DOESN'T LOOK LIKE ONE OF DARKSEID'S BOOM TUBES, AND WHO EVEN KNOWS WHERE IT LEADS.
SHOULDN'T WE LOOK FIRST?
IT LEADS WHERE YOU GO, WOMAN.
TO YOUR DOOM.

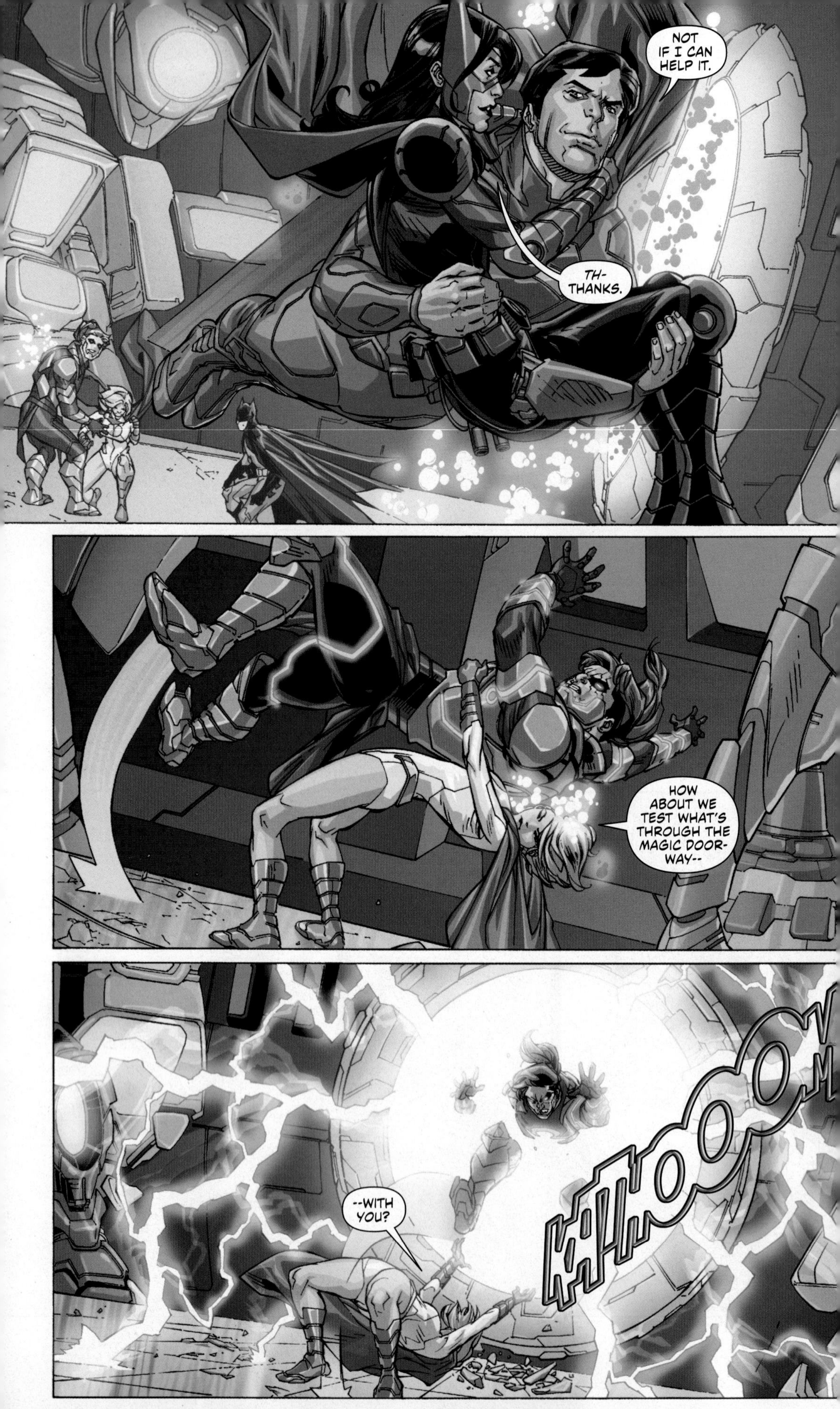
NOT IF I CAN HELP IT.
TH-THANKS.
HOW ABOUT WE TEST WHAT'S THROUGH THE MAGIC DOOR-WAY--
--WITH YOU?
KHHOOOOM

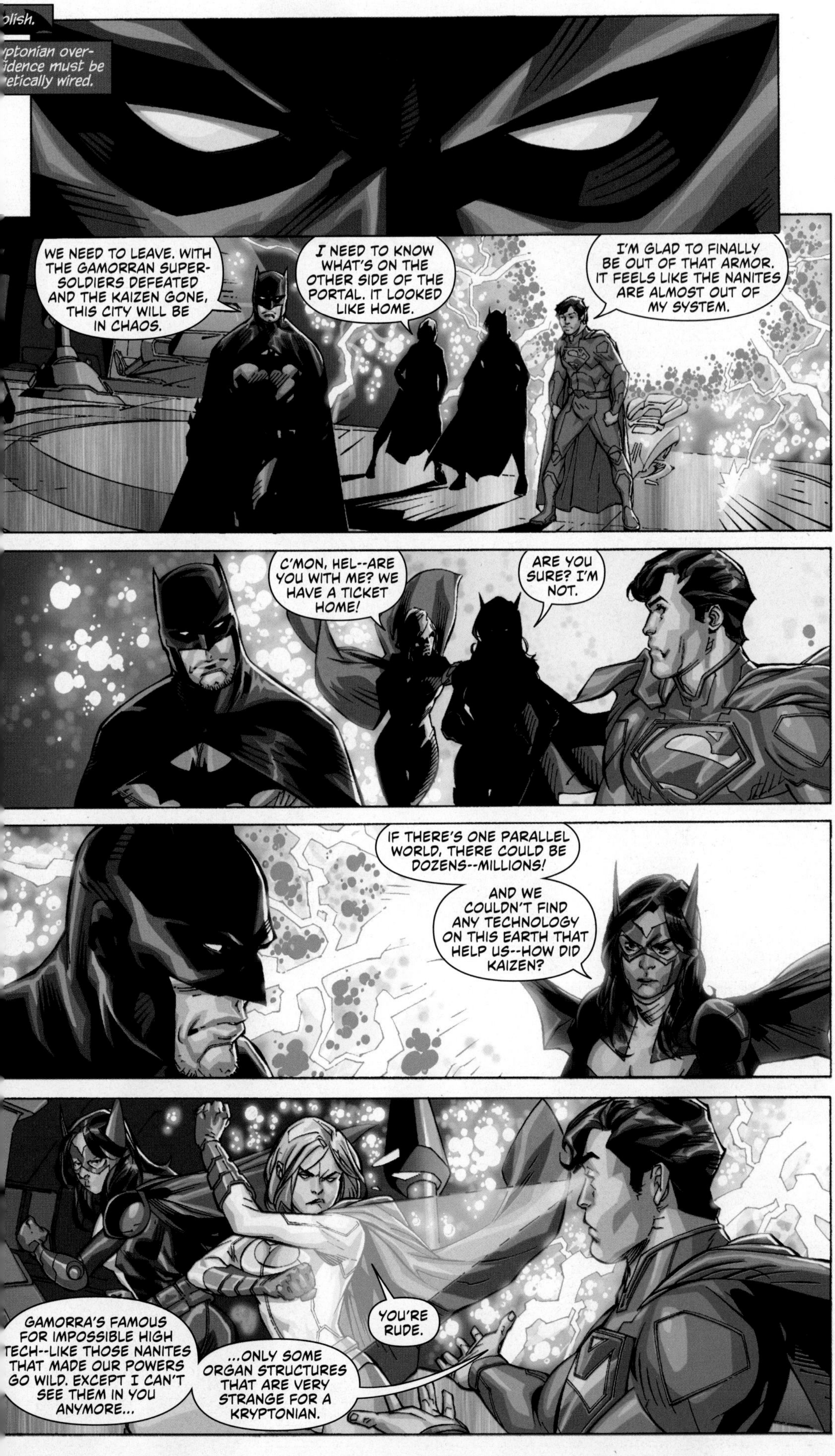
olish.
ptonian over-
idence must be
etically wired.
WE NEED TO LEAVE. WITH THE GAMORRAN SUPER-SOLDIERS DEFEATED AND THE KAIZEN GONE, THIS CITY WILL BE IN CHAOS.
I NEED TO KNOW WHAT'S ON THE OTHER SIDE OF THE PORTAL. IT LOOKED LIKE HOME.
I'M GLAD TO FINALLY BE OUT OF THAT ARMOR. IT FEELS LIKE THE NANITES ARE ALMOST OUT OF MY SYSTEM.
C'MON, HEL--ARE YOU WITH ME? WE HAVE A TICKET HOME!
ARE YOU SURE? I'M NOT.
IF THERE'S ONE PARALLEL WORLD, THERE COULD BE DOZENS--MILLIONS!
AND WE COULDN'T FIND ANY TECHNOLOGY ON THIS EARTH THAT HELP US--HOW DID KAIZEN?
GAMORRA'S FAMOUS FOR IMPOSSIBLE HIGH TECH--LIKE THOSE NANITES THAT MADE OUR POWERS GO WILD. EXCEPT I CAN'T SEE THEM IN YOU ANYMORE...
YOU'RE RUDE.
...ONLY SOME ORGAN STRUCTURES THAT ARE VERY STRANGE FOR A KRYPTONIAN.

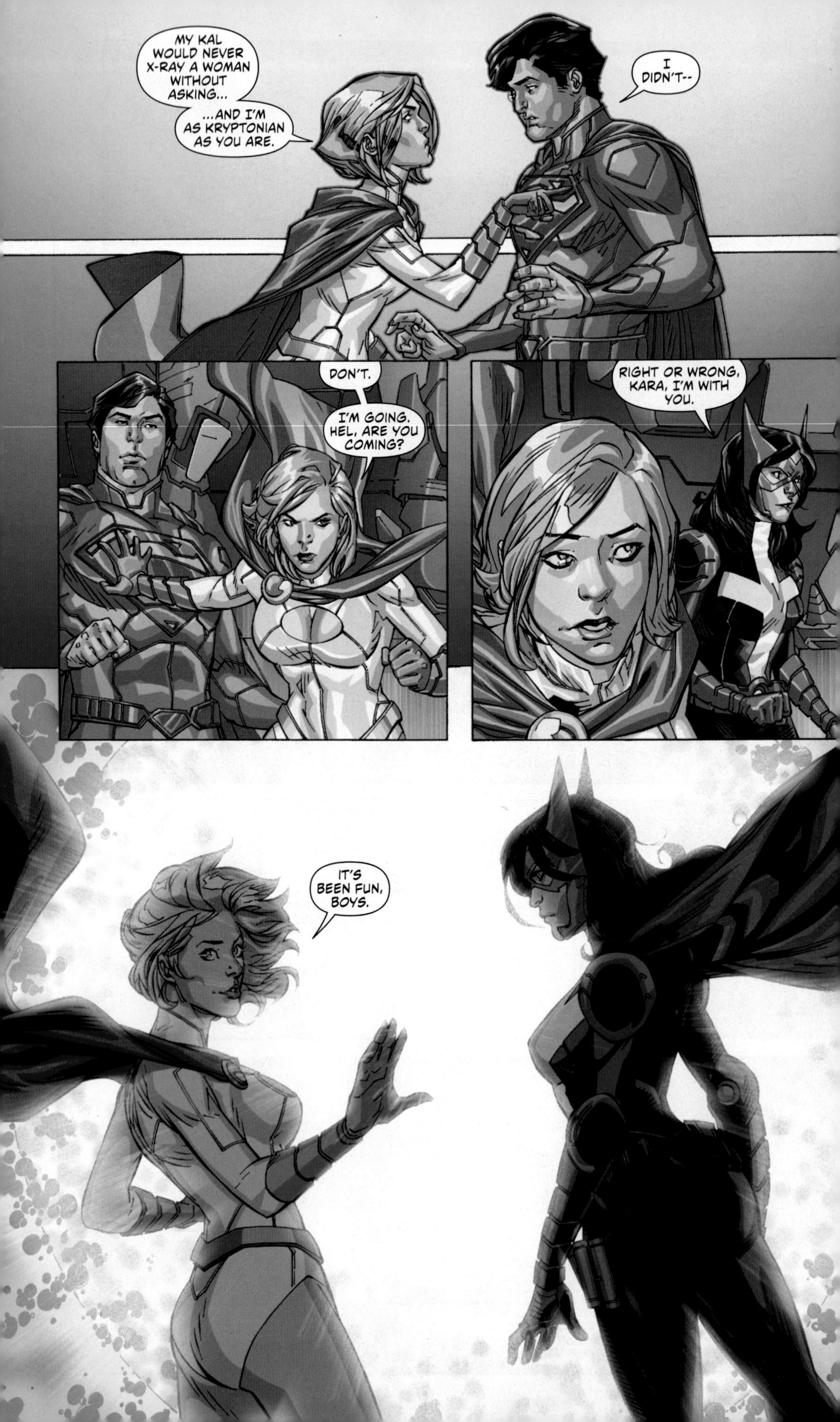
MY KAL WOULD NEVER X-RAY A WOMAN WITHOUT ASKING...
...AND I'M AS KRYPTONIAN AS YOU ARE.
I DIDN'T--
DON'T.
I'M GOING. HEL, ARE YOU COMING?
RIGHT OR WRONG, KARA, I'M WITH YOU.
IT'S BEEN FUN, BOYS.

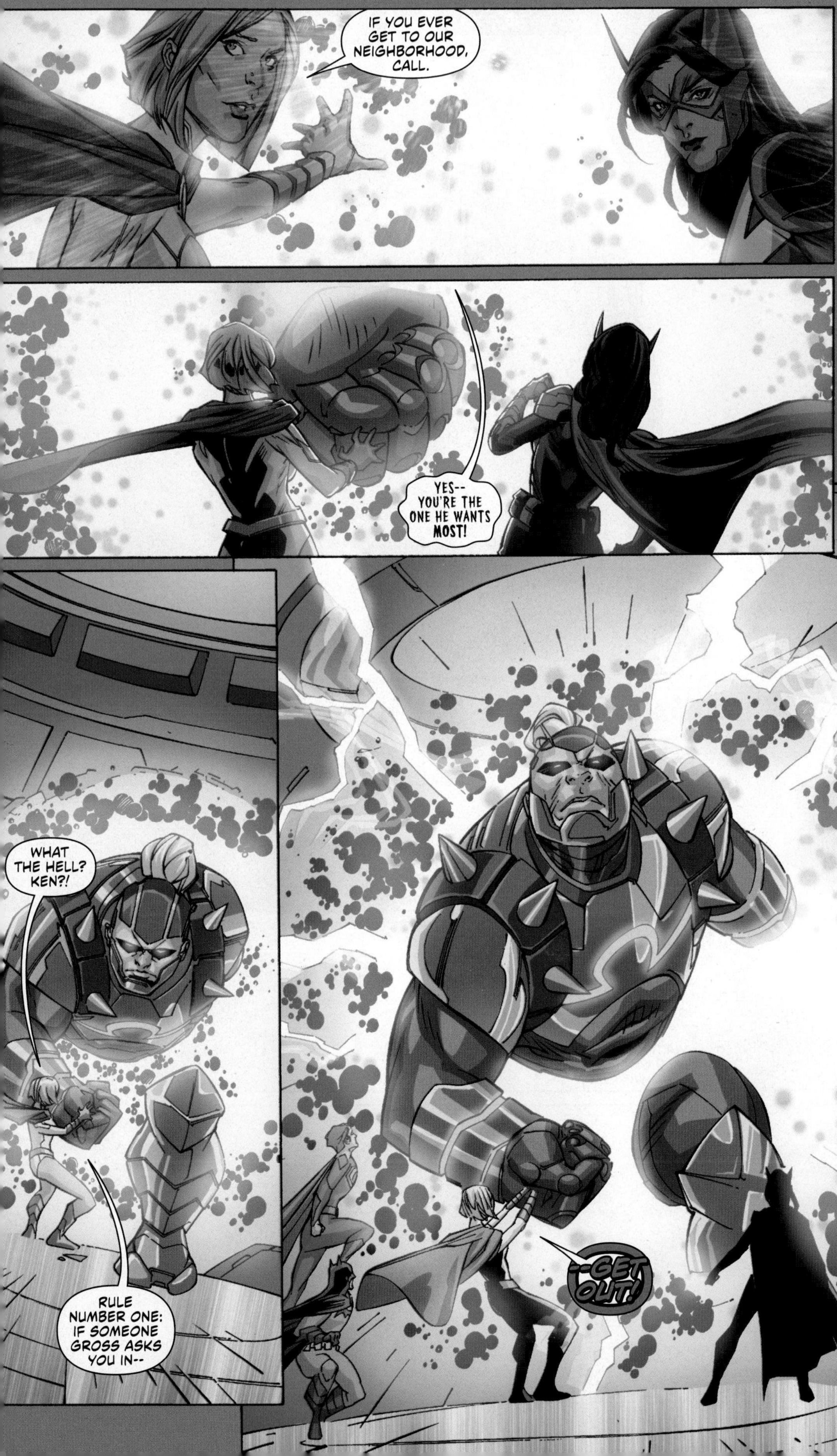
IF YOU EVER GET TO OUR NEIGHBORHOOD, CALL.
YES-- YOU'RE THE ONE HE WANTS MOST!
WHAT THE HELL? KEN?!
RULE NUMBER ONE: IF SOMEONE GROSS ASKS YOU IN--
--GET OUT!

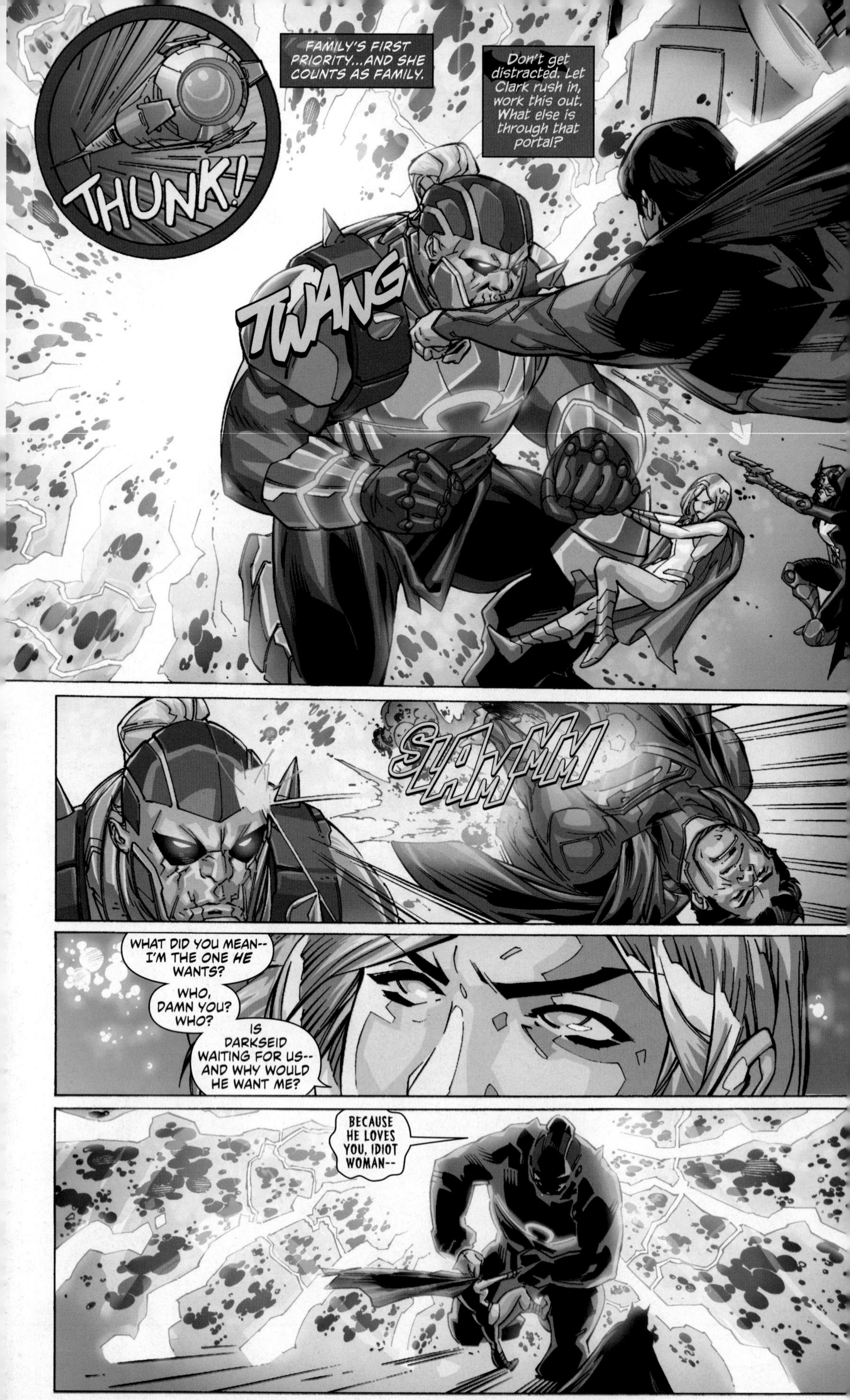

THUNK!
FAMILY'S FIRST PRIORITY...AND SHE COUNTS AS FAMILY.
Don't get distracted. Let Clark rush in, work this out. What else is through that portal?
TWANG
SLAMMM
WHAT DID YOU MEAN-- I'M THE ONE HE WANTS?
WHO, DAMN YOU? WHO?
IS DARKSEID WAITING FOR US-- AND WHY WOULD HE WANT ME?
BECAUSE HE LOVES YOU, IDIOT WOMAN--

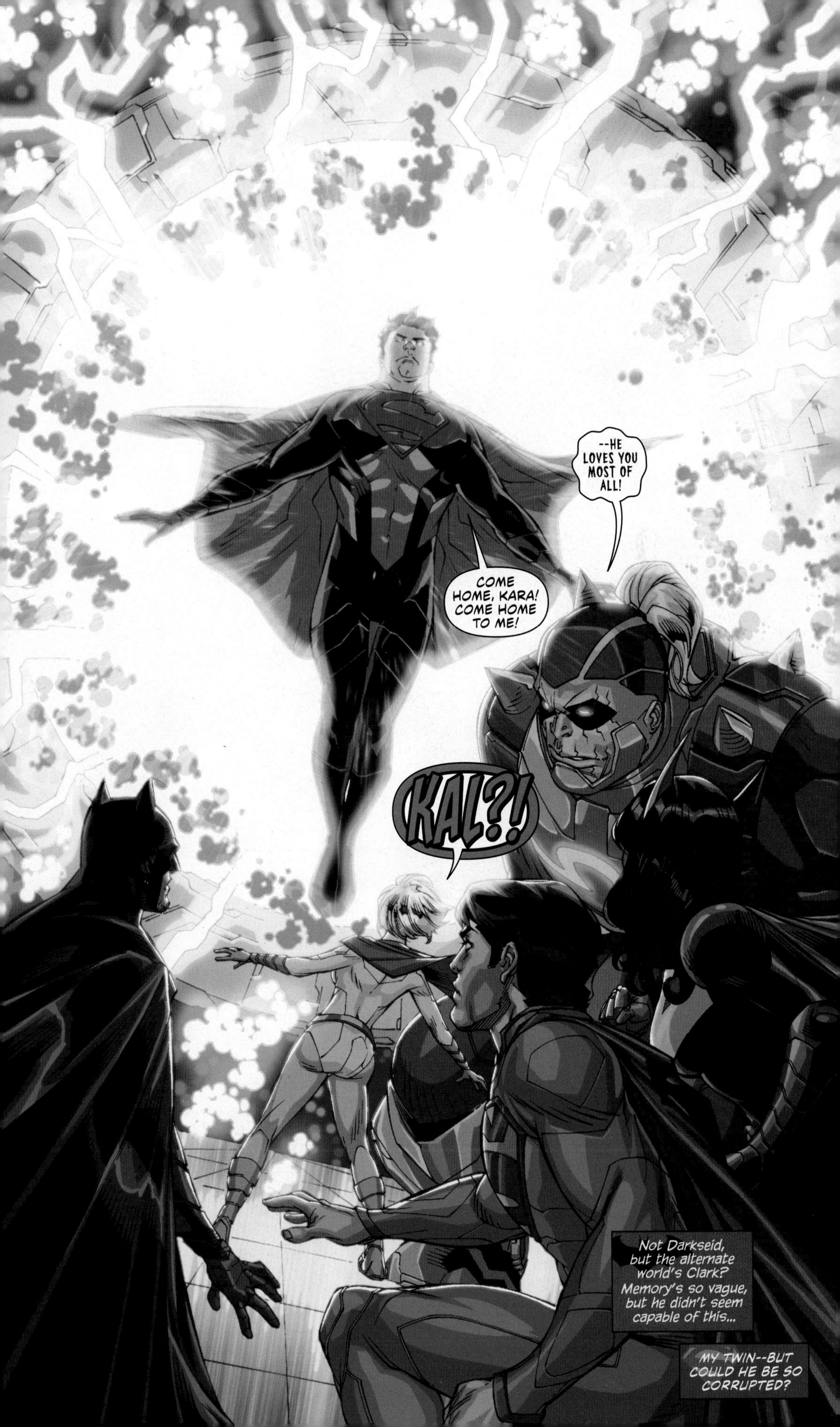
COME HOME, KARA! COME HOME TO ME!
--HE LOVES YOU MOST OF ALL!
KAL?!
Not Darkseid, but the alternate world's Clark? Memory's so vague, but he didn't seem capable of this...
MY TWIN--BUT COULD HE BE SO CORRUPTED?

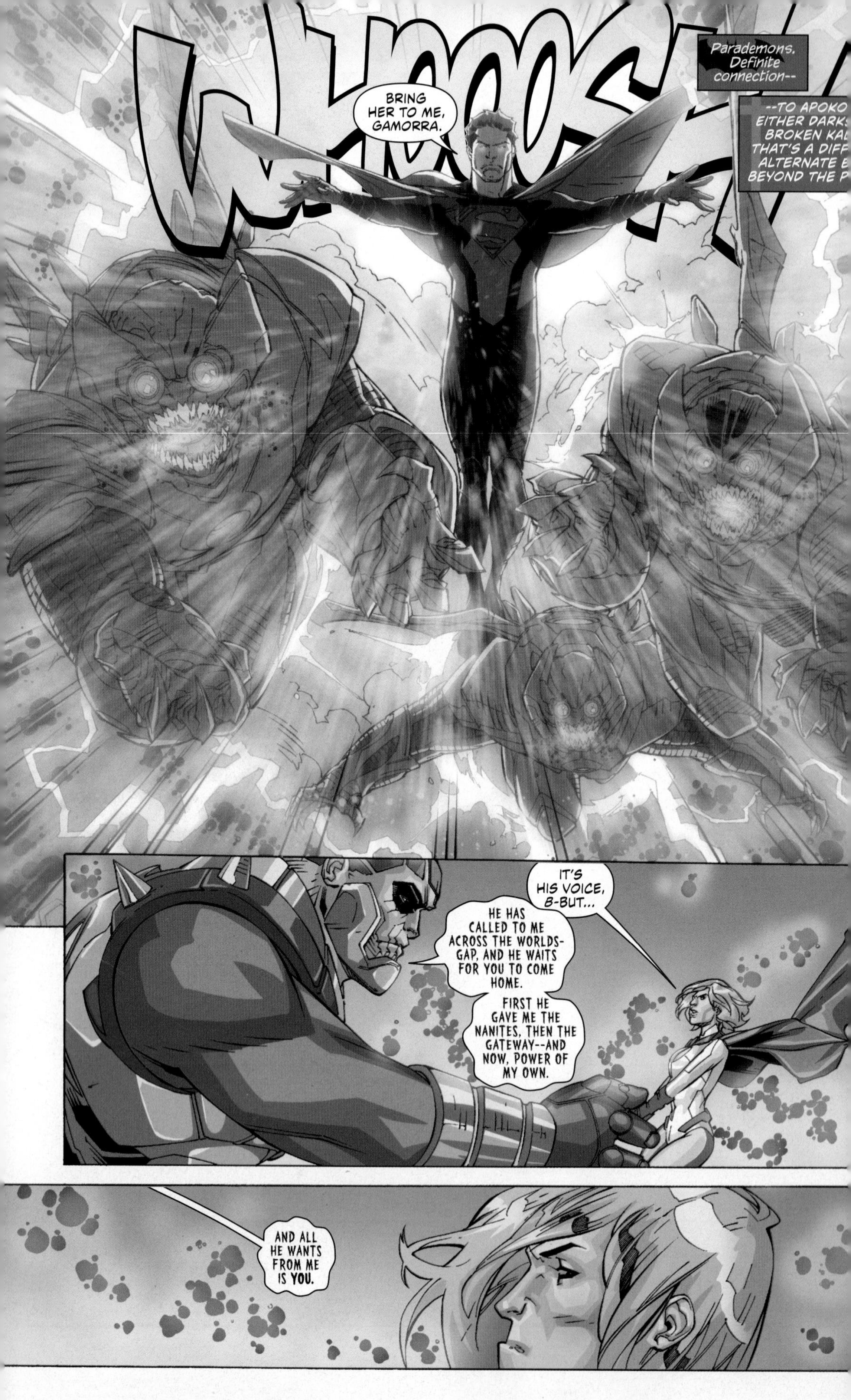
WHOOOSH
Parademons. Definite connection--
--TO APOKO
EITHER DARKS
BROKEN KA
THAT'S A DIFF
ALTERNATE E
BEYOND THE P
BRING HER TO ME, GAMORRA.
IT'S HIS VOICE, B-BUT...
HE HAS CALLED TO ME ACROSS THE WORLDS-GAP, AND HE WAITS FOR YOU TO COME HOME.
FIRST HE GAVE ME THE NANITES, THEN THE GATEWAY--AND NOW, POWER OF MY OWN.
AND ALL HE WANTS FROM ME IS **YOU**.

NOT AT FULL STRENGTH WITH THESE NANITES IN MY SYSTEM, AND THE ARMOR'S EFFECT IS WEAKENING AS IT CRACKS...

THEY'RE STRONG, BUT AWKWARD...AND THERE'S VULNERABLE FLESH UNDERNEATH.

HUNTRESS!

DOWN HERE, NOT-DAD!

SNAP

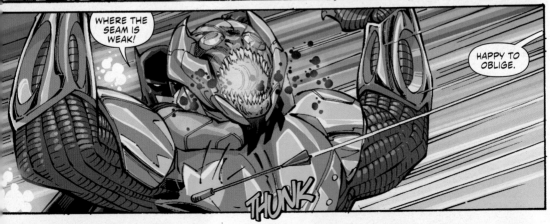

WHERE THE SEAM IS WEAK!

HAPPY TO OBLIGE.

THUNK

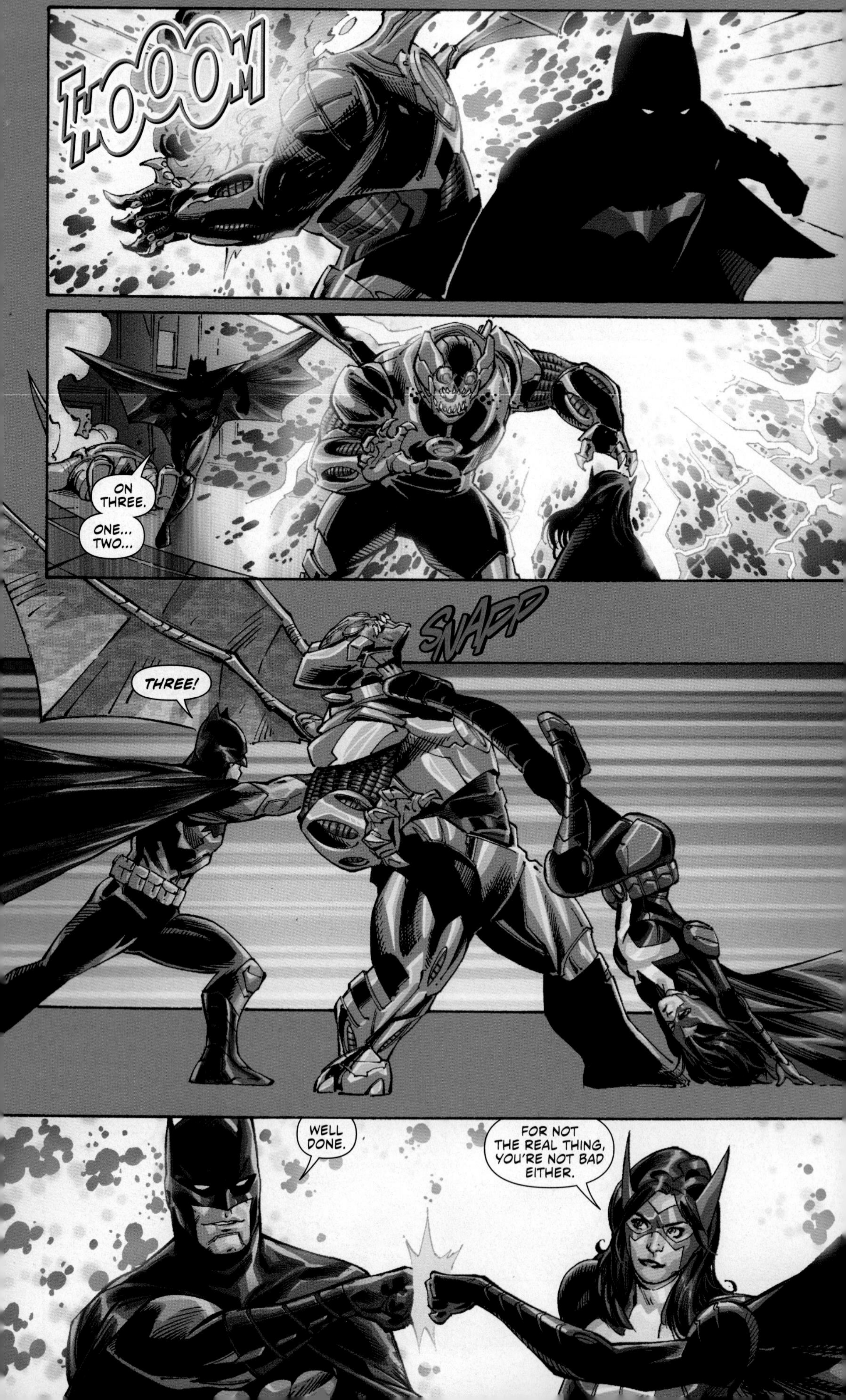
THOOOOM
ON THREE.
ONE... TWO...
SNAPP
THREE!
WELL DONE.
FOR NOT THE REAL THING, YOU'RE NOT BAD EITHER.

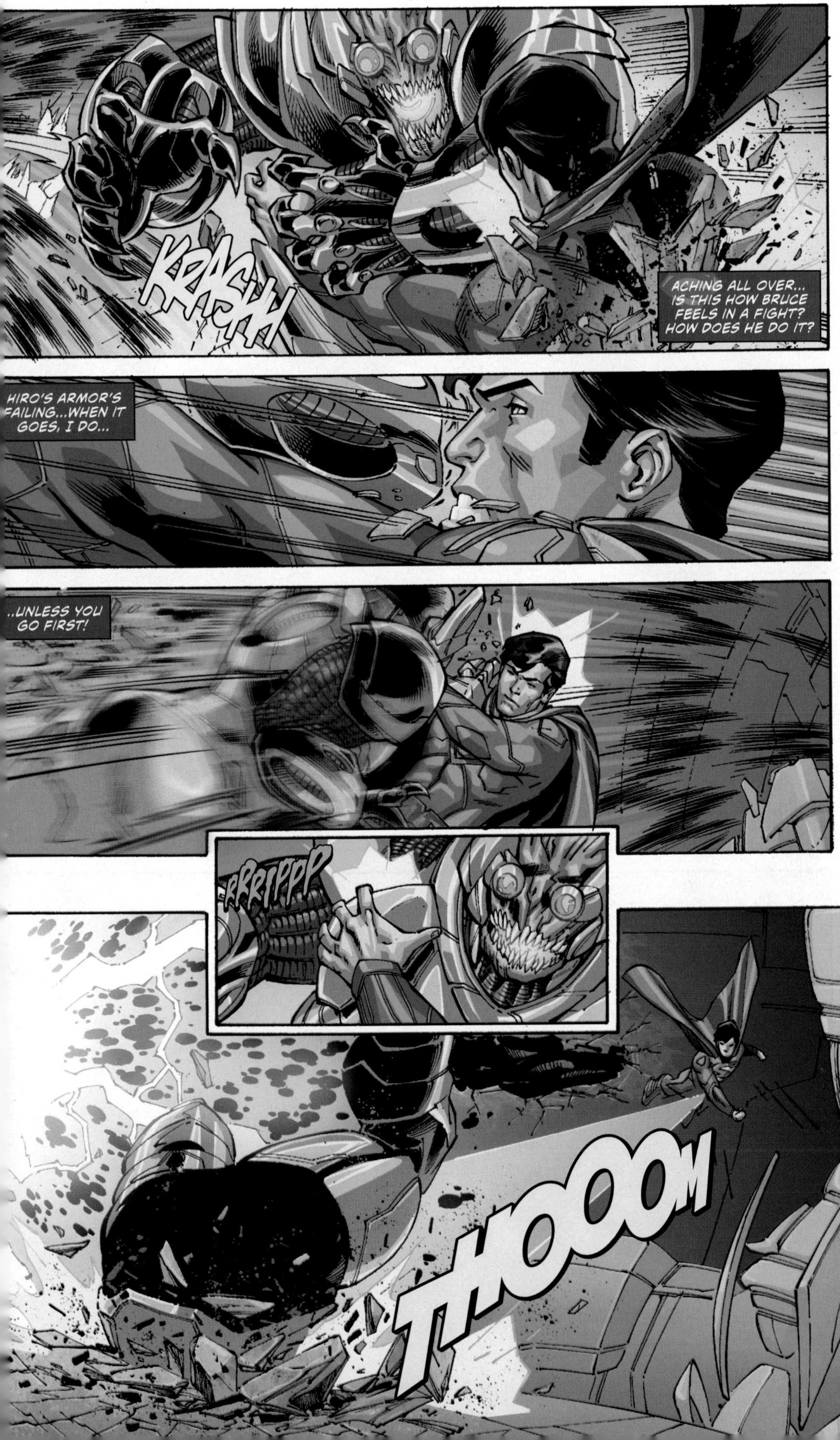
KRASHH
ACHING ALL OVER... IS THIS HOW BRUCE FEELS IN A FIGHT? HOW DOES HE DO IT?
HIRO'S ARMOR'S FAILING...WHEN IT GOES, I DO...
..UNLESS YOU GO FIRST!
RRRIPPP
THOOOM

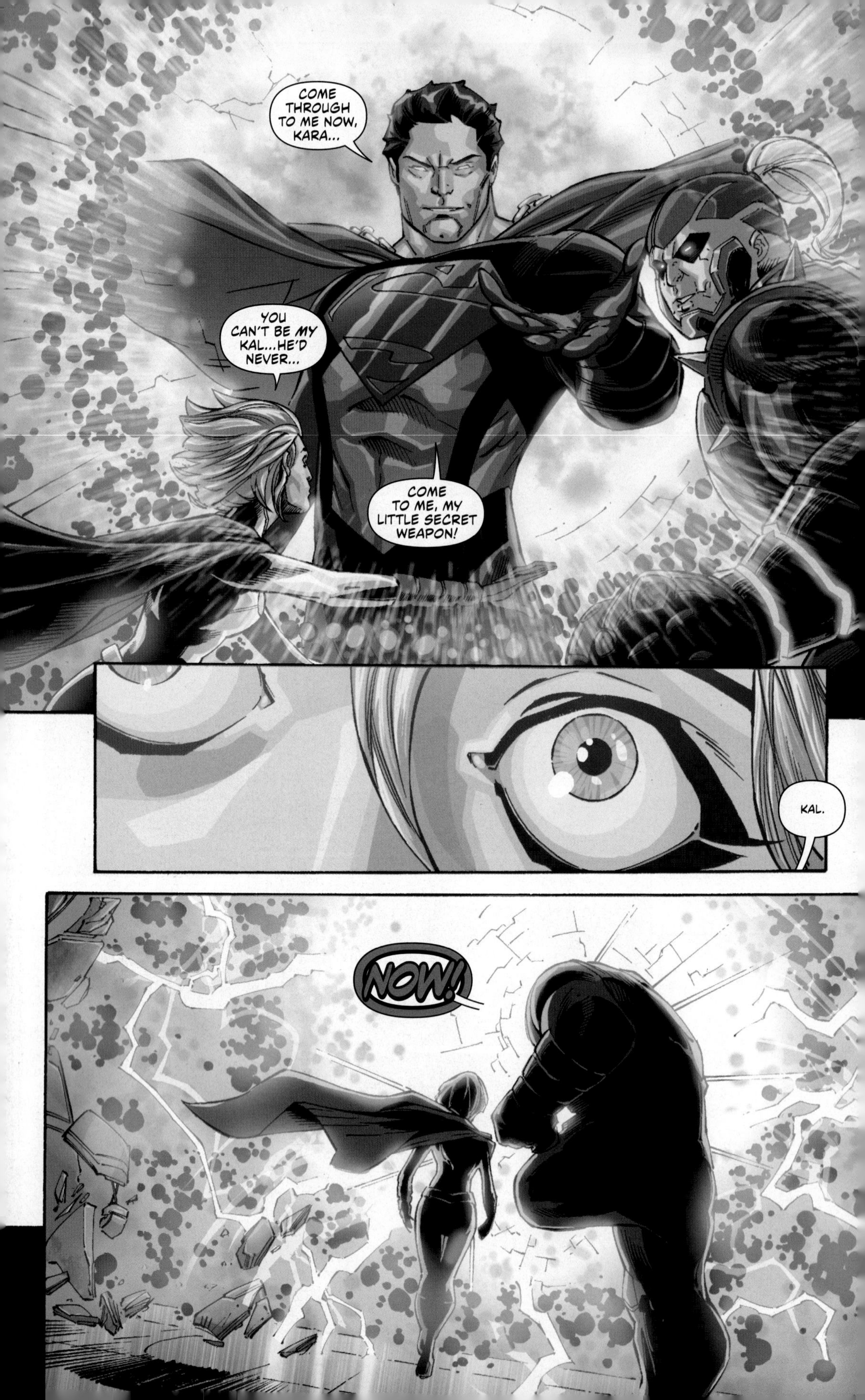
COME THROUGH TO ME NOW, KARA...
YOU CAN'T BE MY KAL...HE'D NEVER...
COME TO ME, MY LITTLE SECRET WEAPON!
KAL.
NOW!

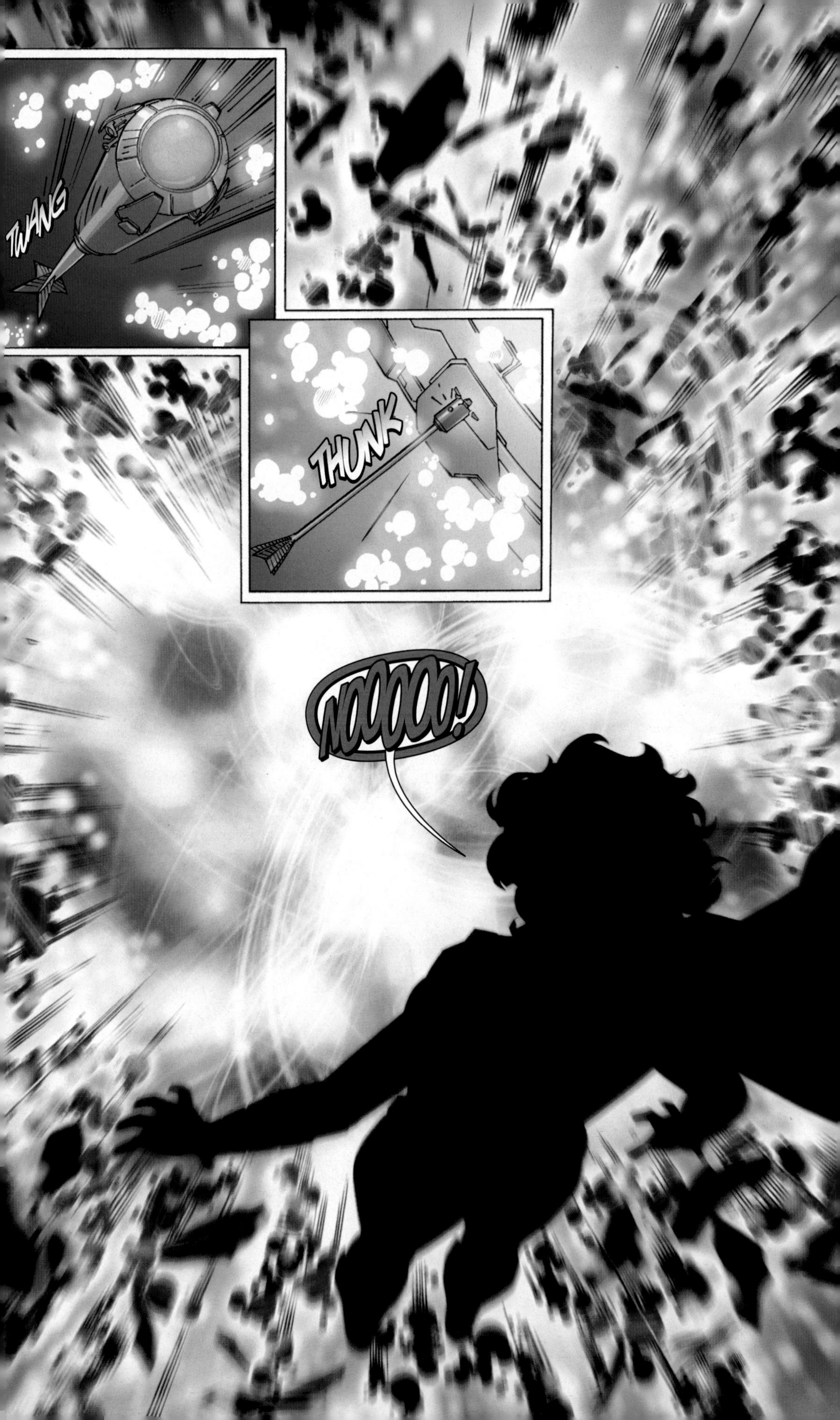
TWANG
THUNK
NOOOOO!

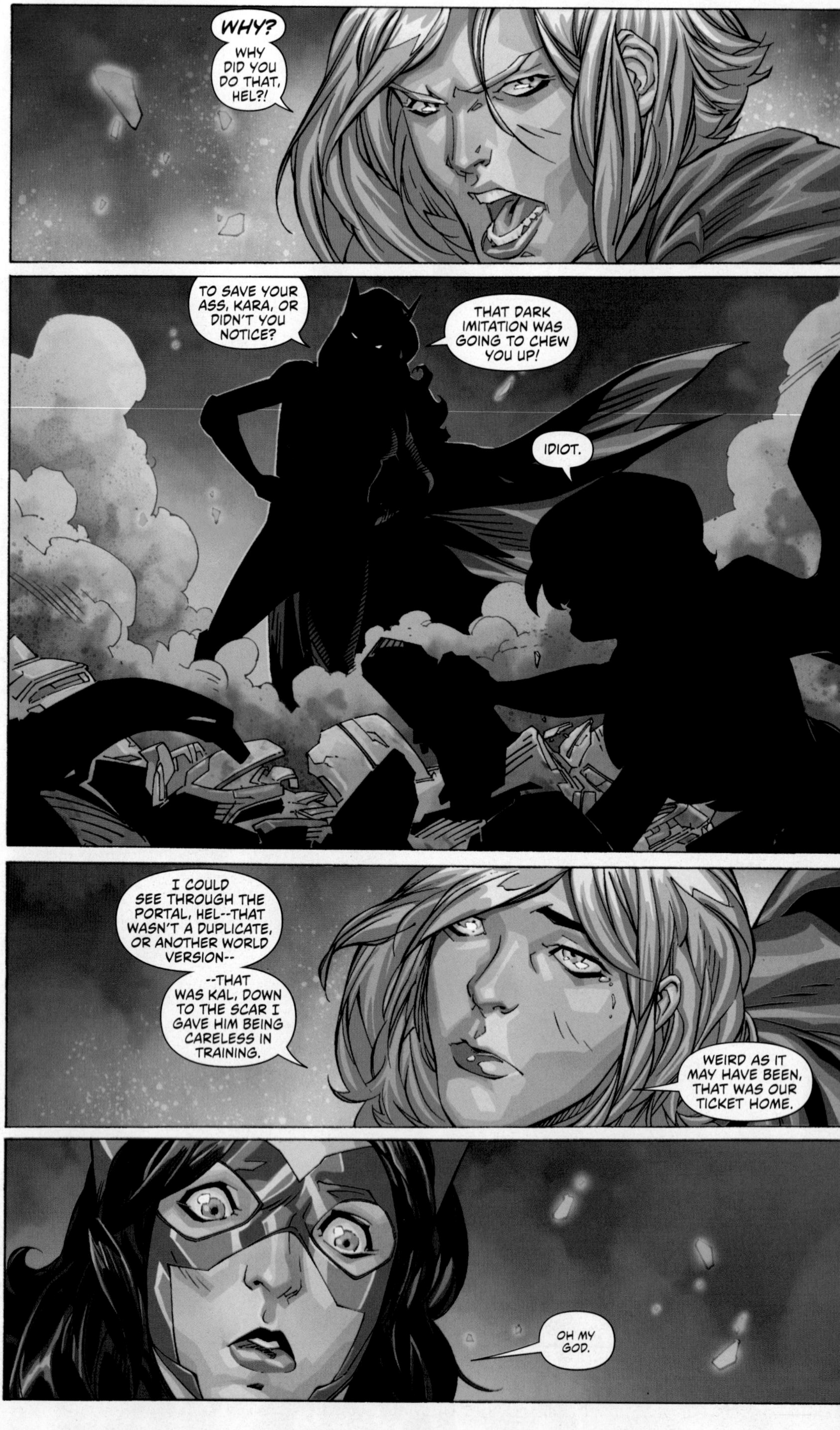
WHY? WHY DID YOU DO THAT, HEL?!
TO SAVE YOUR ASS, KARA, OR DIDN'T YOU NOTICE?
THAT DARK IMITATION WAS GOING TO CHEW YOU UP!
IDIOT.
I COULD SEE THROUGH THE PORTAL, HEL--THAT WASN'T A DUPLICATE, OR ANOTHER WORLD VERSION--
--THAT WAS KAL, DOWN TO THE SCAR I GAVE HIM BEING CARELESS IN TRAINING.
WEIRD AS IT MAY HAVE BEEN, THAT WAS OUR TICKET HOME.
OH MY GOD.

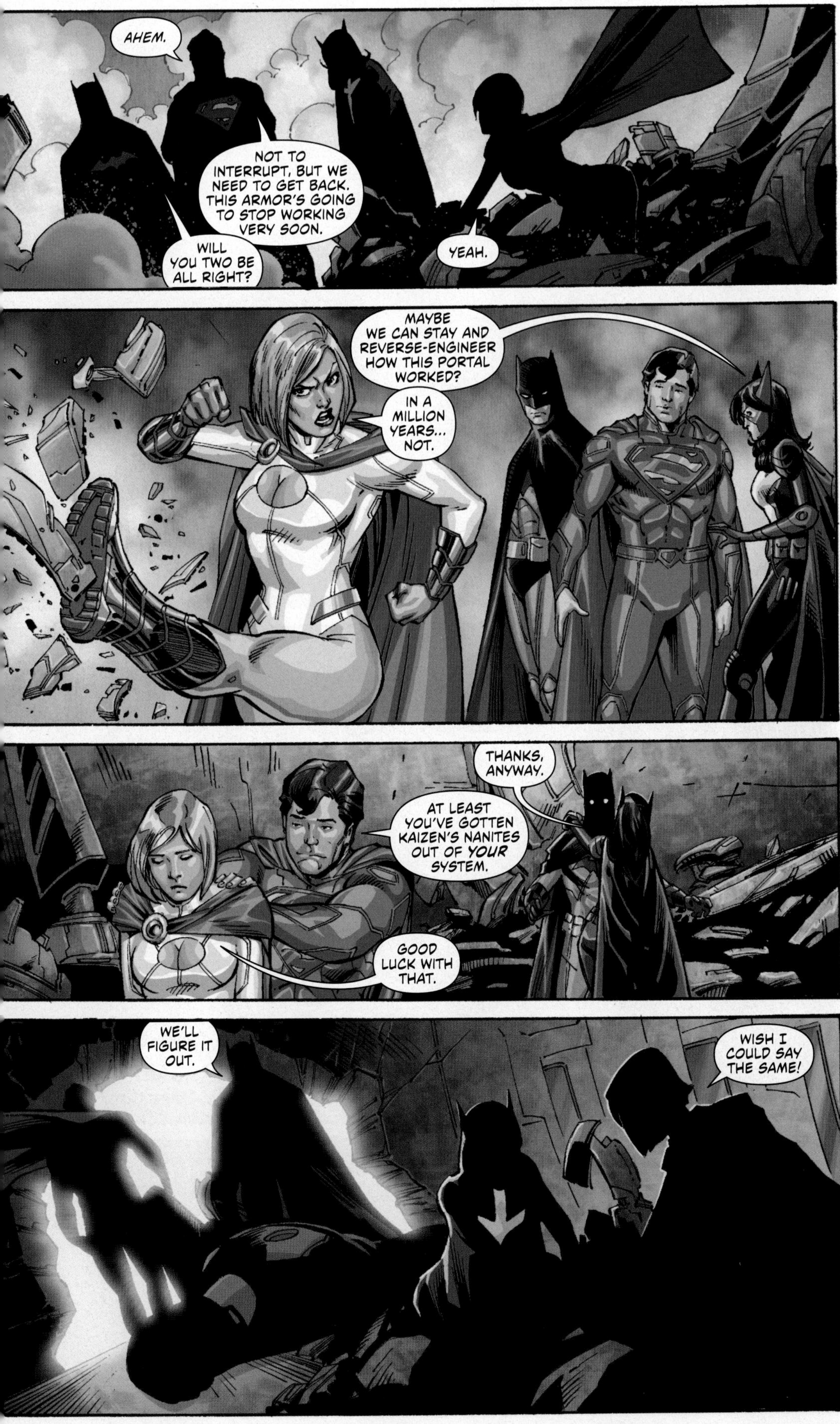
AHEM.
NOT TO INTERRUPT, BUT WE NEED TO GET BACK. THIS ARMOR'S GOING TO STOP WORKING VERY SOON.
WILL YOU TWO BE ALL RIGHT?
YEAH.
MAYBE WE CAN STAY AND REVERSE-ENGINEER HOW THIS PORTAL WORKED?
IN A MILLION YEARS... NOT.
THANKS, ANYWAY.
AT LEAST YOU'VE GOTTEN KAIZEN'S NANITES OUT OF *YOUR* SYSTEM.
GOOD LUCK WITH THAT.
WE'LL FIGURE IT OUT.
WISH I COULD SAY THE SAME!

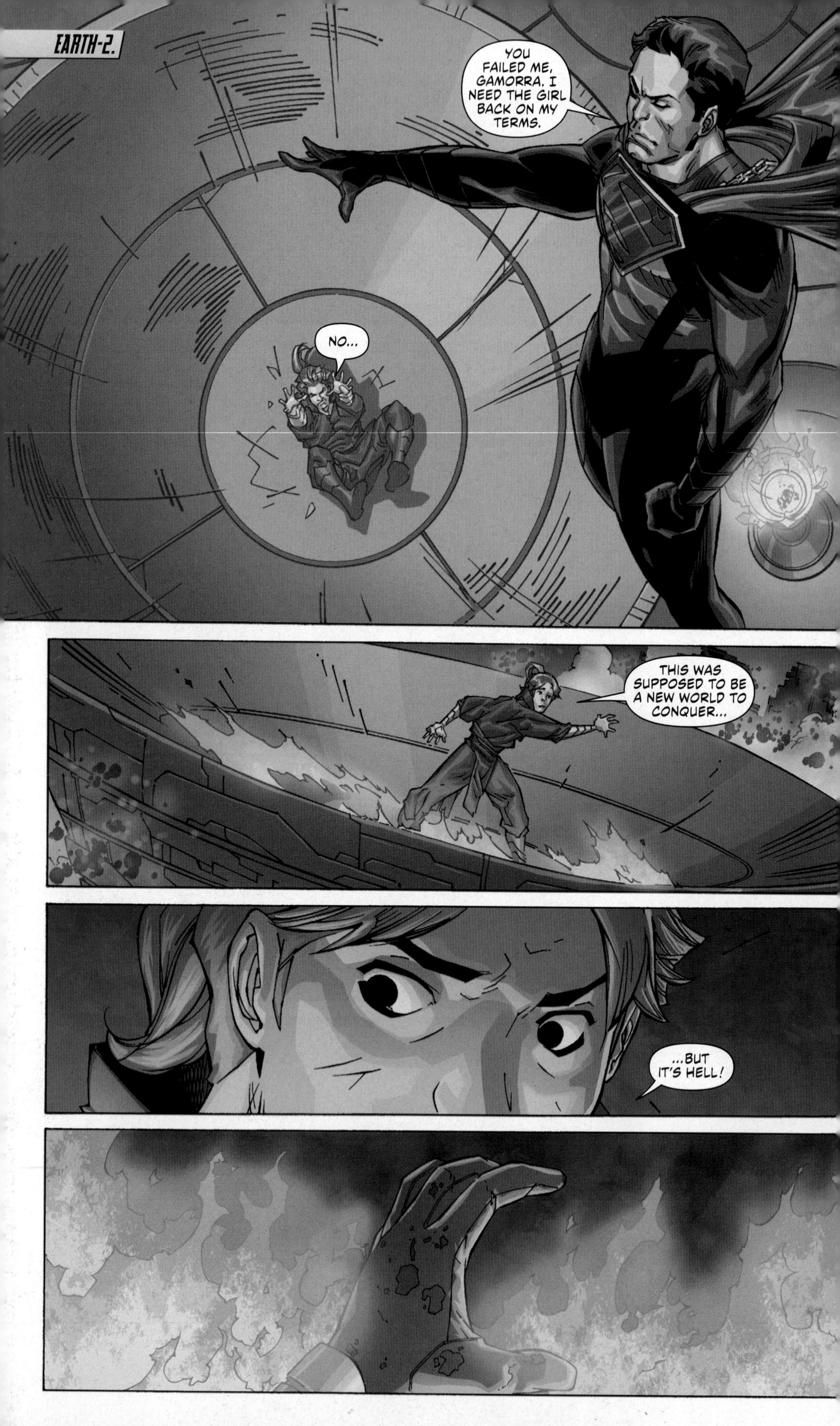
EARTH-2.
YOU FAILED ME, GAMORRA. I NEED THE GIRL BACK ON MY TERMS.
NO...
THIS WAS SUPPOSED TO BE A NEW WORLD TO CONQUER...
...BUT IT'S HELL!

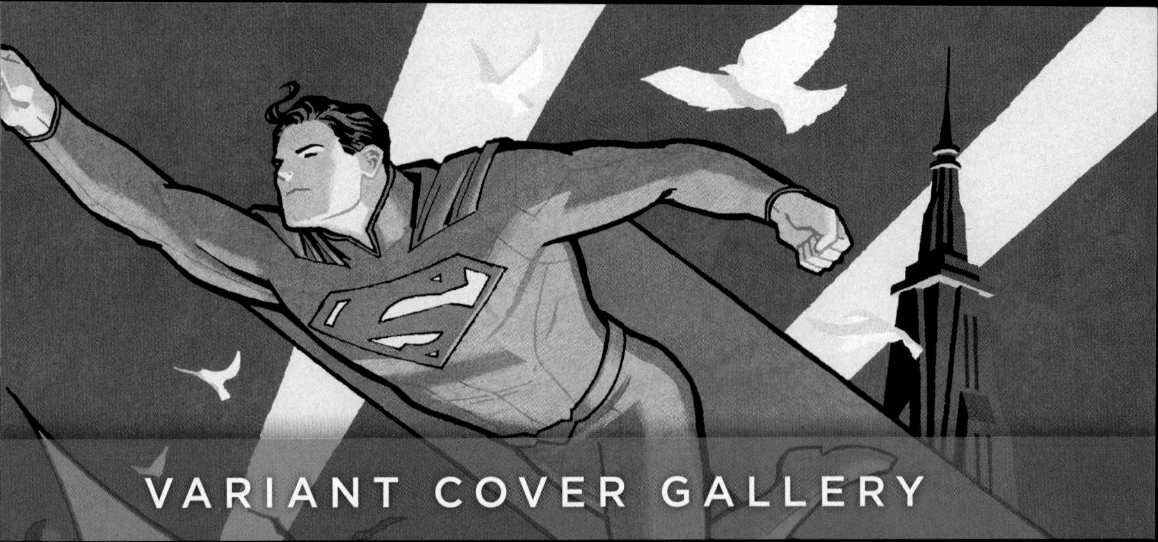

VARIANT COVER GALLERY

BATMAN/SUPERMAN 5
By Jon Bogdanove with Daniel Brown

BATMAN/SUPERMAN 6
By Cliff Chiang

BATMAN/SUPERMAN 7
***Scribblenauts* variant by Jon Katz, after Frank Miller**

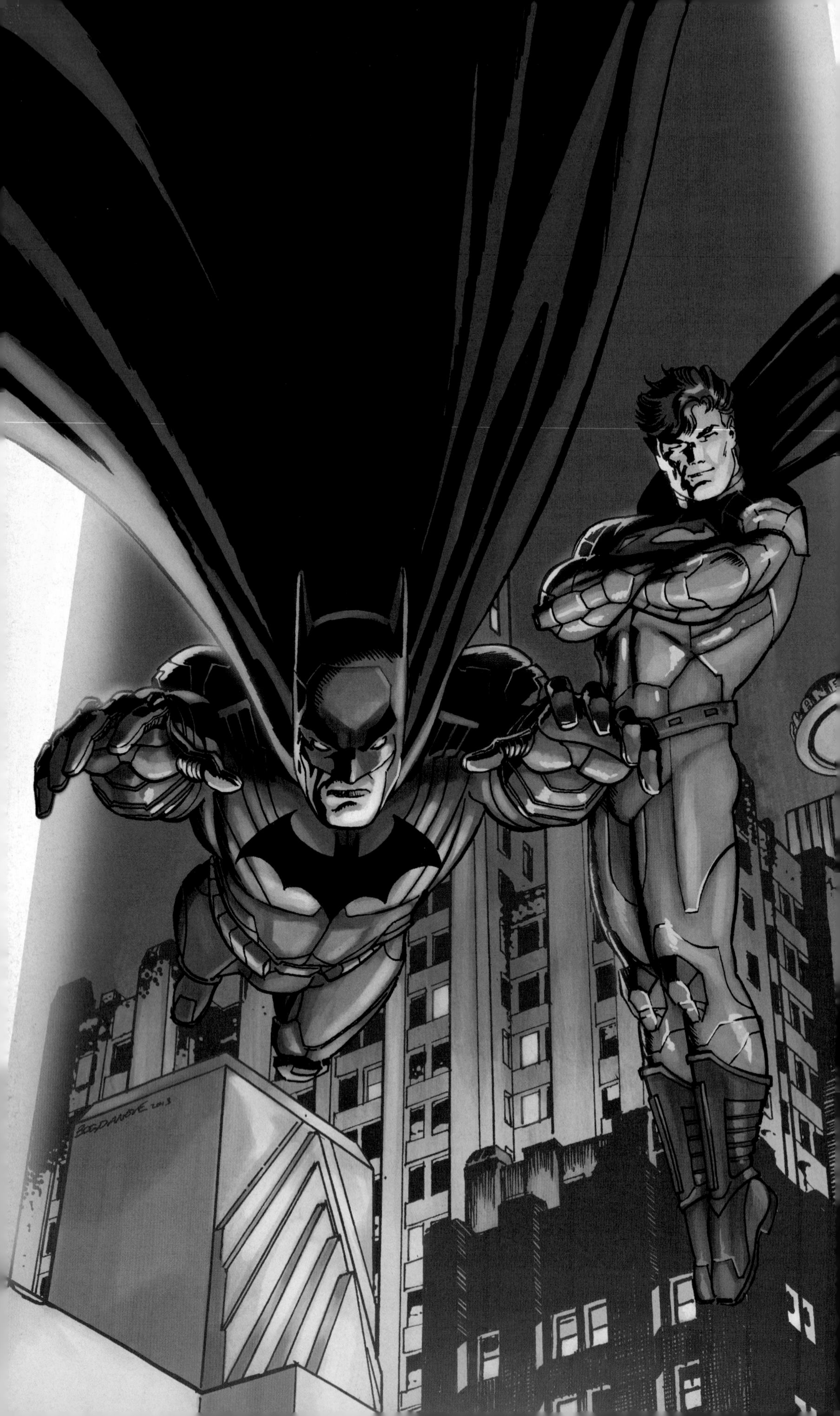

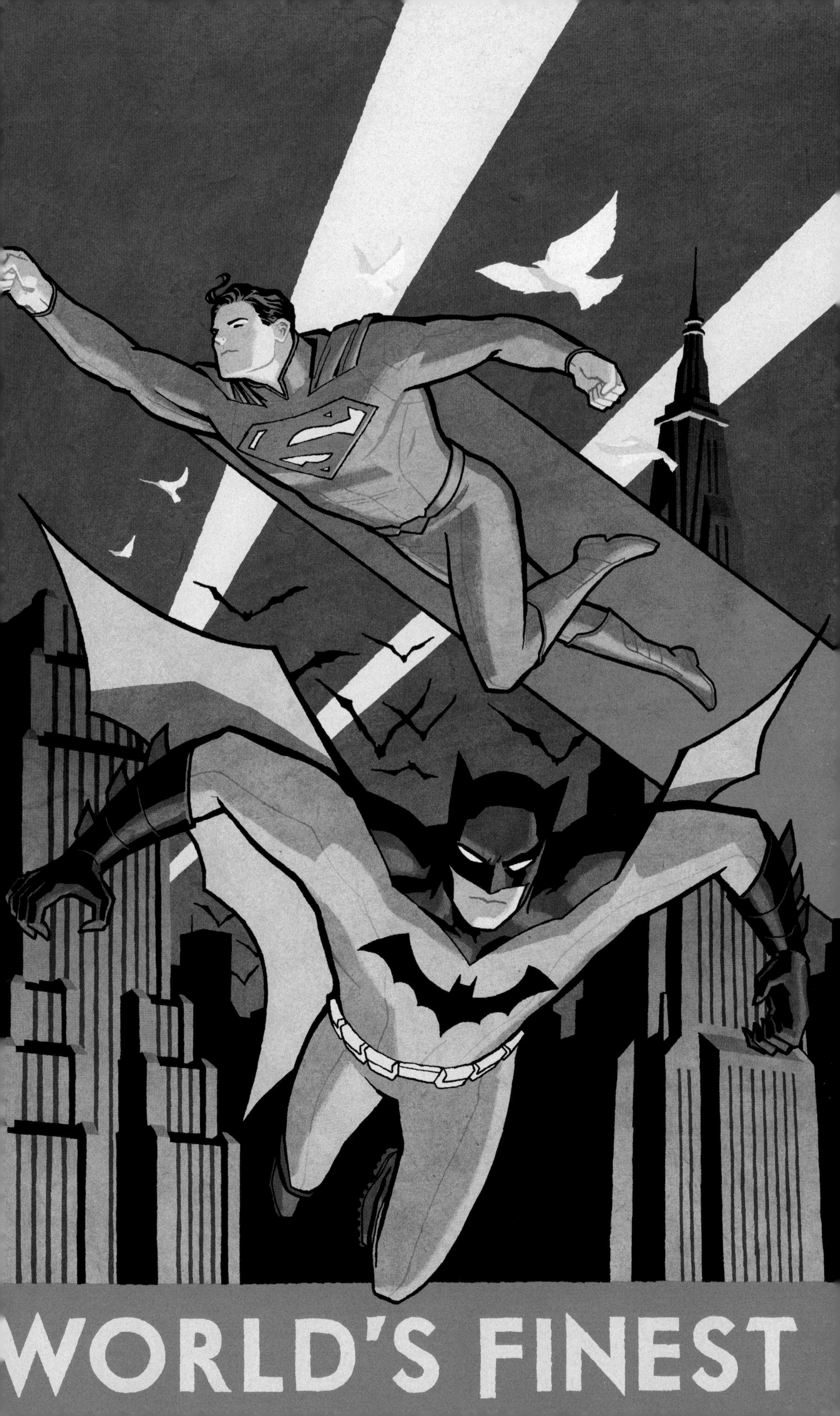
WORLD'S FINEST

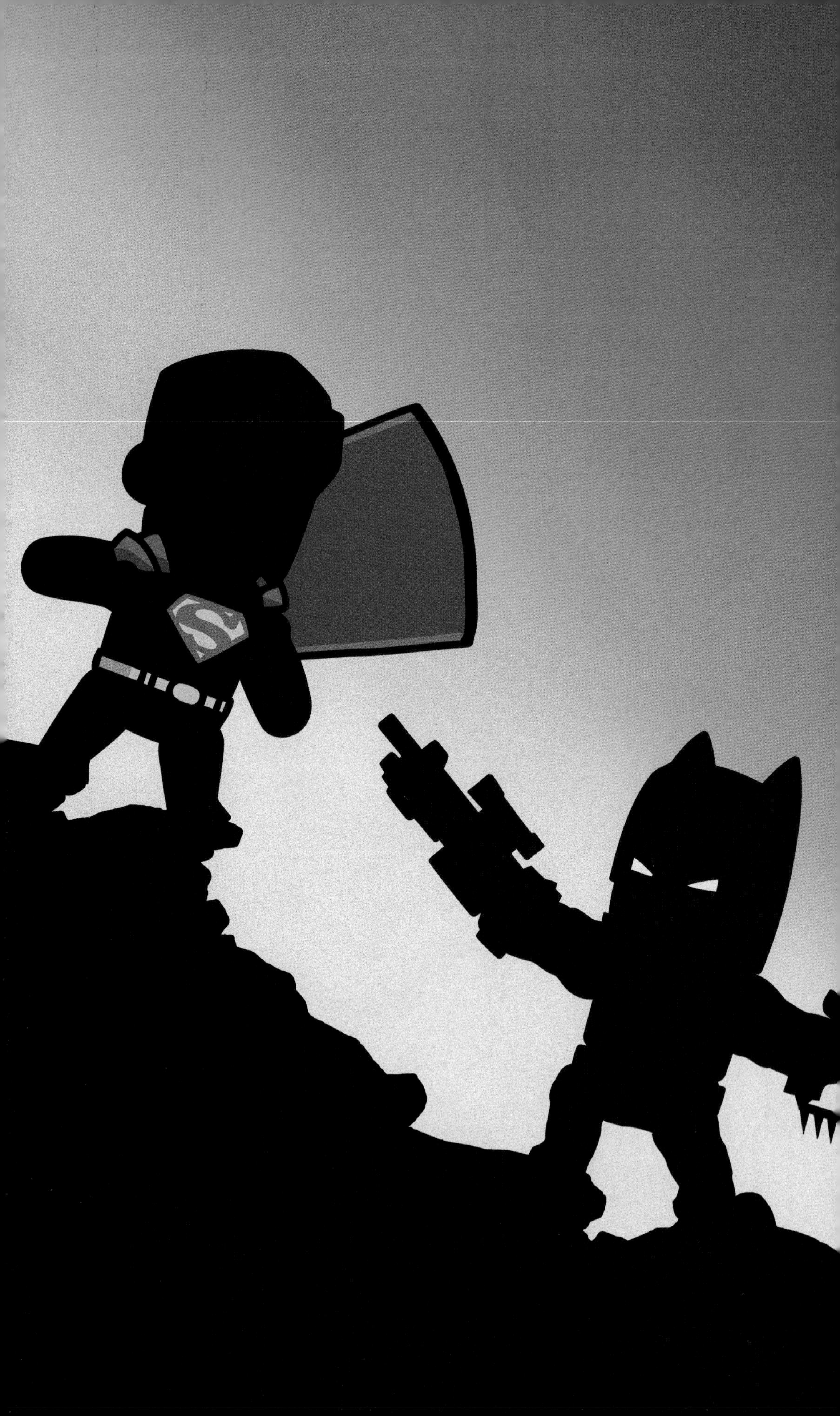

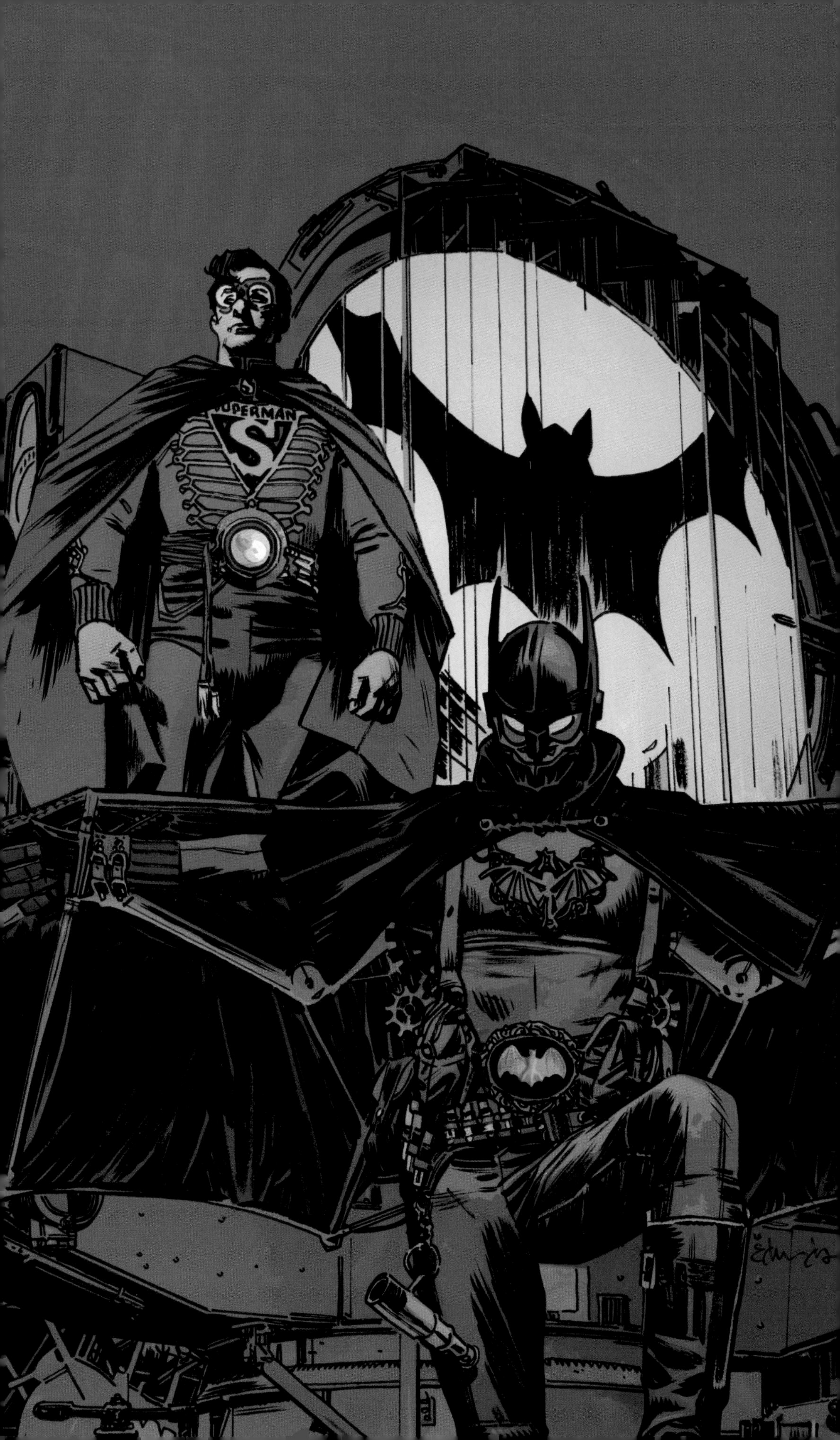
SUPERMAN

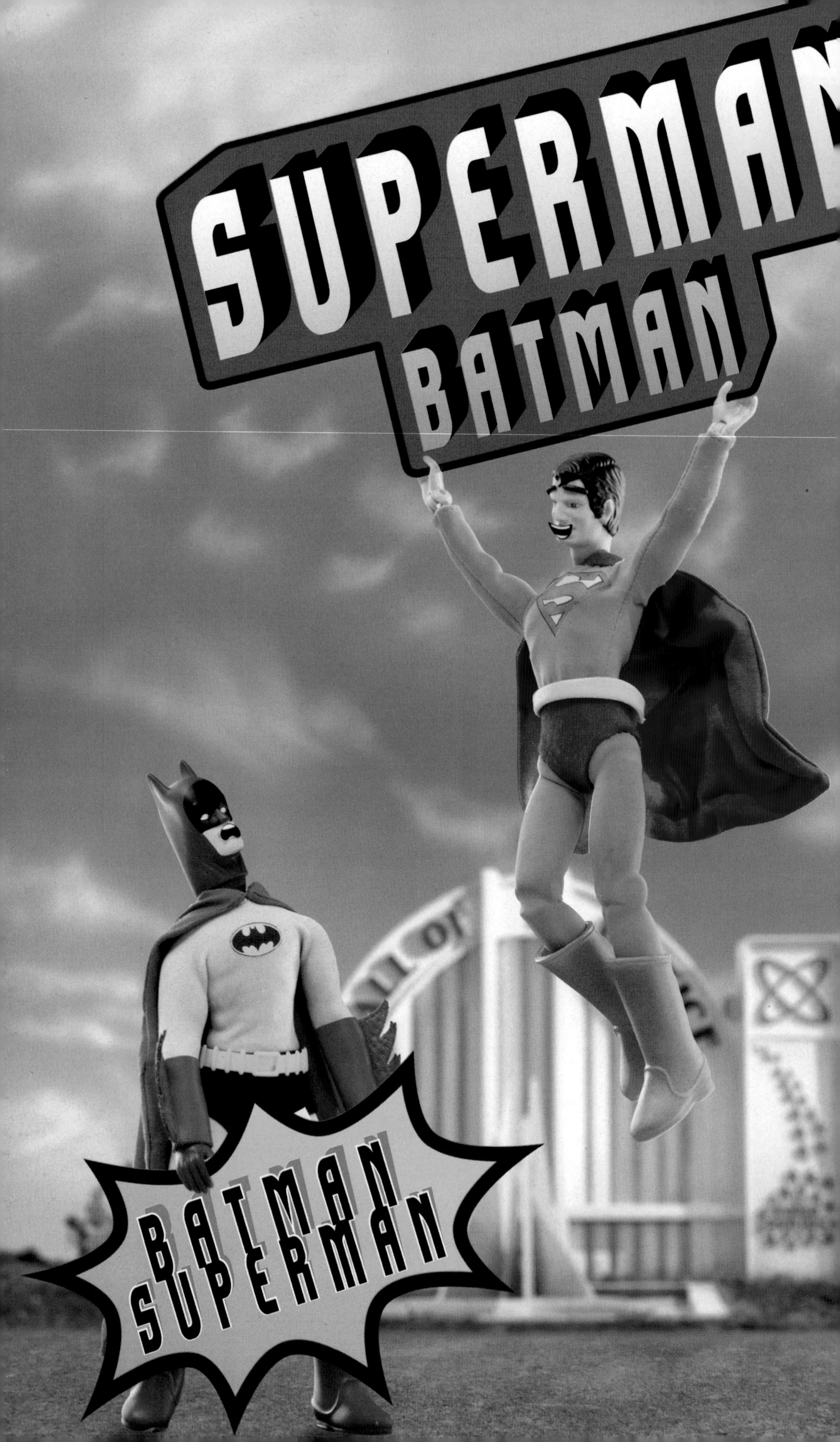
SUPERMAN
BATMAN
BATMAN
SUPERMAN

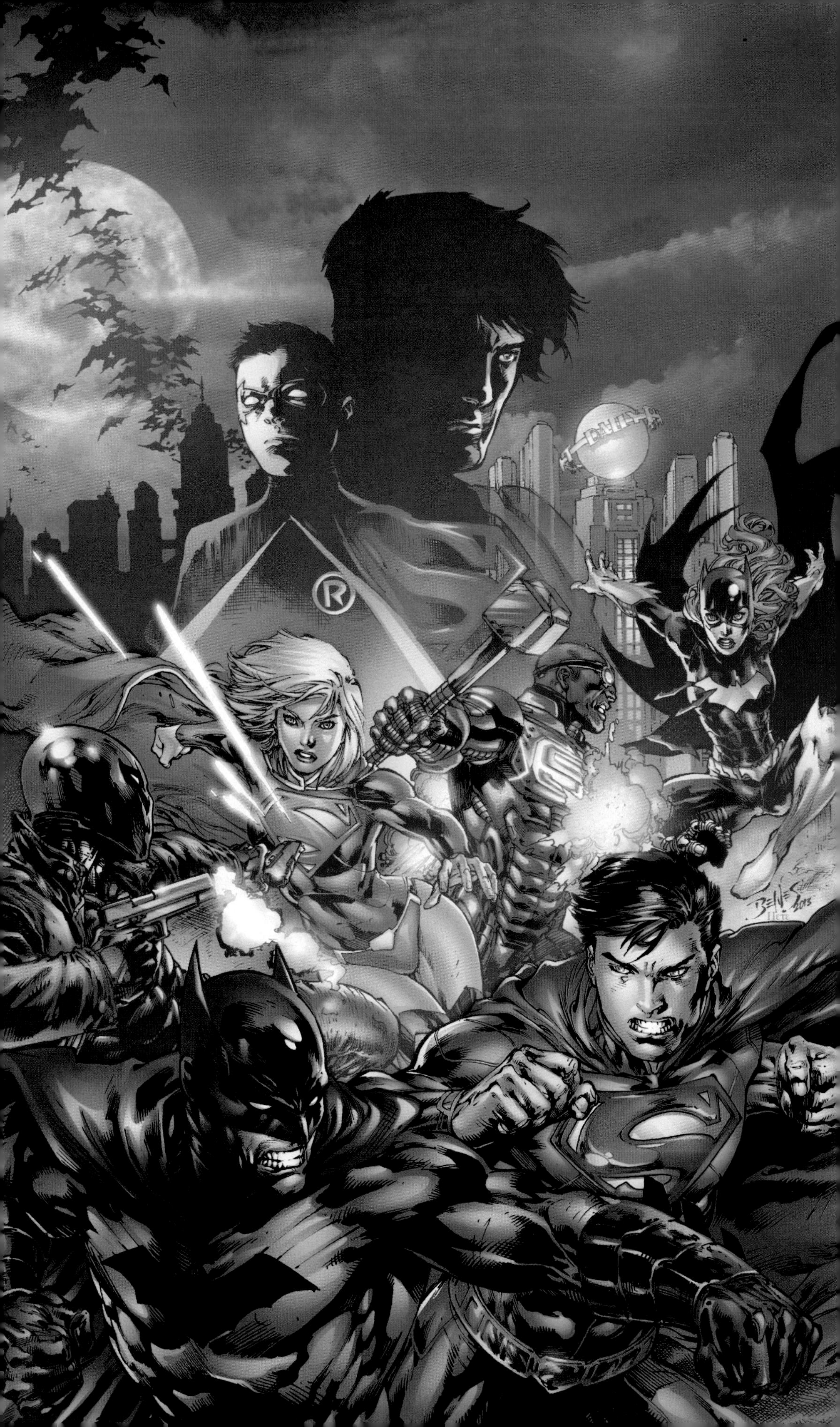

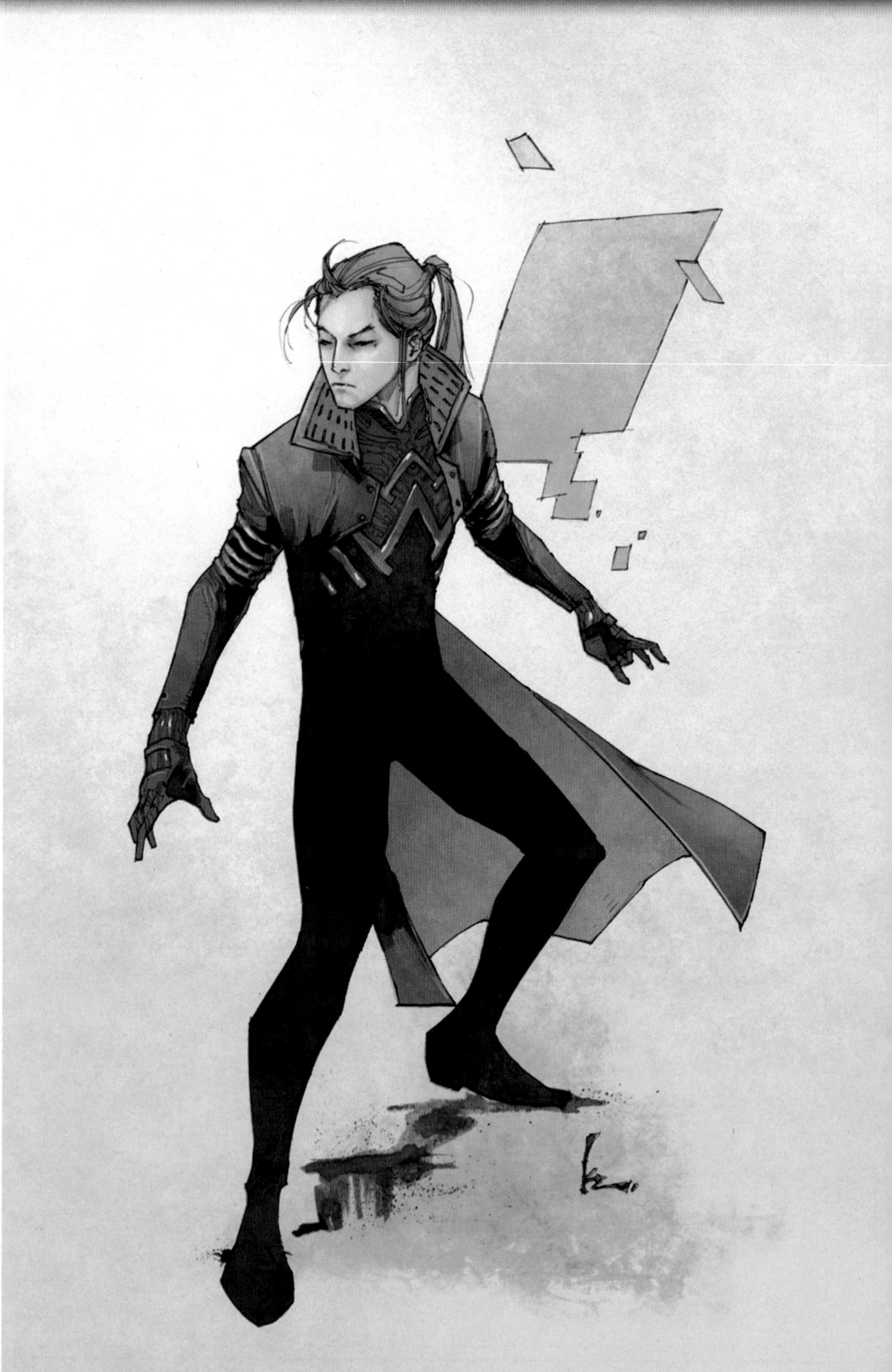

Kaizen Gamorra design by Kenneth Rocafort

Brett Booth's thumbnail layouts and pencil artwork for BATMAN/SUPERMAN #5 cover

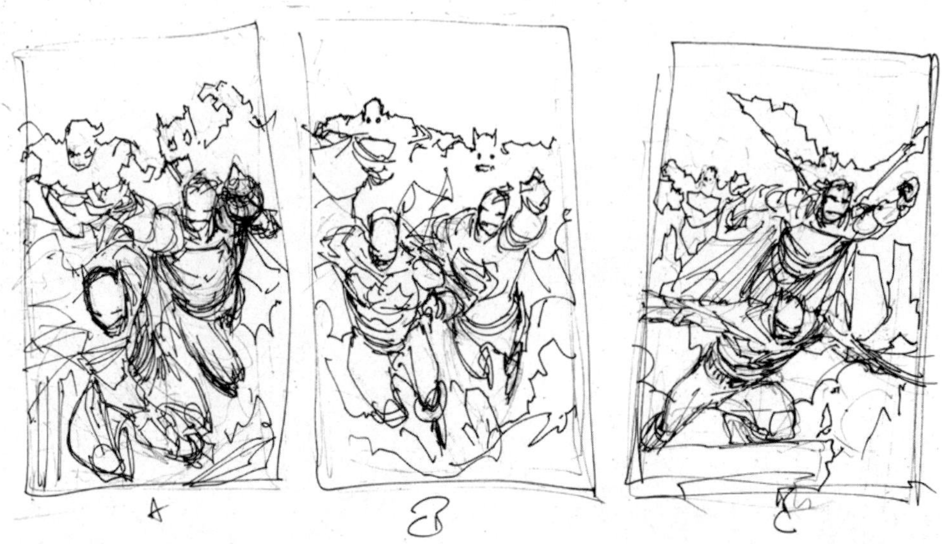
A
B
C

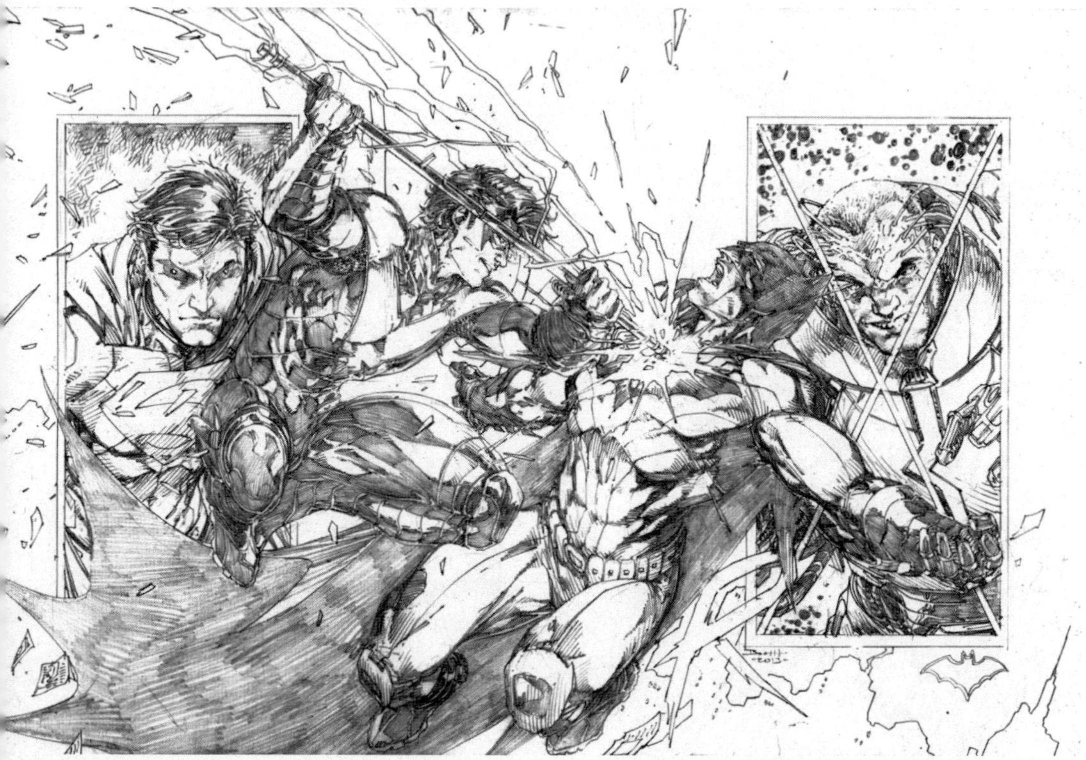

Page progression from layouts to inks for Brett Booth's cover to BATMAN/SUPERMAN #6

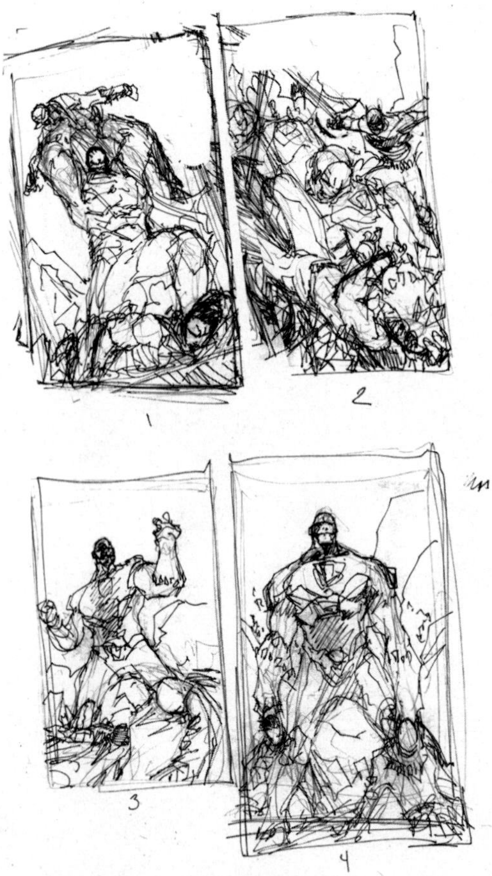
1
2
3
4

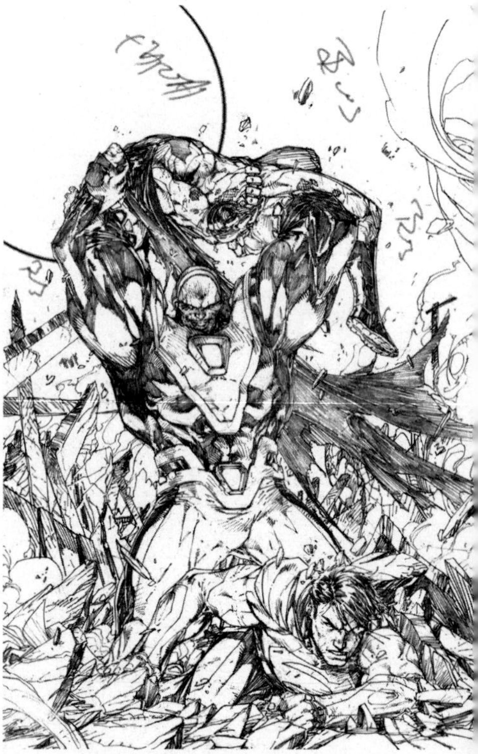

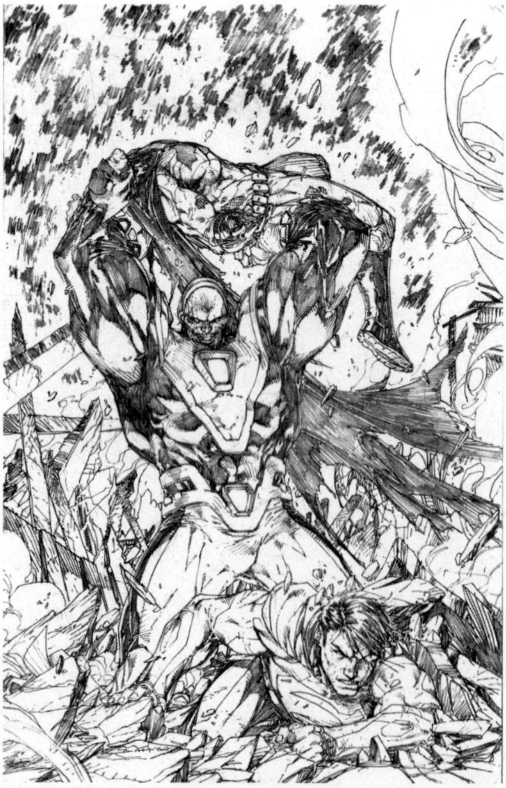

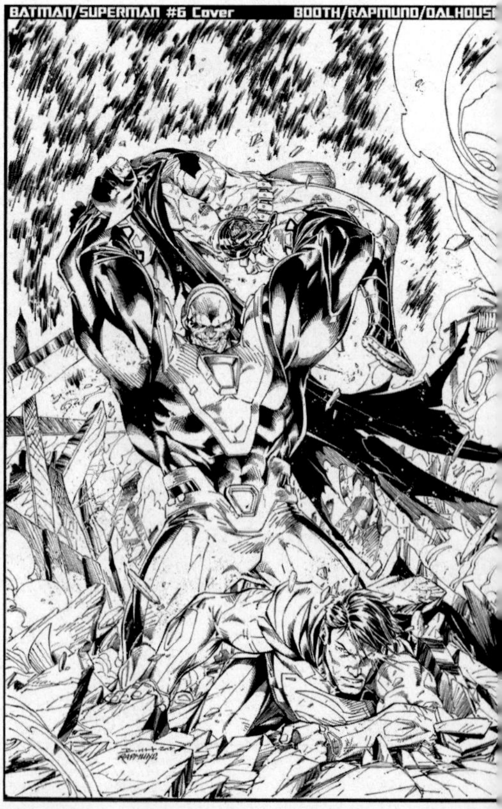
BATMAN/SUPERMAN #6 Cover
BOOTH/RAPMUND/DALHOUS

Original layouts and final pencils for
BATMAN/SUPERMAN #7 cover by Brett Booth

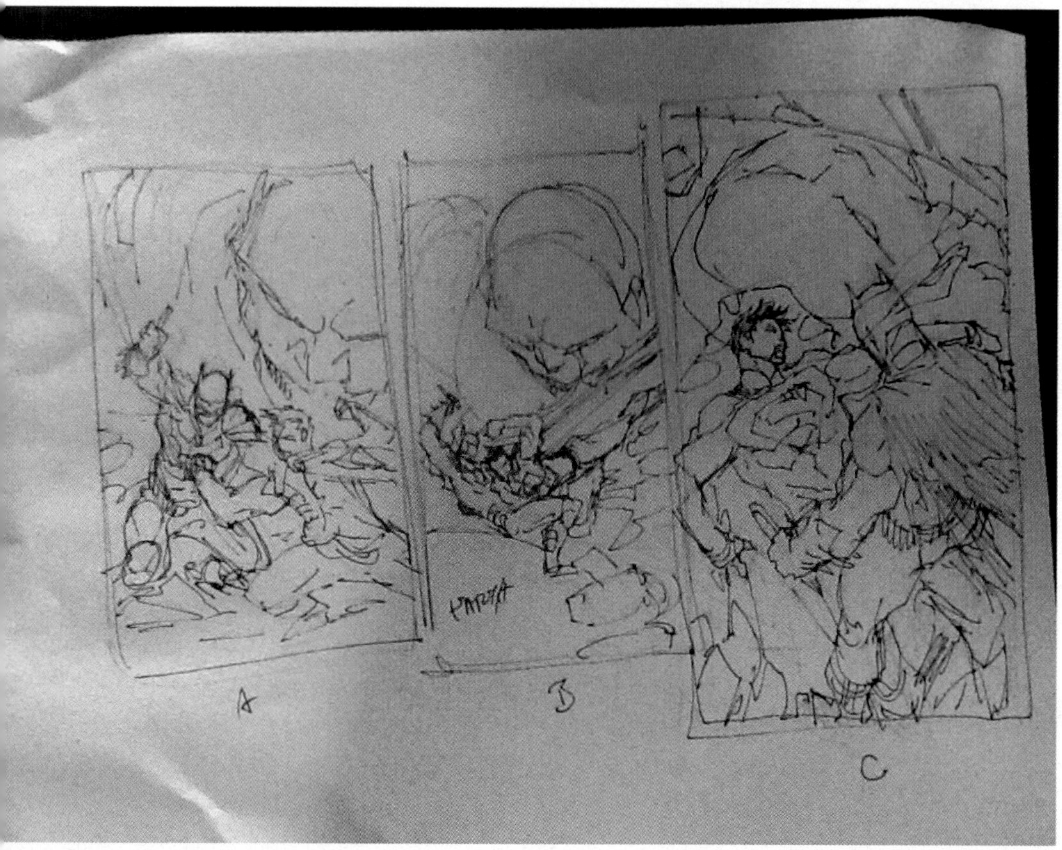
A
B
C

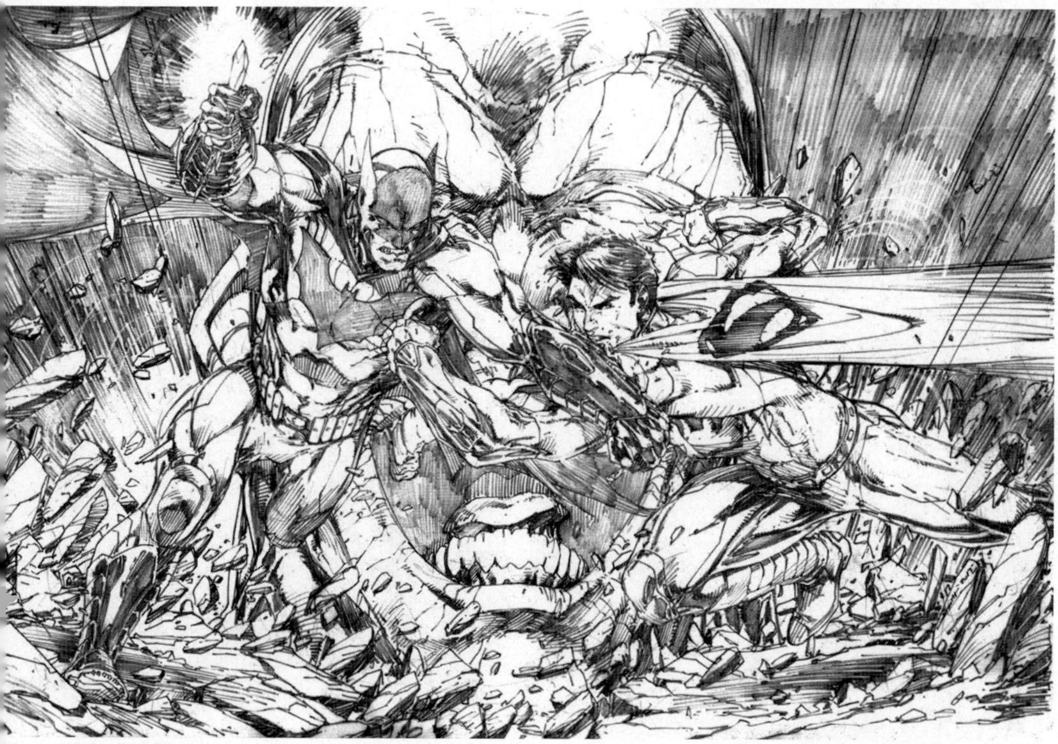

Sketches and pencils fo
BATMAN/SUPERMAN #8 and #9 covers by Jae Le

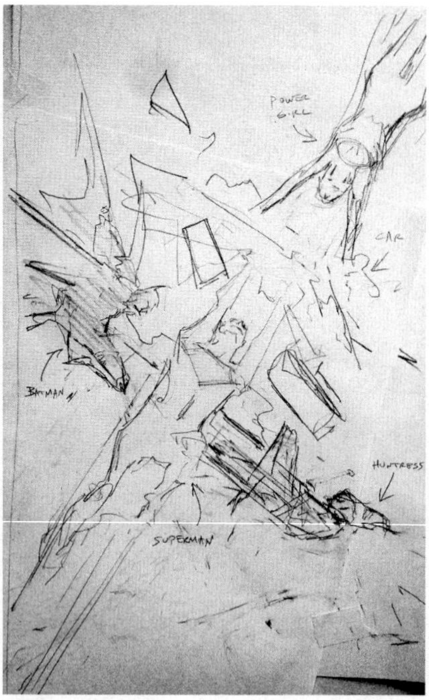
POWER GIRL
CAR
BATMAN
HUNTRESS
SUPERMAN

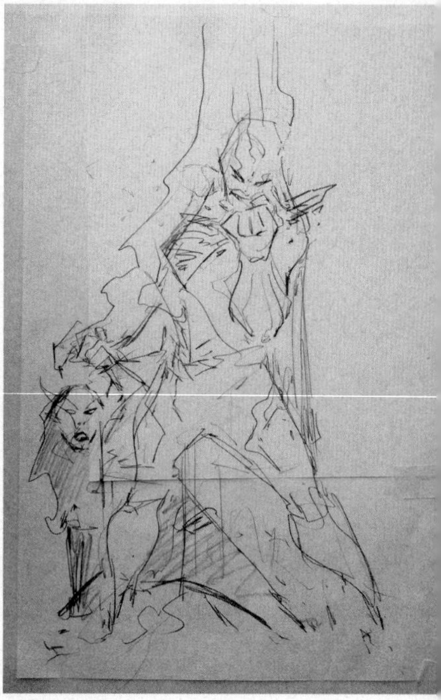

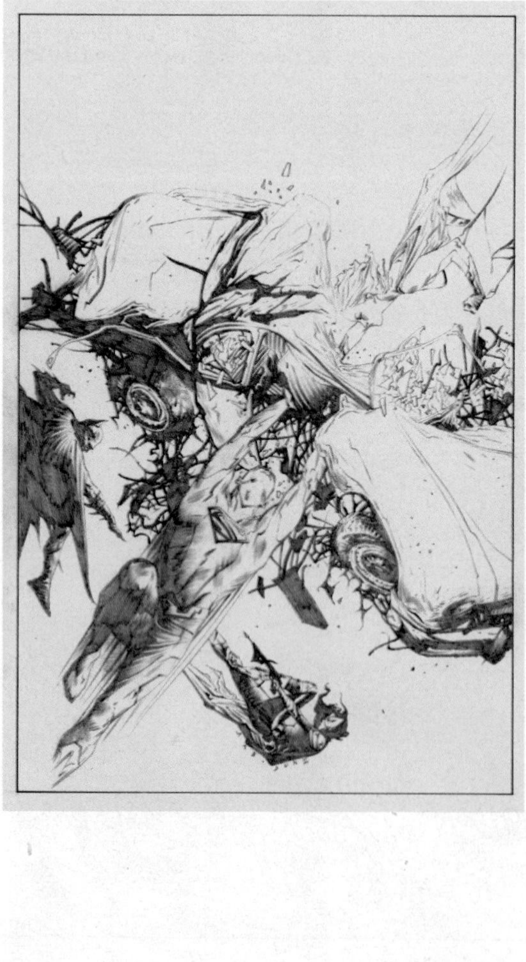

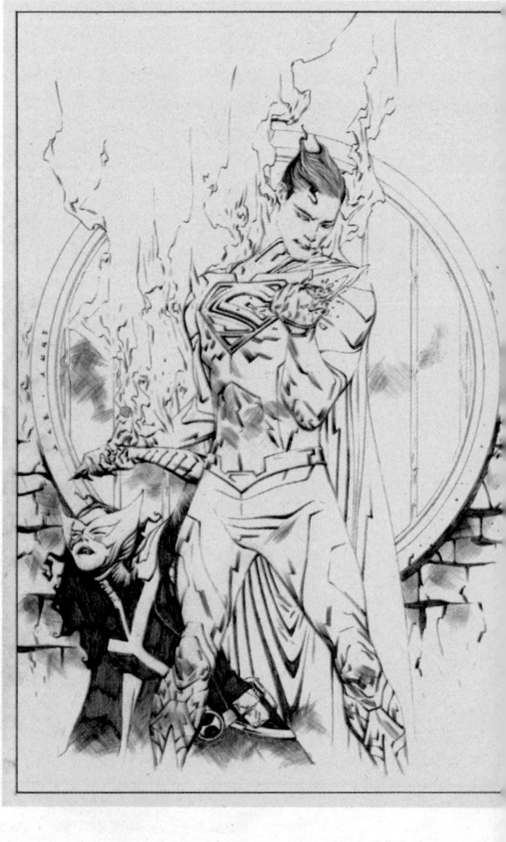

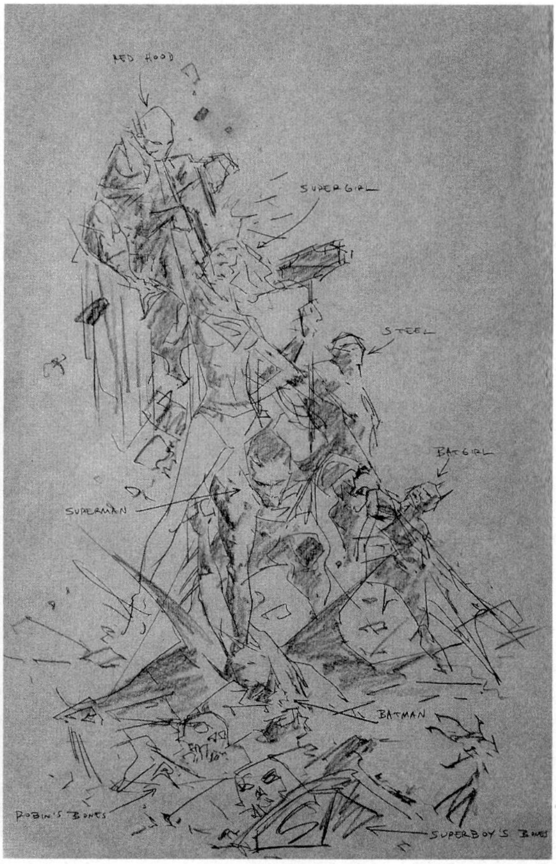
RED HOOD
SUPERGIRL
STEEL
BATGIRL
SUPERMAN
BATMAN
ROBIN'S BONES
SUPERBOY'S BONES

Jae Lee's rough sketch and pencils for
BATMAN/SUPERMAN ANNUAL #1

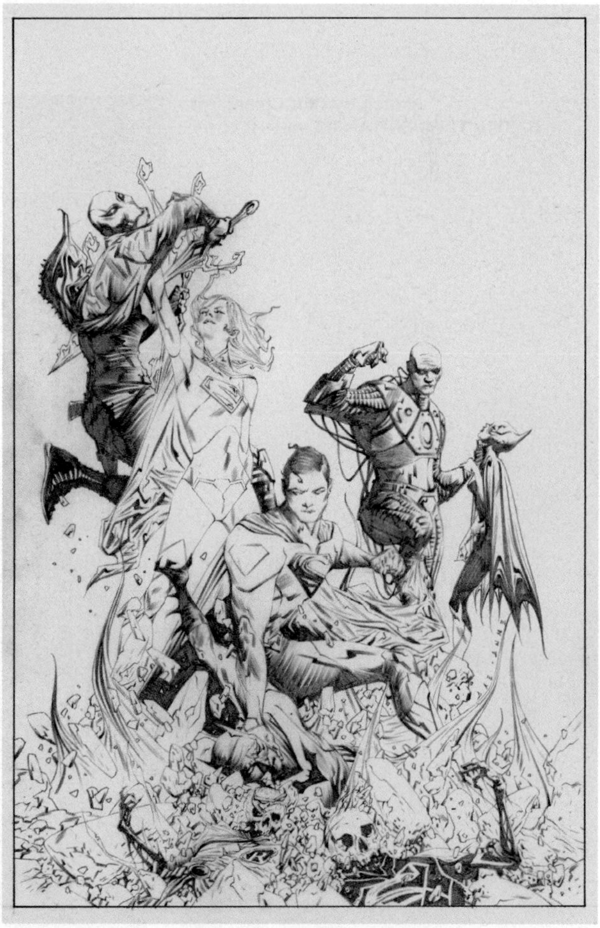

Pencils for BATMAN/SUPERMAN #5
variant cover by Jon Bogdanove

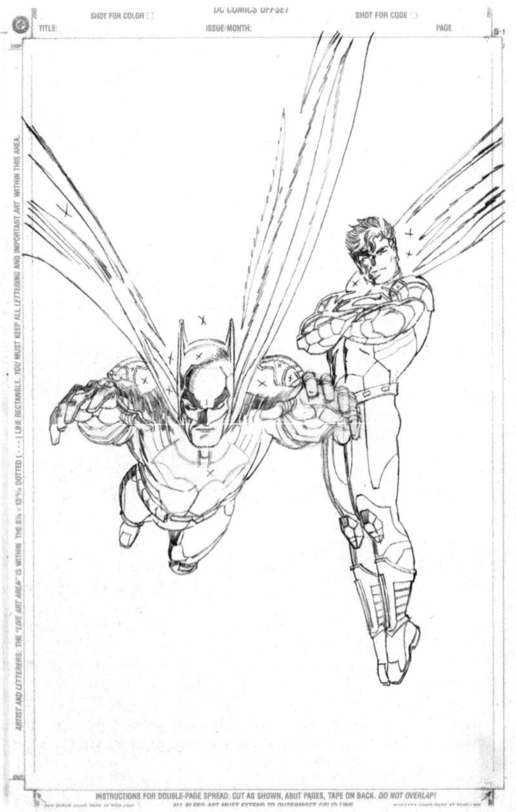
SHOT FOR COLOR
DC COMICS OFFSET
SHOT FOR CODE
TITLE:
ISSUE/MONTH:
PAGE
INSTRUCTIONS FOR DOUBLE-PAGE SPREAD: CUT AS SHOWN, ABUT PAGES, TAPE ON BACK. DO NOT OVERLAP!

Pencils for BATMAN/SUPERMAN ANNU
variant cover by Ed

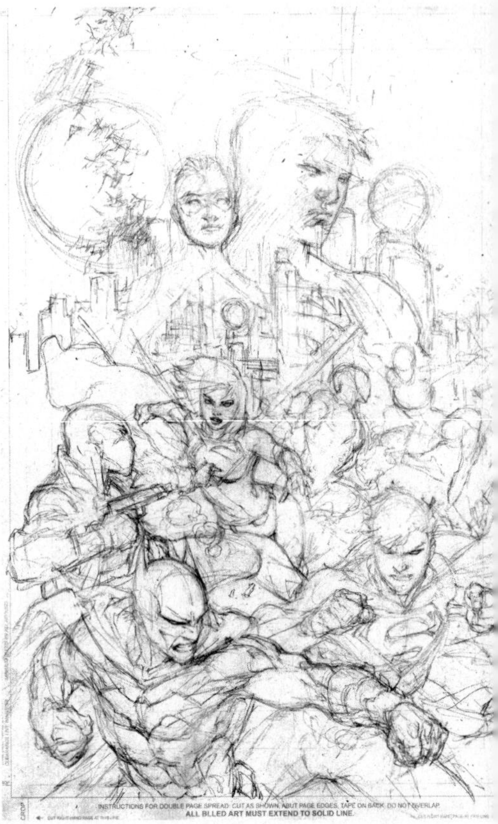
INSTRUCTIONS FOR DOUBLE PAGE SPREAD: CUT AS SHOWN, ABUT PAGE EDGES, TAPE ON BACK. DO NOT OVERLAP.
ALL BLLED ART MUST EXTEND TO SOLID LINE.

Sketch by Cliff Chiang for
BATMAN/SUPERMAN #6 variant cover

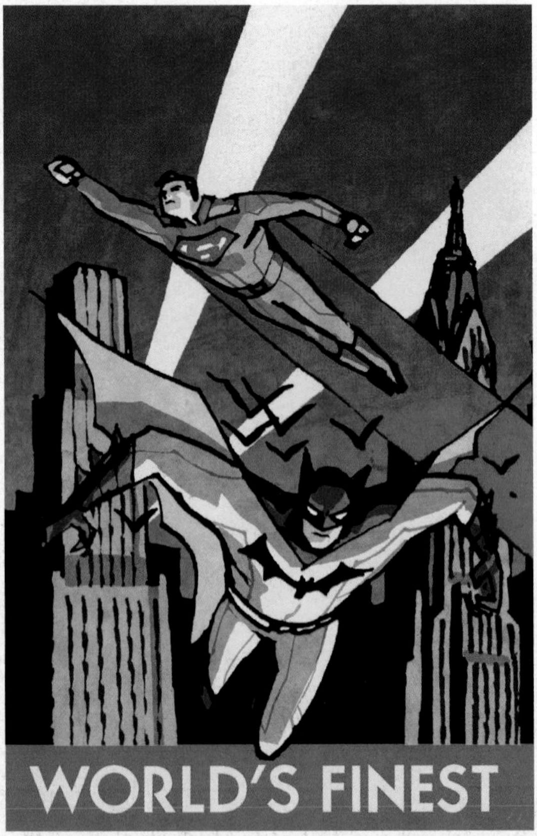
WORLD'S FINEST

"A stunning debut. This is definitely in the top rank of the revamp."
—THE ONION / AV CLUB

"Snyder and Capullo reach new heights of collaboration here, with Capullo making inspired storytelling choices that add additional layers to Snyder's narration and dialog."
—VANITY FAIR

START AT THE BEGINNING!

BATMAN VOLUME 1: THE COURT OF OWLS

BATMAN & ROBIN VOLUME 1: BORN TO KILL

BATMAN: DETECTIVE COMICS VOLUME 1: FACES OF DEATH

BATMAN: THE DARK KNIGHT VOLUME 1: KNIGHT TERRORS

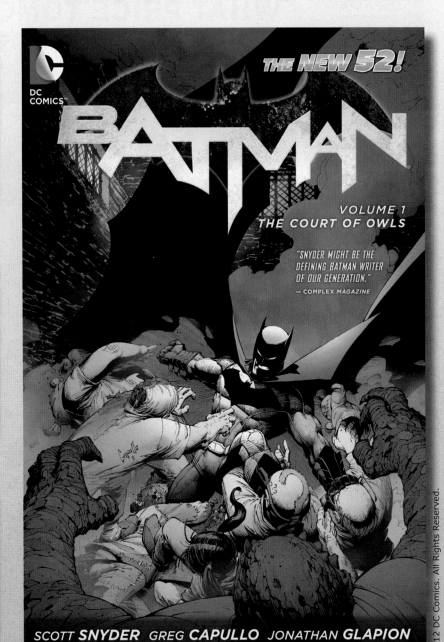

THE NEW 52!

DC COMICS™

BATMAN

VOLUME 1
THE COURT OF OWLS

"SNYDER MIGHT BE THE DEFINING BATMAN WRITER OF OUR GENERATION."
— COMPLEX MAGAZINE

SCOTT **SNYDER**   GREG **CAPULLO**   JONATHAN **GLAPION**

START AT THE BEGINNING

SUPERMAN VOLUME 1
WHAT PRICE TOMORROW

**SUPERMAN VOL. 2:
SECRETS & LIES**

**SUPERMAN VOL. 3:
FURY AT WORLD'S
END**

**SUPERMAN:
H'EL ON EARTH**

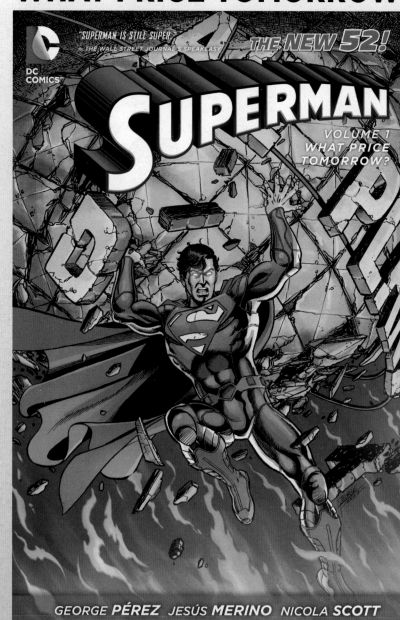

GEORGE **PÉREZ**   Jesús **MERINO**   Nicola **SCOTT**